# Adaptive Governance

*Integrating Science, Policy, and Decision Making*

Ronald D. Brunner, Toddi A. Steelman,
Lindy Coe-Juell, Christina M. Cromley,
Christine M. Edwards, and Donna W. Tucker

COLUMBIA UNIVERSITY PRESS    NEW YORK

COLUMBIA UNIVERSITY PRESS
*Publishers Since 1893*
New York, Chichester, West Sussex
Copyright © 2005 Columbia University Press
All rights reserved

Library of Congress Cataloging-in-Publication Data

Adaptive governance : integrating science, policy, and decision making /
Ronald D. Brunner . . . [et al.].
p. cm.
Includes bibliographical references and index.
ISBN 0–231–13624–2 (alk. paper)
ISBN 0–231–13625–0 (pbk. : alk. paper)
1. Natural resources—United States—Management—Case studies.
2. Natural resources—Government Policy—United States—Case studies.
3. Conservation of natural resources—United States—Decision making—Case studies.
4. Environmental policy—United States—Decision making—Case studies.
I. Brunner, Ronald D.

HC103.7.A69    2005
333.7′0978—dc22                                            2005041414

# Contents

*Preface*

THIS BOOK DOCUMENTS through case studies the emergence of adaptive governance from otherwise intractable conflicts over natural resources in the American West. These conflicts have common historical roots in the rise of scientific management around the turn of the twentieth century. Scientific management aspired to rise above politics, relying on science as the foundation for efficient policies made through a single, central authority, a bureaucratic structure with the appropriate mandate, jurisdiction, and expert personnel. But the aspiration to rise above politics through these policies and decision-making structures was unrealistic, and the remnants of scientific management have become increasingly problematic over the last century with the proliferation of bureaucracies and organized interest groups. The remnants have exacerbated conflict and gridlock, stimulating innovations in the governance of natural resources in three respects.

- *Science.* Local and other kinds of knowledge, in addition to scientific knowledge, are necessary to support policy. Applied science is inevitably incomplete, leaving far too many uncertainties to serve as an exclusive or objective foundation for policy. An integrative, interpretive science is emerging to supplement traditional reductive, experimental science.
- *Policy.* Sound policy integrates multiple interests if possible or balances them if necessary. Efficiency in pursuit of a single target is counterproductive if not politically infeasible when multiple diverse interests are at stake. In the policy process, appraisal and termination of failed policies are at least as important as planning when many uncertainties exist.
- *Decision Making.* Local community-based initiatives can supplement fragmented decision-making structures, overcoming gridlock on particular issues by integrating or balancing the many interests of competing bureaucracies and organized groups to advance their common interest. There is no single, central authority to decide the important issues.

Adaptive governance as we conceive it highlights the interdependence of these innovative practices in science, policy, and decision-making structures. In particular, adaptive governance integrates scientific and other types of knowledge into policies to advance the common interest in particular contexts through open decision-making structures. It has worked well enough in particular cases to recommend for natural resource policy. But adaptive governance is far from inevitable; other outcomes are possible in the future.

The purpose of this book is to clarify how to expedite a transition to adaptive governance for people who are also concerned about problems of gridlock in natural resource policy and are in a position to make a difference. Foremost among these are present and future field officials, their neighbors in the community, their superiors in the agency, elected officials, and other citizens. A transition to adaptive governance will not eliminate traditional science, management targets, rules, bureaucracies, or other mainstays of scientific management. Rather, it will subsume them in the larger pattern of adaptive governance and redefine their roles to facilitate advancing common interests in natural resource policy. Advancing the common interest, we believe, is the appropriate goal and criterion for governance in a democracy. Those who insist on fair consideration of their own environmental, economic, or other priority interest cannot legitimately deny fair consideration of others. Attempts to do so produce more gridlock than progress: Progress for any one interest depends increasingly on accommodating others that are interdependent.

For practitioners in natural resource policy, this book offers five cases in adaptive governance that have advanced the common interest well enough to be considered innovative models for possible diffusion and adaptation in other circumstances. These circumstances include other local communities as well as policies and programs at the state and federal levels.

- In the 15-Mile Reach of the Colorado River above Grand Junction, federal officials led negotiation of an innovative Programmatic Biological Opinion to recover endangered fishes, with the active participation and support of water developers and environmentalists.
- In the Camino Real in northern New Mexico, a district ranger implemented a series of innovations that satisfied most groups, including local land grant people who depended on subsistence use of the Carson National Forest but had been excluded from its management.
- Grassbanks serving multiple interests in rangeland demonstrate the horizontal diffusion and adaptation of an innovation across the West from the original in the Malpai Borderlands of southern Arizona and New Mexico and the first adaptation in northern New Mexico.

- The Oregon Plan for salmon and steelhead recovery demonstrates how the work of local watershed councils can be diffused and adapted vertically to advance the common interest at the state level, with state support but without state co-optation or excessive red tape.
- When community-based forestry went to Washington, D.C., it showed how local initiatives can organize themselves to effect modest but potentially important changes that adapt national legislation to support local initiatives and gain bipartisan support.

Unlike various generalized lessons, formulas, or recipes for success, case studies that are sufficiently comprehensive and detailed (as these are intended to be) allow the practitioner to find the cases most relevant to his or her particular context and to understand each factor and its significance in context. Leadership, for example, is an important factor in every case, but its forms and roles typically differ from one case to the next.

In addition, the concluding chapter offers practitioners an evaluation of business-as-usual scenarios at the national and local levels to buttress the case for a transition to adaptive governance, along with a basic strategy for shaping a transition. Based on the cases and other sources, the basic strategy includes substantive and procedural goals, action alternatives, and integrative politics. It also anticipates certain obvious pitfalls and potentials in a transition to adaptive governance.

For students and scholars, this book builds on several strands in the literature of natural resource policy and suggests how these strands might converge. A thorough review of the literature is beyond the scope of this preface, but it is appropriate to acknowledge some valuable contributions to the literature and to outline some connections with adaptive governance.

The literature on adaptive management reconsiders the role of science in natural resource policy. Most notably, C. S. Holling characterized the traditional "science of the parts" as "essentially experimental, reductionist, and narrowly disciplinary" and called for a supplementary "science of the integration of the parts" that is "fundamentally concerned with integrative modes of inquiry and multiple sources of evidence." We have incorporated these ideas into ideal types of scientific management and adaptive governance because they provide insight into our data. Other versions of adaptive management evidently would restore the privileged role of traditional science in scientific management. For example, Carl Walters asserted, "The application of sound principles of experimental design is the essence of adaptive management." Kai Lee distinguished experiments in adaptive management from trial-and-error interventions. But it is not yet clear how even well-designed experiments can be distinguished from trial and error in practice, which inevitably occurs in open, evolving systems lacking treatment and control groups or the possibility of replicating results. In any case, Holling recognized the limitations of experiments when he wrote that "we have just begun to develop the concepts, technology, and methods that can deal with the generic nature of the problems."[1] As those tools are developed, they might address the practical implications of Holling's larger conception of science for policy and decision-making structures. If so, adaptive management also might converge on some of the same practices we have found in cases of adaptive governance. This latter term is an attempt to set aside the technical and bureaucratic connotations of *management,* which tends to divert attention from politics.

The literature on collaborative decision making reconsiders from the bottom up established structures for making decisions. Collaborative conservation, civic environmentalism, and community-based initiatives are some of the overlapping concepts that draw attention to local groups of people, representing diverse interests, who collaborate to resolve particular policy issues in their own communities, often in response to the failures of established decision-making structures.[2] Emphasizing community-based initiatives to avoid certain policy presumptions in related concepts, adaptive governance builds on the collaborative decision-making literature in three main areas.

- First, the concept explicitly recommends the common interest as the goal of policy, a goal implied by authentic collaboration and supported by national legislation. The common interest includes conservation, environmentalism, sustainable communities, and any other interests that may be valid and appropriate in a particular context.
- Second, the concept recognizes that multiple means are necessary for success in advancing the common interest. For example, adversarial means and processes sometimes are necessary in competition for funds, authorities, or other forms of assistance, even if success depends primarily on collaborative processes involving representatives of diverse interests.
- Third, the concept explicitly includes the diffusion and adaptation of successful innovations. Diffusion and adaptation are necessary to magnify the significance of successful innovations by community-based initiatives. Isolated local innovations are not sufficient for significant reforms nationwide.

We believe these three interrelated points are supported implicitly if not explicitly by democratic commitments and by experience documented in the case study literature. As related concepts are developed, they might address these practical policy implications of collaborative decision making. If so, they also might converge on some of the same practices we have found in the emergence of adaptive governance.

A third reform literature, less integrated than the other two, reconsiders established decision-making structures from the top down in response to cumulative problems. For example, Robert Nelson has made a case for abolishing the U.S. Forest Service. Daniel Kemmis has proposed that Congress transfer sovereignty over federal lands in the American West to the people of the West. Although we are unaware of any specific proposals for wholesale reform of public land law, the Forest Service and Congress have recognized conflict between laws, including regulations and court decisions, as a problem.[3] The problem is that laws affecting public lands often are ambiguous and incompatible, reflecting the diverse interests of a pluralistic society as it has evolved over more than a century. From the standpoint of agency officials, particularly those on the ground, compliance with some legal mandates often means violation of others. The main alternatives are inaction to minimize legal exposure, action that accepts legal risks, or analysis to minimize those risks at the cost of diverting scarce resources. In response to such cumulative problems, reformers may discover that wholesale reform efforts maximize the intensity and scope of opposition by groups organized to compete in fragmented decision-making structures at the national level. If so, reformers might converge on incremental reforms by exemption, informed and guided by the diffusion and adaptation of successful innovations on the ground. This is part of the basic strategy we recommend for a transition to adaptive governance.

Finally, for practitioners and academics whose interests in policy and governance go beyond natural resources, this book offers an application of the policy sciences, the oldest distinctive tradition within the broader policy movement.[4] The conceptual framework and selected propositions of the policy sciences can be traced in the following pages through citations to the work of Harold D. Lasswell and his collaborators. The framework has been used here to organize and integrate data in each case study and to develop the concept of adaptive governance through comparisons between cases. Because translations across frameworks are always possible, it is unnecessary and futile to attempt to promote the policy sciences framework. The point of making it explicit here is to invite comparative evaluations with other frameworks proposed or in use, in an effort to advance policy inquiry. Such evaluations cannot be completed without comparing applications of frameworks according to their purposes. From our standpoint, frameworks and other forms of theory are not ends in themselves, nor are they limited to scientific purposes alone. They are means for improving policy and governance in practice.

NOTES

1. For the quotations from C. S. Holling, see his chapter "What Barriers? What Bridges?" in Lance H. Gunderson, C. S. Holling, and Stephen S. Light, eds., *Barriers and Bridges to the Renewal of Ecosystems and Institutions* (New York: Columbia University Press, 1995), pp. 3–34, at pp. 12–13 and 33. See also Holling's "Two Cultures of Ecology," *Conservation Ecology* 2 (1998), online at http://www.consecol.org/vol2/iss2/art4. The other quotation is from the first author's notes of Walters's remarks to a workshop on "Learning from Regions: A Comparative Appraisal of Climate, Water, and Human Interactions in the Colorado and Columbia River Systems," Aspen Global Change Institute, Aspen, Colo. (June 5–10, 2003). See also Carl Walters, "Challenges in Adaptive Management of Riparian and Coastal Ecosystems," *Conservation Ecology* 1 (1997), online at http://www.consecol.org/vol1/iss2/art1. For an introduction to Kai Lee on adaptive management, see Kai N. Lee, "Appraising Adaptive Management," *Conservation Ecology* 3 (1999), online at http://www.consecol.org/vol3/iss2/art3, and his *Compass and Gyroscope: Integrating Science and Politics for the Environment* (Washington, D.C.: Island Press, 1999).

2. See DeWitt John, *Civic Environmentalism: Alternatives to Regulation in States and Communities* (Washington, D.C.: CQ Press, 1994); Barb Cestero, *Beyond the Hundredth Meeting: A Field Guide to Collaborative Conservation on the West's Public Lands* (Tucson, Az.: Sonoran Institute, 1999); Julia M. Wondolleck and Steven L. Yaffee, *Making Collaboration Work: Lessons from Innovation in Natural Resource Management* (Washington, D.C.: Island Press, 2000); Donald Snow, "Coming Home: An Introduction to Collaborative Conservation," in Philip Brick, Donald Snow, and Sarah Van de Wetering, eds., *Across the Great Divide: Explorations in Collaborative Conservation and the American West* (Washington, D.C.: Island Press, 2001), pp. 1–11; and Ronald D. Brunner, Christine H. Colburn, Christina M. Cromley, Roberta A. Klein, and Elizabeth A. Olson, *Finding Common Ground: Governance and Natural Resources in the American West* (New Haven, Conn.: Yale University Press, 2002), on community-based initiatives.

3. See Robert H. Nelson, *A Burning Issue? A Proposal for Abolishing the U.S. Forest Service* (Lanham, Md.: Rowman & Littlefield, 2000); and Daniel Kemmis, *This Sovereign Land: A New Vision for Governing the West* (Washington, D.C.: Island Press, 2001). In April 1995, the secretary of agriculture directed establishment of a Forest Service task force to evaluate how laws and regulations on the management of national forests relate to one another and the impacts of those relationships on management. The draft report, *Review of the Forest Service Legal and Regulatory Framework,* was not released officially. It was followed up in hearings of the U.S. House of Representatives, Committee on Resources, Subcommittee on Forests and Forest Health, on "Conflicting Laws and Regulations: Gridlock on the National Forests" (December 4, 2001) and on "Process Gridlock on the National Forests" (June 12, 2002). See also Elizabeth Beaver, Gary Bryner, Alicia Gibson, Parke Godar, Carolyn Herb, Ian Kalmanowitz, Doug Kenney, Kathryn Mutz, and Adam Peters, *Seeing the Forest Service for the Trees: A Survey of Proposals for Changing National Forest Policy* (Boulder, Colo.: Natural Resources Law Center, June 2000).

4. On the policy sciences, see especially Harold D. Lasswell, *A Pre-View of Policy Sciences* (New York: Elsevier, 1971); Harold D. Lasswell and Abraham Kaplan, *Power and Society: A Framework for Political and Social Inquiry* (New Haven, Conn.: Yale University Press, 1950); and Harold D. Lasswell and Myres S. McDougal, *Jurisprudence for a Free Society: Studies in Law, Sci-*

*ence, and Policy* (New Haven, Conn., and Dordrecht, The Netherlands: New Haven Press and Martinus Nijoff, 1992). On the policy sciences in the broader policy movement, see Ronald D. Brunner, "The Policy Movement as a Policy Problem," *Policy Sciences* 24 (1991), pp. 65–98; and Ronald D. Brunner, "Policy Sciences," in Adam Kuper and Jessica Kuper, eds., *Encyclopedia of the Social Sciences,* 2nd ed. (London: Routledge, 1995), pp. 622–624.

*Acknowledgments*

THE COAUTHORS ARE pleased to acknowledge and thank the many people who have contributed to this book. We begin with Ted Smith, executive director of the Henry P. Kendall Foundation, who provided encouragement and the funding necessary for a previous book, for some of the field research reported here and later for completion of this book. The coauthors agreed to proceed with the book shortly after a small workshop organized by Christina Cromley in Boulder in February 2002. Behind that agreement was encouragement from practitioners at the workshop—Carol Daly, Cecilia Danks, Maia Enzer, Gerry Gray, and Lynn Jungwirth—and our initial field research. Graduate students at the University of Colorado at Boulder and North Carolina State University read and critiqued earlier versions of the manuscript in the 2003–2004 academic year. Crockett Dumas and Carveth Kramer separately met with graduate seminars in Boulder. Carveth Kramer also carefully read and critiqued chapters 1, 3, and 7. Robin Smith guided the manuscript through acquisition and production at Columbia University Press. Carol Anne Peschke edited the manuscript.

In addition to these people, we are grateful to many others who helped with individual chapters. Art Cooper, Fred Cubbage, Bill Lewis, Lynn Maguire, and Larry Nielsen read and critiqued a draft of chapter 1. In doing so, they helped us refine both our ideas and the presentation of our ideas.

For chapter 2, we thank practitioners in the 15-Mile Reach case who took time from their busy schedules for interviews: Scott Balcomb, Lori Field, Patty Gellat, Eric Kuhn, Jim Lochhead, Dan Luecke, Larry MacDonnell, Henry Maddux, Ralph Morgenweck, Robert Muth, Tom Nesler, Tom Pitts, Dick Proctor, Gerry Roehm, Jim Rooks, Greg Trainor, Brent Uilenberg, Robert Wigington, and Margot Zallen. Ron Brunner, Jim Corbridge, and Larry MacDonnell provided advice, encouragement, and reviews as members of the committee for the master's thesis on which this chapter is based.

For chapter 3, we are indebted to those who took time to meet with us while we learned about adaptive governance in the Camino Real Ranger District: Ernest Atencio, Joane Berde, Max Cordova, Ike DeVargas, Crockett Dumas, George Grossman, Sam Hitt, Pat Jackson, Carveth Kramer, Audrey Kuykendall, Henry Lopez, Kay Matthews, Steve Miranda, Mark Schiller, Luis Torres, and Courtney White. Crockett Dumas, Kay Matthews, Mark Schiller, and Carveth Kramer were especially helpful with comments on earlier drafts.

For chapter 4, we thank the people who took the time to talk about their important work in the innovation, diffusion, and adaptation of grassbanks: Laura Bell, Tony Benson, Ben Brown, Bob Budd, Bill deBuys, Edmund Gomez, Steph Gripne, Claire Harper, Charlie Jankiewicz, Lou Lunte, Bill McDonald, Mark Schiller, Virgil Trujillo, and Courtney White. Bill deBuys, Steph Gripne, Ben Brown, and Bill McDonald provided helpful comments on earlier drafts. Ron Brunner, Sam Fitch, and Anne Keller served as members of the committee for the master's thesis on which this chapter is based.

For chapter 5, we thank those who volunteered their time for interviews about the Oregon Plan: Sybil Ackerman, Ken Bierly, Holly Coccoli, Neal Coenen, Dana Erickson, John Falzone, Jennifer Hampel, Doug Heicken, Roy Hemmingway, Ted Lorenson, Jay Nicholas, Tom Paul, Dave Powers, Dave Sahagian, Louise Solliday, Michael Tehan, Joe Whitworth, Ray Wilkeson, and Mike Wiltsey.

Chapter 6 could not have been completed without input from many busy people who gave time for interviews on community-based forestry and reviews of earlier drafts: Carol Daly, Maia Enzer, Gerry Gray, Lynn Jungwirth, Anne Moote, and Cass Moseley. Congressional staffers, agency officials, environmental and industry group representatives, and community partners also helped the author, then policy director at American Forests, pull together additional information: Andrea Bedell-Loucks, Calli Daly, Cecilia Danks, Lisa Dix, Frank Gladics, Kira Finkler, Michael Goergen, Jonathan Kusel, Arlen Lancaster, Mike Leahy, Laura McCarthy, Mary Mitsos, Susan Odell, Mark Rey, Lloyd Ritter, Eleanor Torres, Alice Walker, John Watts, and many others.

And finally, each coauthor warmly acknowledges the efforts, insights, and support of the others. Each of us took responsibility for one or more parts of the book, and each part is indispensable to the whole. This is indeed a collaborative effort.

*Adaptive Governance*

# 1. Beyond Scientific Management

RONALD D. BRUNNER AND TODDI A. STEELMAN

ON INDEPENDENCE DAY, July 4, 2001 in Klamath Falls, Oregon, farmers and their supporters used acetylene torches and crowbars to open the headgates of an irrigation canal owned and operated by the U.S. Bureau of Reclamation. About a hundred like-minded demonstrators rallied around them. Some protested the bureau's closing of the gates 3 months earlier, shutting off irrigation water in the midst of drought. One carried a sign asking the bureau, "How can you destroy my future?" Others linked arms to block the view. But it was no secret who was involved in trespassing and vandalism on federal property. Their pictures from earlier incidents had been published in a local newspaper and broadcast on local television. As he watched the protesters from his car, the county sheriff, Tim Evinger, declined to intervene on grounds that it was a federal issue. But apparently even the Federal Bureau of Investigation and the U.S. Marshals Service were reluctant to intervene. Neither had yet dispatched officers to Klamath Falls, despite requests for their assistance from the Bureau of Reclamation, which could only strengthen physical barriers to vandalism after each incident. Jeff McCracken, the bureau's spokesperson, explained, "We absolutely do not want to put anyone out there to protect the gates that have been providing water to people the last 94 years." Bob Grasser, co-owner of a local fertilizer business whose revenues were down 85 percent from the previous year, summed up the local standpoint: "Rural people in America, by and large, are true patriots. . . . But we're not too patriotic here anymore. It feels like our freedom is being betrayed. We just can't believe that a great country would do this to our own people." Farmer Paul Arritola went further: "I'm tired of playing by the rules. Nobody's listening."[1]

Behind these dramatic events on Independence Day 2001 is a Klamath Basin water crisis in the making since the Progressive era and many other unresolved conflicts over limited natural resources in the American West today. Such conflicts have common historical roots in the rise of scientific management a century ago, around the turn of the twentieth century. Scientific management aspired to rise above politics, relying on science as the foundation for efficient policies made through a single central authority—a bureaucratic structure with the appropriate mandate, jurisdiction, and expert personnel. But from the outset attempts to implement this aspiration have been frustrated by political interests excluded from scientific management. In recent decades, with the proliferation of organized groups, the remnants of scientific management have done more to exacerbate than to resolve conflicts over natural resources. In certain places, the intolerable costs of such conflicts have stimulated the emergence of adaptive governance. Adaptive governance integrates scientific and other types of knowledge into policies to advance the common interest in particular contexts through open decision-making structures. Related concepts tend to emphasize science, policy, or decision-making structures rather than their integration.[2] As argued in this book, adaptive governance has worked well enough in certain places to recommend it as a new set of practices for finding common ground in the twenty-first century.

The story behind the events on Independence Day 2001 in Klamath Falls is worth telling because it highlights the problems of scientific management and the need to move beyond it. The story also highlights the possibility of moving toward adaptive governance of natural resources in the American West.

## Klamath Basin Water Crisis

The Klamath Falls headgates are part of the Klamath Project, the Bureau of Reclamation's second oldest, begun in 1905. Over the decades it constructed seven dams, eighteen canals, forty-five pumping plants, and 516 miles of irrigation ditches. The project made it possible to farm deep soil in the arid high plain of the Klamath Basin, which straddles the Oregon–California border east of the Cascade Range (figure 1.1). Many residents are descendants of veterans of the two world wars who were lured there by government promises of land and plenty of water. By the end of the century, the project was providing irrigation water for about 1,400 farms covering about 210,000 of the basin's 400,000 acres of farmland. But the project depends on a series of shallow lakes that lack the capacity to store much water from one year to the next. The largest is Upper Klamath Lake, 35 miles long but only 7 feet deep on average; it feeds the Klamath River, flowing south and mostly west from Klamath Falls into the Pacific Ocean. Thus the water available to the project each year depends heavily on the previous winter's snowfall in the surrounding mountains. Nevertheless, the project delivered irrigation water as contracted every year since 1907, except

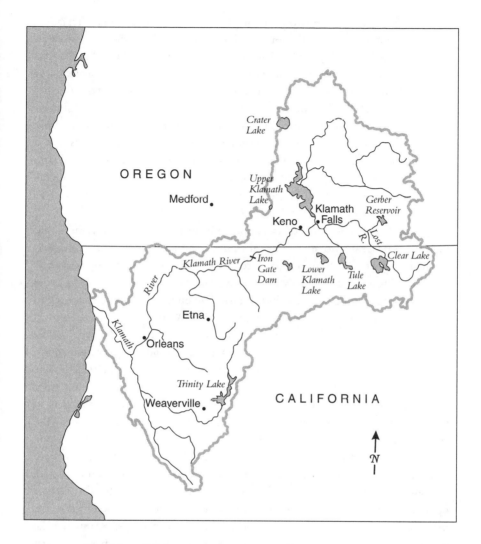

Figure 1.1. The Klamath River Basin. Source: National Research Council Committee on Endangered and Threatened Fishes in the Klamath River Basin.

in 1991 and 1994. In these two drought years it was necessary to cut irrigation water to maintain a sufficient amount and quality of water for the shortnose and Lost River suckers in Upper Klamath Lake, their primary habitat. Thus in the early 1990s, "For the first time, the farmers' claim to the water was shaken."[3]

In 1988 the two sucker species were listed as endangered under the Endangered Species Act (ESA). A species of coho salmon in the Klamath River below Iron Gate Dam was listed as threatened in 1997. On January 22, 2001, to comply with the ESA, the bureau forwarded a biological assessment of the effects of the Klamath Project's proposed 2001 operations on the endangered suckers to the U.S. Fish and Wildlife Service (FWS), requesting initiation of formal consultations. Similarly, on February 13 the bureau forwarded a biological assessment to the National Marine Fisheries Service (NMFS), which has jurisdiction over the threatened coho, requesting consultations. On March 13 and 19, respectively, FWS and NMFS issued draft biological opinions concluding that the proposed Klamath Project operations put the listed fishes in jeopardy and proposed "reasonable and prudent alternatives" (RPAs) for project operations as required under the ESA. In their judgment, the best available science indicated that the listed species needed more water in the coming drought. With reports that the snowpack in the surrounding mountains was 40 percent of normal or less, the bureau informed the NMFS and FWS that water supplies would not be sufficient to comply with both RPAs. Meanwhile, scientists hired by the Klamath Water Users Association concluded that low water was not to blame for sucker kills in Upper Klamath Lake in 1995, 1996, and 1997. Their study, released in March, blamed hot weather and a lack of wind for inhibiting the natural mixing of water in the lake, leaving different strata too poor or too rich in oxygen.[4] In addition, some farmers believed that the release of more warm lake water into the Klamath River would raise water temperatures to levels lethal for coho salmon.[5]

Despite these conflicting estimates of the fishes' needs, the final biological opinions issued on April 6 insisted on the fishes' need for more water. The RPA from FWS mandated a minimum surface water level in Upper Klamath Lake of 4,139 feet above sea level "to increase water quality and the physical habitat for juvenile and adult suckers, and provide access to spawning areas outside the lake."[6] This was a foot higher than the level proposed by the bureau in January. The RPA from NMFS mandated minimum flows in the Klamath River below Iron Gate Dam from a low of 1,000 cubic feet per second in July through September to a high of 2,100 cubic feet per second from June 1 to 15 to increase riparian habitat for the coho there. The minimum flow was more than three times what the bureau had sought earlier for the peak irrigation season. Despite its tradition and distinctive mandate to deliver irrigation water, the bureau was required to incorporate the FWS minimum water levels and the NMFS minimum flows into its Klamath Project 2001 Annual Operations Plan, depriving farmers of water during their growing season. The plan was released on April 6, which is known as "Black Friday" in the community. According to the accompanying press release,

> Federal officials have finalized the biological opinions for the operation of the Klamath Project for this critically dry water year. Based on those opinions and the requirements of the Endangered Species Act, the Bureau of Reclamation announced today that *no water will be available from Upper Klamath Lake to supply the farmers of the Klamath Project.* Furthermore, based on current estimates, Reclamation projects that there will be only about 70,000 acre-feet available for the irrigation of "A" lands on the east side of the basin. That water will be supplied by Clear Lake and Gerber Reservoirs. A full supply for the project would be about 500,000 acre-feet.[7]

Based on the April forecast of the Natural Resources Conservation Service, the Operations Plan anticipated that inflows to Upper Klamath Lake from April through September—a total of about 108,000 acre-feet—would leave 70 percent of farmers' demand unmet.

In addition to the requirements of the ESA, the Operations Plan acknowledged a trust responsibility shared with all federal agencies to maintain sucker and coho salmon fisheries of the Klamath Basin tribes under a treaty signed in 1864. The plan also acknowledged contractual obligations to provide water in an amount necessary to meet reasonable beneficial uses for irrigation but noted that only limited irrigation water would be available. Finally, the plan acknowledged the need to provide suitable habitat for migratory birds and bald eagles in the basin's six national wildlife refuges but noted that water deliveries would be made only for the needs of endangered suckers.[8] The refuges depend largely on water runoff from irrigated fields. The Lower Klamath National Wildlife Refuge hosts 80 percent of the wildfowl in the Pacific Flyway, providing winter prey for the largest concentration of bald eagles in the lower forty-eight states. The final biological opinion from the FWS concluded that the bald eagles would be damaged, but not threatened, by Klamath Project operations.

The 2001 Operations Plan did not mention an important court decision 3 days before, on April 3, 2001. The Pacific Coast Federation of Fishermen's Associations (PCFFA) and several conservation groups had filed a suit almost a year earlier claiming that the bureau was operating the Klamath Project in 2000 without consulting NMFS regarding its effects on the threatened coho and therefore was not in compliance with ESA. Judge Saundra Brown Armstrong agreed. She prohibited delivery of irrigation water below specified levels recommended in a scientific study and until the bureau completed an Operations Plan for the 2001 water year after appropriate consultation with NMFS.[9]

Irrigation interests, including farmer Steve Kandra, filed a suit 3 days after release of the 2001 Operations Plan. Citing their contractual rights to irrigation water, they asked the U.S. District Court to block implementation of the plan and order the bureau to deliver "historic" amounts of irrigation water or, alternatively, to release 262,000 acre-feet of water. That would be enough to lower Upper Klamath Lake 1 foot to 4,138 feet above sea level by the end of September and to allocate the stored water and inflow roughly equally between project irrigators and the fishes. Judge Ann Aiken denied the motion. She explained, "While the court sympathizes with plaintiffs and their plight, I am bound by oath to uphold the law. The law requires protection of suckers and salmon as endangered and threatened species and as tribal trust resources, even if the plaintiffs disagree with the manner in which the fish are protected or believe that they inequitably bear the burden of such protection."[10]

The burden was considerable, whether inequitable or not. In the weeks around the demonstration and civil disobedience on Independence Day 2001, fields without project irrigation water were parched. Estimates of farm losses attributed to the shutoff ranged from $150 million to $250 million. Struggling farmers could not afford high prices for alfalfa to feed their cattle, and hay producers could not take advantage of high prices because they lacked the water to grow a crop. "Already in towns like Klamath Falls, population 17,000, and Tulelake, Calif., population 1,000, businesses have begun to close and school populations have plunged by as much as 30 percent, reflecting an exodus of [migrant] farm workers."[11] Other reports from Klamath Falls mentioned that supplies at food banks were stretched and that demands on county mental health services were up 60 percent over the same period in 2000. "Work at one local hairdressers has 'dropped off like a lead sinker,' one cosmetologist said."[12] Reacting to the shutoff, Don Russell, director of the Klamath Basin Water Users Association, contended, "The Bureau totally betrayed us. The agency could have stood up and said [to the FWS], 'Your science stinks,' but it didn't. . . . I feel funny putting my hand over my heart and saying 'my land of liberty.'"[13]

But it would be a mistake to assume that friends of the environment were clearly winners, judging from their assessments in the spring and summer of 2001. Wildlife biologist Tim Griffiths, who grew up in the basin, was frustrated about the protection of the fish at the expense of other wildlife in the refuges. "When I was studying conservation management at Oregon State University, they drilled it into my head that you manage for the [whole] ecosystem and that if you manage for one species you're in trouble." Phil Norton, manager of the six national wildlife refuges in the basin, was apprehensive. "I don't believe we can have consensus and conservation when we have a community in chaos," he said. "I'll freely admit I think the ESA should be tweaked; everybody's losing under this." Larry Dunsmore, a biologist for the Klamath tribe, agreed. "The ESA has totally polarized the situation at a time when what we need is significant restoration that requires buy-in from the private landowners. I can't help but wonder if we'll look back at this time as a step forward or a step back." Oregon Governor John Kitzhaber, a long-time friend of the environment, told a crowd of angry farmers in mid-April, "The biggest problem with the Endangered Species Act ... is how [it] is implemented. I don't intend to stand by and see this community or the children in the community become extinct."[14]

But Jan Hasselman, an attorney for the Earthjustice Legal Fund in Seattle, insisted, "The Endangered Species Act is working exactly like it's supposed to. It's helping us find a balance between different needs in the basin. The BuRec has given the irrigators every drop of water they've needed since [the agency] opened shop in 1905, but the government has obligations to different people in the basin besides the irrigators."[15] In this and other assessments by participants, there is a tendency to accept the need for balance. But there is little agreement on where the balance lies and little understanding of practical means by which it might be found.

Assessments on all sides were further complicated early in February 2002, when a committee of the National Research Council (NRC) released an interim evaluation of the FWS and NMFS biological opinions on the effects of Klamath project operations on the three listed fish species. Secretary of the Interior Gale Norton and other federal officials had requested the study during the crisis in 2001, in part because the scientific foundations of the 2001 Operations Plan were controversial from the outset. The committee found that the two biological opinions had substantial scientific support except for the parts that mandated shutting off irrigation water under the ESA. In its own words,

> The committee concludes that there is no substantial scientific foundation at this time for changing the operations of the Klamath Project to maintain higher water levels in Upper Klamath Lake for the endangered sucker population or higher minimum flows in the Klamath River main stem for the threatened coho population. The committee concludes that the [Bureau of Reclamation] proposals are also unjustified, however, because they would leave open the possibility that water levels in Upper Klamath Lake and minimum flows in the Klamath River main stem could be lower than those occurring over the past 10 years for specific kinds of climatic conditions.[16]

Lower levels and flows, as initially proposed by the bureau, were lower than any in recorded history and therefore would expose the listed fish to unknown risks. Thus none of the agencies' proposals for Klamath Project operations was based on sound science.

The details of the NRC evaluation highlight scientific uncertainty. For example, the FWS biological opinion and RPA found that "adverse water quality conditions known to stress or kill the endangered suckers are associated with the lowest water levels." But using the same sources as the biological opinions, the committee found no relationship between water levels in the lake and those water quality conditions, especially algae population densities and extremes of dissolved oxygen or pH. "Furthermore, a substantial mortality occurred in 1971, the year of highest recorded water levels since 1950 and, within the last ten years, mortality of adults was highest in 1995, 1996, and 1997, none of which was a year of low water level."[17] The NMFS biological opinion and RPA sought higher flows "to increase the amount of habitat in the main stem, [but] the increase in habitat . . . in dry years is small (a few percent) and possibly insignificant. Furthermore, tributary conditions appear to be the critical factor for this [coho] population; these conditions are not affected by operations of the Klamath Project and are therefore not addressed in the RPA. Finally, and most importantly, water added as necessary to sustain higher flows in the main stem during dry years would need to come from reservoirs, and this water could equal or exceed the lethal temperature for coho salmon during the warmest months."[18] In this respect at least, the NRC committee corroborated the farmers' understanding.

The committee insisted that its tasks "encompass only the scientific and technical issues that are relevant to the three endangered and threatened fish species." But the committee also noted that "the strong and multiple interests of individuals and communities in the Klamath Basin in the conclusions reached by the committee are well recognized by the committee members."[19] In view of these strong and multiple interests, it was not surprising that the committee and its report quickly became ensnared in politics. Different interests criticized or used science to support their previous positions. For instance, Jim Waltman of the Wilderness Society criticized what he perceived as the committee's search for clear-cut proof of the relationships between water levels and the fishes' health. "This is like saying we can't really prove that cigarette smoking causes cancer. It's intuitive: lower lake levels will not help fish." Chuck Cushman of the American Land Rights Association observed, "You can't trust the science, because you can't trust the scientists. They've got a biased point of view, and there's no way for people to fight back." U.S. Rep. John Peterson (R–Pa.) concluded, "'It's reprehensible when junk science is used to put farmers out of business'. . . . Federal land-use decisions should be based 'on sound science and not political agendas.'"[20]

Thus the NRC's interim report, the best available science, did more to reinforce existing positions on the issue than to change them. One member of the NRC committee considered it "a real insult for people to call it junk science, because there has been a lot of good science done. It just hasn't provided a clear-cut answer."[21] But even if the report could have provided a clear-cut answer, it would have been vulnerable to attacks from political interests adversely affected by it. Within weeks of the NRC's interim report, and prompted by the Klamath Basin water crisis, a committee of the U.S. House of Representatives debated bills cosponsored by Greg Walden (R–Ore.) and Richard Pombo (R–Calif.) "to ensure the government uses 'sound science' when it protects vanishing plants and animals."[22] Thus science becomes devalued as an important resource for policy when political interest groups expect and demand more than science can deliver. Science itself is among the interests poorly served in an arena of entrenched political interests.

## The Problem and Its Roots

Stepping back from the details of the Klamath story, it is worthwhile to clarify the problem. The problem is not changes in natural and social conditions, which are unavoidable and unpredictable to a large extent. Nature will continue to produce surprises such as the droughts in the basin in 1991, 1994, and 2001, with or without global climate change. Modern American society will continue to evolve new interests, and new interests will undermine established policies such as reclamation for the development of the West and lead to the establishment of new policies such as protection of endangered species. Moreover, the problem is not exclusively in the damage done to interests in respecting contractual obliga-tions to provide irrigation water and in maintaining suitable habit for migratory birds and bald eagles. These interests were acknowledged as appropriate under the law, along with interests in maintaining fisheries for Klamath Basin tribes and protecting endangered and threatened species. The problem is an inability to integrate valid and appropriate community interests when possible, or to balance them when necessary, to protect or advance the common interest of the com-munity. Interests were hardly balanced when the 2001 Annual Operations Plan allocated all the water in Upper Klamath Lake to the three listed fishes at the ex-pense of irrigators and wildlife in the national refuges. The problem in the Klam-ath Basin water crisis is representative of other problems involving other natural resources elsewhere in the American West and in other issue areas as well.[23]

### The Common Interest

Advancing the common interest is the appropriate goal and criterion of gover-nance in a democracy. "In the simplest terms, the common interest is composed of interests widely shared by members of a community. It would benefit the community as a whole and be supported by most community members, *if they can find it*."[24] Judgments of the common interest depend on assessments of the multiple interests in the particular community. When such judgments differ significantly, the differences must be resolved through politics if the community is to act collectively. This does not require unanimity.[25] In the Klamath crisis, friends of the environment shared interests in managing for the whole ecosystem, not just the listed fishes; in avoiding a community in chaos, from which everybody loses; and in a buy-in to restoration from private landowners, not polarization. At the same time, irrigation interests who filed the Kandra suit shared the interest in protecting listed fishes when they proposed to allocate limited water roughly equally. The common interest was not exclusively an interest in protecting listed fish regardless of the consequences for other interests, nor was it in meeting all needs of the people in the community regardless of the listed fish.

In general, it is difficult both politically and ethically to justify policies that serve the special interests of the few over the common interest of the many in the American political tradition. Today, Americans understand "We, the people" in the preamble to the Constitution as a reference to all the people, not the select few. Similarly, the Pledge of Allegiance reaffirms "liberty and justice for all," not the select few. Those who accept equal rights and insist on fair consideration of their own interests cannot legitimately deny equivalent consideration of competing interests without showing that the competing interests are invalid or inappropriate.[26] Interests are invalid if not supported by the evidence available and inappropriate if not consistent with larger community commitments such as "liberty and justice for all." Interest groups in competition with each other sometimes appeal to their own special interests in attempts to rally their own supporters. This typically does less to achieve dominance by one group over the others than to block collective action and reinforce gridlock. Interest groups sometimes appeal to the common interest in one form or another to broaden community support for their policy positions. This is both expedient in the search for more community support and principled in a democracy. Thus interest groups can and do contribute to advancing the common interest, but some do not. We define a special interest group as one that advances its own interests at net cost to the common interest of the community as a whole.

The common interest also is consistent with Aldo Leopold's land ethic. Leopold wrote, "All ethics so far evolved rest upon a single premise: that the individual is a member of a community of interdependent parts. His instincts prompt him to compete for his place in that community, but his ethics prompt him also to co-operate (perhaps in order that there may be a place to compete for). The land ethic simply enlarges the boundaries of the community to include soils, waters, plants, and animals, or collectively: the land."[27] The land ethic does not divide the community into human and nonhuman parts and recommend the subordination of one part to another. Indeed, Leopold insisted that "conservation is a state of health in the land-organism. Health expresses the cooperation of the interdependent parts: soil, water, plants, and people. . . . When any part lives by depleting another, the state of health is gone."[28] Similarly, a democratic community is unhealthy when special interest groups live by depleting the valid and appropriate interests of other groups in the community. For environmentalists, Leopold's land ethic is a principled basis for accepting the common interest as the purpose and criterion of governance in a democracy.[29]

Judgments of the common interest, it bears repeating, depend on assessments of the multiple interests in the particular community. The common interest typically includes interests represented by environmentalists, such as clean water, clean air, and the sustainability of natural resources, out to the seventh generation in some versions. It typically includes interests represented by employees and employers in a sustainable economy, such as jobs and income that support a decent standard of living. It typically includes interests represented by public officials and citizens in sustaining public services, such as schools, police and fire protection, and recreation. And so on. (Sometimes environmentalists, employees and employers, and officials and citizens are the same people.) Because each community is dynamic and different in some respects, neither the range of potentially valid and appropriate interests nor the possible tradeoffs or integrations between them can be fixed or standardized entirely. Assessments are easier done in a local community than in a community of national or global scope because there are fewer interests, and they are easier done by noting present and near-term problems because our understanding of what is sustainable out to the seventh generation is limited. But assessments must be done despite such practical complications. And different judgments of the common interest must be resolved politically if the community is to act democratically.

### Historical Roots

In short, the problem is an inability to integrate valid and appropriate interests into natural resource policies that advance the common interest. The historical roots of the problem can be traced back to scientific management in the Progressive era. A seminal paper on "A Piece-Rate System" by Frederick W. Taylor in 1895 inaugurated development of a collection of management techniques including time and motion studies, standardized tools and operations, wage incentives, and accounting systems. In 1910, the Taylor system and related systems of management were named "scientific management" in hearings of the Interstate Commerce Commission, hearings that "brought headlines and set off an efficiency craze that swept the nation. Suddenly every problem from governmental sloth to personal inadequacy could be cured by the new methods if properly applied." Scientific management sought "the increase of productivity through rational measurement, the elimination of waste and duplication, and the search for the 'one best way.'" Organized labor resisted changes that sped up work without protection from overwork but gradually made accommodations to scientific management. Since Taylor's paper in 1895, "Scientific Management has worked its way into the fabric of all modern industrial societies, where it is now so common as to go unnoticed by most people."[30]

Progressive conservationists in Theodore Roosevelt's administration led the effort to bring scientific management to natural resource policy. In Samuel Hays's famous account, they preached a gospel of efficiency. "The crux of the gospel of efficiency lay in a rational and scientific method of making basic technological decisions though a single, central authority." Consider the three aspirations manifest here. First is a scientific aspiration, to use "to the fullest extent the latest scientific knowledge and expert, disinterested personnel." Teddy Roosevelt himself "had an almost unlimited faith in applied science." Such faith implies the exclusion of other kinds of knowledge. Second is a policy aspiration, to base decisions on technology and efficiency. Roosevelt and his advisors were appalled by the waste and inefficiency manifest in overgrazing, timber cutting, land monopolization, and water speculation, which they attributed to unrestricted economic competition. "To replace competition with economic planning, these new efficiency experts argued, would not only arrest the damage of the past, but could also create new heights of prosperity and material abundance for the future." Third is a decision-making aspiration, to rely on a single, central authority for making optimal decisions on a national scale and implementing them through a bureaucratic chain of command. Thus in Teddy Roosevelt's administration, the "entire program emphasized a flow of authority from the top down and minimized the political importance of institutions which reflected the organized sentiments of local communities." Policy issues were not to be resolved through partisan politics, interest group compromises, or judicial decisions. That "would defeat the inner spirit of the gospel of efficiency. Instead, experts, using technical and scientific methods, should decide all matters of development and utilization of resources, all problems of allocation of funds."[31]

Overall, the gospel of efficiency was "an attempt to supplant conflict with a 'scientific' approach to social and economic questions."[32] Conflict nevertheless frustrated fulfillment of Progressive conservationists' aspirations for decision making. When they excluded resource users from the important resource policy decisions, resource users naturally sought political means to protect their interests. Some of them were water, cattle, and timber barons who were among the richest and most powerful people in their own areas. They discovered eventually that nationwide pressure groups were their most effective means to influence policy. Pressure groups "concerned with single interests—such as navigation, flood control, or irrigation—joined with administrative agencies in charge of individual programs and congressional committees which deal with specialized subjects to defeat an integrated approach."[33] (Such alliances are now called "iron triangles.") Conservation groups and environmental interest groups eventually engaged resource users in power-balancing politics. They had little choice, other than to abandon the fight. The results are visible today in single interests—such as no commercial logging in national forests—that mirror the single interests of resource user groups.[34] Thus politics were never replaced by the rise of scientific experts and central planning. Instead, politics took various different forms as the context evolved. Even Gifford Pinchot, the leading Progressive conservationist in forestry, wielded his "expertise [as] a political tool that he honed more sharply than his woodsman's ax. Pinchot not only deployed expertise for political gain—he helped define expertise in ways that would yield political benefits."[35]

Politics also frustrated the policy aspirations of Progressive conservationists. "Single-purpose policies . . . became the predominant pattern because they provided opportunities for [resource-user] participation in decision-making." Single-purpose policies once were considered "impractical from the point of view of the conservation ideal of maximum development through scientific adjustment of competing uses" on a national scale.[36] But the agencies nevertheless found it expedient to adapt their policy aspirations to single-purpose policies. For example, the Forest Service harnessed the science and technology of silviculture to help meet the nation's demand for timber, especially after World War II. "In response to growing criticism of its accelerated timber harvest program in the 1960s, the Forest Service defensively asserted its expertise and insisted that its management conformed to sound principles of forestry." Despite the ecological consequences of intensive management for timber harvest, "pressure from the timber industry and optimism about progress from new technology led the agency to repeatedly raise the allowable cut, eventually above levels that were sustainable even under optimistic assumptions." This was hardly sound science or policy, which began to be challenged in the Multiple Use Sustained Yield Act of 1960. The act mandated outdoor recreation, range, timber, watershed, and wildlife and fish as multiple uses of national forests but left the balance between uses to forest managers. In 1960, the Forest Service was still considered a "model of public-spirited bureaucratic efficiency" for its success in timber production. By 1990, it was "assailed from all sides"—once as a "stultifying, almost Stalinesque bureaucracy"—for its persistence in timber production and failure to accommodate demands for multiple uses of national forests.[37]

Similarly, the Bureau of Reclamation once was recognized for its success in meeting demands for water for human settlements throughout the arid West but later was criticized for its failure to accommodate other demands for the water resources it had developed. Thanks to successes in an era long gone, remnants of scientific management still are taken as given in important parts of natural resource policy today. But those remnants now limit our ability to find common interest solutions to problems in natural resource policy.[38] This is illustrated in the Klamath case.

### Remnants Illustrated

First, consider the aspiration in scientific management to apply science as the foundation for policy, to the exclusion of other kinds of knowledge. It survives in basing the 2001 Annual Operations Plan on the "best available science" as required by ESA, in the convening of the National Academy of Sciences (NAS) committee, and in appeals to "science" as justification for partisan positions. For example, Glenn Spain, regional director of the PCFFA, feared political pressure was being exercised "at the highest levels" of government to negate Judge Armstrong's rule in favor of PCFFA. "They're trying to force the agencies to back away from *what science requires* and cut a deal where irrigators get some water," he said in defense of the ruling. Similarly in the Kandra suit, Jan Hasselman of Earthjustice claimed, "Overall, the biological opinions represent the best science, and are required by the Endangered Species Act." Paul Simmons, representing the irrigators, characterized the biological opinions as "fundamentally flawed on technical grounds." Judge Aiken merely stated the obvious in her ruling: "The opposing views and supporting evidence of the parties demonstrate that plaintiffs simply disagree with the scientific conclusions reached by FWS and NMFS."[39] No one argued against using the best available science. But on whose science should policy be based?

That is a political question because applied scientific knowledge always is incomplete and because there was much at stake in how scientific issues were resolved in the 2001 Annual Operations Plan despite the scientific uncertainties. Scientific uncertainties are apparent in the NRC committee review of data limitations pertinent to Klamath Project operations. "While information of a sporadic or anecdotal nature is available over as much as 100 years, routinely-collected data on environmental characteristics and fish [in Upper Klamath Lake] are available only since 1990 or later." Similarly, the committee noted that "standard methods for observing and counting spawning fish are not easily applied [in the main stem of the Klamath River], and the size of the spawning population is not known." Moreover, "the assessment of habitat suitability is difficult and subject to considerable uncertainty. [Assessment methods] require extensive field measurements that are not yet available."[40] In its rejection of the bureau's proposed Operating Plan, the NRC committee recognized that future environmental conditions and population outcomes could range outside the limited scientific record. Consequently, it is not surprising that there is no impersonal scientific basis for the 2001 Annual Operations Plan or any competing plan. The scientific studies commissioned by the bureau, the FWS, the NMFS, the Klamath Water Users Association, and Secretary Norton through the NRC reflect their respective policy positions. Nor is it surprising, given the importance of science in the 2001 Annual Operations Plan, that self-assessed losers attacked science and scientists themselves. Thus the Klamath case calls into question Progressive era faith in applied science as the foundation for policy and as a practical alternative to politics. Decisions nevertheless have to be made, despite scientific uncertainties.

Second, consider the aspiration to make technological decisions on behalf of efficiency—initially on a national scale but later to meet single targets. It survives in the FWS and NMFS biological opinions, including the RPAs, which apparently determined the 2001 Annual Operations Plan under the ESA and drought conditions and were upheld by the courts. Efficiency meant maximizing the benefit—fish recovery, a single target—with little regard for cost. The existence of multiple costs and benefits, and disputes over which is which, call into question efficiency in this narrow sense. So does the existence of scientific uncertainties, unknowns, and omissions in the means selected to realize the target in the Operations Plan. The impacts of prescribed water levels and flows on the target were uncertain according to the NRC committee's report, the best available science. The impacts of other actions prescribed on behalf of the target were unknown. Among them were postponed installation of screens to keep endangered suckers from being sucked into the main irrigation canal. The bureau claimed that it was difficult to design a screen that does not kill fish.[41] Moreover, all conditions unaffected by Klamath Project manipulation of water levels and flows were excluded from the RPAs even if they affected the target. Among them were coho habitats in the tributaries of the Klamath River main stem and human acts that pollute fish habitats throughout the basin. Unrecognized conditions affecting fish recovery exist to the extent that knowledge of this open ecosystem is incomplete. On the cost side, any reasonable claim of efficiency must take into account the costs of the Operations Plan borne by interests other than recovery. But these costs were considered irrelevant under the law.

Moreover, efficiency in the development and use of resources to meet single targets is not equivalent to rationality. Rationality involves the mutual adaptation of ends and means, and the appropriate end, as argued earlier, is advancing the common interest. The Operations Plan sacrificed the valid and appropriate interests of those who support wildlife in the six national wildlife refuges that depend on irrigation runoff, farmers who were denied irrigation water and whatever depends on it, and others in the community, including fertilizer dealers and hairdressers, who depend on the farmers. Groups disadvantaged and frustrated by a policy decision do not necessarily go away. More often they find other means to protect their interests. A rational assessment of the consequences flowing from the Operations Plan also might include civil disobedience, distrust in government, and alienation, as manifest on Independence Day 2001 in Klamath Falls and on other occasions. It is hardly rational to make policy decisions that deplete reserves of faith in structures of governance, as if such reserves were unlimited.[42] Thus the Operations Plan was less than rational or efficient. The Klamath case calls into question Progressive era faith in technological decisions on behalf of efficiency or rationality.

Third, consider the aspiration to make policy decisions through a single, central authority that minimizes the influence of local interests. It survives in the apparent priority of national legislation and its implementation in the Klamath Basin. Despite her sympathy for irrigators in the Kandra suit, Judge Aiken noted, "I am bound to uphold the law": the ESA. The NRC committee elaborated: "The [ESA] sets the framework for determination of future water use and management in the Klamath River basin. The ESA is tightly focused on the requirements for survival of the threatened and endangered fishes, the survival of which is not negotiable under the ESA."[43] However, even the ESA is not a single, central authority. As amended in 1978, the ESA includes a provision to convene a panel of seven cabinet-level officials chaired by the interior secretary to weigh economic and ecological considerations in particular cases. The Bush administration refused to convene this "God Squad" in the Klamath case in July 2001, ostensibly on technical grounds.[44] Moreover, the ESA does not automatically control policy decisions. According to Judge Armstrong's ruling in the PCFFA case, the Bureau of Reclamation did not comply with certain procedural provisions of the ESA in the year before the crisis. Similarly, a year after the crisis, in the midst of an unexpected drought, the Klamath Project gave priority to irrigators without significant changes in black-letter law.[45] Finally, the voluminous national legislation accumulated over the last century is not necessarily consistent with the ESA as written or implemented.[46] For example, the National Environmental Policy Act of 1969 arguably provided authority to open up the bureau's decision process beyond the agencies' biological assessment and opinions to include public comments on a draft Environmental Impact Statement.

The aspiration for a single, central authority was institutionalized in the distinctive mandate and limited jurisdiction of each of the federal agencies involved in the Klamath Basin crisis. The more visible agencies include the Bureau of Reclamation, the Klamath Project, the Federal Bureau of Investigation, the U.S. Marshals Service, the FWS, the NMFS, the National Resources Conservation Service, the Lower Klamath National Wildlife Refuge, and the federally chartered NAS, for which the NRC is the operating arm. But no agency was autonomous even within its own mandate and jurisdiction. For example, despite its mandate to develop and deliver irrigation water through the Klamath Project, the bureau had to take into account the FWS and NMFS, other parts of the executive branch, Congress, and U.S. district courts. Vice President Dick Cheney intervened on behalf of irrigator interests before the Operations Plan, and Secretary Norton announced the release of up to 75,000 acre-feet of irrigation water late in July 2001.[47] Oregon Senator Ron Wyden and Representative Greg Walden, among other elected representatives of the basin, took the lead in seeking federal aid through Congress. State and local agencies and officials, including Governor Kitzhaber, also were involved.

The ideal of a single, central authority becomes even more unrealistic when nongovernment organizations are taken into account. These include the three Klamath tribes (the Klamath, the Modoc, and the Yahooskin Band of Snake) recognized by treaty in 1864, the NRC, and the large number of interest groups involved. Among these are the PCFFA, the Klamath Basin Water Users Association, the Klamath and Tulelake irrigation districts, the Earthjustice Legal Fund, the Wilderness Society, and the American Land Rights Association, all of which are authorized under the First Amendment "peaceably to assemble, and to petition the Government for a redress of grievances." The First Amendment also authorized local, regional, and national news organizations to report demonstrations, civil disobedience, and related events and thereby to bring the crisis to the attention of the general public and officials and interest groups in Washington. It should not be assumed that frustrated groups such as the irrigators will work through the Bureau of Reclamation, the courts, or other authorized structures of government indefinitely. Some, such as Paul Arritola, were tired of playing by the rules in the summer of 2001.[48]

This fragmented decision-making structure systematically frustrates finding common ground on policies that advance the common interest, in the Klamath crisis and on many other issues in natural resource policy. A fragmented structure gives each agency or interest group incentives to defend its own primary interest and attack other interests involved in the issue, even if it accepts those other interests as valid and appropriate. The structure also encourages adversaries to commission their own scientific studies as part of their defense or attack. In the conclusion to her ruling in the Kandra suit, Judge Aiken recognized both the problem with respect to the common interest and the structural roots of the problem.

> The scarcity of water in the Klamath River Basin is a situation ... which demands efforts and resolve on the part of all parties to create solutions that provide water for the necessary protection of fish, wildlife and tribal trust resources, as well as the agricultural needs of farmers and their communities. Continued litigation is not likely to assist in such a challenging endeavor. This court hopes and expects that the parties and other entities necessary to long-term solutions will continue to pursue alternatives to meet the needs of the Klamath River Basin.[49]

The mediation alternatives failed in the Kandra case, in part because the parties and other entities already were polarized and entrenched in their positions. This is characteristic of the "new American political (dis)order," a reference to trends toward more fragmentation and less integration among conflicting interests and to a decline in the representative and deliberative aspects of public participation. According to Robert A. Dahl, a leading democratic theorist, "What is missing, because the framers did not provide for it, is a constitutional process for readily resolving these conflicts" built into the separation of powers and checks and balances between them.[50]

Community-based initiatives have demonstrated some potential to supply the missing piece in the constitutional process.[51] A community-based initiative emerged from the 1994 drought in the Klamath Basin: a twenty-seven–member working group appointed by Senator Mark Hatfield "to develop ways to restore the ecosystem, maintain the economy, and reduce the impacts of future droughts." An informal appraisal claims that the group "created several wetland restoration projects in the Upper Basin and helped to facilitate dialogue between disparate parts of the community. But since Hatfield left office in 1996, the federal agencies haven't given the group enough money to make significant changes, says Alice Kilham, one of the group's original leaders."[52] The group made little apparent difference in the 2001 Annual Operations Plan, although it may yet help find a long-term solution.[53] Not all of the hundreds or thousands of community-based initiatives that have emerged have advanced the common interest. (Nor have all agencies or interest groups, for that matter. There are no sure things in governance.) However, some community-based initiatives have helped significantly in advancing the common interest, despite the limitations of established structures of governance. Included among these are initiatives in the implementation of the ESA in the recovery of endangered fishes in the Colorado River and wolves in the northern Rockies.[54]

## Adaptive Governance

The rise of community-based initiatives marks the emergence of adaptive governance from the remnants of scientific management in certain places, much as scientific management emerged piecemeal from unrestricted competition over natural resources during several decades around the turn of the twentieth century. Community-based initiatives began to rise before the mid-1980s in response to the limitations of established structures of governance, as manifest in apparently intractable issues that could not easily be ignored. They are composed of participants representing quite different interests who interact directly over a period of time in an effort to resolve an issue in the community where they live. The small scale and issue focus of a community-based initiative open up additional opportunities for citizens and officials alike to advance their common interest by integrating their separate interests if possible or balancing them if necessary through new policies. Community-based initiatives are the most promising approach to situations like the Klamath crisis and to similar situations anticipated in the Bureau of Reclamation's 1998 guidebook for field officials: "Today, anyone can delay or even stop your process by lobbying Congress, initiating court action, or rallying grass roots effort to oppose your action. You cannot take away their right to fight. Thus you need to pay attention to their issues and actively seek their participation and consent."[55]

As emerging and as envisioned here, adaptive governance is a pattern of practices; it cannot be reduced to any one thing without serious distortion. Adaptive governance includes the adaptation of policy decisions to real people, not the cardboard caricatures sometimes constructed for scientific or managerial purposes. Real people act on limited subjective perspectives that are diverse, not uniform; they act both rationally and nonrationally on these perspectives; and, though influenced by external factors, their acts are not determined by scientific or public laws. Sound policy is based on people as they are, and in a democracy it seeks to advance their common interests within practical constraints. Adaptive governance also includes the adaptation of policy decisions to experience on the ground as real people interact with each other and the soils, waters, plants, and animals in specific contexts. Sound policy takes differences and changes in their contexts into account. Because of its emphasis on adapting to experience on the ground, adaptive governance is an expression of American pragmatism, not another set of utopian aspirations.[56] Adaptive governance also includes the adaptation of policy decisions to twenty-first–century realities that are still largely denied in the remnants of scientific management. Contemporary experience in Klamath and elsewhere indicates that science is not sufficient as a foundation for sound policies and decision-making structures, even though science can make important contributions. Important policy decisions inevitably are political, even if significant scientific and technical considerations also are involved. And there is no single, central authority to make policy decisions or resolve political issues. Sound policy takes these larger contemporary realities into account. Historically, adaptive governance is not merely scientific management done right.[57]

To help advance the common interest, this book recommends a transition from the remnants of scientific management to the adaptive governance of natural resources on public lands in the American West. The primary purpose is to clarify how to expedite the transition, for those concerned about the problem and in a position to make a difference in practice. Foremost among these are present and future field officials in agencies with jurisdiction over public lands. Field officials make most of the important policy decisions, whether they want to or not, because voluminous and often inconsistent national laws and policies do not determine a single solution to any localized problem. Moreover, their superiors in regional headquarters and the nation's capitol lack sufficient time, information, and other resources to oversee decisions on hundreds or thousands of local problems, even if they are motivated to do so. Faced with a local problem, a field official can choose to defend the agency's interests against other agencies, interest groups, and community-based initiatives. But he or she can also choose to work with representatives of interest groups and other agencies to advance the common interest through a community-based initiative. These roles as agency representative and community member can be reconciled in practice, as documented in this book. But a field official's efforts can be hindered or helped by neighbors in the community, by superiors in the agency, and by elected officials at any level, including Washington, D.C. Therefore these people also are relevant to a possible transition from scientific management to adaptive governance.

The next section develops and compares the concepts of scientific management and adaptive governance, drawing on contemporary sources beyond the Klamath crisis for illustrations. The final section introduces the case studies in subsequent chapters that illustrate a possible transition to adaptive governance and clarify how it has already emerged in certain places. The final chapter harvests experience from these cases to develop suggestions for field officials and for those in a position to help or hinder them in implementing adaptive governance on a broader scale. No one can predict with confidence that expansion of adaptive governance is the future of natural resource policy. But at least it is one vision for real people to consider as their faith in scientific management and American government continues to wither under the cumulative weight of adverse experiences. And those involved can help shape the future through more enlightened decisions on behalf of the common interest.

## Patterns of Governance

To develop the concepts of scientific management and adaptive governance in natural resource policy, it is useful to distill from multiple examples and other sources the practices most characteristic of each pattern. Each pattern of governance consists of distinctive and interdependent practices in science, policy, and the structure of decision making. "Distinctive and interdependent" means that a commitment to traditional science constrains the options for policy and decision-making structures; similarly, acceptance of multiple centers of authority and control in decision-making structures constrains the options for policy and science. These three dimensions are not exhaustive of all relevant differences, nor are the patterns entirely symmetrical. For example, historically scientific management has been sustained by general aspirations, whereas adaptive governance is emerging in response to experience in specific situations, as noted earlier. In the future, movement toward adaptive governance will not eliminate bureaucracies or other mainstays of scientific management but will subsume them in a larger pattern of governance and redefine their roles. The distillation of each pattern nevertheless serves as an ideal type—a hypothetical perfect specimen—useful in identifying deviations from the type in actual specimens and characterizing the few specimens that are close approximations.[58]

### Ideal Types

Scientific management as an ideal type may appear to be something of a straw man, no longer substantial enough or important enough to merit much attention. However, as shown in the Klamath case, remnants of scientific management are institutionalized in national law and policy, government agencies, and other aspects of natural resource policy today. And some scientists and decision makers still find it expedient to invoke scientific management to explain and justify their actions, even if they do not consistently practice it.

In the ideal type, the foundation of scientific management is positivism, the traditional view of science in our culture. C. S. Holling called it the "science of the parts" and described it as "essentially experimental, reductionist, and narrowly disciplinary." "The goal is to narrow uncertainty to the point where acceptance of an argument among scientific peers is essentially unanimous." The preferred method is the controlled experiment in which "a narrow enough focus is chosen to pose hypotheses, collect data, and design critical tests for the rejection of invalid hypotheses." Other rigorous or "hard" methods also are used for critical tests that depend on precise comparisons between quantitative data and predictions deduced from hypotheses. Replications of critical tests presume the existence of stable relationships underlying the diversity of behavior observed across contexts. Hypotheses that survive replications reduce that behavior to simple causal relationships. In principle, such relationships are independent of any particular context and independent of any particular scientist's point of view. They are "objective" in that sense. In Holling's summary assessment, the science of the parts is "appropriately conservative and unambiguous, but it achieves this by being incomplete and fragmentary."[59] This is basic science, the most plausible interpretation of many references to "sound science."

In scientific management, the prerequisite for sound policy and management is sound science. The identification of problems begins with a scientific assessment of the management context, including measurements of the important variables. The selection of problems depends on the scientific relationships available to solve them. Each relationship clarifies the technology by which one or more causes can be manipulated to produce the desired effect—typically a single goal or target—as efficiently as possible. For example, how can an outbreak of spruce budworm infestation be controlled? How can forest fires be suppressed? How can salmon populations be restored?[60] Each target typically is fixed and taken as given or assumed to respect scientific objectivity at the boundary between science and nonscience. Science-based technology also can be applied to determine the necessary conditions for realizing a target. For example, what water level or flow is necessary to protect endangered fishes? What amount of timber harvest is sustainable? Science-based technology independent of particular contexts supports long-term plans and the standardization of planning processes. For example, under the National Forest Management Act (NFMA) of 1976, the Forest Service mandated a "consistent, unified approach to forest planning" through FORPLAN, a computer optimization model used to calculate the allowable sale quantity of timber at minimum cost in the planning process in each national forest.[61] Each forest management plan was expected to serve for 10 to 15 years under the NFMA. Informally, such plans were expected to be approved, funded, and implemented because they were science based. Evaluating the consequences of implementing a plan is less important than planning if the technology is sound and managers respect the goals, procedures, and boundaries authorized by a higher authority.

In the decision-making structure, management plans and the planning process are subsumed under the jurisdiction of a single, central authority such as the Forest Service. Participation by scientific and technical experts is a prerequisite because only they have the necessary knowledge and skills. However, to maximize their expertise and minimize threats to their objectivity, the experts discount public comments and insist on clear management direction from superiors at a higher level of authority.[62] Superiors are responsible for reducing multiple policy goals to clear targets and prescribing boundaries and procedures for realizing those targets. Working within prescribed boundaries and procedures, the experts are responsible for incorporating the best available science and technology into planning to realize the target and sometimes to implement plans after their authorization by higher authority. Implementation depends primarily on the enforcement of rules through the bureaucracy. Experts also advise their superiors on the best available science and technology. Thus technical advice flows up the hierarchy in the bureaucratic division of labor, whereas substantive and procedural direction for management flows down to the experts. In principle, both the experts and their superiors are accountable to elected representatives of the people under the administrative management paradigm.[63]

Adaptive governance as emerging in practice and envisioned here is less well defined. It begins with recognition that established practices are increasingly problematic and that politics are unavoidable amid twenty-first–century realities. No important policy issue is purely technical, if "technical" is understood as an issue that is reducible to scientific or administrative rules and therefore nonpolitical. "Politics" are best understood as the exercise of power, the giving and withholding of support in making important decisions. Politics are deplorable when they serve special interests at net cost to the community as a whole. Politics are necessary to advance the common interest through public policy and commendable when they do.[64]

In the ideal type of adaptive governance, authority and control over policy issues in the overall decision-making structure are fragmented. Thus the overall structure depends on community-based initiatives to integrate the valid and appropriate interests at stake in the local issue, which is unique if viewed from the bottom up.[65] A community-based initiative is open in principle to representatives of any person, group, or agency with enough at stake to justify participation from their own perspectives, but exceptions may be warranted in practice. For example, it may be prudent to exclude people with no tolerance of other interests if the goal is to find common ground or to proceed without people who are unwilling or unable to participate.[66] The interests of participants are diverse but interdependent, so that protecting or advancing one interest depends on accommodating others. (If interests were not diverse, there would be no issue to resolve; if interests were not interdependent, there would be no reason to participate.) Thus politics are unavoidable. Within a community-based initiative, participants in search of common ground have opportunities to integrate local and scientific knowledge, to resolve factual issues through first-hand observations, and to negotiate face to face. But outcomes also depend on the knowledge, authorities, funds, and other resources brought to the table by participants, their capacity to develop mutual respect and trust, and their willingness to exploit conflicts and other ambiguities in applicable laws and regulations. If negotiations succeed, the outcome is a consensus (not necessarily unanimity) on policy expected to advance their common interest. If implementing the policy advances their common interest, the policy tends to be diffused as a model and adapted by similar communities elsewhere and to be used as a resource for reforms at higher levels in the decision-making structure. In any case, participants in the community-based initiative assume responsibility and accountability for the policy because they must live with the direct consequences of implementing it.

From a policy standpoint, the multiple goals of a consensus policy reflect the common interest of the participants, integrating their valid and appropriate interests where possible and balancing them where necessary. The problem addressed by the policy consists of discrepancies between these goals and past or projected trends in the particular local context. Descriptions of these trends and inferences about the multiple factors shaping them depend on the best scientific and other knowledge available to the participants, including knowledge of the local context. The uncertainties resulting from the limitations of this knowledge are taken into account, not simply acknowledged and ignored, in the invention, evaluation, and selection of action alternatives for ameliorating the problem. Often it is necessary to act on alternatives in the face of significant uncertainties. It is rational to do so if the alternatives are modest enough to fail gracefully if they fail and to allow participants to learn from the experience in a timely fashion and modify future courses of action accordingly. From a procedural standpoint, improvements in policy over time and across local communities depend on an evolutionary process, one that relies on trying various alternatives, selecting what works, and building on the successes. But the process is better described as quasi-evolutionary because the alternatives are goal directed, not random.[67] Planning can improve the alternatives, but in the face of uncertainties the burden of decision making shifts to monitoring and evaluating and to terminating policy alternatives that fail. No policy can be a permanent solution because interests, knowledge, and other significant details of the context are subject to change.

Finally, the science applied in adaptive governance is contextual, necessitating interpretations and judgments that integrate what is known about the particular context. (A consensus on the results of controlled experiments does not imply a consensus on an application to any particular context.) Interpretations and judgments of facts and values are needed because each context is a unique combination of policy-relevant considerations not completely covered in scientific or public laws. These considerations include the behaviors of human beings and other living forms, behaviors subject to change through learning and adaptation as the context evolves. The boundary between applied science and nonscience is tenuous because judgments of facts and values are connected. Each statement of fact is directed toward the goal values of the application and may affect the interests at stake in the particular context.[68] Thus interpretive, qualitative, and other "soft" methods are used, along with any "hard" or rigorous methods that may be relevant and practical. Holling recognized much of this in his "science of the integration of the parts," a second stream of science that is "historical, analytical, and integrative" and "fundamentally concerned with integrative modes of inquiry and multiple sources of evidence." The premise is that "knowledge of the system we deal with is always incomplete. Surprise is inevitable. Not only is the science incomplete, but the system itself is a moving target, evolving because of the impact of management" and other factors.[69] Thus it makes sense to integrate the best available science with other kinds of knowledge, including local knowledge. Local knowledge is equivalent to the "science of the concrete" that served human communities for ten thousand years before the rise of the exact sciences and remains the foundation of modern civilization.[70]

## The Committee of Scientists

To illustrate these ideal types, consider the Committee of Scientists named by Secretary of Agriculture Dan Glickman in December 1997 to address persistent and pervasive controversies in planning in the U.S. Forest Service. (This illustration also shows how the ideal types can shed light on documents of a kind familiar to field officials and other specialists in natural resource policy.) The committee's report, published in March 1999, was important enough to elicit comments from a variety of differently informed perspectives in forest management. The report includes characteristics of both patterns, as if the committee itself were caught up in a transition from scientific management to adaptive governance. Nonetheless, as documented in this section, the establishment of the committee (as distinguished from its report) closely approximates the pattern of scientific management.

Secretary Glickman took formal responsibility for establishing the committee. To recruit the necessary experts, a notice in the *Federal Register* (August 15, 1997) solicited nominations of people who had knowledge of the national forests but were not employees of the Forest Service and collectively represented diverse scientific specialties and academic disciplines. The thirteen nominees selected for the committee met these conditions.[71] Forest Service Chief Mike Dombeck expected that "the breadth of expertise and experience represented by this Committee will ensure that our new planning regulations are scientifically based. We cannot make management decisions that maintain healthy ecosystems without a fundamentally sound planning structure in place." Undersecretary of Agriculture James Lyons urged the committee "to develop a conceptual framework for land and resource planning that could last at least a generation." The committee itself recognized that "its role is not to dictate specific management practices for the Forest Service, but rather to provide advice that the Secretary and Chief may act on as they deem appropriate." The committee also distinguished between science-based and value-based decisions in clarifying the role of the scientific community. "While the scientific community can help estimate the risk associated with different management strategies, decisions about an acceptable level of risk are value based, not science-based decisions."[72]

Turning to the committee's report, it is not difficult to find characteristics of scientific management. While recognizing the interdependence of ecological, economic, and social sustainability, the committee concluded that "the first priority for management is to retain and restore the ecological sustainability of these watersheds, forests, and rangelands for present and future generations." The priority of ecological sustainability was fixed and justified on scientific, legal, and political grounds. Scientifically, continued economic and social benefits from these natural resources depended on their sustainability. A review of a century of legislation concluded that "individually and collectively, our environmental laws express a profound commitment to the protection of plant and animal species and of our air, water, and soil. While the laws allow considerable discretion in their interpretation, their thrust is clear." Finally, the committee appealed to a "national consensus on the importance of sustaining the lands and resources of the national forests and grasslands." Ecological sustainability was not yet a quantifiable target, however. The committee noted that "sustainability is broadly aspirational and can be difficult to define in concrete terms." Nevertheless, "sustainability has spawned a worldwide movement to develop a common set of criteria and indicators."[73] In any case, the committee's report replaced the traditional target, timber harvest, with a new target: ecological sustainability.

Given the priority of sustainability, the committee recommended "building stewardship capacity through a process of collaborative planning" at the regional level. (We emphasize planning here and the collaborative component later.) "Collaborative planning begins by finding agreement in a common vision for the [desired] future conditions of the national forests and grasslands and their unique contributions to different regions of the country." It may be inferred that a common vision was expected to set politics aside and to allow planning to proceed on a scientific foundation from the top down. The committee suggested habitat conservation through "a scientific assessment of the characteristics, composition, structure, and processes of the ecosystems," with an emphasis on native "focal species" because assessing the viability of all species is "impossible from a practical standpoint." Such assessments provide "independent information" "for developing regional, scientifically credible conservation strategies." Large landscape strategies should "build proposed pathways" from current conditions as disclosed by bioregional assessments to desired future conditions. Then these large landscape strategies are worked out at lower levels in the decision-making structure: "Assessments at the more local level, such as watersheds, will be needed to help translate strategic plans for large landscapes into site-specific management actions."[74]

The committee recommended influential roles for scientists to "ensure the development of scientifically credible conservation strategies" in the decision process. These included roles in the ecological assessment and definition of conservation strategies, independent scientific review of proposed conservation strategies before their publication, and "a national scientific committee to advise the Chief of the Forest Service on scientific issues in assessment and planning." Clearly, there was plenty of faith in applied science and plenty of work for scientists.[75] There is also an implication that science is key to credibility.

More characteristic of adaptive governance in the committee's report is the focus on more local collaborative planning, with the emphasis on *collaborative*. (This should be distinguished from regional planning, emphasized earlier.) It is "the process in which scientists, citizens, and other public and private stakeholders come together to debate and discuss how to use and manage the national forest system." Thus it opens up decision processes to additional interests beyond experts' and to the consideration of "lands and communities beyond the boundaries of the national forests and grasslands. National forests and grasslands are open systems that are affected by the land uses outside their boundaries." The committee also acknowledged other considerations more characteristic of adaptive governance. It noted that policy direction is not always clear and consistent: "At times there may be conflicts between the requirements of different statutes and their implementation." Moreover, "within the context of sustaining ecological systems, planning must take generous account of compelling local circumstances. This approach includes the needs of ranching, farming, timber and mining communities as well as Indian communities relying on treaty obligations and Hispanic communities depending on the resources in former Spanish and Mexican land grants." Furthermore, "because of the wide variation in site-specific practices and local environmental conditions, impacts of management practices may not always be well understood or predicted." This implies a need for continuous monitoring to "detect unanticipated changes and allow the introduction of new elements to the system." This also implies a need to preserve policy options as "a way of explicitly acknowledging our incomplete knowledge of complex ecological systems." Overall, "policy and management must evolve according to natural dynamics and disturbances as well as social events, economic changes, and political values." Finally, the committee acknowledged some limitations of science. "Uncertainty arises from an incomplete understanding of how ecological systems work and from insufficient information." Uncertainty is compounded by the fact that ecological systems "are not in equilibrium; inherent dynamics are natural features in these systems."[76]

As manifest in the committee's report, the characteristics of scientific management and adaptive governance are not necessarily compatible. Indeed, certain conflicting directions reveal the many tensions inherent in any transition from scientific management to adaptive governance. Consider the following questions not answered clearly or satisfactorily, and certainly not once and for all, within the constraints of the committee's charter.

- What happens when differently informed scientists, citizens, and public and private stakeholders involved in collaborative planning disagree?
- What happens when their interpretation of the conflicting requirements of statutes concludes that ecological sustainability should not be the priority in their own local circumstances?
- If policy and management must take account of compelling local circumstances and related jurisdictions, what happens when Forest Service regulations standardize local adaptations?
- If policy and management must evolve according to natural and social dynamics and disturbances, what happens when national laws and policies inhibit adaptations over time?
- Given uncertainty arising from incomplete understanding of ecological system dynamics and insufficient scientific information, what are the proper roles of science in decision processes?

Perhaps such questions underlie the reaction of one district ranger now retired from the Forest Service: "Take a look at the Committee of Scientists' 12 recommendations. I defy any line officer to recognize their intent after they were converted to CFR's! It is difficult to create change when the direction is so cloudy."[77] Nevertheless, each line officer answers such questions one way or another, for better or for worse, in each significant decision, and decisions, including "no action," have to be made despite the lack of clear management direction from higher authorities. The questions are not hypothetical, even if they cannot be resolved at the national level.[78]

Regulations based on the committee's recommendations were approved, but to our knowledge their consequences have not been evaluated systematically and comprehensively. That would be a formidable if not prohibitively expensive task involving 155 national forests and 20 national grasslands, including more than 600 ranger districts covering more than 191 million acres. However, if anyone expected that the committee's independence and scientific credentials—as applied to improvements in the Forest Service planning process nationwide—would resolve major management problems in the Forest Service, he or she was mistaken. A few months after publication of the committee's report, the *Journal of Forestry* (May 1999) published comments on it as a special issue. Taken together, the comments from nearly a dozen differently informed perspectives make it abundantly clear that the priority target, the focus on planning, and responsibilities for outcomes were still quite controversial, despite the committee's best efforts.

First, the priority of ecological sustainability among policy goals was challenged in the special issue, along with the alleged national consensus. The priority was controversial even within the committee. An independent consultant, Perry Hagenstein, reported, "The major dispute within the committee was over the proposal in draft reports that the overriding goal for management of the national forests be 'ecological sustainability.'" A veteran ecologist, Arthur Cooper, confirmed that the committee "had to revise planning regulations in an environment where basic policy was disputed (committee members themselves were almost unable to agree how their recommendations should reflect sustainability) and in the face of often-conflicting legislative and administrative direction." Similarly, a member of the Committee of Scientists, Roger Sedjo, described the committee's priority as mission shift. "Its recommendation that 'sustainability should be the guiding star for the stewardship of the national forests' is fundamentally different from the concept of 'sustainable production of multiple outputs.' The latter was the objective of . . . the current statutory legislation governing the management of the National Forest System."[79] The reconciliation of multiple policy goals is an essential task but less science based than value based. The committee stepped over the boundary but had little choice within the framework of its scientific management charter.

Second, the focus on planning was challenged as unrealistic in the special issue. Cooper observed, "The problems of the National Forest System cannot be resolved, not even by the best planning system in the world, because the problems are policy issues, and planning does not resolve policy issues." He believed that "the [planning] process as originally envisioned was never given a fair chance to succeed" because of politics. Sedjo concurred when he wrote that "many forest plans have never been implemented or are only partly implemented because of political considerations or implementation budget shortfalls." Andy Stahl, a spokesman for Forest Service Employees for Environmental Ethics, also concurred: "It's not that NFMA planning has failed, as many say; it has never been tried." Also concurring was Jim Geisinger, a spokesperson for the Northwest Forestry Alliance. He wrote that the "agency has failed to fully implement any of its plans" because of funding shortages, short-term political interference by the White House, and administrative appeals, among other impediments. He attributed part of the failure of current forest planning regulations to "the myriad existing laws that govern land management. These laws have accumulated over the years and have been interpreted and reinterpreted by many courts. The result is that the agency can't do anything without violating the letter of the law." A former Forest Service planner, Harold Nygren, projected that "much of the current tension between the choices for management of national forest land will likely continue because much of the polarity between competing interests, and even between legal mandates, will not be resolved by the [committee's] recommended changes."[80] Nevertheless, the committee was caught up in a ritualistic celebration of scientific management planning aspirations that had only tenuous connections with actual experience on the ground over the previous quarter century.

Third, the special issue included arguments that planning could work if those outside the Forest Service lived up to their responsibilities. For example, Cooper wrote, "Policy issues should be resolved by legislators and politicians, and it is their failure to do so that we are now suffering." "The tragedy is that there are no statesmen or stateswomen at the national level to step forward and resolve the issues." He added, "At some point, Congress and the interest groups together have to ask what is the best thing for the country." Nygren also located responsibility for the problem outside the planning process: "Planners and managers have learned that a planning process cannot resolve the issues; rather the interests involved must come to some accommodation. Management decisions have been held hostage to processes that are not allowed to succeed." A task force of the Society of American Foresters broadly concurred. According to a summary in the special issue, "New legislation must clarify which of the many legitimate public values are now most important and must balance the economic and ecological consequences of human management of forest and rangeland resources. This task, which lies at the heart of the matter, will entail a political struggle of enormous consequence."[81] These arguments can be interpreted as both defenses of scientific management and assignment of blame for the disappointments and frustrations of scientific management.

Such defenses are incomplete at best. They leave the future of scientific management dependent on an aspiration that is unrealistic in the absence of evidence that Congress and the interest groups can reconcile their multiple interests at the national level. Decades of experience indicate that they cannot. Meanwhile, there are more promising possibilities to pursue than improvements in Forest Service planning regulations. According to Nygren, "Experience has shown that 'bridge scientists' and 'bridge managers' . . . can be instrumental in developing good plans." These are "scientists who understand management situations and needs and managers who seek out and apply scientific knowledge and expertise."[82] Such people might be trained, recruited, encouraged, and rewarded in larger numbers. Moreover, they have better opportunities to use their expertise in interpersonal relations to good effect from the bottom up, through community-based initiatives, because problems of policy and management are much more complex from the top down. For example, the Committee of Scientists in principle had to consider more than six hundred different ranger districts in different ecosystems around the country. The complexity is even more overwhelming when other federal agencies are considered.[83] As Randal O'Toole pointed out in the special issue, "Centralized planning cannot work because no one can collect or integrate the huge amount of data needed to understand a forest or the alternative ways of managing that forest. Planners have no special insights into the future, and most of the predictions that they build in their computer models turn out to be wrong. Most important, planning gives interest groups incentives to polarize the public, not to cooperate with the Forest Service and one another."[84] The experience of community-based initiatives indicates that incentives to polarize are easier to overcome at the local level.

It is important to emphasize that these issues were not new in 1997 or 1999. In the introduction to the special issue, Hagenstein placed the committee's mandate and report in historical context. The national forests, he wrote, "are valued for many purposes—outdoor recreation, range, timber, watershed, and wildlife and fish. It is the character of the national forests that has given rise to what seems to be never-ending clamor over their uses. Faced with demands from the various interests in those uses, Congress has never settled on an appropriate balance among them. Instead, it gave the Forest Service the job of setting priorities." The most recent precedent was the NFMA of 1976, in which "Congress reaffirmed the list [of multiple uses] and again told the Forest Service it must make the choices." Hagenstein did not consider it strange that Congress would devolve the difficult decisions to the Forest Service: "The character of the national forests and demands placed on them vary widely from place to place. These call for local decisions." He did consider it peculiar that Congress decided in NFMA that a Committee of Scientists "would be best qualified to provide political guidance."[85]

Arthur Cooper, the chair of the first Committee of Scientists appointed under NFMA in 1977, concurred that "the task of the second Committee of Scientists still resembles that of the first" with two differences. The second committee dealt with a planning process in place, thanks to the work of the first, and "there was little way the [second] Committee could fail to make sustainability the principle underlying all its recommendations" in the absence of clear policy direction from above. Ironically, both committees nevertheless understood that their task was essentially political. According to Cooper, "The first Committee of Scientists was not naïve. We understood that we were helping to resolve policy issues that had been sidestepped by policymakers." According to Roger Sedjo, "We on the [second] committee were warned early on that this assignment was essentially political. It is political, and properly or improperly, the committee has de facto taken sides."[86] Remarkably, the experience of the first committee was not harvested to reframe the charter for the second. This is a testament to extraordinary faith in the aspirations of scientific management, the constraints of expertise narrowly aligned with those aspirations, and the subordination of actual experience that might otherwise call that faith into question. Planning for the future is the priority in scientific management, not appraisals of actual experience.[87]

## Summary and Comparison

Table 1.1 provides a summary and comparison of two patterns of governance: scientific management and adaptive governance. The columns draw attention to the logical and behavioral connections between scientific, policy, and decision-making practices within each pattern. As such they summarize each ideal type and, to a lesser extent and more abstractly, the specimens of the types examined in this chapter: the establishment of the Committee of Scientists in 1997, the committee's report in 1999, and the predecessor committee appointed in 1977. As these specimens suggest, it would be a mistake to assume that the two patterns are mutually exclusive or exhaustive alternatives. Rather, they represent an incomplete evolution in the history of natural resource policy. Scientific management could persist where the science is sound, the policy problem is technical, and the decision-making structure is uncomplicated by multiple centers of authority and control. And the possible outcomes of the evolution include other patterns of governance; certainly multiple proposals for reform are on the table.[88] Thus the extent to which the historical evolution will move toward adaptive governance remains to be seen. Meanwhile, table 1.1 can be visualized as a snapshot of two patterns of governance in motion, with the pattern in the first column retreating from areas where it fails to resolve issues that cannot be ignored and the pattern in the second column expanding into some of the ecological niches opened up by the retreat.

*Table 1.1. Two Patterns of Governance: A Summary and Comparison*

| Scientific Management | Adaptive Governance |
|---|---|
| SCIENCE | SCIENCE |
| Relationships underlying observed behaviors are stable if not universal (reductionist). | Relationships evolve; the behaviors of living forms depend on the context (contextual). |
| Relationships are tested by experimental, quantitative, and other "hard" methods. | Multiple methods are necessary, including qualitative, interpretive, and integrative. |
| Verified relationships are independent of any particular context or point of view. | Verifiable explanations of behaviors differ from one particular context to the next. |
| Knowledge of closed (experimental) systems is unambiguous but fragmentary. | Knowledge of open systems is contingent and incomplete; surprises are inevitable. |
| POLICY | POLICY |
| Goals are single targets to be realized efficiently; they are fixed, given, or assumed to separate science from nonscience, and progress is measurable. | Multiple goals are to be integrated if possible or traded off if necessary; they depend on judgments in the particular context and are subject to change. |
| Problem definition depends on scientific assessments within procedures and boundaries established by higher authority. | Problem definition depends on human interests and other contextual considerations, including law and policy. |
| Science-based technologies are prerequisites for solving problems and gaining support. | Local and scientific knowledge are both relevant to solving policy problems. |
| Policy alternatives focus on how to realize the target, discounting uncertainties. | Modest incremental steps minimize the unintended consequences of policies. |
| Planning is the priority in policy process; monitoring and evaluating are not. | Policy process often depends on monitoring, evaluating, and terminating failed policies |
| DECISION MAKING | DECISION MAKING |
| Management proceeds from the top down under a single, central authority. | Policy integration proceeds from the bottom up under fragmented authority and control. |

(*continued*)

*Table 1.1. (continued)*

| Scientific Management | Adaptive Governance |
|---|---|
| DECISION MAKING | DECISION MAKING |
| Only the experts are qualified to make and implement sound management plans. | Participation is open to almost any person or group with a significant interest in the issue. |
| Bureaucracies are necessary to enforce uniform rules and regulations. | Community-based initiatives can compensate for the limitations of bureaucracies. |
| Expertise and authority to enforce rules and regulations are the necessary resources. | Local knowledge, respect, and trust are a few of many resources necessary for success. |
| Plans and planning processes are standardized and stabilized over long periods of time. | Successful policies are diffused and adapted elsewhere, at the same and higher levels. |
| Science replaces politics through clear policy direction from elected officials. | Politics are unavoidable and are commendable when they advance the common interest. |

The rows of table 1.1 invite comparisons across distinguishable practices characteristic of the two patterns.[89] The distinguishable practices are quite different and quite important: Like the last transition to scientific management a century ago, the next major transition in natural resources policy will proceed piecemeal, practice by practice, person by person, and place by place.[90] Where science leaves many uncertainties, the policy issue is political, and multiple centers of authority and control complicate the decision-making structure, evolutionary niches exist for the practices of adaptive governance to take hold. As those practices help resolve otherwise intractable issues, the remnants of scientific management will be redefined through use. For example, bureaucratic structures will not disappear, but agency officials can depend more on community-based initiatives for the interest integration necessary to get their jobs done. Public participation as ritual rationalization or legitimization of decisions by the experts will not disappear,[91] but public participation can be used more as a tool for clarifying and advancing common interests through policy. Science and technology will not be ignored, but they can be integrated along with other kinds of knowledge in policy decisions, including knowledge of local contexts.

In these ways, the remnants of scientific management can be redefined and subsumed within the larger pattern of adaptive governance. And the practices of adaptive governance will continue to evolve.

The rows in table 1.1 also clarify in the abstract some of the major choices and decisions to be made by field officials and others who will shape the future of natural resources policy in the American West. For example, the people involved are in a position to choose

- Whether to rely on the incomplete but unambiguous results of the science of the parts or to accept the uncertainties of the science of the integration of the parts in particular contexts
- Whether to derive policy and management decisions from general laws, public and scientific, or to explore the particular policy context with these general constraints in mind
- Whether to ignore the politics in fragmented decision-making structures or to accommodate multiple valid and appropriate interests in the particular context to the extent practical

Thus in practice, adaptive governance is not scientific management done right. To evaluate the consequences of the choices made, experience on the ground and a historical baseline are essential. Progress with respect to a historical baseline is possible; perfection is not. For that reason alone, utopian aspirations are self-defeating.

It should be emphasized that adaptive governance is scientific in an inclusive sense. Pragmatist Abraham Kaplan put it well when he wrote that "policy must be scientific to be effective. . . . But to say scientific is not to speak [only] of the paraphernalia and techniques of the laboratory; it is to say realistic and rational—empirically grounded and self-corrective in application. Policy is scientific when it is formed by the free use of intelligence on the materials of experience."[92] This concept of science leaves room for both traditional reductive and experimental science and an emerging integrative and interpretive science. It also is compatible with local knowledge based on cumulative experience in particular contexts—approximately what one anthropologist called the "science of the concrete." "This science of the concrete . . . was no less scientific and its results no less genuine [than the exact sciences]. They were achieved ten thousand years earlier and still remain at the basis of our own civilization."[93]

Finally, it should be noted that remnants of scientific management and tendencies toward adaptive governance are not limited to natural resources in the American West. Similar patterns can be found in management, social policy, the workplace, climate change policy, and, more generally, critiques of failed totalitarian schemes in the twentieth century.[94]


## Looking Ahead

The next five chapters are case studies in the emergence of adaptive governance, presented in sufficient detail for the reader to assess its potential to resolve persistent problems of governance rooted in the past. They include studies of innovations on the ground that have been successful enough to be diffused and adapted in other local communities around the American West. They also include studies of how such experience on the ground has been used to modify policies at higher levels in the structure of American government, in order to advance multiple interests represented at the state and federal levels and in community-based initiatives at the same time.

Chapter 2 illustrates how the recovery of endangered species can be integrated with other interests through adaptive governance. Lindy Coe-Juell considers efforts by the FWS to recover endangered fishes in the Upper Colorado River Basin since establishment of a recovery program in 1988. Insufficient progress threatened to break down the fragile consensus supporting the program in 1996. But then officials focused the recovery effort on an ideal habitat for the endangered fishes—the 15-mile reach of the Colorado River above Grand Junction, Colorado—and opened up management of the 15-mile reach to the multiple interests involved. By 1999 they had agreed to a set of actions expected on the best available knowledge to accommodate recovery, water development, and other interests. To incorporate scientific uncertainties, they made the policy contingent on and adaptable to the response of the fish populations. This innovative approach has been successful enough to maintain the support of the multiple interests and to be adapted in other parts of the Upper Colorado Basin and elsewhere—in contrast to many other recovery efforts, including those in the Klamath Basin.

Chapter 3 illustrates how national forest management can be adapted to protect the land and serve the people, even under the most difficult circumstances. Toddi A. Steelman and Donna W. Tucker examine the evolution of policies in the Camino Real Ranger District in the Carson National Forest in northern New Mexico. In 1991, after almost a year on the job, District Ranger Crockett Dumas concluded that old management practices could not work and rather abruptly began to evolve a new approach that relied on "horseback diplomacy": listening to people from Hispano land grants and other parts of the local community. Under his leadership, permitting procedures, timber sales, stewardship, and grazing policies were adapted to multiple interests well enough to eliminate appeals and lawsuits after 1993, to sustain the policies through a crisis in 1995, and to earn recognition through national awards in 1997 and 1998. Envy aroused by the awards and personnel turnover have tarnished the success, but Camino Real's experience in the 1990s is still relevant to policy and management elsewhere.

Chapter 4 shifts attention to the diffusion and adaptation of successful innovations. Christine A. Edwards focuses on grassbanks, beginning with an innovation in the Malpai Borderlands in southern Arizona and New Mexico in 1993. Some ranchers exchanged conservation easements on their ranches for grazing privileges on a large grassbank, the Gray Ranch, to help sustain ranch lifestyles and livelihoods, reduce subdivision of the land, and reintroduce fire to improve the rangeland. The innovation was diffused and adapted to restoring grazing allotments in the Santa Fe National Forest in northern New Mexico by allowing permittees to graze their animals temporarily on the privately owned Valle Grande Grass Bank. Since 1999, a number of other communities throughout the West have used the Gray Ranch or Valle Grande as a model to establish or operate their own grassbanks. These experiences and others like them suggest ways of correcting malfunctions in diffusion and adaptation processes to help realize more of their potential in adaptive governance.

Chapter 5 shifts attention to the possibilities for adaptive governance at the state level. Lindy Coe-Juell examines the Oregon Plan, signed into law in 1997, part of a long, continuing evolution. Under the threat of federal listing and control of coastal coho salmon, the new governor in 1995, John Kitzhaber, sought an effective approach that would avoid the hardships and resentments of earlier "timber wars" over spotted owls in the Northwest. He decided to build on the progress in salmon and watershed recovery of twenty model watershed initiatives supported under a state program established in 1993 and to coordinate state agencies in providing more technical and financial support for watershed initiatives. The number of watershed initiatives with state support increased to ninety under the Oregon Plan, which survived federal listing of the coho in 1997 and won support on a ballot initiative and in the legislature. The experience suggests how multiple local and state interests can be integrated through community-based initiatives with state support without co-opting the initiatives or tying them up in red tape.

Chapter 6 shifts attention to the possibilities for adaptive governance at the national level. Christina M. Cromley examines how practitioners of community-based forestry have made progress in gaining support in the national legislative arena since the mid-1990s. They have made their experience available to people in the executive branch and the Congress through regional organizations and through American Forests, the Pinchot Institute, and related organizations headquartered in Washington, D.C. Experience demonstrating that community-based forestry serves both the ecological and economic health of forest-dependent communities often turns out to be interesting and persuasive across partisan lines, with only minimal promotion. Under some circumstances, that experience has been decisive in gaining additional funding, technical assistance, or authorities for community-based forestry. Analysis of the successes and failures of relevant bills clarifies those circumstances and sheds some light on how to advance adaptive governance on behalf of the common interest at the national level.

In chapter 7, the concluding chapter, we harvest experience from these five case studies and other sources. The purposes are to clarify alternative possible transitions in the future of natural resource policy and to recommend how field officials and others involved in the process might be more effective in advancing the common interest through adaptive governance. The recommendations emphasize means of educating, organizing, and supporting people who are interested in shaping the future in that direction. Adaptive governance is not inevitable; it is only one of the possible outcomes in the current transition from the remnants of scientific management. However, if enough of us are willing and able to use our collective experience, adaptive governance on behalf of the common interest is achievable.

NOTES

1. McCracken and Grasser are quoted in Douglas Jehl, "Officials Loath to Act as Water Meant for Endangered Fish Flows to Dry Western Farms," *New York Times* (July 9, 2001), p. A8. Arritola is quoted in Craig Welch, "Both Sides Harden in Ore. Water Dispute," *Seattle Times* (July 9, 2001), p. A1. For background, see Rebecca Clarren, "No Refuge in the Klamath Basin," *High Country News* (August 13, 2001), pp. 1, 8–12.

2. The preface to this book locates adaptive governance with respect to related concepts in the literature, including adaptive management.

3. Jeff Barnard, "Drought Pits Farmers Against Fish in Klamath Basin," *Associated Press State and Local Wire* (March 28, 2001).

4. "Farmers Rally to Demand Water for Crops over Wildlife," *Associated Press State & Local Wire* (March 9, 2001); Beth Quinn, "Water Fight May Go to the Top," *Oregonian* (March 15, 2001), p. B7; and Barnard, "Drought Pits Farmers Against Fish."

5. Tracey Liskey, "Bald Eagles and Farmers Both Left High and Dry by Act," *Oregonian* (April 18, 2001), p. B9.

6. U.S. District Judge Ann Aiken's ruling in *Kandra v. U.S.,* 145 F. Supp.2d 1192 (D. Ore. 2001), which reviews the history of the water crisis before her ruling on April 30, 2001.

7. Jeffrey S. McCracken, "Water Allocation Decision Announced for Klamath Project"

(Klamath Falls, Ore.: Klamath Basin Area Office, U.S. Bureau of Reclamation, April 6, 2001); emphasis added.

8. *Klamath Project 2001 Annual Operations Plan* (Klamath Falls, Ore.: Klamath Basin Area Office, U.S. Bureau of Reclamation, April 6, 2001).

9. *Pacific Coast Federation of Fishermen's Associations v. U.S. Bureau of Reclamation,* 138 F. Supp.2d 1228 (N.D. Cal. 2001).

10. *Kandra v. U.S.,* 145 F. Supp.2d 1192 (D. Ore. 2001). The other plaintiffs were David Cacka, the Klamath Irrigation District, and the Tulelake Irrigation District. There were a number of defendants and intervenors.

11. Douglas Jehl, "Cries of 'Save the Suckerfish' Rile Farmers' Political Allies," *New York Times* (June 20, 2001), p. A1.

12. Welch, "Both Sides Harden." See also Hal Bernton, "Farm Country Gone Dry," *Seattle Times* (July 1, 2002), p. A1.

13. Clarren, "No Refuge," p. 10.

14. All four are quoted in Clarren, "No Refuge," at pp. 1, 10, 10, and 8, respectively.

15. She is quoted in Clarren, "No Refuge," at pp. 10–11.

16. The NRC Committee on Endangered and Threatened Fishes in the Klamath River Basin, *Scientific Evaluation of Biological Opinions on Endangered and Threatened Fishes in the Klamath River Basin* (Washington, D.C.: National Academy Press, February 2002). This is the pre-publication copy taken from Web site of the National Academy of Sciences.

17. NRC Committee, *Scientific Evaluation,* p. 13.

18. Ibid., p. 3.

19. Ibid., p. 8.

20. Waltman and Cushman are quoted in Michael Grunwald, "Scientific Report Roils a Salmon War," *Washington Post* (February 4, 2002), p. A1, which broke the story 2 days before scheduled release of the interim report on February 6. Peterson is quoted in Eric Bailey and Deborah Schoch, "Biologists on the Defensive in Klamath Water Fight," *Los Angeles Times* (February 9, 2002), part 2, p. 1.

21. Quoted anonymously by Allen Foreman, chair of the Klamath tribes, in "No Time for Delay," *USA Today* (February 11, 2002), p. 15A.

22. Katherine Pfleger (Associated Press), "Bill Would Define 'Sound Science,'" *Boulder (CO) Daily Camera* (March 21, 2002), p. 4B.

23. The general problem is considered more fully in Ronald D. Brunner, Christine H. Colburn, Christina M. Cromley, Roberta A. Klein, and Elizabeth A. Olson, *Finding Common Ground: Governance and Natural Resources in the American West* (New Haven, Conn.: Yale University Press, 2002).

24. Brunner et al., *Finding Common Ground,* p. 8, from a section on "The Common Interest," pp. 8–18; emphasis added.

25. "Unanimity is a euphemism for minority veto power, in which the negative decision of one community member enforces policies on all." Myres S. McDougal, Harold D. Lasswell, and W. Michael Reisman, "The World Constitutive Process of Authoritative Decision," in Myres S. McDougal and W. Michael Reisman, eds., *International Law Essays* (Mineola, N.Y.: Foundation, 1981), pp. 191–286, at p. 202. See also Robert E. Goodin, "Institutionalizing the

Public Interest: The Defense of Deadlock and Beyond," *American Political Science Review* 90 (June 1996), pp. 331–343; and Harold D. Lasswell, "The Common Interest: Clarifying Principles of Content and Procedure," in Carl J. Friedrich, ed., *The Public Interest: Nomos V* (New York: Atherton, 1962), pp. 54–79.

26. See Robert A. Dahl, *After the Revolution?* (New Haven, Conn.: Yale University Press, 1970), ch. 1, which generalizes the criterion of personal choice as a basis of democratic authority to other members of the community through the doctrine of political equality.

27. Aldo Leopold, *A Sand County Almanac: And Sketches from Here and There* (New York: Oxford University Press, 1989), pp. 203–204.

28. Aldo Leopold, "Land Use and Democracy," *Audubon* 44 (September–October 1942), pp. 259–265, at p. 265. See also Philip Brick, "Of Impostors, Optimists, and Kings: Finding a Political Niche for Collaborative Conservation," in Philip Brick, Donald Snow, and Sarah Van de Wetering, eds., *Across the Great Divide: Explorations in Collaborative Conservation and the American West* (Washington, D.C.: Island Press, 2001), pp. 172–179.

29. A parallel argument based on expediency can be constructed from the history of the modern environmental era. For example, Richard N. L. Andrews suggests that further progress in environmental policies might depend on finding common ground with other interest groups in a section on "A 'Next Generation' of Environmental Policies?" in *Managing the Environment, Managing Ourselves: A History of American Environmental Policy* (New Haven, Conn.: Yale University Press, 1999), pp. 366–368. See also the section on "Environmental Groups" in Brunner et al., *Finding Common Ground,* pp. 221–229.

30. Judith A. Merkle, "Scientific Management," in Jay M. Shafritz, ed., *International Encyclopedia of Public Policy and Administration,* vol. 4, pp. 2036–2040 (Boulder, Colo.: Westview Press, 1998), at pp. 2036, 2040. James C. Scott places Taylorism and scientific forestry in the larger historical context of high-modernist ideology, which is "best conceived as a strong, one might even say muscle-bound, version of the self-confidence about scientific and technical progress, the expansion of production, the growing satisfaction of human needs, the mastery of nature (including human nature), and above all, the rational design of social order commensurate with the scientific understanding of natural laws." See his *Seeing Like a State: How Certain Schemes to Improve the Human Condition Have Failed* (New Haven, Conn.: Yale University Press, 1998), p. 4.

31. Samuel P. Hays, *Conservation and the Gospel of Efficiency: The Progressive Conservation Movement, 1890–1920* (Cambridge, Mass.: Harvard University Press, 1959), pp. 266–267, 271–272. For more on scientific management in natural resource policy, see Robert H. Nelson, "The Future of the National Forests," *Society* 34 (November–December 1996), pp. 93–98; Robert H. Nelson, "The Religion of Forestry: Scientific Management," pp. 4–8; and Jack Ward Thomas and James Burchfield, "Comments on 'The Religion of Forestry: Scientific Management,'" pp. 10–13, both in the *Journal of Forestry* 97 (November 1999); and Brian Balogh, "Scientific Forestry and the Roots of the American State: Gifford Pinchot's Path to Progressive Reform," *Environmental History* 7 (2002), pp. 199–225.

32. Hays, *Conservation and the Gospel of Efficiency,* p. 267.

33. Ibid., p. 275, which includes a brief analysis of the political interests served by these iron triangles. "Through policies devoted to the development of a single resource, Congress found protection against independent executive action, administrative agencies discovered a

means to prevent coordination of their work with other bureaus, and local interests created programs of direct benefit to themselves and under their control." See also Mark Sagoff, "The View from Quincy Library: Civic Engagement in Environmental Problem-Solving," in Robert K. Fullinwider, ed., *Civil Society, Democracy, and Civil Renewal* (Lanham, Md.: Rowman & Littlefield, 1999), pp. 151–183.

34. The special report by Tom Knudson, published in five parts in the *Sacramento Bee* (April 22–26, 2001), alleges that environmental groups now resemble the industry groups they sought to oppose.

35. Balogh, "Scientific Forestry," p. 200.

36. Hays, *Conservation and the Gospel of Efficiency,* p. 275.

37. Paul W. Hirt, *A Conspiracy of Optimism: Management of the National Forests Since World War II* (Lincoln: University of Nebraska Press, 1994), pp. xvii, xxviii, xvi.

38. For more case material on the remnants of scientific management, see "Bison Management in Greater Yellowstone" by Christina Cromley and the role of local Forest Service officials in "Forest Policy and the Quincy Library Group" by Christine Colburn, in Brunner et al., *Finding Common Ground,* chs. 4 and 5, respectively.

39. Spain is quoted in Eric Brazil, "Suit May Bar Klamath Farmers from Irrigating," *San Francisco Chronicle* (April 6, 2001), p. A4; emphasis added. Hasselman and Simmons are quoted in "Water Users File Lawsuit to Reverse Irrigation Decision," *Associated Press State & Local Newswire* (April 10, 2001). Aiken's statement is from *Kandra v. U.S.*

40. NRC Committee, *Scientific Evaluation,* pp. 12, 17, and 17–18, respectively.

41. Bailey and Schoch, "Biologists on the Defensive," part 2, p. 1.

42. Ronald D. Brunner, "Myth and American Politics," *Policy Sciences* 27 (1994), pp. 1–18.

43. NRC Committee, *Scientific Evaluation,* p. x.

44. Deborah Schoch and Eric Bailey, "Bush Administration Won't Intervene to Reconsider Fairness of Endangered Species Act," *Los Angeles Times* (July 14, 2001), part 2, p. 9. See also Jeff Barnard, "Klamath Basin Irrigation Conflict Could Go to God Squad," *Associated Press State & Local Wire* (March 14, 2001). The ESA also includes exemptions from some rules for "experimental and non-essential" populations of endangered species, but these provisions were not invoked in the Klamath crisis.

45. Jonathan Brickman, "Klamath Water Supply Shrinks," *Oregonian* (July 12, 2002), p. A1. See also Dean E. Murphy, "California Report Supports Critics of Water Diversion," *New York Times* (January 7, 2003), p. A12. "Black-letter law" refers to law codified in print, which may differ from the law invoked or applied in particular cases.

46. Thomas and Burchfield, "Comments on the 'The Religion of Forestry,'" p. 11, observe, "We have on our bookshelves a tome entitled *The Principal Laws Relating to Forest Service Activities* (USDA-FS 1993) that occupies 1,163 pages of fine print and includes 196 laws. Only five of these laws existed at the time of the Transfer Act (1905), which established the Forest Service in the Department of Agriculture."

47. Eric Brazil, "Klamath Water to Be Released—But Too Late to Help Farmers," *San Francisco Chronicle* (July 25, 2001), p. A3.

48. Others considered working outside the rules, but most residents of the basin were careful not even to hint at violence. See Welch, "Both Sides Harden."

49. *Kandra v. U.S.,* p. 37 of typescript.

50. Robert A. Dahl, *The New American Political (Dis)order* (Berkeley: Institute of Governmental Studies, University of California, 1994), pp. 1–2, 5.

51. This point is developed more fully in Brunner et al., *Finding Common Ground,* especially ch. 1. On the concept of "community-based initiative," see in the same source, pp. 7–8 (including notes 26 and 27) and pp. 37–38. The concept excludes communities of interest (or single-interest groups) but is more inclusive than collaborative conservation groups.

52. Clarren, "No Refuge," p. 1.

53. See Jones & Stokes (consultants), *Situation Assessment Memorandum for the Upper Klamath Basin Working Group Proposed Restoration Planning Process* (Sacramento, Calif.: Stokes & Jones, October 2001).

54. On endangered fish recovery in a 15-mile reach of the Colorado River, see ch. 2. On wolf recovery in the northern Rockies, see ch. 3 by Roberta A. Klein in Brunner et al., *Finding Common Ground.* See also the literature cited in that book, including especially Brick, Snow, and Van de Wetering, eds., *Across the Great Divide.*

55. Bureau of Reclamation, *How to Get Things Done: Decision Process Guidebook* (Denver, Colo.: U.S. Department of the Interior, Bureau of Reclamation, Summer 1998), p. 22.

56. For an introduction to pragmatism, which calls it "the most distinctive and major contribution of America to the world of philosophy," see H. S. Thayer, "Pragmatism," in Paul Edwards, ed., *Encyclopedia of Philosophy* (New York: Macmillan and The Free Press, 1968), vol. 6, pp. 430–436. Abraham Kaplan, *American Ethics and Public Policy* (New York: Oxford University Press, 1963) is an expression of pragmatism.

57. The utopian aspirations and blinders of scientific management have been challenged in adaptive management as developed by C. S. Holling and his colleagues, especially in the critique of traditional science. But *management* connotes the technocratic and apolitical aspirations of scientific management, and governance is more than science management. See C. S. Holling, "What Barriers? What Bridges?" in Lance H. Gunderson, C. S. Holling, and Stephen S. Light, eds., *Barriers and Bridges to the Renewal of Ecosystems and Institutions* (New York: Columbia University Press, 1995), pp. 3–34. See also C. S. Holling, "Two Cultures of Ecology," *Conservation Ecology* 2 (1998), online at http://www.consecol.org/vol2/iss2/art4.

58. On ideal types, see Harold D. Lasswell and Abraham Kaplan, *Power and Society: A Framework for Political and Social Inquiry* (New Haven, Conn.: Yale University Press, 1950), p. xxiii.

59. Holling, "What Barriers? What Bridges?" pp. 12–13. The NRC Committee's interim report may be characterized in these terms. For a seminal and still authoritative account of positivism in the social sciences, see Milton Friedman, "The Methodology of Positive Economics," in *Essays in Positive Economics* (Chicago: University of Chicago Press, 1953), pp. 3–43.

60. These are among the targets included in Holling's review of twenty-three cases of ecosystem collapse in "What Barriers? What Bridges?" pp. 6–8.

61. "On December 3, 1979, Associate Chief Douglas Leisz sent a letter to regional foresters and staff directors designating FORPLAN as the primary analysis tool to be used in forest planning. FORPLAN was chosen because it addressed two key issues in forest planning: cost efficiency, and an allowable timber sale quantity within constraints. With FORPLAN, the Forest

Service felt it would have a consistent, unified approach to forest planning." U.S. Congress, Office of Technology Assessment, *Forest Service Planning: Accommodating Uses, Producing Outputs and Sustaining Ecosystems,* OTA-F-505 (Washington, D.C.: U.S. Government Printing Office, February 1992), p. 132.

62. Compare Sagoff, "The View from Quincy Library," p. 164: "A bureaucracy may implement clear political goals, but it is hopeless when it tries to resolve what are essentially political disputes."

63. The administrative management paradigm is reviewed and vigorously defended by Ronald C. Moe in "The 'Reinventing Government' Exercise: Misinterpreting the Problem, Misjudging the Consequences," *Public Administration Review* 54 (March–April 1994), pp. 111–122.

64. For insight into how power can ennoble as well as corrupt, see Arnold A. Rogow and Harold D. Lasswell, *Power, Corruption, and Rectitude* (Englewood Cliffs, N.J.: Prentice Hall, 1963).

65. A local issue construed as somewhat unique is a much simpler policy problem, politically and scientifically, than many local issues construed as somewhat similar and aggregated to regional or national scale.

66. For examples of warranted exceptions to the principle of affected interests, see ch. 5 on the Quincy Library Group by Christine H. Colburn in Brunner et al., *Finding Common Ground.* For a critique of the principle of affected interests, see ch. 2 in Dahl, *After the Revolution?* Inclusive participation may be complicated by scientific or technical experts or bureaucrats who lack tolerance or respect for politics or lack the interest or skill to participate effectively and responsibly in politics. Note that experts as such are seldom trained in politics and that bureaucrats are socialized in bureaucracies designed to avoid politics in favor of the impersonal application of standard rules.

67. Adaptive governance relies on behavioral models of rational decision making (based on people as they are, or real people) as distinguished from normative models (based on people as they should be). On the behavioral models, see Harold D. Lasswell, *A Pre-View of Policy Sciences* (New York: Elsevier, 1971), on the maximization postulate and its implications; and see Herbert A. Simon, *Reason and Human Affairs* (Stanford, Calif.: Stanford University Press, 1983), for an introduction to the principle of bounded rationality and its implications. Simon considers evolutionary processes in "The Architecture of Complexity," in *The Sciences of the Artificial,* 3rd ed. (Cambridge: MIT Press, 1996), pp. 183–216. For an introduction to this literature and the distinction between behavioral and normative models, see Ronald D. Brunner, "Predictions and Policy Decisions," *Technological Forecasting and Social Change* 62 (1999), pp. 73–78.

68. On the interdependence of scientific facts and moral values in particular policy contexts, see Kaplan, *American Ethics and Public Policy,* especially the section on the "Methodology of Morals," pp. 90–101. In "The Methodology of Positive Economics," p. 25, Friedman concedes that interpretations and judgments are unavoidable in applications of positive science.

69. The quotations from Holling can be found in "What Barriers? What Bridges?" p. 13. For a more general analysis of scientific limits, see Naomi Oreskes, Kristin Schrader-Frechette, and K. Beliz, "Verification, Validation, and Confirmation of Numerical Models in the Earth Sciences," *Science* 263 (February 4, 1994), pp. 641–646.

70. On the science of the concrete, see Claude Lévi-Strauss, *The Savage Mind* (Chicago: University of Chicago Press, 1966), p. 16.

71. The members (and their areas of expertise) were identified in the report of the Committee of Scientists, *Sustaining the People's Lands: Recommendations for Stewardship of the National Forests and Grasslands into the Next Century* (Washington, D.C.: U.S. Department of Agriculture, March 15, 1999), pp. vi–vii, as follows: chair, Dr. K. Norman Johnson (forest management and policy), Dr. James Agee (forest ecology), Dr. Robert Beschta (forest hydrology), Dr. Virginia Dale (landscape ecology), Dr. Linda Hardesty (range ecology and management), Dr. James Long (silviculture), Dr. Larry Nielsen (fisheries and public administration), Dr. Barry Noon (animal ecology), Dr. Roger Sedjo (natural resource economics and policy), Dr. Margaret Shannon (sociology and organizational theory), Dr. Ronald Trosper (forest economics and Native American studies), Charles Wilkinson (natural resource law), and Dr. Julia Wondolleck (public administration and dispute resolution).

72. Committee of Scientists, *Sustaining the People's Lands,* p. xvi. The quotations from Dombeck and Lyons can be found in the same source, pp. ix and xiii, respectively.

73. The quotations are from Committee of Scientists, *Sustaining the People's Lands,* pp. xiv and xv, respectively.

74. The quotations are from Committee of Scientists, *Sustaining the People's Lands,* pp. xv, xxx, xviii, xxvi, xxvii, xxx, xxvii, xix, and xix, respectively.

75. The quotations are from Committee of Scientists, *Sustaining the People's Lands,* p. xix.

76. The quotations are from Committee of Scientists, *Sustaining the People's Lands,* pp. xxv, xviii, xli, xxi, xvii, xviii, xviii, xvi, xvii, and xvii, respectively.

77. Crockett Dumas, personal communication, November 11, 2002. CFRS are codes in the *Federal Register*.

78. Alternatives to the establishment of another committee of scientists at the national level are explored and developed in ch. 7 to advance the common interest through adaptive governance.

79. From the following articles in the *Journal of Forestry* 97 (May 1999): Perry Hagenstein, "Changing Course: A Wide, Slow Turn," p. 5; Arthur W. Cooper, "The *Second* Committee of Scientists: Moving Forward While Looking Back," pp. 16–18, at p. 18; and Roger A. Sedjo, "Mission Impossible," pp. 13–14, at p. 13. In the same issue, Jim Geisinger, "Nonscience from the Committee of Scientists," pp. 24–25, at p. 24, agreed on mission shift: The committee's report "deviates from the charter by recommending a new mission for the Forest Service. The mission, 'to retain and restore the ecological sustainability of these watersheds, forests, and rangelands for present and future generations,' goes way beyond existing laws."

80. Harold T. Nygren, "The Planning Process: Panacea or False Hope?" *Journal of Forestry* 97 (May 1999), pp. 37–40, at p. 39. For the quotations, see Cooper, "The *Second* Committee of Scientists," pp. 18, 17; Sedjo, "Mission Impossible," p. 14; Andy Stahl, "The New Question," *Journal of Forestry* 97 (May 1999), p. 23; and Geisinger, "Nonscience from the Committee of Scientists," pp. 25, 24.

81. Donald W. Floyd, Kelsey Alexander, Charles Burley, Arthur W. Cooper, Arthur DuFault, Ross W. Gorte, Sharon G. Haines, Bruce B. Hronek, Chadwick D. Oliver, and Edward W. Shepard, "Choosing a Forest Vision," *Journal of Forestry* 97 (May 1999), pp. 44–46, at p. 46. The

quotations can be found in Cooper, "The *Second* Committee of Scientists," pp. 16, 18, and 18; and Nygren, "The Planning Process," p. 37.

82. Nygren, "The Planning Process," p. 39. For a concrete example of a bridge manager in a forest planning setting, see the role of Gil Churchill in Toddi A. Steelman, "Elite and Participatory Policy Making: Finding Balance in a Case of National Forest Management," *Policy Studies Journal* 29 (2001), pp. 71–89.

83. For example, Upper Klamath Lake is only one of the 348 reservoirs operated by the Bureau of Reclamation, which also operates 58 hydroelectric plants and manages in partnership 308 recreation sites. The U.S. Fish and Wildlife Service has nearly 700 field units managing more than 520 national wildlife refuges, thousands of small wetlands and other special management areas, 66 national fish hatcheries, 64 fishery resource offices, and 78 ecological field stations. Such data on the agencies can be updated through their Web sites.

84. Randal O'Toole, "Reforming the Forest Soviet," *Journal of Forestry* 97 (May 1999), pp. 34–36, at p. 35. The other quotations are from Nygren, "The Planning Process," pp. 37, 39.

85. Hagenstein, "Changing Course," p. 5.

86. Sedjo, "Mission Impossible," p. 14. The quotations are from Cooper, "The *Second* Committee of Scientists," pp. 18, 17, and 17, respectively.

87. The absence of systematic appraisal of the work of the first committee was an issue in "A Symposium of the Committee of Scientists," *Forest & Conservation History* 36 (July 1992), pp. 117–131. On faith in scientific management aspirations, see Mary A. Munson, "Good News for Wildlife and Ecological Sustainability," *Journal of Forestry* 97 (May 1999), pp. 26–28 for an example; and Nelson, "The Religion of Forestry," for a critique.

88. In the works previously cited, see the proposals in O'Toole, "Reforming the Forest Soviet"; Floyd et al., "Choosing a Forest Vision"; and the Bureau of Reclamation, *How to Get Things Done*. Other proposals are considered in ch. 7, including Robert H. Nelson, *A Burning Issue? A Proposal for Abolishing the U.S. Forest Service* (Lanham, Md.: Rowman & Littlefield, 2000), and Daniel Kemmis, *This Sovereign Land: A New Vision for Governing the West* (Washington, D.C.: Island Press, 2001).

89. Table 1.1 and this book apply the conceptual framework of the policy sciences but do not attempt to elaborate or promote that framework. For an introduction, see Lasswell, *A Pre-View of Policy Sciences*. In table 1.1, *Science* in each pattern is described in terms of basic perspectives, doctrine, and formula but not miranda. *Policy* includes both substantive policy outcomes and the policy process. The tasks of the problem orientation (goals, trends, conditions, projections, and alternatives) underlie descriptions of substantive policy outcomes; functions modifying policy outcomes (planning, promotion, prescription, invocation, application, appraisal, and termination) underlie descriptions of the policy process. *Decision Making* refers to constitutive decisions—decisions about how to make decisions—described in terms of social process categories (participants, perspectives, situations, base values, strategies, outcomes, and effects). Constitutive decisions are structural in that they tend to change more slowly than ordinary policy decisions (the policy outcomes of constitutive process).

90. On basic patterns and dynamics of political and social change, see Lasswell and Kaplan, *Power and Society,* especially ch. X; and Harold D. Lasswell, Daniel Lerner, and Ithiel de Sola Poole, *The Comparative Study of Symbols: An Introduction* (Stanford, Calif.: Stanford University

Press, 1952), ch. 1. For a compatible account based on the history of science, see Thomas S. Kuhn, *The Structure of Scientific Revolutions,* 3rd ed. (Chicago: University of Chicago Press, 1996).

91. According to one informed source, standard practice among Forest Service officials is to "develop the plan you want, announce a public comment period and then do what you want to do." Chris Wood, former senior advisor to the Forest Service chief, quoted in Katharine Q. Seelye, "Flooded with Comments, Officials Plug Their Ears," *New York Times* (January 17, 2002), sec. 4, p. 4.

92. Kaplan, *American Ethics and Public Policy,* p. 92.

93. Lévi-Strauss, *The Savage Mind,* p. 16.

94. See Gifford Pinchot and Elizabeth Pinchot, *The End of Bureaucracy and the Rise of the Intelligent Organization* (San Francisco: Berrett-Koehler, 1993); Hedrick Smith, *Rethinking America: A New Game Plan from the American Innovators: Schools, Business, People, Work* (New York: Random House, 1995); Lisabeth B. Schorr, *Common Purpose: Strengthening Families and Neighborhoods to Rebuild America* (New York: Doubleday, 1997); Thomas Petzinger Jr., *The New Pioneers: The Men and Women Who Are Transforming the Workplace and the Marketplace* (New York: Simon & Schuster, 1999); Steve Rayner and Elizabeth L. Malone, "Ten Suggestions for Policy Makers," in Steve Rayner and Elizabeth L. Malone, eds., *Human Choice & Climate Change,* Vol. 4: *What Have We Learned* (Columbus, Ohio: Battelle Press, 1998), ch. 4; Scott, *Seeing Like a State;* and the writings of Vaclav Havel, including "The End of the Modern Era," *New York Times* (March 1, 1992).

## 2. The 15-Mile Reach: Let the Fish Tell Us

LINDY COE-JUELL

ON DECEMBER 12, 1994, the Ute Conservancy District, a municipal water provider in the Grand Valley of western Colorado, applied to the Bureau of Land
Management for a permit to enlarge its raw water pipeline. The request triggered federal involvement by the U.S. Fish and Wildlife Service (FWS) under
the Endangered Species Act (ESA) because the project would affect four species
of endangered fishes managed by a recovery program in the Upper Colorado
River Basin. In response to this request, the FWS flexed its regulatory muscles.
It included the Ute Conservancy District's historic water use, not just the water
involved in the proposed project, in the consultation required under Section 7
of the ESA. Furthermore, the FWS asserted that the recovery program, established
in 1988, had not made sufficient progress to serve as the reasonable and prudent
alternative (RPA) to offset the project's harm to the fish. This decision surprised
and threatened water users throughout the basin. Thus the working consensus
supporting the recovery program was about to blow up and thereby jeopardize
negotiations in Congress to extend appropriations for the recovery program's
capital construction projects.

However, in contrast to the Klamath Basin water crisis, representatives of the
different interests involved—including water users, environmentalists, the FWS,
and other federal and state agencies—decided to initiate negotiations in what
amounted to a community-based initiative. They focused on the management
of a small part of the Colorado River with potentially ideal habitat for the endangered fishes, the 15-Mile Reach above Grand Junction, Colorado, where the
Gunnison River flows into the Colorado (figure 2.1). In December 1999, the
FWS issued a Programmatic Biological Opinion (PBO) that secured agreement
among the various interests involved in the negotiations. The PBO prescribed
increased water flows to the reach to benefit endangered fish species at critical
times, development of as much as 120,000 acre-feet of new water, and other
management actions. (An acre-foot is the amount of water that would cover

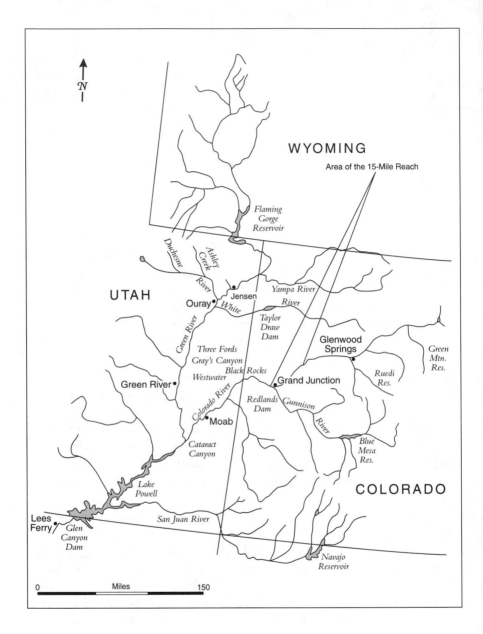

Figure 2.1. The 15-Mile Reach and the Upper Colorado River Basin. Source: Department of the Interior Recovery Implementation Program.

1 acre of land to a depth of 1 foot, or roughly the amount used by a family of four in 1 year.) The PBO also reduced uncertainty about the regulatory environment for all concerned, despite acknowledged scientific uncertainties about the needs of the endangered fishes. Essentially, the participants agreed to monitor the response of fish populations to the recovery actions prescribed in the PBO, to "let the fish tell us" whether those actions are sufficient to meet recovery goals, and to adapt water depletions and recovery actions accordingly. Among those involved in the negotiations, success is not disputed. The 15-Mile Reach has advanced their common interest, according to their own accounts and their continuing support and implementation of the PBO. The community-based approach and the PBO also have been diffused through the recovery program and adapted to circumstances in other subbasins of the Upper Colorado River Basin and outside.[1]

The 15-Mile Reach PBO is a model of adaptive governance worth consideration by officials and others struggling to implement the ESA and to reconcile species recovery with the other valid and appropriate interests involved in each place. The purpose of this chapter is to clarify and illustrate adaptive governance by harvesting experience from the 15-Mile Reach and the larger recovery program of which it is a part. The first section describes the biological and historical background of the recovery program. The second tells the story of the recovery program, including the crisis that threatened to blow up support for it. The third focuses on the 15-Mile Reach PBO, covering the negotiations, the outcomes, the implementation, and the outlook. The fourth section offers an appraisal from a common interest standpoint. The conclusion summarizes the 15-Mile Reach experience as an example of adaptive governance.

## Background

Four native fishes once thrived in the warm water reaches of the Colorado River Basin: the Colorado pikeminnow (*Ptychocheilus lucius*), the humpback chub (*Gila elegans*), the razorback sucker (*Xyrauchen texanus*), and the bonytail chub (*Gila cypha*). As the dominant predator in the Colorado River, the Colorado pikeminnow grew as long as 6 feet and could weigh nearly 100 pounds. (Today these fish rarely exceed 3 feet in length or weigh more than 18 pounds, although some are estimated to be 45 to 55 years old.) The other three species did not grow to such a spectacular size but could not be called small fry at 2 to 3 feet in length. The fish were notable not only for their size but also for their prevalence in the Upper Basin and their use as food by Native Americans and early settlers. Residents living along the Colorado River in the 1930s and early

1940s reported observing several thousand razorback suckers during the spring runoff. Similarly, the Colorado pikeminnow reportedly was prevalent in the late nineteenth century along the Green River in Utah.[2]

The Colorado pikeminnow, the razorback, the humpback chub, and the bonytail are now listed as endangered under the ESA. Scientists attribute the decline of these fish primarily to habitat loss and other environmental changes associated with reduced and regulated flows on the Colorado River. In the last 80 years of the twentieth century, the Bureau of Reclamation constructed ten major dams in the Upper Basin to capture the spring peak flows for irrigation, municipal use, and power production. In the Upper Colorado River main stem, the magnitude of spring flows has declined by about 30 to 45 percent since the early twentieth century. The dams and reservoirs, other diversions, and water use practices have greatly altered the seasonal flow patterns to which the fish had adapted. Historically, the high spring flows washed away sediment, cleaning the cobble and gravel substrates that were ideal habitat for spawning and egg incubation in upstream reaches. As the sediment-laden waters continued downstream, they would slow and warm, creating bottomland nursery habitat ideal for native fish larvae that drifted with the currents. The young adults eventually would migrate back upstream, where higher water clarity allowed greater production of algae to feed the invertebrates that were the native fishes' prey and where the spring floodwaters would again create spawning habitat.[3]

The harnessed river provides less suitable habitat for the native fishes, and the cool, clear water released from the dams has provided an ideal habitat for nonnative fishes such as trout. Other nonnative fishes including the northern pike, channel catfish, and red shiner compete with the native fishes for habitat and prey on their young. The dams and diversions further limit the native fishes' available habitat by presenting insurmountable barriers to what was their historic range. The range of the Colorado pikeminnow and razorback sucker, which fishery biologists know better than the other two species, has been reduced by 80 percent. Once found in the warm waters of Wyoming, Colorado, and south to the Gulf of Mexico, these fishes are now limited to river reaches above the Glen Canyon Dam. In addition to nonnative species, pressures on the native fishes include the toxic effects of selenium from irrigation return flows and bank-stabilizing shrubs that have flourished with lower spring peak flows.[4]

Although most of the available range is not ideal for the endangered fishes under current conditions, a few reaches of the Colorado River are very important to the struggling populations. One is the 15-Mile Reach, from the confluence of the Gunnison River 15 miles upstream to the Grand Valley Irrigation Company diversion dam near Palisade, Colorado. Located in the 33-mile-long Grand Valley on the west slope of Colorado, the 15-Mile Reach is considered by the FWS to be important habitat for adult Colorado pikeminnow and the nearly extirpated razorback sucker. The largest concentrations of adult Colorado pikeminnow in the Colorado River are located in the 15-Mile Reach, and the last known captures of razorback occurred in and directly below the reach. Biologists believe the habitat there has the optimal balance of food supply, water temperature, and spawning substrate for the adult fish. Douglas Osmundson summarized the policy significance of the 15-Mile Reach and the FWS's position, based on years of research: "The quality and quantity of habitat in the 15-mile reach must be protected and enhanced if Colorado River populations of [the] two endangered species are to be maintained and recovered."[5]

Just as the water in the 15-Mile Reach is valuable for the recovery of endangered fish populations, it is also valuable to the surrounding agricultural communities in the Grand Valley. Federal reclamation projects and the long growing season in the higher-elevation lands in the eastern part of the valley made this area ideal for producing fruit, including the grapes that support a budding wine industry. Water diversion has reduced suitable habitat for endangered fishes here, as in much of the Upper Colorado River Basin. Of the habitat ranges on the Colorado River above Glen Canyon Dam, the 15-Mile Reach is particularly sensitive to flow regulation. It is located downstream from several large diversions and upstream from the confluence of the Gunnison River, which adds a significant amount of flow to the Colorado River. The flows to the 15-Mile Reach have been greatly reduced by the upstream water depletions, especially during the irrigation season, which runs from April through October.[6]

As the FWS and other conservation interests sought to improve flows to the 15-Mile Reach, water users sought to continue full use of their water rights and to develop more water under state laws and within the Colorado River Compact, which allocates water between the states.[7] This set the stage for the struggle between interest groups over the 15-Mile Reach from 1996 through 1999, culminating in the PBO. According to those involved, the story of that struggle must be told in the larger context of the Recovery Implementation Program for Endangered Fish Species in the Upper Colorado River Basin.

## The Recovery Program

The Upper Basin recovery program was formally established in 1988. The origins can be traced back to tensions in the early 1980s between the competing claims of water development interests and conservation interests backed by the Endangered Species Act of 1973. Section 4 of the ESA directs the secretary of the interior through the FWS to develop and implement recovery plans to protect and recover threatened and endangered species. Section 7 requires that all federal agencies ensure that actions "authorized, funded, or carried out by them do not jeopardize the continued existence of such endangered species or result in the destruction or modification of habitat of such species." Thus, federal agencies must enter into Section 7 consultations with the FWS to determine whether proposed projects will jeopardize listed species.[8]

A nexus between a private entity and the federal government also triggers a Section 7 consultation. The nexus often is triggered in the upper basin because of the large number of federal water storage and diversion projects and contracts with private water users.[9] For example, a federal nexus could be triggered by a water user seeking to lease water from a reservoir operated by the Bureau of Reclamation. The result of a Section 7 consultation with the water user is a biological opinion from the FWS, which determines whether and how the project may proceed. A nonjeopardy biological opinion means that no harm to the listed species is expected, allowing the project to go forward as originally planned by the water user. A jeopardy opinion means that the FWS must decide whether to terminate the project or allow it to go forward if there is an RPA to offset the expected harm.

By the early 1980s, the FWS had issued nearly a hundred biological opinions concluding that individual water development projects had the cumulative effect of jeopardizing the continued existence of the endangered Colorado River fishes. The individual mitigation actions required by the jeopardy opinions were costly to water interests. In addition, in 1983 the FWS released a report that laid out conservation plans for keeping an ambitious amount of water instream for the endangered fishes. The water establishment of the Upper Colorado River Basin viewed the conservation plans and jeopardy opinions as a direct threat to its water use. It joined with state representatives to lobby against the FWS recovery plans. The affected state, federal, and private interests realized that the impending confrontation was unlikely to result in progress toward fish species recovery and could result in great uncertainty for future water resource development in the Upper Basin.[10]

As an alternative to unwanted litigation, the FWS, the Bureau of Reclamation, the states of Wyoming, Colorado, and Utah, water user representatives, and environmental interests began discussions in 1984. Three years of negotiation resulted in a 1987 framework document issued by the FWS. This document outlined a recovery program with the dual goal of identifying and implementing measures for recovering the endangered fishes while allowing new water development to proceed in the Upper Basin. On January 22, 1988, the secretary of the interior, the governors of the three states, and the administrator of the

Western Area Power Administration signed a Cooperative Agreement. This established the recovery program, based on the framework document.[11]

Members of the newly formed recovery program recognized an underlying problem from the perspectives of both the water users and the FWS: the fragmentation of the FWS process for prescribing mitigation responses in Section 7 consultations. The issuance of separate jeopardy opinions meant that each project owner had to develop and fund a unique mitigation plan or contribute monetarily to the recovery effort. This was expensive and time-consuming for everyone. The FWS staff viewed the fragmented process from an administrative and biological management perspective as difficult to monitor and time consuming. The recovery program participants determined that a comprehensive program consisting of broad measures for recovering the species would be a better approach. Such a comprehensive recovery program could serve as an RPA for all projects in the Upper Basin subject to Section 7 consultations.[12] The 1987 framework document directed the comprehensive plan to consist of five conservation elements: habitat management; habitat development and maintenance; native fish stocking; nonnative species management; and research, monitoring, and data collection. Recovery actions under each element have been reviewed and updated annually by program participants and then implemented by the FWS. The 1987 framework document also created an implementation committee with representatives for all participating interests. The committee oversees and endorses program implementation through consensus rule.

Under the comprehensive program, water users no longer provided individual mitigation plans in the case of jeopardy opinions. If their project would directly and adversely affect the endangered fishes by obstructing migration routes or causing another physical alteration of occupied habitat, the FWS worked with the project owner to develop a reasonable and prudent mitigation alternative. For indirect impacts caused by a project that entailed new water depletions, water users have been required to make a one-time $10 per acre-foot contribution, adjusted for inflation, to support the program that serves as that project's RPA. Substantial funding for the recovery program has been dedicated through congressional appropriations for base program funding, and the Bureau of Reclamation has contributed annually for capital projects.[13] In addition, as long as the recovery actions under the comprehensive program were proceeding with "effective and continued" progress, new water development projects could move forward.[14] As Tom Pitts understood it, "The coordinated actions of the program put the burden [of recovery] on the Recovery Program as a whole rather than individuals."[15] Pitts is one of the original developers of the program and remains active as a water users' representative to the program.

Nearly 15 years after the recovery program was established, members are still very positive about its inclusive and consensual procedures. Ralph Morgenweck, regional director of the FWS, believes that this attitude has enabled program participants to incorporate different values and ideas in making decisions. Brent Uilenberg of the Bureau of Reclamation believes that the search for consensus often leads to clarification of long-standing disagreements by members of the program and to creative solutions. This creativity, he believes, results largely from the ability of any member across the range of interests in the Upper Basin to protest a group decision. Several other program members, including Morgenweck and Bob Muth, the director of the recovery program, observed that commitments to a group decision are much stronger when all interest groups work to find a consensus solution.[16]

Through the 1990s, the recovery program members realized several positive achievements for both resource development and conservation. By 1998, the recovery program had served as the RPA for approximately 400 water projects.[17] Recovery program biologists gained a great deal of knowledge about the needs of the rare fishes. Procedures to control the stocking and impact of nonnative fish species were implemented. Furthermore, efforts to protect habitat, such as a coordinated reservoir release plan, were completed or under way. Despite these accomplishments, recovery program members were troubled by several problems that are more apparent with the benefit of hindsight.

One problem was that the recovery program lacked specific goals with interim indicators for fish recovery. The 1987 framework document states that recovery and delisting of the species is the ultimate goal of the program. However, as the agency ultimately responsible for administering the ESA, the FWS did not establish specific fish recovery goals until the fall of 2001. Henry Maddux, former director of the recovery program, said that the general nature of the recovery goals had been a weak point in the program for many years. The lack of specific recovery goals created uncertainty among the program members as to the progress being made toward the ultimate goal of fish recovery. Additionally, under the recovery program the process for evaluating sufficient progress for the program to continue to provide ESA compliance was unclear to the water users. This uncertainty made the water users uneasy because the program was meant to provide ESA compliance for their projects in return for their support.[18]

In an attempt to clarify criteria of sufficient progress for the recovery program, the implementation committee amended the framework document in 1993. The revisions established the Recovery Implementation Program Action Plan (RIPRAP) on October 15, 1993.[19] The RIPRAP is updated annually by program participants. It contains a timetable with recovery actions that must be completed as scheduled to show that the program has made sufficient progress and may continue to serve as a comprehensive RPA for offsetting harm from water development. For example, the fiscal year 2000 RIPRAP listed recovery actions for the Colorado River main stem approved by the implementation committee. Included under habitat development and maintenance was construction of a fish passage device at the Roller Dam, a diversion dam above the 15-Mile Reach, for completion in March 2002. This recovery action and its completion date were tracked by the implementation committee as part of the effort to evaluate progress of the recovery program under RIPRAP.[20]

An article published in *Conservation Biology* in 2001 pointed to the RIPRAP as evidence that a bureaucratic process and criterion had displaced the goal of fish recovery.[21] It claimed that completion of recovery actions according to the RIPRAP timetable was the recovery program's criterion of progress. This criterion is not equivalent to fish recovery, the primary goal. The article also claimed that through its consensus-based approach, the recovery program has surrendered its authority to issue sanctions in the event of further decline of the endangered fish. Allegedly, this surrender of authority allowed goal displacement to continue under RIPRAP, despite the responsibility of the FWS to recover the endangered fishes as the agent of the federal government.

Recovery program participants considered these criticisms in the context of the program's primary purpose and alternatives, formal and effective agreements, and biological complications. Some conceded that the RIPRAP process probably did detract to some extent from species recovery, the primary goal of the recovery program, but there was no acceptable alternative under the circumstances. Bob Muth acknowledged, "Yes, the Program is bureaucratic. Obviously it is. We have lots of interests on all sides of the fence. I think that the Program has to be bureaucratic to a point because if we didn't have this broad support across all interests, we wouldn't have a program."[22] Ralph Morgenweck agreed that the alternative to the recovery program is unacceptable. "The alternative is us [the FWS] doing things on our own and then people suing us. That stuff just takes a lot of time and cost with lawyers, and in the end, in situations as complex as this, you often don't get a very satisfactory response from the courts. The courts won't, and probably can't, get into all of the nuances and many problems that need to be solved along the way. They are going to render some kind of decision, and we may be left with a set of problems to deal with even after the lawsuits are all done."[23]

According to formal agreements between program members, the FWS never surrendered its regulatory authority. Part 1.3 of the 1987 framework document states, "Under this program, it is expected that all parties will implement the Implementation Committee's recommendations as legally appropriate. However, this program cannot, and does not in any way, diminish or detract from or add to the [Interior] Secretary's ultimate responsibility for administering the Endangered Species Act."[24] Furthermore, the "Framework for Agreement" section of the 1993 revisions states, "The Fish and Wildlife Service has ultimate authority and responsibility for determining whether progress is sufficient to enable it to rely upon RIP as an RPA and identifying actions necessary to avoid jeopardy."[25] Moreover, Bob Muth insists that the FWS has the authority to determine whether the program can continue to serve as the RPA for development: "We have never abrogated our ESA authority; that hammer is always sitting there. It can be wielded if the Service believes that the fish are not doing what they need to do."[26]

The 1993 revisions accepted by the implementation committee also acknowledged biological complications in the evaluation process. "The participants accept that certain positive population responses to the RIPRAP initiatives are not likely to be measurable for many years due to the time required for the endangered fishes to reach reproductive maturity, limited knowledge about their life history and habitat requirements, sampling difficulties and limitations, and other difficulties."[27] Tom Nesler, a fishery biologist with the Colorado Department of Wildlife and member of the recovery program, put the limitations of available scientific knowledge in context. "Part of the experiment of the Recovery Program is to see if these fish can maintain themselves given the amount of water development we are having in the system."[28] Another part of the context is what FWS biologists *do* know. Colorado pikeminnow are not reproductively mature until they are 7 years old. That means that if the fish stocked by the recovery program survived, it could still take years to see a noticeable population change. Despite these limitations, by the time the *Conservation Biology* article was published, some signs of recovery had occurred. The estimates for adult Colorado pikeminnow in the Colorado River main stem had tripled since 1991 to 650 individuals, according to a 2001 recovery program report. The humpback chub numbers had held steady in the Upper Basin, with 6,500 individuals at the Colorado–Utah border. In 2001, Tom Nesler believed that the trends for the Colorado pikeminnow populations, at least, had been very positive, giving him hope that the fish were on the road to recovery.[29]

In short, judgments of ultimate success or failure with respect to the primary goal were premature, but the FWS maintained authority and control sufficient for the recovery program to serve as an RPA for new water development. The 1993 RIPRAP had clarified the specific actions and timeframe, but the criteria for gauging sufficient progress and ultimately recovery remained ambiguous. In allowing water development to continue according to state laws and compact entitlements, the recovery program's framework document states that recovery and delisting of the species is the ultimate goal of the program. However, those goals were largely unspecified because there was "insufficient information about these species to adequately define the parameters of self-sustaining viable populations." For example, the recovery goal for the Colorado pikeminnow was to "maintain and protect self-sustaining populations and natural habitat."[30]

This uncertainty was the problem, not the bureaucratic process. It was coupled with the problem that the program's goal of continued water development was not quantified by location or amount, thereby giving the impression that water users had been given a blank check. This impression was reinforced by use of the recovery program as the RPA for several hundred water development projects undergoing Section 7 consultations. Another fundamental problem was the scope of the recovery program. The program covered the entire Upper Colorado River Basin and was so large that effective responsibility for fish recovery was distributed thinly. The unintended consequence was uncertainty about who would be responsible for insufficient progress in recovery. This in turn exacerbated uncertainty about where and how much water development would be allowed. Negotiations over the 15-Mile Reach PBO emerged from this context.

## The 15-Mile Reach PBO

In 1996, the FWS flexed its regulatory muscles. The Ute Conservancy District, a municipal water provider in the Grand Valley, applied to the Bureau of Land Management for a permit to enlarge its raw water pipeline in December 1994.[31] The application triggered a federal nexus, necessitating a biological opinion from the FWS. The FWS ruled that the recovery program had not made sufficient progress to serve as an RPA for the project. This decision marked a turning point for the recovery program. Throughout the early 1990s, the FWS had automatically approved requests for projects involving fewer than 3,000 acre-feet without undergoing Section 7 consultations. Before the Ute Conservancy District's request, most of the applications had been small enough to fall below the threshold. In another significant decision, the FWS decided to include in the Section 7 consultation the Ute Conservancy District's historic water use, not just the water involved in the new project.[32] The district would not be able to use the recovery program as an RPA, and they would have to develop and fund a conservation plan to offset the impact their historic water use had on the endangered fishes.

This turn of events disturbed not only the Ute Conservancy District but also many water users on the Colorado River above Glen Canyon Dam. Big water users such as the Denver Water Board and the Northern Colorado Water Conservancy District were especially concerned. They divert water from the main stem of the Colorado River above the 15-Mile Reach and pump it over the continental divide to more populated areas on the east slope. They understood that what happened to the Ute Conservancy District could happen to them as well. They began to worry that any future application for a federal permit could be problematic. For example, if the Denver Water Board needed to repair Dillon Reservoir, they would need clearance from the Army Corps of Engineers under Section 404 of the Clean Water Act.[33] The 404 review would qualify as a federal action that requires a Section 7 consultation with the FWS. If the FWS ruled that the recovery program was not making sufficient progress, the board would be responsible for funding recovery actions individually. This was the situation before the recovery program was established. Furthermore, the big water users were upset that despite their financial and political support for the recovery program, it was no longer supporting their historic and new developments.

At the time of the FWS's decision regarding Ute Conservancy's request, both the FWS and the water users were frustrated with what they perceived as failures under the recovery program. FWS biologists believed that the recovery program had failed to do enough to protect the habitat in the 15-Mile Reach. [34] Water users wanted further clarification in program policies guiding Section 7 consultations, specifically concerning the amount of new and historic development that would be approved by the FWS in return for their support of the program. The tension among the recovery program members was high, and the water users were threatening to walk away from the program. Other recovery program members knew that the program was in danger of failing because losing the water users' support probably would mean an end to congressional support.[35]

Bob Muth explained the program's dependence on appropriations and broad support: "The Recovery Program requires money for doing major things to try and restore some semblance to the natural system to recover the fish. We need the broad support for the Program. When we go back to Congress and ask for funding for the Recovery Program, the water users, the enviros, the Park Service, Fish and Wildlife Service, and others stand toe to toe and fight together for funding the program. I never thought that we would see it happen, we have Environmental Defense Fund people standing next to a water group and saying that we are going to join arms here and fight for this common goal."[36] Negotiations were under way in Congress in the spring of 1996 to extend appropriations for the program at $100 million over 10 years, for capital projects such as the construction of fish ladders and screens over culverts.[37]

Program participants needed to find a new approach to implementing the program in order to sustain it. Returning to the situation before the recovery program was not an attractive alternative because recovery efforts had stalled then. According to the FWS's Patty Gellatt, the bottom line was that the FWS would not be able to carry on a recovery effort on its own. The FWS and the program's environmental representatives recognized that several projects to increase flows—through more efficiency in the delivery of irrigation water, for example—had been planned but not implemented. Water users in the Grand Valley held the water rights and operated the systems for such projects. Thus the FWS needed the cooperation of water users. At the same time, water users wanted greater certainty about relief from the ESA in return for their cooperation and support of the recovery program. Robert Wigington recalled that he and Dan Luecke, the other environmental representative, considered a comprehensive biological opinion a plausible approach. "Instead of being taken hostage, let's negotiate. Let's see if we can end up with a flow protection that may be worth trading for some kind of ESA relief." By the end of 1996, the recovery program decided that a comprehensive biological opinion was a plausible approach.[38]

Jim Lochhead, executive director of the Colorado Department of Natural Resources at that time, understood that no one really wanted to see the program fall apart. He believed that a different approach to implementing the ESA could help to resolve the program uncertainties. Early in 1997, Lochhead convened a series of meetings among representatives of the FWS, water users, the state of Colorado, and environmentalists. He was able to persuade the parties to reinitiate face-to-face discussions based on what became known as programmatic regulation.[39] Under programmatic regulation, the FWS would consider all of the water projects above the confluence of the Gunnison River in one comprehensive consultation. However, programmatic regulation would also include all historic depletions plus an allotment for future development. Thus a Programmatic Biological Opinion (PBO) issued by the FWS would prescribe recovery actions to serve as the RPA for a specific amount of development. Furthermore, the process for developing recovery actions would be opened to water users above the 15-Mile Reach, in addition to recovery program members. The recovery program had already been inclusive in the sense that all relevant interests had a representative on program committees. With the initiation of programmatic regulation, more water users—those most affected by consultation outcomes involving the 15-Mile Reach—were included in the planning of recovery actions.

Programmatic regulation was a new approach to water and species management in the upper basin and a way to work through problems in the recovery program. No one knew what path the negotiations would take. Ralph Morgenweck recalled, "We all trusted that we were trying to get an end goal of harmonizing our interests. None of us knew how in the world we would get there, but we knew that if we kept at it, we'd get it figured out."[40] The PBO process provided an arena for all groups with an interest in the 15-Mile Reach.

The water users' priority interest was and is to be able to use their water rights for irrigation or municipal purposes that support their livelihoods and well-being.[41] Some do not appreciate the endangered fish or the value of attempts to recover them. This is understandable because in a previous management era the endangered fishes had the status of trash fish.[42] When dams created excellent habitat for introduced species in the Colorado River, the Colorado Department of Natural Resources initially focused on popular game fish, such as the rainbow trout. Nevertheless, irrigation interests want to operate their water systems in compliance with the ESA. Dick Proctor, manager of the Grand Valley Water Users Association, felt that his customers probably do not like so much attention and money being given to the endangered fish, but they want to figure out how to deal with it because it is the law. In addition, they value keeping more water instream to improve water quality and to enhance the aesthetics of a free-flowing river. Water users took the opportunity to participate in the PBO because they believed their interests could be addressed there. As Jim Rooks put it, "The protection of water rights is one of the major things that I feel needs to be done as the manager of the Orchard Mesa Irrigation District. We have to deliver a good supply of water to the water users. And [the PBO] was one method of doing it. Within the scope of the PBO there are extra [water] releases for the fish which come down the river which also enhances the water quality."[43]

Also represented in the 15-Mile Reach process were corporate water users such as American Soda, which mines soda ash, and Copper Mountain Inc., which runs a skiing resort and area sanitation service. Attorneys Scott Balcomb and Lori Field represented several of the corporations with water interests above the 15-Mile Reach. Their clients were also concerned about what could happen to their water rights when they needed to apply for a federal permit. Their clients have not readily expressed an interest in recovering endangered fishes, but they do value avoiding confrontations over their water rights. The water is too valuable to lose by not participating in a process that could affect their rights in the present or in the future, when they apply for federal permits.[44]

FWS officials were and are interested in carrying out their mission to recover the endangered fishes. Representatives of the state agencies also involved, such as the Colorado Department of Wildlife, share this interest. Fishery biologists in the department are interested in recovering the endangered fishes and in their research on recovery. Furthermore, a positive response of the fish populations to the recovery program was very important to the work of the environmentalists. For this purpose, environmental representatives in the recovery program worked to purchase instream flow rights for the program and to change reservoir operations to be more beneficial for the endangered fishes.[45] Because of such efforts, lawyers representing private corporations, irrigators, and others in the Grand Valley believe that the environmentalists and some officials in the federal and state agencies simply want to curtail the development of water on the west slope. Thus trust between the interests represented was not complete. But the PBO process nevertheless was an opportunity for representatives of these diverse interests to find common ground.

### The Negotiations

In August 1997, approximately fifty people began meeting monthly in large and small groups to discuss how to resolve problems on the 15-Mile Reach through a PBO.[46] Generally, the participants could not recall a formal method of recruitment. Word of mouth apparently was adequate to attract those interested. For example, Jim Rooks thought it was "automatic" that he would participate as manager of one of the six irrigation companies in the Grand Valley, but he could not recall how he became aware of the meetings.[47] Brent Uilenberg of the Bureau of Reclamation thought all of the water users would have known about controversy over the 15-Mile Reach through the Colorado Water Congress, an organization that provides education and information to promote wise management of the state's water resources. It serves as a network for communication between water users in the state. Ralph Morgenweck did not recall any formal method to make the 15-Mile Reach PBO more inclusive than the typical biological opinion. To him it seemed to be a self-selected group. Each participant had a big enough stake to endure many, many meetings and the travel necessary to get to them.[48] Those interviewed agreed that all the interests with a significant stake in the issue were represented.

Robert Wigington and Dan Luecke from The Nature Conservancy and the Environmental Defense Fund, respectively, remained the environmental representatives in the 15-Mile PBO negotiations.[49] They did make an effort to reach out to the larger environmental community by continuing the "fish caucus" that had met throughout the history of the recovery program and to update the broader environmental community on significant program developments. They held a fish caucus early in the 15-Mile Reach PBO negotiations, but other environmental groups did not express much interest or feel compelled to participate actively in the negotiations. Apparently, the larger environmental community believed it had less at stake in the 15-Mile Reach negotiations than water users, or perhaps they perceived their participation costs to be higher.

Throughout the negotiations, participants appreciated the immediate benefit of a stake in the process and other benefits of the open, collaborative approach.

Henry Maddux, the recovery program director at the time of the negotiations, thought that the open, collaborative process was very important because it drew in interests that could have later attacked the final decisions of the group. Margot Zallen, head regional solicitor for the Department of the Interior and recovery program participant, agreed that the credibility of the negotiation outcome was established up front because of the wide spectrum of interests represented in the negotiating process. Another benefit was access to the practical local knowledge of water users. For example, Dick Proctor, manager of the Grand Valley Water Users Association, was able to propose a strategy to deliver water more quickly to the 15-Mile Reach when needed because of his experience with the association's irrigation delivery system.[50]

The participants also appreciated the commitment of agency officials and other interest group leaders to the slow but important process of addressing everyone's concerns. Dick Proctor credited Ralph Morgenweck and Henry Maddux with willingness to let the negotiations develop at a pace that assured everyone that their interests were being considered. "Even though he [Maddux] was a federal Fish and Wildlife employee, he allowed some of these things to come up from the water users and he was patient enough to allow things to develop and to accept some of these ideas." Jim Rooks also expressed an appreciation for the openness demonstrated by FWS employees: "I think that a lot of us learned that there are some people in the federal agencies that you can trust and that have the clout to convince their superiors that what they [local people] are saying is correct and that it can happen that way." Rooks credited Tom Pitts, a water user representative in the recovery program, for keeping all of the water users motivated and willing to work together. Both Proctor and Rooks used the word *cohesive* to describe the working relationship that developed in the 15-mile PBO negotiations.[51]

At the outset of the negotiations in August 1997, more than fifty participants split themselves up into five or six subgroups to work through various problems in delivering more water to the 15-Mile Reach. These were problems such as the logistics of coordinating reservoir releases, finding an appropriate legal mechanism to deliver surplus water from Green Mountain Reservoir, and drafting a legally binding recovery agreement for the PBO participants. Each problem was complex and time consuming; any one of them could have preoccupied the whole group for a very long time. The work of the subgroups was enhanced by the tendency of participants to choose subgroups according to their primary interests and areas of expertise. For example, Dick Proctor was involved with a subgroup considering how the recovery program could legally protect water that would be saved through improvements in the irrigation system that he manages. Ralph Morgenweck considered the subgroups an important approach to governance that emerged from the PBO process. The process as a whole was able to move forward more quickly and effectively by distributing the important subproblems to different subgroups working concurrently.[52]

Long-standing differences between water users on the east and west slope were a big challenge early in the negotiations. Users from both sides of the continental divide divert water above the 15-Mile Reach, so both affect the amount of habitat available for the endangered fishes. Therefore both groups needed to contribute to the solution. Jim Lochhead, director of Colorado's Department of Natural Resources at that time, met with the water users weekly for about a month to work out some of the issues before coming back to the larger PBO process. The PBO participants considered this to be very important to the success of the negotiations. Jim Rooks thought that "the scope of the PBO [negotiations] got the west slope and east slope water people together.... I think that we became a more cohesive group. We are also learning that east slope and west slope interests can sit down and discuss the issues and come to a consensus opinion on something like the PBO." Lochhead's leadership helped east and west slope water users see the potential benefits of taking a united position to the PBO negotiations.[53]

The PBO negotiations took 2 to 3 years to complete, partly because of an important informal consensus rule for making decisions. Participants did not move forward until a consensus on an issue had been reached. Cohesive working relationships helped make this work, but the important factor was that everyone understood the need for support from most if not all participants. Any participant could potentially block agreement on a comprehensive PBO, but the go-it-alone alternatives to such an agreement were expected to be worse. As Dick Proctor observed, "We were just trying to make everyone happy because it [the PBO agreement] needed everyone to be involved and to go along with it. I think that everyone knew that almost every water user on the river has a federal nexus somehow and they would be brought up for a consultation. I think that was the motivation to keep people involved with it and to keep their nose to the grind stone. They needed to resolve this thing, and it was better to resolve it as a group than individually."[54]

The group operated under another informal rule that helped make the negotiations work. Participants agreed not to use the news media to air complaints in public or to promote a position on an issue. That would disrupt negotiations within the subgroups. Margot Zallen agreed to review working ideas from the water users and comment on the position of the FWS as the collaborative process moved along. But under the rule, that information was expected to stay in the group, and not leak to the press, until consensus had been reached. Robert Wigington recalled that there were a few press leaks every now and then, but avoiding negotiations through the newspapers was important despite these oc-casional breaches of the rule. "Being patient and being able to negotiate face to face in a structured way was important" to their success, he said.[55]

## The Outcomes

The outcome of this process was a final PBO for the 15-Mile Reach released by the FWS in December 1999. The PBO provides the ESA-mandated RPA for all historic water development and for specific amounts of future development above the confluence of the Gunnison River, provided that the endangered fish populations respond positively to the implementation of specified recovery actions for the 15-Mile Reach. There was no federal nexus for all the his-toric depletions and new development at the same time. The solution carefully crafted by the authors of the PBO was to consult on the implementation of the program itself. Thus the federal nexus was action to implement the recov-ery program by the Bureau of Reclamation and the FWS. Participation in the PBO, like participation in the recovery program, is voluntary and discretionary. However, most of the area water users have chosen to participate because the PBO clarifies critical uncertainties that had plagued the recovery program and because they are motivated to avoid the alternative. The alternative to meet-ing the requirements of the PBO was reinitiation of the Section 7 consultations without the PBO as an RPA. The conclusion to the PBO specifies the conditions under which reinitiation would occur. The main conditions are described here, in a review of specific provisions on water development, positive fish response, and recovery actions.[56]

Consider first water development. Specification of the amount of future depletions to be allowed under the PBO required some accommodations from participants in the negotiations. At the outset, according to Henry Maddux, the FWS wanted a conservative 50,000 acre-feet of new depletions to be the maximum allowed. The first suggestion from the environmental representa-tives was 100,000 acre-feet. Robert Wigington recalled that the water users, especially from the west slope, thought that this was not enough. They thought that with only 100,000 acre-feet allowed under the PBO, all of the new deple-tions would go to the east slope because the east slope already had projects under way that could deplete that amount. The proposal that reconciled these differences was to split the new water developments into two blocks of 60,000 acre-feet apiece above the confluence with the Gunnison River. Development of the first block could go forward without delay, but devel-opment of the second block was contingent on a positive response of fish populations. Total depletions of 120,000 acre-feet would be calculated as a

10-year moving average, in view of extreme variability in hydrology and demand patterns.[57]

The FWS concluded that historic depletions and 120,000 acre-feet in new depletions were not likely to adversely affect critical habitat for the endangered fish populations, provided the recovery actions in the PBO were implemented. (Historic depletions were defined as those from federal and private projects that were operational on the Colorado River above the 15-Mile Reach as of September 30, 1995, a total of about 1 million acre-feet per year according to modeling estimates.[58]) But instead of assuming that a positive population response would follow the implementation of recovery actions on schedule, the PBO specifies practical means to determine fish population responses in the long run and on an interim annual basis. The credit for this innovative proposal varies a bit from one participant to the next. However, the bottom line is that determination of a positive response of the fish populations is the glue that holds the PBO together. It made more specific the recovery goals and the evaluation process and opened the way for recovery goals later developed for the recovery program as a whole.

Consider next the provision to determine a positive population response, or the lack of it. Only yearling fish and adults hatched in the wild are included in population counts, and only the Colorado pikeminnow and humpback chub are counted.[59] Because their life histories are better known, their population responses were taken as surrogates for the razorback and bonytail for 10 years as research continues on the latter. Moreover, the FWS expected the fish populations to take perhaps 15 years to exhibit a positive response because fish stocked to improve the health of the population take several years to reach reproductive maturity. Consequently, the PBO established a long-term review in the year 2015, or after new depletions under the first block reach 50,000 acre-feet, whichever comes first. At that review, a positive population response is defined as more than 1,100 individuals in the Colorado River from Rifle, Colorado, downriver to the confluence with the Green River, including the 15-Mile Reach. A positive response would allow the second block of new water developments, depleting up to 60,000 additional acre-feet of water. A negative population response would trigger reinitiation of the PBO consultation if the population declined to 350 adults. For example, the FWS could insist on delivery of more water to the 15-Mile Reach or greater efforts to control nonnative fish predators. By comparison, the service estimated that 600 adult pikeminnow populated the stretch of Colorado River from Rifle to the confluence of the Green River in the 1993 to 1995 timeframe.[60]

The FWS also takes interim population measurements on an annual basis as part of the effort to obtain new information affecting the listed species or their critical habitat "in a manner or to an extent not considered in this PBO."[61] Measurements from one unusual year may not indicate that the fish population as a whole is declining, or increasing for that matter. But a significant decline would allow reinitiation of the consultation by the FWS. "Significant decline" means "a decline in excess of normal variations in the population... .The Service retains the authority to determine whether a significant decline in population has occurred, but will consult with the Recovery Program's Biology Committee prior to making a determination. In the event of a significant decline, the Service is to rely on the Recovery Program to take actions to correct the decline."[62] The interim reviews and reports give program participants the option of adapting policy in light of new information before the long-term review in 2015 or at 50,000 acre-feet of depletions. These specifications of "positive response" in the PBO are specific to the subbasin that includes the 15-Mile Reach and will serve as the indicator of sufficient progress by the recovery program participants in the Upper Colorado River main stem. The FWS also released recovery goals and criteria for downlisting or delisting the endangered fishes for the entire Upper Colorado River Basin in September 2001. In the estimation of the FWS, when these goals are reached the endangered fishes can maintain self-sustaining, genetically diverse populations in the Upper Basin; in other words, they will have recovered.

The water user clients of Lori Field were pleased that the PBO clarified the rules for Section 7 consultation and means to determine how the recovery process is working. Bob Muth concurred that "with the 15-Mile PBO there is certainty given to the water users. There is equal certainty given to the Recovery Program and the Fish and Wildlife Service. We can hold people's feet to the fire. You have to do these things [recovery actions]. And so the certainty was on both sides, the resource side and also on the water use side." Dan Luecke simply noted that they decided to "let the fish tell us" how well the recovery actions were working.[63]

### Recovery Actions

Finally, consider the recovery actions in the PBO. Some were already implemented or planned by the recovery program at the time of the PBO negotiations; others were developed during the negotiations. In either case, their timely implementation is necessary to maintain ESA relief for water users and avoid reinitiation of the PBO consultation. This review begins with efforts to improve instream flows during the two critical periods for the fish: spring peak flows, usually between April and July; and late summer and early fall, after spring runoff has subsided and when demands for irrigation water are high, usually in

August, September, and October. It concludes briefly with the other four kinds of recovery actions.

Before the PBO negotiations, two instream rights were granted to the Colorado Water Conservation Board by the water courts in September 1997. These rights protect irrigation return flow and the minimum amount of flow in the 15-Mile Reach during the late summer. The return flow comes from water that seeps back to the river from unused irrigation water and water returned to the top of the reach from a federal hydropower plant. Greg Trainor, utility manager for the city of Grand Junction, claims that the 15-Mile Reach never had run dry. There was always some flow of irrigation water that seeps through the soil and returns to the river. Eric Kuhn, manager of the Colorado River Water Conservation District, agrees that irrigation return flow contributes a substantial amount of water several miles into the reach. However, he argues, records show several years in which the flow at the top of the reach was only a trickle because upstream water users had diverted all the water that they could to fill their rights. Thus the water protected by the decrees is junior to all other uses above the 15-Mile Reach, and the decrees do little to protect flow at the top of the reach during the peak irrigation season.[64] A third right, held by the Bureau of Reclamation, allowed the recovery program to secure "wet" water for late summer or early fall. The Bureau of Reclamation can release from Ruedi Reservoir into the 15-Mile Reach 5,000 acre-feet annually, and an additional 5,000 acre-feet 4 out of 5 years at times the FWS determines would be the most helpful for the fish.[65]

During their PBO negotiations, participants found ways to increase total flows in the reach during late summer by approximately a factor of four over what had been previously protected by the recovery program. The FWS used models to estimate the amount of late summer flow expected with the implementation of the PBO recovery actions and 60,000 and 120,000 acre-feet of new depletions. Based on the models, actual flow conditions were expected to meet flow recommendations developed by the FWS in the 1990s for the 15-Mile Reach in late summer. The increased flows in the late summer were expected to provide more preferred habitat in the reach for the adult Colorado pikeminnow and open backwater areas to serve as nursery habitat for young Colorado pikeminnow and razorback suckers. These habitat improvements, in turn, were expected to help increase populations of those two endangered species.[66] Of the new ways to increase late summer flow incorporated in the PBO, two warrant discussion as innovations or concessions by water users made possible by their active participation in the PBO negotiations.

In the first significant agreement, water users agreed to deliver an additional 10,825 acre-feet per year to the 15-Mile Reach, to be split equally between east and west slope water users. The PBO makes it clear that "reinitiation of this consultation will be required if the water users fail to provide 10,850 acre-feet/ year on a permanent basis."[67] The agreement alleviated some tensions. Going into the PBO negotiations, many west slope users thought that east slope water users had not contributed equally to the recovery program. According to Dick Proctor, "Everybody had to share in the pain to make it [the PBO] work." Eric Kuhn agreed that Denver's contribution to the PBO helped improve relationships between east and west slope water users. The water users have stuck to their agreement, delivering the late summer flows every year since the PBO was finalized.[68]

The second significant agreement to augment instream flow in the 15-Mile Reach involves improvements in the old Government Highline Canal, a 1996 settlement of the Orchard Mesa Check Case, and a new Palisade pipeline. This agreement illustrates the complicated dance sometimes necessary to increase instream flow under western water regimes. It is so complicated that the story is best told separately, in the following subsection.

Efforts to augment peak spring flows in the 15-Mile Reach, to improve spawning habitat for the endangered fishes, were less successful. In 1997, after the PBO negotiations began, recovery actions implemented by the recovery program improved peak flows in the reach through coordination of federal and private reservoirs that maintain storage water above the reach. The effort is called Coordinated Reservoir Operations for the Colorado River. In 1998, it was able to add 2,000 cubic feet per second (cfs) to the 15-Mile Reach during a 10-day period of the spring runoff period.[69] Currently, recovery program participants are studying additional ways to increase the peak spring flow, including possibilities for a new storage project for instream water dedicated to the fish and more coordinated reservoir releases. However, the recovery program's efforts to increase peak spring flow remain controversial. The main point of contention is that water users and their representatives are not convinced by scientific studies sponsored by the FWS estimating the amount of flow needed by the fish.[70] They consider the supporting evidence insufficient.

Water users also believe the FWS may be too concerned with peak spring flow and not concerned enough with other threats to the endangered species, such as nonnative fish populations. Jim Rooks, Dick Proctor, and the attorneys representing the corporate water users mentioned that the 15-Mile Reach negotiations alleviated some of their concerns because the recovery actions include efforts beyond increasing instream flow to the reach. However, they remain concerned that the scientific evidence is too thin to warrant a significant effort to augment the spring flows. Eric Kuhn of the River District agreed. He thinks the problem is not a lack of good science but not enough studies to conclusively understand and address the many factors that have contributed to the decline of the endangered fish. On the other hand, he also recognizes that studying the endangered species is a difficult task because of their limited numbers. "I have some concern about what is known about the science. We have to temper that with the reality that these are very rare fish. If we knew enough about them it would probably mean that there were sufficient numbers for them not to be endangered. That is the reality."[71]

In any case, FWS models project that under the PBO, recovery actions will meet flow recommendations for late summer during most years but will not meet flow recommendations for the spring. Nevertheless, the FWS expects the combination of flow and nonflow management activities under the PBO to off-set the impacts of existing and new depletions and allow a positive population response.[72] Whether missing the recommended peak spring flow is a critical problem for the recovery program is a question for which "there is no good answer," according to Ralph Morgenweck. In the early 1990s, the recovery program hired a renowned fishery biologist, Jack Stanford, to review the science supporting the flow recommendations of the FWS. According to Stanford, numerous studies indicate that the reductions in peak flow have contributed to the decline of the endangered fishes. However, cause-and-effect relationships are difficult to understand because of many uncertainties and confounding variables, including the limitations of flow models and the impacts of introduced species. Still, Stanford concluded that scientific knowledge about the relationship between flow and fish response in the Upper Basin was sufficient to justify the FWS flow recommendations.[73]

Stanford's recommendation was to implement the FWS flow recommendations with an emphasis on monitoring population responses, monitoring critical uncertainties, and preparing a management alternative for flows if the fish do not respond positively. In essence, Stanford's recommendation was to implement the flow recommendations and to learn from what happens. He called this "adaptive learning" and referred to the need for an ecological understanding of the fishes' needs based on their response to their environment. Stanford also recognized the practical difficulties of an experimental approach given political realities in the Upper Basin, where holders of water rights are hesitant to experiment. Recovery program participants including Tom Nesler and Ralph Morgenweck agree that returning to predevelopment flows in the Upper Basin is not politically realistic. According to Morgenweck, "All of the people who would like to see recovery move faster or see flows return to historic levels want to live in Colorado too. What are they going to drink? What will they wash their car with? This is part of the reality that we have to face."[74]

The PBO negotiation process could not secure the peak spring flows recommended for the 15-Mile Reach by the FWS. However, the negotiations did secure a goal and criterion for positive fish response under the spring flow conditions to which the parties agreed and established conditions for reinitiation if the PBO fails. The coordinated reservoir releases provide a point of departure for clarifying the amount of peak flow needed for positive fish response. Margot Zallen observed, "It might be possible that we don't need the water that is in the flow recommendations. However, we won't know that until we go out and do all of these other efforts and see if the fish respond. You have to experiment. These numbers, the flow recommendations, are just numbers that people assume the fish need. It is a best guess, but we don't know until we try." Ralph Morgenweck agreed: "In essence, the fish will tell us as time goes on how they are doing. If we are able to improve the fishes' status without meeting those [spring] flow targets, then that is fine because our interest is in the fish. Our interests are not in some number of cfs."[75]

The other four parts in the 15-Mile Reach PBO, in addition to instream flows, are habitat development, native fish stocking, nonnative fish control, and research and monitoring activities. Habitat development actions are concentrated on the restoration and protection of floodplain habitats and the construction of fish passageways. Two major floodplain restoration projects have been completed, and propagated razorback sucker were found to be using the new habitat in early evaluations. Under the PBO, a fish ladder was constructed at the Grand Valley Irrigation Company's diversion dam at the top of the 15-Mile Reach. The fish ladder is a configuration of rocks forming a series of pools that gradually ascend the diversion to allow adult fish swimming upstream to pass the diversion more easily. The recovery program plans to construct two additional fish passageways at the abandoned Price–Stubb Dam and at the Roller Dam to open up an additional 50 miles of habitat that has been closed to the endangered fishes for nearly 100 years. However, FWS biologists are not sure how the fish will respond. Water temperature in the new habitat above the dams may be too cold for fish growth.[76]

The recovery program maintains several facilities for rearing the endangered fishes. A plan to release young razorback suckers, bonytail, and Colorado pikeminnow fishes (the three rarest species) was approved by the recovery program and announced in the 15-Mile Reach PBO. The PBO also includes a plan for controlling nonnative fish populations. In January 1999, the Colorado Wildlife Commission adopted regulations that limit the stocking of nonnative fishes in private ponds in an effort to help the endangered fishes. The commission also removed the catch limit for all nonnative fishes to increase the number of nonnative fish removed by anglers. Colorado also agreed in the PBO to close river reaches to fishing when it might harm the endangered fishes. The PBO further called for the Colorado Division of Wildlife to plan and implement a nonnative fish control effort. The division has formulated a plan for wildlife management for the Colorado River and is planning for several other subbasin regions in the Upper Colorado River Basin.

The fifth element of recovery actions in the PBO is research, monitoring, and data management. This effort consists of measuring endangered fish catches annually and estimating population sizes. In short, participants in the PBO recognized scientific uncertainties, recovery and the other goals at stake, and bureaucratic, legal, and political realities. They established goals and criteria for positive fish response previously missing from the recovery program, secured more water for the late summer and the spring peak flows, implemented other recovery actions, and agreed to adapt to what they learned from experience. This is adaptive governance.

## The Complicated Dance

As noted earlier, the carefully constructed dance that secured more water for the fish is so complicated that the story is best told separately. It is worth telling because it demonstrates why such decisions are best devolved to people on the ground: No one else knows enough of the relevant details and how to integrate them into politically feasible and rationally effective action. In the early 1900s, the U.S. Bureau of Reclamation decided to build a dam in Debeque Canyon, about 4 miles northeast of the town of Palisade, to provide more irrigation water to support the burgeoning orchard business in the Grand Valley.[77] Technically, Debeque Canyon was a good site for the dam because its higher elevation and location east of the Grand Valley would allow water delivery to more than 20,000 acres of farmland. However, the bureau faced a challenge in obtaining a substantial water right for the project because of several senior projects located downstream.

Below Debeque Canyon, the Palisade Irrigation District and the Mesa County Irrigation District operated the Price–Stubb diversion dam (figure 2.2). This structure generated electricity to pump water up to the canals owned by the two irrigation districts. The two districts had a right to about 600 cfs to be used solely to pump their remaining water right of 300 cfs to the canals.[78] Two other irrigation companies, the Grand Valley Irrigation Company and the Orchard Mesa Irrigation District, had significant senior rights for water from the Colorado River. These established water rights limited the amount of water that the Bureau of Reclamation would be able to claim for a dam in Debeque Canyon. To obtain a better water right, the bureau offered to divert water from a Debeque Canyon dam and deliver it to the Palisade and Mesa Country irrigation districts' headgates at no cost if they would give up their senior pumping

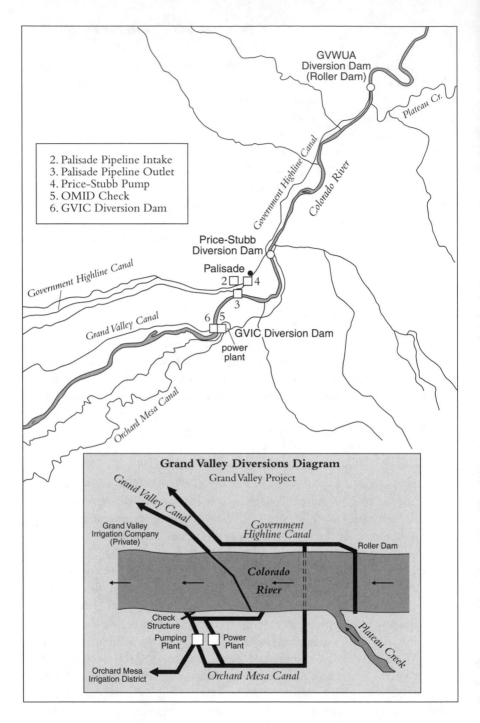

Figure 2.2. Site of the complex dance. GVIC, Grand Valley Irrigation Company; GVWUA, Grand Valley Water Users Association; OMID, Orchard Mesa Irrigation District. Source: Adapted from the Colorado River Water Conservation District.

right. The irrigation districts, whose pumping systems had been less than reliable, agreed and abandoned the Price–Stubb diversion dam.

Having obtained a more substantial water right, the bureau constructed in Debeque Canyon the Roller Dam, which diverts water from the Colorado River into the Government Highline Canal. This canal is 55 miles long and runs through the Grand Valley roughly parallel to the river. The Grand Valley Water Users Association was formed in 1905 to manage this dam and diversion project, which together are known as the Grand Valley Project.[79] The association also diverts water from the Colorado River for delivery to the Orchard Mesa Irrigation District and a hydropower plant owned by the federal government. Both the district and the plant operate just above the beginning of the 15-Mile Reach.

The Government Highline Canal is a gravity flow system that carries water from the diversion at Debeque Canyon to landowners' headgates located along the canal. Recovery program participants had known for a long time that the canal was not a very efficient delivery system because of its design. The canal is dug deep into the ground, but the headgates used to deliver water to the various landowners are located high in the structure. According to Dick Proctor, during the irrigation season the Grand Valley Water Users Association historically diverted about 450 cfs into the canal in order to make deliveries, but not all of that water was used for irrigation. Nearly half was used to carry the irrigation water high enough in the canal to make deliveries to the headgates. Unfortunately for the endangered fish, all of the "carrying" water was returned to the Colorado River below the critical 15-Mile Reach. Around 1992, the bureau began to look for a way to increase the efficiency of the association's delivery system. A more efficient system would reduce the diversion needed at the Roller Dam, which could then increase the amount of water available to the 15-Mile Reach.[80] The bureau's study showed that the best way to reduce the water needed to make deliveries along the Government Highline Canal would be to construct several check dams in the canal. These structures would work as a series of locks to maintain water levels high enough to make deliveries to the high headgates on a rotated basis.

However, western water law posed another problem. As Larry MacDonnell explained in his study of water conservation in the Grand Valley, the problem is that water saved or salvaged by increasing the efficiency of an existing use is subject to a "call," or demand for use, by senior appropriators. In other words, the water saved might not remain instream. It becomes subject to use by senior appropriators until their rights have been completely filled. Thus even with funds from the recovery program and incentives under the ESA, recovery program participants would not have a legal basis for keeping the saved water instream for the endangered fishes. However, with most of the water users who could claim the saved water at the negotiating table, the PBO participants found a way to solve the problem. Robert Wigington recalled that the water users wanted the PBO to work as much as everyone else, so they said in effect, "Don't worry, the water will be there."[81]

This is where the dance gets complicated. If the demand for water at Roller Dam is reduced by a more efficient delivery system, then water savings in the valley will reduce reliance on the Green Mountain storage reservoir from which the Grand Valley Water Users Association draws supplies. So theoretically, the excess water from Green Mountain Reservoir could be released and delivered to the 15-Mile Reach when the FWS determines that the fish need the water—that is, if the bureau could determine when there was surplus water in the reservoir beyond what other appropriators need and if there was a way to legally protect the water to the reach. In the settlement of the Orchard Mesa Check Case in 1996, the bureau produced a graph showing the reservoir's multiple managing entities how much surplus existed in Green Mountain Reservoir in a given period. Because of that settlement, water users who draw supplies from the reservoir have a good idea of how much surplus water is available for the fish. A portion of the saved water from the reservoir could be delivered to the federal hydropower plant just above the 15-Mile Reach, used to generate power, and then returned to the river. But this delivery would protect only a portion of the saved water. The problem was how to protect the remaining water to be saved from increases in efficiency.

Again, it is not clear who came up with the idea, but Grand Junction, Palisade, and Fruita provided legal protection for the remaining water. These cities agreed to serve as the delivery point for water contracted for nonconsumptive municipal or recreational uses. Recreational use is a purpose recognized in the operating policy for water from Green Mountain Reservoir, so the release of water from the reservoir could be legally protected through the 15-Mile Reach to increase available fish habitat. The cities of Grand Junction, Palisade, and Fruita, as well as the rest of the water user community, have been willing to allow the water to be delivered at the times FWS determines it is needed for the fish. Technically, the agreement to deliver the contracted water to the three municipalities is subject to legal challenge because the real purpose is to benefit the fish. However, from interviews with those involved in the negotiating process, it seems clear that the agreement will not be challenged, partly because there is justifiable pride in the innovation on the part of those involved. But more importantly, it is in everyone's interest to make the PBO and the recovery program work, and the agreement is an important part of that.

According to Margot Zallen, "This whole thing about contracting water with Grand Junction and Fruita, that is innovative. There are people who could have challenged that and said that it was very flaky, that [delivery for recreational purposes] is not real. But, no one is going to challenge it now, because it is part of the deal." Greg Trainor, the PBO representative from Grand Junction, agreed. "I don't think that people will challenge it. Because all of the other purposes for Green Mountain Reservoir have been met. Certainly boaters, kayakers, and other recreational interests wouldn't challenge it because there is additional water in the river. The people that boat on the river say that having that extra water in there is great. The people who walk along the river like it. The people downstream in Utah certainly are not going to complain about it because that is extra water going downstream to them. So, who does that leave to challenge it? That could possibly be junior water right holders upstream like Northern Colorado Conservancy District. But they wouldn't challenge it either because it is one of the components in the Recovery Program in the 15-Mile Reach PBO that everyone has agreed to."[82]

Seven manual check structures in the Government Highline Canal and the Palisade pipeline were completed in the winter of 2000, making it possible to deliver saved water to the fish in the 15-Mile Reach. In 2003, recovery program technicians completed work to make the check structures automated. The check structures reduced irrigation diversions by 16 percent, or 45,000 acre-feet, in 2002 and 12 percent, or 33,000 acre-feet, in 2003. These results surpassed the recovery program's expectations for 28,000 acre-feet to be saved in average years. The Palisade pipeline was Dick Proctor's idea. It allows water to be delivered directly from the Roller Dam to the 15-Mile Reach rather than through the canal that delivers water to the hydropower plant. This reduces the time needed to change flows in the reach from 48 hours to 12 hours, to benefit the fish.[83]

The managing entities of the surplus water from Green Mountain Reservoir are the Grand Valley Water Users Association, the Orchard Mesa Irrigation District, the Grand Valley Irrigation Company, the FWS, the Bureau of Reclamation, the U.S. Geological Survey, the National Weather Service, and the National Oceanic and Atmospheric Administration; the cities of Grand Junction, Fruita, and Palisade; the Colorado Water Conservation Board; and the Northern Colorado Water Conservation District, the Denver Water Board, and Ruedi Water and Power. Every summer, their representatives meet weekly, or more often, to determine how much water to release beginning in August to augment late summer flows to the 15-Mile Reach, based on the water users' needs, weather, surplus water forecasts, and fish needs.[84] Thus the complicated dance of cooperation continues in operations, well after the necessary engineering, legal, and political structures were put in place.

## The Outlook

So far, the trends for Colorado pikeminnow populations in the Colorado River are promising. Updates from the recovery program, reported in September 2003 and March 2004, show the estimates for adult Colorado pikeminnow in Colorado main stem at 700 and 780, respectively. These numbers show an increase over the estimated population of 650 adult pikeminnow in 2001. The FWS expects that increased flows will also benefit humpback chub and bonytail chub downriver to Lake Powell because there are few major diversions below the 15-Mile Reach. However, less is known about the life history needs and population trends of the species other than the Colorado pikeminnow. The species in the worst shape is the bonytail chub. Currently, there are no self-sustaining bonytail populations in the wild, and only eleven adults have been reported in the upper basin since 1977. Tom Nesler commented that all expectations for the bonytail are speculative at this point because information about their biological needs is limited.[85] From a practical perspective, the success of the 15-Mile Reach PBO is predicated on improvements in the populations of all four species.

Future challenges to the PBO agreements are possible. The bonytail could continue to exist only as a hatchery-augmented species. The Upper Basin could experience several consecutive years of drought, causing the Colorado pikeminnow population to decrease. The long-term response of the Colorado pikeminnow population could be negative as a result of natural or human pressures. Will participants in the PBO and the recovery program be able to find common ground on working solutions that advance their common interest under such circumstances? Robert Wigington concedes that a negative fish response will be a serious test of the 15-Mile Reach PBO agreements. A negative response would require participants to struggle again to reintegrate or rebalance other water uses with recovery of endangered fishes. Scott Balcomb expects other water uses would be severely challenged under a negative fish response. Underlying this expectation is the belief in the water user community that curtailing water development is the primary interest of environmentalists and other fish advocates. In fact, environmental participants in the 15-Mile Reach negotiations considered the depletion cap for the Upper Colorado River to be a very important accomplishment of the PBO.[86]

Despite possible future problems and remaining disagreements over priorities, participants have confidence in the approach taken in the 15-Mile Reach PBO. Eric Kuhn, Scott Balcomb, and Robert Wigington all agree that the 15-Mile Reach community-based initiative and outcomes so far represent only one chapter in an evolving story of resource management in the Upper Basin. However, they also agreed that the programmatic, community-based approach developed by the 15-Mile Reach participants will be the best way to address future problems. Scott Balcomb noted an opinion widespread among resource managers that the courts rarely provide a satisfactory solution. Robert Wigington added that future recovery and evaluation efforts would have little chance to succeed without the working relationships that have been developed. So, although a negative population response would raise difficult problems, participants in the 15-Mile Reach PBO already have a collaborative, community-based decision-making structure in place for that contingency.[87]

The 15-Mile Reach PBO is now being used as a model by other subbasins of the Upper Colorado River. In particular, community-based initiatives for endangered species recovery and water management were under way for the Yampa and Gunnison River subbasins in 2002 and planned for the White River. Recovery program participants call this model the programmatic approach. For them it consists of establishing a discussion group, open to local stakeholders and recovery program participants, to negotiate the terms of a biological opinion for continued and new water development in the basin. Tom Nesler visualizes the influence of the 15-Mile Reach model as small circles representing subbasin recovery programs encircled by the larger recovery program.[88] The subbasins develop their own recovery program with recovery goals and wildlife management plans, and these become recovery actions of the recovery program. The recovery program still has species recovery goals for the entire Upper Basin and still provides expert advice from FWS biologists and other resources for the subbasins, but the subbasin programs address local management problems.

The 15-Mile Reach programmatic approach has become the new management paradigm for the Upper Basin of the Colorado River because people in the other subbasins recognized that it works: It has satisfied the interests involved in the 15-Mile Reach so far. This experience nurtures expectations that it might work elsewhere and boosted motivations to try in the White, Yampa, and Gunnison river subbasins. Compared with the previous recovery program practices, this would open up negotiations to local interests in those subbasins. These include water users, anglers, and environmentalists, to name a few. Inspired by experience in the 15-Mile Reach, participants in other subbasins hope to clarify the process for Section 7 consultations and the recovery actions that must be undertaken to satisfy ESA requirements. Recovery program directors believe that the programmatic approach also establishes a firm basis for clarifying responsibilities for fish recovery at the subbasin level for the entire Upper Basin.[89]

At the basin level, recovery program participants such as Tom Nesler believe that the programmatic approach is the right thing to do because it allows all interests to be heard. However, they are quick to point out that they expect deviations from the 15-Mile Reach model, because personalities and circumstances differ in the other subbasins. For example, the Yampa River experience will be a bit different because there are not nearly as many federal projects as there are around the 15-Mile Reach. The Gunnison River presents a new set of problems because the potential exists for transmountain diversions, even though the infrastructure has not been developed yet. East slope interests would like to see an allowance for potential transmountain diversions built into the PBO there. West slope interests oppose setting aside any water for use on the east slope of the continental divide.[90]

Despite the challenge of adapting to new personalities and circumstances, recovery program leaders expect the new subbasin PBO negotiations to improve on the 15-Mile Reach model. Ralph Morgenweck acknowledged that the process is "not elegant, it's not clean, and it is not easily described." However, he also believes that sustaining a viable recovery program of practical use to the subbasin communities involved is far better than returning to the old way of doing business, in which the FWS planned recovery actions alone and was sued at every turn. Dick Proctor agreed that the 15-Mile Reach PBO helped keep the recovery program operational and that the alternative is very unattractive. "Life without the Recovery Program is a scary thought.... If we were on our own out there we would have eventually had to pay for some capital construction on our own. Right now, the PBO allows us to continue as we were. We can enjoy our water rights and still allow for the fish to be recovered."[91] For all interests involved in or affected by the recovery program, the 15-Mile Reach PBO represents the best alternative discovered so far for managing resources and implementing the ESA on the Colorado River.

Officials outside the Upper Basin Recovery Program have taken notice of the 15-Mile negotiations. Henry Maddux reported that federal agency representatives responsible for endangered fish recovery in other rivers such as the Rio Grande in Colorado and New Mexico and the Trinity River in California had called him to ask about the process in the 15-Mile Reach. At some of the later meetings in the 15-Mile Reach process, Eric Kuhn saw solicitors and managers from as far away as Billings and Salt Lake City. This interest from federal managers shows that a community-based approach to the implementation of ESA is another alternative to consider, at least, outside the Upper Colorado River Basin. In some places this interest has led to action based on the model. Similar programs are in various stages of development in the Platte River and San Juan River basins. Ralph Morgenweck, Margot Zallen, Brent Uilenberg, and other recovery program participants noted that knowledge transfer or diffusion has facilitated the development of these programs. In their view, knowledge transfer takes place primarily because people who have worked on the recovery program for the Upper Colorado River Basin are also involved in the other programs. Sometimes trust and friendship established in the Colorado River Basin have also transferred to other basins. This made recovery work easier in the Platte River Basin, according to Margot Zallen.[92]

Jim Lochhead, who has worked with recovery programs in several other river basins, believes that the model has the potential for further diffusion. In his experience, the 15-Mile Reach approach is more sophisticated than any other available for quantifying specific recovery actions and clarifying the extent of ESA relief that the water users can anticipate. Lochhead also believes that to the extent the 15-Mile Reach model has been documented, other decision makers should look to the experience of participants there to inform their own decisions.[93] Ideas for greater transfer of the model include knowledge sharing between federal agency managers through outreach between regional divisions. Forums could also be established by water users for the exchange of information between those affected by the ESA.

## An Appraisal

Whatever surprises the future may bring, it is reasonable to conclude that the 15-Mile Reach PBO has advanced the common interest of the local and larger communities. The priority interest of the FWS, environmentalists, and others in recovering the four endangered species through improvements in instream flow and other recovery actions is appropriate under the ESA and still a valid possibility in light of the limited scientific knowledge and practical experience available in the Upper Colorado Basin. Similarly, priority interests in delivering water for agricultural, municipal, and other purposes are appropriate under a host of more traditional public policies and private contracts still in force and valid in light of extensive practical experience in making these deliveries over the last century. Such interests are shared to some extent by everyone who takes or uses water from the Colorado River main stem above Grand Junction. All those involved in the PBO also share interests in clarifying their responsibilities under the ESA and in developing means of monitoring progress to meet those responsibilities, despite the many scientific uncertainties inherent in the situation. These valid and appropriate interests were integrated where possible and balanced where necessary in the PBO, which put the recovery program on a sustainable basis after it nearly blew up in 1996. Consider the evidence from previous sections.[94]

All participants in the 15-Mile PBO signed a voluntary letter of commitment to recovery and the implementation of recovery actions, as a condition of sharing in the benefits. This indicates formally their expectation that the PBO serves their priority interests. Scott Balcomb considered it his clients' best interest to sign the letter of agreement, and if any had not signed, that was probably because they had not yet had to go through a federal permitting process since the PBO negotiations began.[95] In addition, all participants interviewed reported that they were satisfied that the PBO serves their priority interests, often without compromising the priority interests of the others involved. Dick Proctor's comment on improvements in the Grand Valley Water Users Association system through the PBO is a case in point. "The [improvement] is good for us. We can participate in some water conservation that is of no cost to us. As long as [the PBO] operates as it is supposed to, we get full enjoyment of our water deliveries and can also have the ability to leave water in the river and help the fish."[96] Such words are corroborated by deeds. Each participant retains the right under the PBO to go it alone, by bureaucratic fiat, by filing suit, or by taking other actions against other participants. No participant has exercised that right, evidently expecting that the PBO serves individual and group interests better than any known alternative. The pragmatic baseline used by these practitioners for assessing progress is the historical situation before the PBO or before the recovery program or expectations about a hypothetical future without them.

Whether the goal of recovery can or will be achieved remains to be seen. It is still too soon to expect a positive fish response, and there are too many uncertainties about conditions necessary for recovery. Nevertheless, flow improvements in the 15-Mile Reach are significant accomplishments if present scientific knowledge is valid and present commitments to implement recovery actions are met. The PBO and the recovery program have increased the flow in late summer by a factor of four, to the level recommended by the FWS. They have also increased the peak flow by 2,000 cfs for a 10-day period in the spring and are trying to find more water to meet the recommended peak spring flow. To incorporate biological and other uncertainties inherent in the situation, the PBO also includes agreement among the participants on what constitutes a positive response of the fish population and how population response is estimated. The lack of a positive response in 2015, or when depletions reach 50,000 acre-feet per year, whichever comes first, will trigger reinitiation of negotiations on implementation of the ESA in the basin. So will a significant population decline in the years before that mark. And so will a failure to implement recovery actions, including delivery of 10,850 acre-feet per year to assist the endangered fishes in late summer. Reinitiation would be a significant setback for all concerned. Therefore the participants are motivated to help realize positive fish responses and are accountable if they fail.

Thus it is no longer the case, as alleged in the *Conservation Biology* article in

2001, that implementation of recovery actions has displaced the goal of recovery. Nor has the FWS ever given up its authority to evaluate the recovery program's ability to serve as an RPA for new water development. The FWS exercised that authority in response to the Ute Conservancy District's request in 1996, the relevant precedent.

Multiple interacting factors have contributed to the success of the PBO and the recovery program in advancing the common interest. Perhaps the most important are decisions that restructured the decision process and at the same time factored the overall recovery problem into more tractable parts, making progress possible. The ESA of 1973 structured the recovery process nationally and motivated action around the country, including the recovery program in the Upper Colorado River Basin. Jim Rooks of the Orchard Mesa Irrigation District understood the significance of the ESA. "We had these federal rules and regulations that a lot of us don't like, but they are there and we have to keep the impacts of our actions to a minimum. That is basically the driving force behind everyone getting together and saying that we needed this PBO."[97] Thus progress was motivated by the ESA but not determined by it. The ESA can be wielded as a weapon on behalf of recovery, regardless of costs to other interests, as it was in the Klamath Basin water crisis in 2001. The ESA also can be used as a tool to motivate negotiations between multiple interest groups to find their common interest, as it was in the Upper Colorado. The difference lies not in the ESA itself but in implementation.

The second structural decision was establishment of the PBO negotiating group on the 15-Mile Reach in August 1997, in response to long-standing problems that threatened to disrupt the recovery program. Among other things, this decision simplified the recovery problem in the upper basin as a whole on a geographic basis, making it possible to focus limited time and attention and other resources on the most critical subbasin for recovery of the endangered fishes. This also opened up the possibility of effective participation by all interest groups with a significant claim on water in or above the 15-Mile Reach and participation by self-selected veterans of the recovery program with a stake in making it work. But the PBO group as a whole was too large—more than fifty participants—to cope effectively with the complexity of the recovery problem even in one subbasin. The third structural decision was to set up five or six subgroups within the PBO group to work in parallel on such distinguishable subproblems as coordinating reservoir releases and finding legal means to protect surplus water. This simplified the recovery problem in the 15-Mile Reach by factoring it on a functional basis rather than a territorial basis.

These structural decisions allowed the PBO group to organize as a community-based initiative, opening up opportunities for finding the common interest in the 15-Mile Reach. The PBO became more inclusive than the recovery program because the focus on the reach attracted nearly all significant interests in the reach. Those with water rights considered them too valuable not to participate in a process that could significantly affect their historic and new depletions. They brought with them practical local knowledge of the intricacies of water systems affecting the reach to integrate with the scientific knowledge available to the FWS and other agencies. They made the most of their specialized areas of expertise on behalf of their particular interests by sorting themselves into subgroups to work on important subproblems. They pulled together working solutions to those subproblems, for example, in the complicated dance that eventually released and protected more water from Green Mountain Reservoir on a timely basis, when the fish need it in late summer. Their local knowledge was an essential resource for finding such creative solutions, along with the motivation to try.

Through their participation in the PBO, individuals and groups were able to clarify and reinforce their initial interests in the recovery program and the PBO and their initial commitments to making them work. They recognized, if they had not already, that they could not realize their priority interests on their own. Advocates of recovery understood that they needed to cooperate with water users who understood and controlled the intricate water systems in and above the reach. Water users understood that they needed to cooperate with the FWS to be confident about the continued operation and development of those systems in the ESA era. The modification of perspectives was easier because they were able to interact face to face over months and years within the community-based initiative and to resolve factual issues by reference to specific observations. Regional or national aggregate data are ineffective in modifying perspectives. In larger or more conventional structures for making decisions than the PBO, participants faced with opposition tend to have more incentives to defend their initial positions by appeal to constituencies outside the negotiations, sometimes through the news media, in order to mobilize more support. The negotiations within the PBO produced enough interim progress to nurture constructive working relationships and some trust, as well as confidence that the effort could succeed. Like political support, these are important resources for advancing the common interest.

Some strategies were important in increasing the resources available and making good use of them. One strategy was to put all depletions, recovery goals and criteria, and recovery actions on the table for all to consider and reconsider. This opened up more space for integrating interests where possible or balancing them where necessary. Negotiations restricted to some part of the space would have limited the possibilities for finding common ground. Another strategy was collaboration under the consensus rule. FWS leaders did not allow the negotiations to go forward until consensus on an issue had been achieved. Thus they devolved some degree of control to other agencies and interest groups and took the time necessary to work out an accommodation. If "listening" had been little more than a ritualistic prelude to bureaucratic fiat, participants eventually would have taken their grievances outside the negotiations. A related strategy was to use solidarity based on consensus and interim progress to maintain the resources available to the PBO and the recovery program from outside. With solidarity, they defended substantial appropriations for capital projects and retained control over the important decisions. Without solidarity, they easily could have lost the appropriations from Congress and lost control of the decisions as self-described losers sought a better deal in the courts, in Congress, or in some other arena.[98]

Making these structural and strategic decisions were people, of course. Success in advancing the common interest depended on leaders in the FWS, including Ralph Morgenweck, Henry Maddux, and Bob Muth. Success also depended on other leaders including Jim Lochhead, who was credited with bringing together the east and west slope water users early in the PBO negotiations; Tom Pitts, who was credited with keeping the water users motivated and willing to work together; and Dick Proctor, who with many others contributed significantly to turning efficiency improvements in the Government Highline Canal into improvements in instream flow for the fish in the 15-Mile Reach. Success also depended on people willing to support these leaders and to take the lead on occasion. The complicated dance could not have been performed successfully without many leaders and followers who sometimes exchanged roles. Given the many failures to advance the common interest on natural resource policy issues in the American West, it is not difficult to imagine that different personalities with different interests could have turned the opportunities for success in the 15-Mile Reach and the upper basin into failure.

The significance of the structural decisions should not be underestimated, however. The structural decisions allowed these able and well-motivated people to factor the larger national, Upper Basin, and 15-Mile Reach recovery problems into more tractable subproblems and then to assemble working solutions to the subproblems into solutions and potential solutions to problems at larger scales. This is the architecture of complexity, the general structure for finding better working solutions to complex problems through evolutionary or quasi-evolutionary means. According to Herbert Simon, the assembling of partial solutions is necessary to account for the pace of evolution observed in nature. More importantly for policy, real people like us do not have the cognitive capacity necessary to find optimal, global solutions to complex problems or even to come close. Under these circumstances, better working solutions to complex policy problems are evolved from the bottom up, even if they are motivated from the top-down, as in the case of the ESA.[99] Unlike the personalities involved, the architecture of complexity is not context specific. It can be diffused and adapted elsewhere.

In conclusion, it is worthwhile to review this experience as an example of adaptive governance, as developed in chapter 1. Authority and control in the decision processes organized around the recovery of endangered fishes in the Upper Colorado River Basin are fragmented between dozens of public agencies and private interests. They could not have made much progress without a structure for reconciling their differences. The community-based initiative established by the 15-Mile Reach PBO negotiations included at the outset nearly all organized groups that could have blocked an agreement. Despite the multiple legal and bureaucratic constraints on participants from the public and private sectors, the initiative made it possible for them to work out their differences. Given those differences, politics—as the giving and withholding of support in making important decisions—were unavoidable. But politics were also essential in clarifying and advancing the common interest. Progress depended on factoring the larger national and Upper Basin problems of recovery down to the local problem in the 15-Mile Reach and then proceeding with working solutions in the reach diffused and adapted regionally and potentially nationally.

As a substantive policy, the 15-Mile Reach PBO reconciled the multiple goals of these diverse participants well enough to secure consensus on allowable new depletions, specific recovery goals and criteria, and recovery actions—and commitments to making them work. To accommodate uncertainties about whether these policies would be sufficient for recovery of the endangered fishes, these policies were made contingent on positive responses of the fish populations. The lack of a positive response at the long-term review or a significant population decline in the interim will trigger reinitiation of negotiations between the agencies and groups involved. These policies incorporated the best available science, but they depended on the practical local knowledge of water users in and above the 15-Mile Reach. Without ready access to that local knowledge, it would have been difficult or impossible to perform the complicated dance that augmented instream flows in the 15-Mile Reach in the late summer and early fall. In other words, these policies were adapted to local circumstances, including the multiple goals and means brought to the table through the programmatic approach. This was a major factor in stimulating creativity. Initial and sustained support for these PBO policies depends on serving the common interest of those most directly involved, not on their scientific foundations.

The scientific foundations included the models used by the FWS to justify its recommendations to increase instream flow as necessary for recovery of the endangered fishes. The water users strongly objected to the FWS peak spring flow recommendations and pointed to limitations of the scientific knowledge and information incorporated into the models. The FWS retained Jack Stanford, the expert in fishery biology, to review the flow models. He reported that, in his opinion, flow models are good tools for establishing a better understanding of the ecosystem but cannot include all the complex interactions in a natural system that are necessary for confidence in predictions.[100] His recommendation was to implement flows that were as close as possible to the recommendations and to adjust the management effort in the light of experience. Thus Stanford and others recognized the inherent limitations of the best available science for practical purposes and based the 15-Mile Reach PBO policy and decision process on the results of practice. Practice can reveal some of the significant factors omitted or misunderstood in scientific models as the situation continues to evolve.[101]

NOTES

1. "Feds Finalize Plan on Endangered Fish," *Associated Press State and Local Wire* (December 21, 1999); Nancy Lofholm, "Grand Junction Water-Use Pact to Benefit Humans and Endangered Fish," *Denver Post* (December 22, 1999), p. B6; author's phone interview (November 30, 2000) with Henry Maddux, former director of the recovery program and then with the FWS in Salt Lake City; author's interview (October 21, 2001) in Glenwood Springs with Eric Kuhn, general director of the Colorado River Water Conservation District in Glenwood Springs.

2. U.S. Department of the Interior, FWS, *Final Programatic Biological Opinion (PBO) on the 15-Mile Reach* (Denver: FWS, 1999), cited hereafter as the *Final PBO;* Harold M. Tyus, "Ecology and Management of Colorado Squawfish," in W. L. Minckley and James E. Deacon, eds., *Battle Against Extinction* (Tucson: University of Arizona Press, 1991), ch. 19; Douglas B. Osmundson and Lynn R. Kaeding, *Studies of Colorado Squawfish and Razorback Sucker Use of the "15-Mile Reach" of the Upper Colorado River as a Part of Conservation Measures for the Green Mountain and Ruedi Reservoir Water Sales, Final Report* (Grand Junction, Colo.: U.S. Department of the Interior, FWS, 1989).

3. Data show that yearling and adult Colorado pikeminnow experience optimal growth at 25°C. Egg development and hatching are most successful in somewhat lower temperatures, approximately 20°C. For more on the connection between life cycle and habitat, see Jack A. Stanford, *Instream Flows to Assist the Recovery of Endangered Fishes of the Upper Colorado River Basin* (Washington, D.C.: U.S. Department of the Interior, National Biological Survey, 1994); Lawrence J. MacDonnell, *From Reclamation to Sustainability* (Niwot: University Press of Colorado, 1999); *Final PBO;* Douglas B. Osmundson, *Importance of the "15-Mile Reach" to Colorado River Populations of Endangered Colorado Pikeminnow and Razorback Sucker, Final Report* (Grand Junction, Colo.: U.S. FWS Position Paper, 2000).

4. Tyus, "Ecology and Management of the Colorado Squawfish"; *Final* PBO; Stanford, *Instream Flows;* Douglas B. Osmundson, Patrick Nelson, Kathy Fenton, and Dale W. Ryden, *Relationship Between Flow and Rare Fish Habitat in the 15-Mile Reach of the Upper Colorado River* (Grand Junction, Colo.: U.S. Department of the Interior, FWS, 1995).

5. Osmundson, *Importance of the "15-Mile Reach,"* p. i. See also *Final* PBO.

6. See the *Final* PBO and MacDonnell, *From Reclamation to Sustainability.* Author's interview (September 21, 2002) in Grand Junction with Dick Proctor, manager of the Grand Valley Water Users' Association in Grand Junction, Colo.

7. The Colorado River Compact was established in 1922 to reach a compromise between the states in the Upper and Lower Basins of the Colorado River. The Upper Basin states (Colorado, Utah, Wyoming, and New Mexico) were concerned that the Lower Basin states (Arizona, California, and Nevada) were developing more quickly and would claim and develop a large amount of Colorado River water before they could make use of it. The Upper Basin states knew they eventually would have to develop more Colorado River water to meet the needs of growing areas such as Denver. The compact divided the waters of the Colorado River between the two basins at 7.5 million acre-feet each, on an annual basis. In 1949 the Upper Colorado River Basin Compact further divided the Upper Basin's apportionment among the Upper Basin: Colorado, 51.75%; Utah, 23%; Wyoming, 14%; and New Mexico, 11.25%. See Dan A. Tarlock, James N. Corbridge, and David H. Getches, *Water Resource Management: A Casebook in Law and Public Policy,* 4th ed. (Westbury, Conn.: Foundation Press, 1993).

8. *Endangered Species Act of 1973* (P.L. 93-205), 16 U.S.C.A. §§1531-43. See also MacDonnell, *From Reclamation to Sustainability,* and Deborah L. Freeman, "Nuts and Bolts of the Endangered Species Act," *Emerging Challenges for Colorado Water Management* (Denver: Continuing Legal Education in Colorado, 1994), sec. 2.

9. Furthermore, under the Clean Water Act, nearly every storage or diversion project is subject to approval by the Army Corps of Engineers. See Tarlock et al., *Water Resource Management,* p. 734.

10. See R. S. Wydoski and J. Hamil, "Evolution of a Cooperative Recovery Program," in W. L. Minckley and J. E. Deacon, eds., *Battle Against Extinction: Native Fish Management in the American West* (Tucson: University of Arizona Press, 1991), pp. 123–139; Tarlock et al., *Water Resource Management;* Ann Brower, Chanel Reedy, and Jennifer Yelin-Kefers, "Consensus Versus Conservation in the Upper Colorado River Basin Recovery Implementation Program," *Conservation Biology* 15 (2001), pp. 1001–1007. See also author's interview (September 26, 2001) in Boulder with Robert Wigington, recovery program participant and attorney with The Nature Conservancy in Boulder, Colo.

11. *Final* PBO, p. 4, lists the participants and purpose. On the five-part approach to recovery efforts, see U.S. Department of the Interior, *Final Recovery Implementation Program for Endangered Fish Species in the Upper Colorado River Basin* (Denver: FWS, 1987), sec. 4, p. 11.

12. *Final Recovery Implementation Program* (1987); author's interview (September 21, 2001) in Lakewood with Gerry Roehm, instream flow coordinator for the recovery program in Lakewood, Colo.

13. *Final* PBO, p. 6. Federal agencies contribute approximately $3.3 million annually for im-

plementation of recovery actions under the base funding component of the recovery program. Additionally, reclamation contributes approximately $7 million annually for capital projects.

14. *Final Recovery Implementation Program* (1987), sec. 4, p. 6, and sec. 5, pp. 1–6.

15. Author's phone interview (October 15, 2000) with Tom Pitts, water users' representative to the recovery program from Loveland, Colo.

16. Author's interviews with Ralph Morgenweck, who also chairs the Recovery Program Implementation Committee, in Lakewood, Colo. (September 18, 2001). Morgenweck also mentioned that in the interest of maintaining the program's inclusiveness, new voting members such as the National Park Service and the Colorado Energy Distributors' Association have been added along the way as interest developed. Author's interview with Brent Uilenberg, the bureau's representative to the Recovery Program Management Committee, in Grand Junction (September 18, 2001); and author's interview with Robert Muth in Lakewood (September 19, 2001).

17. Colorado Department of Natural Resources, "New Proposal to Expedite Endangered Fish Recovery in the Colorado River" (2001), online at http://www.dnr.state.co.us/cdnr_news/edo/2001195104711.html.

18. *Final Recovery Implementation Program* (1987), sec. 1, p. 1; Maddux interview.

19. U.S. Department of the Interior, FWS, *Recovery Implementation Program for Endangered Fish Species in the Upper Colorado River Basin: Section 7 Consultation, Sufficient Progress and Historic Projects Agreement and Recovery Action Plan* (Denver: FWS, 1993). Cited hereafter as RIPRAP (1993).

20. RIPRAP (updated 2001).

21. Brower et al., "Consensus Versus Conservation."

22. Muth interview.

23. Morgenweck interview.

24. *Final Recovery Implementation Program* (1987), sec. 1, p. 7.

25. RIPRAP (1993), p. 3.

26. Muth interview.

27. RIPRAP (1993), p. 1.

28. Author's interview (September 11, 2001) in Ft. Collins with Tom Nesler, fishery biologist with the Colorado Division of Wildlife in Ft. Collins, Colo., and the division's representative in the recovery program.

29. U.S. FWS, *Recovery Program Director's Update* (March 2001), accessed online at http://www.r6.fws.gov/coloradoriver/Index.htm; Nesler interview.

30. *Final Recovery Implementation Program* (1987), sec. 1, p. 2 and p. 1, respectively.

31. U.S. Bureau of Land Management, *Plateau Creek Pipeline Replacement Project: Final Environmental Impact Statement* (Grand Junction, Colo.: Camp Dresser & McKee Inc., 1998).

32. Author's interview (September 18, 2001) in Lakewood with Margot Zallen, lead regional solicitor for the Department of the Interior in Lakewood, Colo., and its representative in the Water Acquisition Committee of the Recovery Program; and interviews with Uilenberg and Wigington.

33. Uilenberg interview; Tarlock et al., *Water Resource Management.*

34. Zallen interview.

35. Wigington interview.

36. Muth interview.

37. Legislation to extend federal funding for another 10 years was signed on October 30, 2000 (P.L. 106-392, 2000). Several recovery program participants have credited the success of this legislation to the 15-Mile Reach PBO and the agreements that helped to maintain broad support for the program.

38. *Final* PBO; Wigington interview; author's phone interview (November 28, 2000) with Patty Gellat, FWS, Grand Junction, Colo.

39. Author's interview (November 30, 2001) via phone with Jim Lochhead in Glenwood Springs, former director of the Colorado Department of Natural Resources.

40. Morgenweck interview.

41. Proctor and Uilenberg interviews.

42. On September 4, 1962, state game and fish departments poisoned the Green River with retenone to eliminate local trash fish before a new dam (Flaming Gorge) was closed on the Green River in Wyoming, just above the Utah border. This gave a head start to rainbow trout introduced later. P. B. Holden, "Ghosts of the Green River," in W. L. Minckley and J. E. Deacon, eds., *Battle Against Extinction: Native Fish Management in the American West* (Tucson: University of Arizona Press, 1991), pp. 123–139. See also Fred Quartarone, *Historical Accounts of Upper Colorado River Basin Endangered Fish* (Denver: Recovery Implementation Program for Endangered Fish of the Upper Colorado River Basin, 1993).

43. Author's interview (September 24, 2001) in Palisade with Jim Rooks, manager of the Orchard Mesa Irrigation District in Palisade, Colo.; and Proctor and Uilenberg interviews. The quality of irrigation water in the Grand Valley often is impaired by high salt content from the shale that underlies the valley and irrigation return flows. Drinking water in the Lower Basin can be impaired by high salinity. MacDonnell, *From Reclamation to Sustainability.*

44. Author's interview (October 19, 2001) in Glenwood Springs with Scott Balcomb, attorney with Balcomb and Green in Glenwood Springs, Colo.

45. Author's phone interview (December 5, 2001) with Dan Luecke, Environmental Defense Fund and Senior Environmental Representative to the Recovery Program, Boulder, Colo.

46. Zallen and Uilenberg interviews; *Final* PBO.

47. Rooks interview. Rooks's Orchard Mesa Irrigation Company is one of the six. The other five are the Grand Valley Irrigation Company, the Grand Valley Water Users' Association, the Mesa County Irrigation District, the Palisade Irrigation District, and the Redlands Water and Power Company. Phil Bertrand, Max Schmidt, Dan Crabtree, and Karen Fogelquist, *Landowner's Guide to Incorporating Irrigation Ditches and Laterals* (Grand Junction, Colo.: U.S. Bureau of Reclamation and Mesa Soil Conservation District, 1996).

48. Uilenberg and Morgenweck interviews.

49. Wigington interview.

50. Maddux and Proctor interviews.

51. Maddux and Rooks interviews.

52. Zallen and Morgenweck interviews.

53. Morgenweck and Rooks interviews.

54. Proctor interview.

55. Zallen and Wigington interviews.

56. The reinitiation section is on pp. 73–77 of *Final* PBO.

57. *Final* PBO, p. 7; Maddux and Wigington interviews.

58. This is the estimated average depletion per year from 1975 to 1991. The minimum depletion was about 877,000 acre-feet in 1983, and the maximum was about 1,172,000 acre-feet in 1978.

59. Although the adult population numbers are the primary indicator, the FWS also considers two other indices of population health. One is the adult age class structure of the population. A population is considered less stable if most of the population is represented by only a few age classes because it is susceptible to mass mortality when those classes reach their life expectancy. The other is the number of yearling fish spawned in the river rather than the hatchery.

60. *Final* PBO, p. 73. When the Colorado pikeminnow population exceeds 1,100, the FWS will define a new population baseline for further review.

61. See the section on "Effects of the Action," pp. 44–67 of the *Final* PBO. The quotation is from p. 73.

62. *Final* PBO, p. 73.

63. Author's interview (October 19, 2001) in Glenwood Springs with Lori Field, attorney with Balcomb and Green in Glenwood Springs, Colo.; and Muth and Luecke interviews.

64. *Final* PBO; author's interview (September 24, 2001) in Palisade with Greg Trainor, utility manager for the City of Grand Junction and its representative in the 15-Mile Reach negotiations; Kuhn interview.

65. *Final* PBO, p. 8.

66. *Final* PBO.

67. *Final* PBO, p. 75.

68. U.S. FWS, *Recovery Program Director's Update* (September 2003 and March 2004), accessed online at http://www.r6.fws.gov/coloradoriver/Index.htm.

69. *Final* PBO.

70. The studies include Lynn R. Kaeding and Douglas B. Osmundson, *Biologically Defensible Flow Recommendations for the Maintenance and Enhancement of Colorado Squawfish Habitat in the "15-Mile" Reach of the Upper Colorado River During July, August and September: Final Report* (Grand Junction, Colo.: U.S. FWS, 1989); Douglas B. Osmundson and Lynn R. Kaeding, *Recommendations for Flows in the 15-Mile Reach During October–June for Maintenance and Enhancement of Endangered Fish Populations in the Upper Colorado River: Final Report* (Denver: U.S. Department of the Interior, FWS, 1991); and D. B. Osmundson, P. Nelson, K. Fenton, and D. W. Ryden, *Relationships Between Flow and Rare Fish Habitat in the 15-Mile Reach of the Upper Colorado River* (Grand Junction, Colo.: U.S. Department of the Interior, FWS, 1995.)

71. Rooks, Proctor, Balcomb, Field, and Kuhn interviews.

72. *Final* PBO, p. 64.

73. Morgenweck interview; Stanford, *Instream Flows*.

74. Morgenweck and Nesler interviews; Stanford, *Instream Flows*.

75. Zallen and Morgenweck interviews.

76. Osmundson, *Importance of the "15-Mile Reach."*

77. MacDonnell, *From Reclamation to Sustainability.*

78. Proctor and Kuhn interviews.

79. Proctor interview; MacDonnell, *From Reclamation to Sustainability;* Bertrand et al., *Landowner's Guide.*

80. *Final* PBO and Proctor interview.

81. MacDonnell, *From Reclamation to Sustainability;* Wigington interview.

82. Zallen and Trainor interviews.

83. U.S. FWS, *Recovery Program Director's Update* (September 2003 and March 2004), accessed online at http://www.r6.fws.gov/coloradoriver/Index.htm; Proctor interview.

84. Proctor and Rooks interviews.

85. U.S. FWS, *Recovery Program Director's Update* (September 2003 and March 2004), accessed online at http://www.r6.fws.gov/coloradoriver/Index.htm; *Final* PBO; U.S. FWS, *Recovery Goals for the Bonytail [Gila elegans] of the Colorado River Basin: Draft Final* (Denver: FWS, 2001); Nesler interview.

86. Wigington, Balcomb, and Luecke interviews.

87. Kuhn, Balcomb, and Wigington interviews.

88. Nesler interview.

89. Kuhn, Muth, and Roehm interviews.

90. Nesler and Kuhn interviews.

91. Roehm, Muth, Morgenweck, and Proctor interviews.

92. Maddux, Kuhn, Morgenweck, Zallen, and Uilenberg interviews.

93. Lochhead interview.

94. For guidance in assessing the common interest, see Ronald D. Brunner, Christine H. Colburn, Christina M. Cromley, Roberta A. Klein, and Elizabeth A. Olson, *Finding Common Ground: Governance and Natural Resources in the American West* (New Haven, Conn.: Yale University Press, 2002), especially pp. 1–18 and the sources in the policy sciences cited there. The latter include Harold D. Lasswell, *A Pre-View of the Policy Sciences* (New York: Elsevier, 1971), which includes criteria for appraisal of decision process from a common interest standpoint on pp. 85–97.

95. Balcomb interview.

96. Proctor interview.

97. Rooks interview.

98. These political dynamics represent an informal mechanism of democratic accountability if a community-based initiative fails to advance the common interest of its participants. If participants in the initiative represent the multiple interests involved in an issue, and the initiative advances the common interest, there is no need in practice or in democratic theory to involve others.

99. See Herbert A. Simon, *The Sciences of the Artificial,* 3rd ed. (Cambridge: MIT Press, 1996), which provides an introduction to human cognition and bounded rationality, and concludes with a chapter on "The Architecture of Complexity," pp. 183–216.

100. Stanford, *Instream Flows.*

101. Ronald D. Brunner and Tim W. Clark, "A Practice-Based Approach to Ecosystem Management," *Conservation Biology* 11 (February 1997), pp. 48–58.

## 3. The Camino Real: To Care for the Land and Serve the People

TODDI A. STEELMAN AND DONNA W. TUCKER

ONE DAY IN 1991 Crockett Dumas wore his uniform to work as the district ranger for the Camino Real Ranger District (CRRD) of the Carson National Forest in northern New Mexico. But some Native Americans at a nearby Picuris Pueblo told him they did not appreciate the uniform. Shortly after that, Dumas had an epiphany and switched permanently to jeans. According to a colleague, Carveth Kramer, "It was like Crockett was struck by lighting one day while riding his horse." As Dumas himself later explained, he suddenly understood that "you don't get power from a green Forest Service truck, badge or uniform. You get it from relationships. Bureaucrats want to assert their power to apply the rules by saying 'no' to the public, but they lose public support in doing so. To get power you must find an appropriate way to say 'yes.'"[1] After 22 years in the U.S. Forest Service (USFS), Dumas realized that his personal and professional commitment to the agency's mission—"To Care for the Land and Serve the People"—could not be served without the respect, trust, and ultimately the political support of the people who depended on the land they inhabited. Without these crucial resources, his efforts to serve the mission would continue to be frustrated by appeals, litigation, and other forms of obstruction.

The challenges Dumas faced in the CRRD were not unlike the problems other USFS district rangers faced. Multiple publics demanded different amenities from the district, and Dumas was expected to integrate or balance these competing demands. He faced lawsuits and appeals from environmentalists, animosity from local residents, and a hostile environment in which it was increasingly difficult to manage vegetation, including timber. Dumas met the challenge by developing respect, trust, and support to advance his mission. He and others in the district practiced horseback diplomacy. They listened to people in their homes and elsewhere, sought out their opinions and concerns, developed relationships, and gave people ownership in the management of the land on which they depended, in many cases, for survival. This strategy made possible an array of substantive policies that served the mission of the USFS and were flexible and pragmatic in response to the dynamic challenges of governance experienced in the CRRD. These policies provided for new permits and procedures for taking firewood for personal use, smaller-scale timber sales for local community members, stewardship blocks for forest restoration, and new grazing management practices. They emerged gradually in the early 1990s and worked well for most of the decade. Collectively they can be called the CRRD policy.[2] However, national recognition and jealousy began to undermine the personal relationships on which the policy depended, and Dumas's departure from the district in 1999 compounded the difficulties.

The CRRD policy is an example of adaptive governance in the common interest. It was guided by the USFS motto and mission, "To Care for the Land and Serve the People," and maintained flexibility to adjust and adapt as events unfolded in unexpected ways in the district. Flexibility and innovation were possible because a stable base of political support provided the latitude necessary to work within gray areas of the larger framework of rules that apply to the USFS and often bog down effective action. The CRRD experience shows how to capitalize on the flexibility that exists within an elaborate structure of laws and regulations accumulated over a century or more and within a large bureaucracy. The CRRD experience also shows how adaptive governance in the common interest is possible even under difficult historical and cultural conditions. The purpose of this chapter is to harvest this experience for public officials and others who might adapt it to the management of public lands elsewhere—people for whom the USFS mission is more than empty rhetoric.

## Historical and Cultural Context

Land ownership is an emotionally charged subject in northern New Mexico. Conflict, frustration, fierce uprisings, civil disobedience, and litigation have typified the relationships between the USFS and inhabitants of the picturesque mountains and valleys of northern New Mexico for decades. Traditional Hispano settlers, environmentalists, USFS employees, and nonprofit groups all have somewhat different interests in the forests in the region. At times these various groups have forged management directions that serve their common interest. At other times they gave in to violence because one interest was subjugated to others.

Before the Treaty of Guadalupe Hidalgo that ended the U.S.–Mexican War in 1848, the lands now in the Carson National Forest were under the jurisdiction of Mexico and inhabited by Hispano pioneers encouraged to settle the frontier. Portions of these lands were given to the settlers on an individual and communal basis, and the communities that remained on them became known as land grants. Over time the lands were acquired, sometimes through dubious practices, by predominantly Anglo landholders in the region. Although the acquisition of lands in northern New Mexico may be considered lawful under the American legal system, the practices were perceived as unfair by the people who historically inhabited the region and abided by different customs. The consequence is a lingering perception that the traditional owners were deprived unjustly of lands their ancestors had inhabited as early as 1598. In the 1880s, expansion of the railroad industry led to an increase in commercial ranching, farming, and mining operations. Several decades of exploitation by these private interests led to soil and vegetation loss. In poor shape, the lands were given over to public ownership in 1908, when the Carson and Santa Fe national forests were established. Aldo Leopold was appointed the first supervisor of the Carson National Forest in 1912. The CRRD is one of six districts there; the others are Canjilon, El Rito, Jicarilla, Questa, and Tres Piedras. Ownership of these lands remains contested in the region today because of the complicated history of land transactions. The enduring sentiment among Hispano residents is that 22 percent of the Carson and Santa Fe national forests come from land that once belonged to Hispano settlers in the region.[3]

Since the late 1940s, several attempts have been made to forge a policy that better serves the multiple interests in the region. Recognizing that the needs of poor, resource-dependent communities were neglected, the federal government established the Vallecitos Federal Sustained Yield Unit in 1948 in the Carson National Forest. It was one of five federal sustained yield units established throughout the country with the Federal Sustained Yield Unit Act of 1944. The Vallecitos Unit was intended to provide communities with stable employment and forest products but for the most part failed to serve its purpose. From the outset, the USFS decided that a single large operator would best serve the Vallecitos Unit. The thought was that economic benefits in the form of cutting and milling wage labor jobs would trickle down to the local community. Local Hispano-owned businesses, too small to achieve the industrial scale envisioned by the USFS, were turned down when they requested designation as operators in the unit. As a result, for the first 20 years the operators of the unit failed to hire sufficient labor from the local communities and lost their contracts, or the land sat idle without a contractor. Contractors claimed that an absence of skilled workers in the region made hiring local help difficult. In 1972, Duke City Lumber, a subsidiary of a London-based multinational corporation, took up the contract. Duke City also was accused of failing to support community interests and hire local workers but nonetheless held onto the contract for 22 years.[4] In a scene replayed all over the United States in the 1970s and 1980s, the interests of the USFS bureaucracy and large, industrial operators took preference over the needs of local communities.

Discontent among the Hispano communities became explosive in the late 1960s. Local activists took matters into their own hands, fueled by the lingering perception that they had been deprived of their land unjustly, reinforced by the USFS inattention to local needs while serving industrial corporations and invigorated by a groundswell of activism, especially among minority populations, throughout the nation. Enigmatic leader Reies Lopez Tijerina and other activists under the banner of Alianza Federal de Pueblos Libres (Federated Alliance of Free Communities) commanded national attention when they took over the Echo Amphitheater in the El Rito District to establish their rights to the land. USFS employees descended onto the amphitheater and were taken hostage. They pressed charges against Tijerina, who was imprisoned for 2 years. To protest Tijerina's imprisonment, a crowd stormed the Tierra Amarilla Court House. Several law enforcement officials were wounded, and one was killed in the gun battle that ensued. Secret groups such as the Gorras Blancas (White Caps) and the Mano Negra (Black Hand) burned and bombed USFS property and made threats of personal injury. The local uprising and national attention led to the development of another policy for the management of the forests in northern New Mexico in 1972, one that explicitly recognized the special connection that the people of northern New Mexico have to the land and better served the common interest.[5]

This Northern New Mexico Policy began to emerge when William Hurst, then regional forester, recognized the need to adapt national forest management to the distinctive circumstances in northern New Mexico in a memo penned in 1967. Milo Jean Hassell expanded on the memo in a 1968 report titled "The People of Northern New Mexico and the National Forests," which detailed ninety-nine policy recommendations for the region. The Hassell report provided the basis for a 1972 directive that was circulated to the forest supervisors and district rangers in the Carson, Cibola, and Santa Fe, the three national forests with the greatest concentration of land grant peoples and the least likely to resist changes in management. The Northern New Mexico Policy called for the three forests to recognize the unique cultural connection of the Hispano descendants to the land and included changes in timber sales to make them more compatible with the needs of local communities; grazing policy to accommodate small permit numbers to better fit the needs of the Hispano communities; firewood and building material policy to provide communities with dead wood and small-diameter trees for poles, posts, and vigas; attention to Indian ceremonial areas and religious shrines; and attitudes of the USFS employees to acknowledge the uniqueness of northern New Mexico. Through this policy, the USFS was expected to serve the common interests of the agency and the Hispano communities in the region.[6]

Initially the Northern New Mexico Policy enjoyed great financial and political support from the regional and Washington offices of the agency. However, as resources were withdrawn over time, the agency reverted to status quo practices. The policy was implemented under conditions that did not support lasting change. For instance, the budget for each forest was calculated based on the board feet of timber cut. Budgets tied to the quantities of timber cut were not conducive to creating smaller timber sales for local populations. Moreover, there were no sanctioning mechanisms in place to rebuke agency employees who did a poor job operationalizing the new procedures or to reward employees who performed well. On the contrary, if an employee organized a big timber sale to get more timber cut, he or she was more likely to be rewarded. Without changes in the larger management structure and culture in which the Carson, Cibola, and Santa Fe were embedded, the three forests reverted to their old ways when the money dried up.

Despite such attempts, the history is dominated by failure to acknowledge and integrate into the management of Carson and Santa Fe national forests the unique cultural ties of the Hispano population to the lands. These failures are the historical basis for misunderstanding and conflict in the region. A USFS culture steeped in principles of scientific management for efficiency, including large-scale projects and an impersonal bureaucratic operating style, fit poorly with a local culture that valued community tradition, small-scale agriculture, and personal relationships. Consider some of the misunderstandings in grazing and timber practices over the decades.

To restore damaged lands to health in the early 1900s, the USFS introduced new grazing policies. For centuries, the Hispano communities grazed small numbers of cattle and larger numbers of sheep and goats on what is now national forest land. The communities relied on the cattle, goats, and sheep to provide food and as emergency stores of wealth for times of need. In some cases, cattle were grazed in the same ancestral areas for hundreds of years. However, as ownership of the land changed, the USFS gained control over how cattle could be managed. The USFS reduced stock numbers, moved toward rotational grazing systems, relocated animals, forced grazers to construct fences and water developments for the animals, and instituted grazing fees. All of these changes had profound impacts on the Hispano villagers. These descendants of the original land grantees, who saw the lands as theirs to begin with, resented these changes, and enmity between them and the USFS grew.[7]

Although it is fair to say that some local residents needed to change their land management practices to improve the land, the means used by the USFS to impose these changes showed little respect for the people. The USFS was a strong-armed agency eager to demonstrate its power over locals, not unlike the agency portrayed in John Nichols's famous novel *The Milagro Beanfield War*. Max Cordova, an important participant in the CRRD policy, remembers from his childhood in the 1960s that the agency installed cattle guards. Cordova's father had a horse that wandered onto one of the guards and became trapped when its legs fell through. The USFS "solved" the problem by removing the horse's legs with a chain saw. Two days later the agency notified the family that their horse had been destroyed. Additional battles arose when permittees and private land-owners on national forest land failed to maintain their fences, and cattle from the land grants had no reason to abide by arbitrary property lines unenclosed by fences. The agency regularly found cattle on public land and fined land grant peoples $500—for them an enormous sum—or jailed them for 6 months. In time the USFS encouraged the permittees to fix their fences and the problem was solved, but not without generating great hostility between the parties.[8]

Likewise, changes in timber practices had a deleterious impact on the His-pano villages. When the USFS assumed management of the lands in 1908, timber cutting slowed in recognition of the unsustainable rate at which timber was harvested in the previous decades. However, in response to the growing market demand for railroad ties, the timber cut reached 83.8 million board feet from 1921 to 1925 in the Carson. The pace of cutting then slowed again until the housing boom after World War II increased the demand for timber.[9] During the timber booms, the timber industry and Congress preferred large-volume sales that favored industrial operations. Responding to the demands of Congress and industry and to its own culture of scientific management, the USFS imple-mented a nationwide policy of large-volume timber sales.

Additional animosity followed the arrival of environmental activists who migrated to northern New Mexico in the late 1960s and 1970s as part of the back-to-the-land movement. Large-volume timber cuts attracted their attention in the 1980s. Often embracing environmental values, these new residents were interested in maintaining the quality of life that attracted them to the region and drew greater attention to the environmental impacts of logging. Carson Forest Watch, the Forest Guardians, and the Sierra Club, among other environmental groups, drew attention to the devastation of the local forests by industrial opera-tors. La Comunidad and other Hispano community groups with an environ-mental interest also began to play a more activist role in the region. Beginning in the late 1980s and early 1990s, a more mobilized and activist environmen-tal presence blocked timber sales and raised ecological concerns about timber practices by filing appeals and lawsuits. As a consequence, the Carson National

Forest, which consistently harvested 26 to 29 million board feet of timber per year throughout the 1980s, saw its timber harvest levels drop to 1 to 2 million board feet per year.[10] By the early 1990s new environmental groups moved to the area, including the Forest Conservation Council and the Southwest Center for Biological Diversity. Opposing proposed timber sales and grazing permits through legal processes, these groups in conjunction with the preexisting groups forced the USFS to change the way it managed national forests.

## Discontent and Innovations

By the late 1980s and early 1990s, discontent was high in and around the CRRD, providing an opportunity for policy innovations. Morale in the CRRD was low. Forest Service employees wanted to manage vegetation, including timber, but were bogged down in appeals and litigation. Environmental groups wanted increased ecological diversity, improved forest health, and reduced environmental impacts from large-volume timber sales. Traditional local people wanted more employment opportunities from the large industrial operators in the region and better and easier access to timber for personal uses.[11]

### A New Ranger

Like other people in and around the forest, people in the Truchas Land Grant had little hope that their concerns would be addressed by the new district ranger. Located between the Carson and Santa Fe national forests, as indicated in figure 3.1, the Truchas Land Grant is recognized as Hispano communal property. It is one of the few that partially survived the vagaries of ownership transfers after the Mexican–American War; about 319 families and a total of about 1,200 people now live there. Despite the contentious history, some of the people from Truchas nevertheless went to see the new district ranger, Crockett Dumas, soon after his official arrival in the CRRD on February 5, 1990. Among them were Max Cordova, a local businessperson and president of the Truchas Land Grant, and Mary Mascarenas, a local postmaster. They expressed their concerns about road closures and access to fuelwood.

Access to fuelwood was a matter of survival, they explained, not convenience. At an average elevation of about 8,000 feet above sea level and lacking money to buy propane, most people in the Truchas Land Grant used wood to cook their food and heat their homes, as their ancestors had for centuries. Each family needed on average six to nine cords of wood to stay warm through the long, cold winter. The USFS issued too few permits to meet their needs, and they had

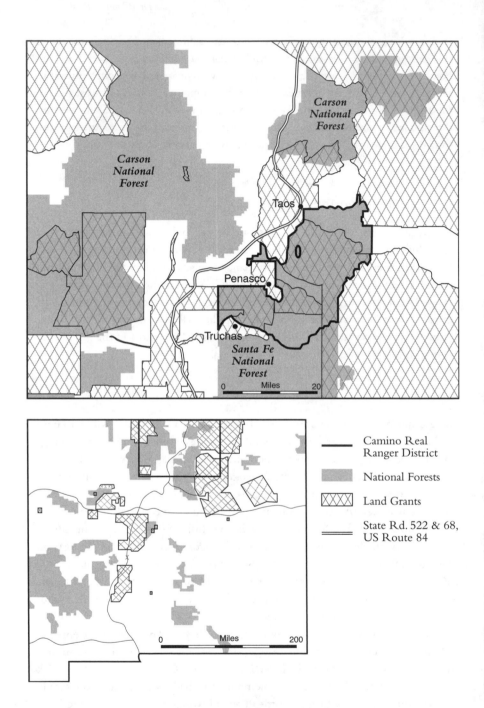

Figure 3.1. Northern New Mexico national forests and land grants. Source: Virginia F. Kunkel, North Carolina State University graduate student.

to drive long distances and wait in long lines at inconvenient times to ensure that they could obtain a permit. The USFS also closed roads and prohibited access to prime cutting areas. In that first meeting Dumas just "sat there and didn't say 20 words."[12] Thus the initial relationship between Dumas, Mascarenas, and Cordova was unproductive. And that was not uncharacteristic of relationships that had existed between USFS officials and the land grant peoples for decades.

The newly arrived Crockett Dumas found controversy over timber sales as well. Local community and environmental groups such as La Comunidad and Carson Forest Watch were unhappy with the size of the Alamo/Dinner timber sale. Proposed in 1988, the Alamo/Dinner sale catered to large industrial timber operations and activated opposition because of its potential ecological impacts. In January 1989 a controversial proposal for the 10,132-acre Angostura timber sale in the Rio Pueblo watershed caught the attention of environmentalists and community members, as did a May 1990 proposal for the 11,595-acre Ojos/Ryan timber sale in the Rio Grande del Rancho watershed. Both the Angostura and Ojos/Ryan were too large for local timber companies to bid on and were slated to take place in sensitive ecological areas. Bogged down with appeals to these sales and general hostility toward the district, Dumas was unable to respond adequately to the concerns of opponents to the various timber sales. He realized that the district "had lost trust with the people it was supposed to serve."[13]

The opposition to the timber sales motivated Dumas and district employees to rethink their approach to timber management. Carolyn Bye, director of public affairs for the USFS regional office in Albuquerque, suggested that Dumas try to improve relationships with the community by engaging in a door-to-door survey, and Dumas followed through.[14] This entailed initiating conversations with the various local people and groups around the CRRD. But years of animosity between district employees and the locals did not make for immediate, effortless, and open conversation. However, things began to change when Mary Mascarenas became Dumas's confidant. She helped him understand the historical aspects of land ownership and the cultural, economic, and spiritual connections to the land, especially among the Hispano villagers. This relationship, and the new understanding that came with it, opened the door to an entirely new strategy of outreach in the CRRD.

In March 1991, with the encouragement of Bye and insight of Mascarenas, CRRD employees began "horseback diplomacy." Dumas and nearly all of his staff—thirty-eight out of forty-two employees in the district—got on their horses or into their trucks and rode out to thirty-two rural communities in or adjacent to the district to listen to the concerns of residents in their own homes. The employees arrived in pairs with an English and Spanish speaker solely for the purpose of listening to what the community had to say. Dumas explained, "Communication begins by listening. I am going to people's homes to listen."[15]

Through horseback diplomacy employees in the CRRD learned more about various problems in the community related to cutting firewood, vigas, and latillas. (Vigas are crossbeams used in the construction of adobe houses; latillas are posts used to support roof structures and to construct fences.) People from the villages use these building materials from the forests for their own houses and to sell to others. For years, residents had problems with the location, timing, and number of USFS permits necessary to obtain these materials and firewood. For example, permits to cut firewood were issued in October, but they were needed from May to December. Likewise, too few permits were issued to meet the needs of the community members, and USFS employees reserved permits for their own use instead of the community's. Consequently, residents had to drive long distances to the Carson National Forest Headquarters in Taos to line up at 2 or 3 o'clock in the morning to secure a permit to cut wood.[16] Closed roads in the forest forced people to drive longer distances or prevented people from collecting wood in traditionally valued areas. Almost immediately, Dumas and his employees altered the permitting procedures to demonstrate their commitment to change. Thus, the CRRD policy began by corroborating the concerns initially expressed by Mascarenas and Cordova a year earlier and by acting on them.

Concurrent with outreach through horseback diplomacy, Dumas and other district employees worked on timber management problems. Redesigning timber sales was another key to serving the community better. Mascarenas coached Dumas through the Alamo/Dinner timber sale, encouraging him to rethink the sale to meet the needs of smaller timber companies and communities in the area. The redesigned sale was authorized to proceed and did so without local opposition in October 1991. But the change in policy was not comprehensive. Other timber sales failed to take into consideration community interests. In June 1992 a notice about the 9,500-acre La Cueva timber sale was sent out. The La Cueva, Ojos/Ryan, and Angostura sales were still large-volume sales designed for a few big operators, without provisions for smaller community operators, as in the redesigned Alamo/Dinner sale.[17] Not surprisingly, these large sales were appealed by local and regional groups, including La Comunidad, Carson Forest Watch, and the Forest Guardians. At this point, Dumas and his employees realized that all timber sales would have to be reconfigured from large projects with products going outside the community to small projects with products used in local communities. "Dumas said he was sick and tired of every project that the USFS was promoting was appealed and litigated and that obviously the era of the big timber sale was over." From that turning point, "he decided to get out of commodity production of saw timber and [get] oriented to providing wood to sell to communities."[18] That coincided with Dumas's epiphany on how to care for the land and serve the people. He switched to wearing blue jeans, leaving his USFS badge at home, and driving his own truck, until the day he retired from the USFS in 2002.

By 1993 the land grant community was meeting with the USFS on a regular basis at Los Siete, an artists' cooperative featuring traditional weaving run by Max Cordova. About twenty people, including land grant community members, environmentalists, and USFS representatives, participated in the series of meetings at Los Siete. At the meetings, according to Cordova, they made great progress on the permitting problems and other issues. Dumas continued the district's strategy of horseback diplomacy to the villages, and Cordova often accompanied him. Clearly, a good working relationship had evolved since the first meeting with Mascarenas and Cordova in which Dumas sat nearly mute.[19] Through the meetings, Cordova and Dumas realized they could manage timber and vegetation to improve the health of the forest, and the concept of forest restoration emerged as a possibility.

Cordova had his own epiphany at this time. "Max went from 'this is my land, my products, who are you to tell me what I need' to seeing the ecological benefits from [forest restoration] and getting very excited about it."[20] For Cordova, forest restoration embodies both understanding the broader ecosystem and imparting knowledge and skills. "Forest restoration and logging are two different things," explains Cordova. "In forest restoration you leave the best [trees], while in logging you take the best [trees]." To implement the forest restoration goal, small-diameter trees had to be cut, the slash had to be cleared away, and the canopy of the forest opened up. This entailed training local people to understand the consequences of these forestry practices and teaching the skills necessary to carry them out accordingly. Imparting these skills invariably tied community health to forest health according to Cordova, by giving people means for better living while also improving the forest.[21]

In addition, Henry Lopez, a forest technician in the CRRD, came up with the idea of stewardship blocks to serve individual parties. A lifelong resident of the area, Lopez had insight into what might work with local community members. Stewardship blocks are 1- to 4-acre allotments for personal use firewood. Within the stewardship blocks local community members contracted to thin badly overgrown tracts to a prescribed condition and take home the fuelwood and small-diameter trees they harvested. After the firewood was cut, they cleared the slash so that grass began to grow and the wildlife returned to the areas.[22] To implement both forest restoration and stewardship blocks, the agency needed a supply of qualified people and resources to support them. The twofold strategy for success was access and education. "Dumas had small greenwood fuel areas that were right by the communities and he set them up so they could access them . . . and then [he] educated people in the communities as to why they were doing this."[23]

### CRRD Policy

By 1993 the CRRD policy was composed of three principal changes in procedures and substantive policy involving the location, timing, and number of permits for personal use timber; timber sales better targeted for smaller-scale community interests; and forest restoration work in the form of small contracts and stewardship blocks. These changes in policy were achieved through continuous outreach to the community, including listening, horseback diplomacy with or without the horse, and various meetings. Dumas and his staff addressed the problems brought to their attention by the community. These responses were prompt, flexible, and pragmatic, in accord with the broader mission to care for the land and serve the people. These aspects of the CRRD policy were worked out in pieces in practice over time and later formalized in the East Entranas Ecosystem Management Plan.[24]

The East Entranas Ecosystem Management Plan documented local perceptions of current conditions of the forest and the vision they had for the future. It also laid out how they could achieve their vision. The idea behind this localized and scaled-down version of a plan came from the Carson Forest planner, Carveth Kramer, and his small core team of USFS employees. Kramer advocated shorter planning processes to create documents more responsive to local needs. Dumas was the only ranger in the Carson to appreciate the value of Kramer's suggestions and move forward with the idea.[25] Dumas and Kramer began working with various local people in late 1995 to incorporate their current understanding of resource conditions and their future needs. By the spring of 1996 they had a plan that represented a joint vision for the region. The East Entranas Ecosystem Management Plan "shows how thin and abstracting a public planning document can be when the public has ownership and trust in it."[26] The plan, only twelve pages long, was short on detail, long on action, and issued in July 1996. This vision for planning fit in well with Dumas's operating style. In his view, "A plan shouldn't be very thick or it will not be read."[27] Planning was short term and led quickly to action because things always are changing. The forest supervisor at the time, Leonard Lucero, was opposed to this scaled-down version of planning, but this did not deter Dumas or Kramer.

The CRRD policy ended appeals and lawsuits in the district after 1993. Neighboring districts continued to experience conflict and controversy. Despite its success, a major challenge to the policy and its implementation occurred in August 1995. The Forest Guardians, a regional environmental group, in conjunction with several other environmental groups, brought suit against Region 3 of the USFS. The result was a court injunction that prohibited all timber-cutting activity in the national forests in the region. This included cutting under the new permitting procedures, small-scale timber projects, and forest restoration, effectively blindsiding the CRRD policy. Neither the lawsuit nor the subsequent injunction explicitly targeted the CRRD policy or the various interests served by the policy. But the injunction nevertheless had grave consequences for the Hispano communities that relied on the forests to provide wood for their cooking and for heating during the long winter.

Plaintiffs included activists involved in the northern spotted owl controversies in the Pacific Northwest in the late 1980s who relocated to the Southwest and formed new groups, including the Forest Conservation Council and the Southwest Center for Biological Diversity, to protect the Mexican spotted owl. In addition to these two groups, plaintiffs included the Forest Guardians, Biodiversity Legal Foundation, Carson Forest Watch, Maricopa Audubon Society, Robin Silver, and Diné Citizens Against Ruining Our Environment. They brought suit under the Endangered Species Act out of concern for old-growth habitat for the owl. In 1993 the U.S. Fish and Wildlife Service (FWS) listed the Mexican spotted owl as a threatened species. In 1994 the agency released a plan to designate 4.8 million acres in New Mexico and Arizona as critical habitat for the owl.[28] Approximately 2,700 owls are located throughout the Southwest, and 1,000 are believed to live in New Mexico and Arizona. The case against the USFS was intended to force a reevaluation and comprehensive review of the standards and guidelines for timber, grazing, recreation, and wildlife programs in the region to provide better management for the owl.[29]

The Forest Guardians emerged as the most active and vocal interest group on behalf of the owl in the Carson National Forest. Located in nearby Santa Fe, the Forest Guardians advocate a no-compromise "zero-cut" and "zero-cow" stand on public lands, meaning that they actively oppose measures to harvest timber and graze national forest lands. Their ultimate goal is the decommercialization of natural resources on public lands. They bring timber sales and grazing practices to a halt while cases are appealed and litigated. Since the late 1980s the Forest Guardians have filed nearly 100 lawsuits.[30] Efforts to gain support for the CRRD policy from the Forest Guardians were limited and unsuccessful in the face of their no-compromise commitments. The Forest Guardians' zero-tolerance policy on public lands also precludes their meaningful involvement in other efforts to manage land in the CRRD.

## The Injunction

In response to the suit, U.S. District Judge Carl Muecke ordered a halt to all timber harvesting in the eleven national forests in Region 3 of the USFS on August 24, 1995. The intent was to allow the USFS, in conjunction with the FWS, to assess cumulative biological impacts on the spotted owl from the many timber sales in the region. The order effectively put twenty-six timber sales and 85 million board feet of timber off limits to the southwestern timber industry. This represented 80 percent of the volume under contract at that time, with considerable financial impacts on the contractors. The injunction also prohibited the collection of personal use timber. The lead plaintiffs in the suit, the Forest Guardians and the Forest Conservation Council, reached an agreement with the USFS in October 1995, 2 months after the injunction came down, to release an initial 1,000 projects throughout the region. Two months later, in December 1995, negotiations allowed twenty-five small timber projects in the Carson and Santa Fe national forests to move forward if restrictions were placed on firewood gathering.[31] Areas considered critical habitat were placed off limits, and the cutting of standing deadwood was prohibited except in designated areas. As a result, many of the most popular and culturally significant places for cutting firewood in the Carson National Forest were placed off limits, including those in the CRRD.

The plaintiffs demanded restrictions on firewood gathering because they believed that Hispano villagers received preferential treatment in their collection of firewood, to the detriment of the habitat for the owl. Sam Hitt, then executive director of the Forest Guardians, claimed that heavy use of firewood in northern New Mexico resulted in a crisis for the Mexican spotted owl, with firewood being logged off "at more than seven times the sustainable rate."[32] According to Hitt, "It's unbelievable. You go into the forest and its like Mexico or third world countries in Asia. There's not a stick left. It's creating huge problems for the wildlife."[33] From the perspective of the Forest Guardians, dead and downed timber provides important habitat for the Mexican spotted owl. Believing that the Carson had fewer snags and dead and downed timber than other forests because of intensive firewood gathering, the plaintiffs called for an end to what they saw as preferential treatment of firewood collecting in the Carson.[34]

However, the perceptions of Sam Hitt and his Forest Guardians were contradicted by an FWS biological opinion issued in September 1995, a month after the injunction and a month before the restrictions on firewood were imposed. This opinion stated that fuelwood gathering in the Carson National Forest would not "adversely jeopardize the continued existence of the Mexican Spotted Owl nor will it destroy or adversely modify the Mexican spotted owl's critical habitat." The opinion specifically addressed the impacts of firewood cutting and concluded that fuelwood programs would not interfere with the owl's ability to nest, roost, or travel. The opinion did recommend restrictions on cutting snags.[35] An additional 8-year, $1.5-million study by the New Mexico Game and Fish Department found that no owls inhabited the CRRD.[36] Carveth Kramer explained that the Forest Guardians were using the owl as a means to protect trees. "You have to understand what the Forest Guardians are about. They want old growth preserve. Their vision is not to cut any trees. If they had their druthers, they wouldn't allow any timber to be cut, no firewood. And they are not into compromise or consensus."[37]

The October 1995 deal between the USFS and the plaintiffs allowed other timber projects to move forward, ignored the Hispano people's ties to the land, and excluded them from the table where the deal was made. The Carson National Forest has more people dependent on firewood than any another national forest in the Southwest and allows a greater volume of firewood to be collected from its lands. People cut a great deal of timber from the communal property of the Truchas Land Grant, but they also need access to public lands for the rest of their needs. For instance, in 1995 land grant members cut 660 cords of wood from their properties and were dependent on the USFS land for the remaining 1,200 cords to meet their needs for the winter. Before the new restrictions, families could roam freely to collect dead and fallen wood anywhere, except for wilderness areas, with "free permits." Dead standing trees also could be cut, except for ponderosa pines. Often returning to the areas where their ancestors had collected wood for centuries, residents maintained a historical and cultural connection to the land. "The Forest Service lawyers and the environmentalists both sat down trying to decide what we need," recalled Cordova. "They should have come and asked us. We're stuck right in the middle. We really feel this is our land they are talking about." However, because the plaintiffs were communicating through lawyers, there was little room to involve others without lawyers, even those who might be harmed by their actions.

Nearly a hundred families in the mountain village of Truchas did not have adequate firewood for the upcoming winter, and twenty-two of them were in immediate need of wood because fuel supplies were low or nonexistent. The other thirty-one timber-dependent communities faced similar circumstances. A survey of homes in Truchas revealed that the families were short 1,800 cords of wood to get them through the impending winter. Wood is the sole source of heat and cooking for many of these families and not an auxiliary fuel source. Cordova expressed his aggravation, "People don't understand that we have a real crisis up here. That is what's so frustrating. We can't seem to get through to them. . . . The lands used to belong to our people. Now they belong to everybody. Yet the rest of America doesn't seem to realize that we depend on these forests for our survival."[38] In response to the restrictions, a group called Herencia de Nortenos Unidos organized to protest the callousness of the Forest Guardians and other plaintiffs toward the nortenos, or people of northern New Mexico. Led by charismatic and outspoken Antonio "Ike" DeVargas, the group labeled the Forest Guardians "a bunch of hypocrites, everything they're doing, they're doing at our expense."[39]

Toward the end of November 1995, Herencia de Nortenos Unidos staged a mock hanging of Sam Hitt and John Talberth, leaders of the head plaintiff organizations. The effigies were hung from an 8-foot wooden beam in the main plaza in Santa Fe, the state capital, in front of the Forest Guardians' office, while a hundred people looked on. Hitt and Talberth maintained that the USFS should have been the real focus of the anger and civil action. DeVargas made clear that he blamed them for their actions: "This protest is meant to let these people know that they cannot hide behind the rhetoric that their actions are to protect the Mexican spotted owl or that the U.S. Forest Service is responsible for litigation that is initiated by them."[40] According to a petition signed by two hundred residents of the mountain communities, "Well meaning judges" are denying wood "to people unable to travel the great distances required to gather fuel. Faced with no alternative, we become lawbreakers just to exist, in a system that is out of control."[41]

To avoid the looming disaster in Truchas, Cordova needed wood, and there was only one place to get it. He placed a call to Dumas, "I am going to send my people to cut wood. You can either send people to mark trees or we are just going to cut the trees." Dumas replied, "Max, you don't understand, a federal judge has handed down an injunction that we cannot violate." Cordova replied, "Hey, the federal judge doesn't live here. We need help."[42] Dumas faced a tough decision. He could abide by the court order to uphold the law. In doing so, he risked a violent confrontation resulting in further injustice to those who depended on the firewood. Alternatively, he could violate the injunction to allow Cordova and his people to take the wood they needed. In doing so, he would prevent an injustice to the community and conserve the trust on which the CRRD policy and the larger mission depended. He would also assume legal liability and put his job at risk. Dumas agreed to send his people to mark the trees. "It was the right thing to do," he said. The next day Cordova and his people cut the marked trees and hauled wood to heat their homes.

Cordova also sent Lorrie Osterstock, ranger for Espanola District in the neighboring Santa Fe National Forest, a letter stating that they would gather firewood near Truchas on her side of the forest with or without the needed permits. An armed standoff between community members and law enforcement officials ensued. The standoff lasted several hours until Osterstock received approval from the U.S. attorney in Arizona to issue the $15 permits to fourteen families to allow them to gather two cords of wood each.[43]

Community self-sufficiency became the topic of a candlelight vigil and march through Santa Fe in December 1995. About 350 people marched from the capitol to Our Lady of Guadalupe Church. According to Maria Varela, a local resident and long-time norteno activist, the march "reflect[ed] the hunger in our communities which has deepened this winter by court action halting the gathering of firewood for home and for income."[44] Community residents from the north were joined by ranchers from the south upon hearing that the Forest Guardians planned to sue the USFS to prevent grazing on federal land because it threatened the habitat for mice, the food for Mexican spotted owls.[45]

The injunction persisted for another year. In October 1996, U.S. District Court Judge Carl Muecke ordered the USFS and plaintiffs to meet until they reached an agreement for the Mexican spotted owl. Hispano community members again were absent from the negotiation, but not by choice. The USFWS fulfilled its obligation to issue a biological opinion on Mexican spotted owl habitat on November 25, 1996. On Wednesday, December 4, 1996, U.S. District Court Judge Roger Strand lifted the controversial ban on logging from the eleven national forests.[46]

## The Policy Evolves

After the controversy over the Mexican spotted owl and the injunction, the CRRD policy continued to evolve as attention focused on grazing issues. The Santa Barbara Grazing Association, a grazing group in the CRRD, noticed that forage on their land was decreasing, the density of trees was increasing, and the weight of their cattle was declining.[47] In 1998 the Rio Pueblo/Rio Embudo Watershed Protection Coalition made arrangements for the Quivira Coalition, a regional environmental group, to facilitate a workshop with grazing stakeholders in the region. Out of this workshop emerged a proposal that allowed the grazing association to move their cattle from the Santa Barbara allotment to another area outside the CRRD, the Valle Grande Grass Bank, so the USFS could undertake forest restoration work and replenish the lands.

While the livestock were gone, multiple projects were proposed. Thinning projects would provide jobs for locals. Dead and down permits would be sold to locals to reduce fuels in the area. Prescribed burning would mitigate the fire risk and activate the strong seed bank in the soil. Earthen tanks to hold water would be constructed to distribute livestock, decrease pressure in riparian areas, and provide water for wildlife.[48] The grazing association, the Quivira Coalition, the Santa Fe Sierra Club, *La Jicarita News,* and the Rio Pueblo/Rio

Embudo Watershed Protection Coalition supported the grassbank and forest restoration project. Local environmentalists from the Rio Pueblo/Rio Embudo Watershed Protection Coalition and the grazing association held a meeting and agreed that 203 cows would be moved to the grassbank. Restoration activities were funded through the USFS, U.S. Environmental Protection Agency (EPA), and New Mexico Environmental Department (NMED), mostly through EPA 319 funds that can be used to address non-point source pollution.

The successes of the CRRD policy did not go unnoticed. In 1997 Vice President Gore's Hammer Award for Reinventing Government was given to the people in the CRRD for their ability to cut red tape and make government work more efficiently. In 1998 the Ford Foundation, in partnership with Harvard University and the Council for Excellence in Government, honored the Camino Real Policy with an Innovations in American Government Award, including $100,000 for the district. This was one of only ten awards selected from 1,400 applications nationwide.

After the national awards, jealousy and envy began to undermine personal relationships within the district and the forest. Cordova calls it *la envidia,* which means that "some people cannot appreciate their own blessings for worrying about the blessings of others."[49] District employees and community members wanted more recognition for what they had done with the CRRD policy. "We were being interviewed by national papers and all this stuff and I think some people felt like they weren't interviewed."[50] The forest supervisor felt slighted because he did not receive credit, even though he did not support Dumas's efforts. Counterintuitively, the perceived success of the policy and the attention it attracted had an overall detrimental effect on the policy.

In 1999 Dumas transferred from the Camino Real to a ranger district in Utah. Increasingly Dumas felt that his supervisors in the Carson National Forest and Region 3 did not support him or his actions. He felt that another district ranger might gain the support of his superiors. The transfer was also an opportunity to move his wife from the local Hispano culture, in which she was still not quite comfortable, and return to land they owned in Utah, where they had long planned to settle down.

Upon Dumas's departure, the personal relationships and continuous outreach on which the CRRD policy depended began to atrophy for reasons beyond *la envidia.* Timber permitting for personal use, stewardship blocks, and grazing improvements were formalized but arguably are no longer as effective. Cordova says the CRRD policy was less vibrant in 2001 than it was in 1999 when Dumas left. There have been no meetings with the community, and the focus on forest restoration has been diluted. Since Dumas left all of the administrative staff in the Camino Real have been replaced, leading to a lack of contact with the community, withering relationships, and misinterpretation of the original intent of the changes in policy.

The contract forest restoration program and the Santa Barbara Grazing Allotment Rehabilitation Project in the Camino Real have survived a change of the entire administrative staff. Many delays and misunderstandings, especially ones having to do with National Environmental Policy Act (NEPA) compliance, have threatened the projects.[51] For instance, people connected with the grass-bank project increasingly are discouraged with their ability to move projects forward and use funds that are available only for limited timeframes. The funding for the Santa Barbara project was acquired before the completion of the NEPA process. Before his departure, Dumas had categorically excluded from the NEPA process a 400-acre area in the Santa Barbara Allotment that was thinned, burned, and had earthen tanks constructed on it, but the remainder of the project, some 12,000 acres, was too large to avoid a more thorough NEPA review. After Dumas left, an additional 300 acres had been treated by 2001; another 800 acres was awaiting NEPA approval.[52] Delays in the NEPA work meant that money went unspent and the projects remained incomplete. Working in conjunction with the NMED, the USFS applied for numerous extensions on the EPA 319 money. Nonetheless, the USFS did not complete the work by midsummer 2001, when the final extension ran out. Only $69,661 of the $107,850 allocated for the project was spent.[53]

Cordova misses Dumas's presence, what it meant for creating change in the community, and how it has led to policy changes. "My feeling was that the Forest Service never really understood the true nature of what we were trying to do [after Dumas left], how we were trying to connect community health to forest health." Since Dumas left, "all of the people here have an idea that [forest restoration] is something else." For instance, some USFS employees think forest restoration is embodied only in parceling out stewardship blocks. But Cordova thinks "that doesn't allow the community to build its own capacity and there is no training going on to enhance people's skills or help them understand the ecological importance of what they need to do and why." Fewer people are participating in restoration activities, and the impacts in the community are lessened. "Right now the Forest Service is having problems connecting with the community," Cordova added. "I don't see enough restoration work being done."[54]

## Policy Appraisals

Not surprisingly, those who felt discontented in different ways with the previous policy of large-volume timber sales to industrial operators considered the

CRRD policy and outcomes an improvement over the previous policy. Before 1993, when large-volume timber sales to industrial operations outside the community were the norm, the district was bogged down in appeals and litigation, little vegetation was managed, forest health was declining, and local populations were underserved by the USFS. From this perspective, there have been clear advances in serving the common interest. But different people and groups appraise the policy and policy outcomes differently. The criteria they apply and the evidence they use highlight some aspects while omitting other criteria and evidence. Consequently, before reviewing the appraisals, it is worthwhile to summarize the policy itself.

According to Dumas, the essence of the CRRD policy was really the mission of the USFS at large. The CRRD policy sought to care for the land and serve the people. Dumas clarified that he was especially concerned with maintaining soil stability and watershed quality in his attempts to take care of the land. To serve the people, he emphasized that the USFS does not own the land; rather, the agency manages national forest lands for the people.[55] To accomplish these ends, the CRRD policy effected major changes in the location, timing, and number of permits for personal use timber; timber sales targeted for smaller-scale community interests; contracts and stewardship blocks for forest restoration; and grassbanks and other measures for restoration of existing grazing lands.

From the view of the personal timber users in the Hispano communities, the CRRD policy is a success in terms of better and more timely access to wood for cooking, heating, and other purposes. The new permitting policies for personal timber use were supported by the land grant communities that benefited from them, namely Cordova and the Truchas Land Grant peoples. The stewardship block program also helped people meet their personal timber use needs while restoring overly dense forest stands.

In contrast to personal timber users, small commercial users evaluate the CRRD policy in terms of improved forest health and community health. The larger forest restoration projects were supported by Cordova, who runs a small nonprofit timber operation called La Montana de Truchas, and by the people who found new employment opportunities though the forest restoration activities. Also supportive of these efforts was Picuras Pueblo, the local Native American reservation, and Ike DeVargas, owner of La Compania de Ocho, another small commercial timber operation.

Some environmentalists, like the small commercial users, also evaluate the policy in terms of forest and community health. For the Santa Fe Sierra Club, El Grupo, La Comunidad, and *La Jicarita News* editors Mark Schiller and Kay Matthews, the smaller-scale forest restoration projects held great promise to diversify the area ecologically while also sustaining the tradition and culture of the land grant peoples. Joanie Berde of the Carson Forest Watch offered that the CRRD policy has been positive but could have done more. "Thinning is good for forest health, and it is good that the community is getting firewood. There have been a couple small efforts to move cows to grassbanks. Those are good efforts and we support them, however, they seem like token efforts."[56] According to Ernie Atencio, a local environmentalist and writer, the policy embodies the notion that "rather than the typical top-down imposition of policy, forest management projects are designed to enhance the ecosystem and biodiversity while providing resources and income for community members."[57]

The evidence supports these appraisals, and it is difficult to isolate improvements in community health from forest health. Since the end of 1996, at least six separate forest health projects on approximately 1,500 acres of land in the CRRD supplied more than 3,000 cords of woods to local communities.[58] Local groups have been incorporated into a variety of projects with the CRRD. For instance, cooperative agreements with the Forest Trust (an environmental and community development nonprofit), La Montana de Truchas Woodlot, Picuris Pueblo (a Native American organization), the Santa Barbara Grazing Association permittees (a local trade group), and the Valle Grande Grass Bank (a conservation nonprofit) resulted in successful thinning and restoration projects. These projects benefited local ranchers and the villagers who rely on fuelwood and other forest resources.[59] More reliable timber was available for communities, and the majority of the woodcutting in the Carson National Forest has been for local use.[60] Between 1992 and 1994 large businesses[61] received the largest share of wood from the Carson National Forest. In 1997–1999 personal use permits received the largest share. In the Carson National Forest in 1994, 600 permits were sold, as were 1,216 cords of firewood. In 1996, 739 permits were sold and 1,478 cords of firewood collected.[62] Over the same period of time, the portion of wood for personal use decreased in the Santa Fe National Forest, and the portion going to large businesses increased.[63] Commenting on the innovations, Jan-Willem Jansens, a local forest consultant in 2001, stated, "Camino Real Ranger District identified new ways of making contracts that were unheard of. These were pioneered 5–10 years ago and make small forest thinning and product sale possible for the local community."[64]

Consider the specific instance of La Montana de Truchas in this broader context. Cordova's company conducted forest restoration contracts on about 600 acres in the Carson in 2000 and completed work on another 600 acres in 2001.[65] The benefits from the forest restoration efforts are multifaceted, as the monitoring of progress revealed. In the words of Cordova, "We've started telling people, 'Don't look at volume or acres that we've cut. . . . When we evaluate the work that we've done we say, not only how many acres did we cut, but how many jobs did we create? For example, we created 30 jobs in that year. . . . The other thing that happens is, as we restored areas, elk moved into the areas. . . . There's more quantitative water that we can measure. There's more herbs that we can measure. . . . And as we've restored areas, the biggest impact I've seen is the animals moving in and then the meat will stay with the families here so, you know, it adds to their larder, basically, in having more to survive."[66] For small commercial users, timber sales were conducted on a smaller scale to help facilitate bidding from local timber companies. Forest health improved in the areas where forest restoration work, through stewardship blocks, grassbanks, and larger projects, took place. The benefits of improving the health of the forest included a return of species and satisfaction among community members that they were contributing to better forest conditions, obtaining valuable job skills, and providing jobs to the local community as they harvested products from the forests.

The USFS evaluates the CRRD policy according to different criteria. They view the policy as a success because it broke the cycle of formal appeals and litigation and involved the constituents of the district. The main criterion for assessing success for the district employees was avoiding litigation and appeals. The goal was to devise a plan that was a "customer-driven and supported program that meets the customer's needs, while improving forest conditions without expensive and lengthy litigation."[67] By these criteria it was indeed successful. According to Dumas, "We haven't had an appeal since 1993. We pull people and communities together and talk. Our management style is to work to prevent problems."[68] Bill deBuys, an environmentalist involved in the grassbank, reflected,

> When you have people that are really interested in their jobs, interested in the people, and their needs, and have the kind of openness displayed by Ranger Dumas where he and his staff went door-to-door. Good things happen as a result of that. . . . There was a "love fest" for the USFS in Truchas as a result of this. The village of Truchas held a party for the USFS. . . . Career forest people at that meeting were so choked up they could not speak because they were crying because all their careers they hoped something like this would happen and finally it did. These were people who had been working hard for a long time in an organization where it is hard to get the right thing done.[69]

Because they broke the cycle of litigation and appeals on the projects devised through the CRRD policy, district employees were able to get back to work managing vegetation, including timber. The policy also boosted morale and freed up resources in the CRRD. Money and time previously spent litigating appeals was channeled to projects in the forest. Dumas raised the rhetorical question, "Where [does the public] want [their] money spent? On attorneys and litigation or on managing your land and producing goods and services for you?"[70] Indeed, the record shows that since 1993 no small timber projects in the Camino Real have been appealed, and at least nine wildlife and fishery projects have been completed without appeal or litigation.[71]

Two national awards acknowledge the success of the CRRD policy and use similar criteria for success as the USFS. Vice President Gore's Hammer Award was given to the CRRD policy on the grounds that it overcame the litigious nature of timber sales and worked with the local community. The Hammer Award recognizes teams of federal employees and their partners who "look for ways to make government work better, cost less, and get results Americans care about."[72] The criteria for the Ford Foundation Innovations in American Government Award are "novelty judged by the degree to which the program demonstrates a leap of creativity; effectiveness demonstrated by evidence that the program has made substantial progress toward its goals; significance indicated by the degree to which the program successfully addresses an important problem of public concern; and transferability defined as the degree to which the program shows promise of inspiring successful replication by other government entities."[73]

The Forest Guardians do not offer a direct appraisal of the CRRD policy. But their actions and comments are inconsistent with the common interest goals of the CRRD policy. The Forest Guardians' policy is driven by the single purpose of decommercializing public lands through litigation, as if this were the best or only way to preserve and restore public lands. The continued presence of commercial timbering and grazing on public lands, even at a small scale, is against their overarching policy. According to Sam Hitt, former executive director of Forest Guardians, "There is no conclusive evidence to justify the effectiveness of restoration based on commercial extraction. Instead, it is widely acknowledged that commercial logging and livestock grazing are major causes of ecosystem decline." Hitt adds, "Grassbanks are an inappropriate use of public lands. We support forage utilization by native species on public land and removal of exotic species such as cattle that compete with native species."[74] Nevertheless, evidence suggests that the CRRD policy made some progress in improving watersheds, reducing fuel that could contribute to catastrophic wildfire, and creating conditions for better tree growth and range conditions, all of which could contribute to better wildlife habitat for many species, including the owl.

The interests manifest in the Forest Guardians' policy and lawsuit are best characterized as a special interest that could be accommodated only at significant cost to the community as a whole. This was demonstrated when the Forest Guardians and others succeeded in getting the injunction that temporarily halted commercial timber activities, of any scale, throughout Region 3. The CRRD employees were deprived of legal opportunities to continue to allow fire-wood removal for personal use and forest restoration, in accord with their mission to protect the land and serve the people. The land grant communities were deprived of fuelwood until they took the law into their own hands openly, as an act of civil disobedience. Moderate environmentalists' interest in continuing the restoration projects were frustrated as well. Moreover, the Forest Guardians' interest in protecting the spotted owl was invalid if one credits the scientific evidence provided by the FWS or the local knowledge of people such as Max Cordova. No spotted owls were observed in the CRRD, but elk, water, herbs, and the like were observed to be returning to the areas affected by the CRRD policy. The Forest Guardians' actions on its single interest are inappropriate in a democracy insofar as they deny in practice consideration of other interests that are valid and appropriate. The actions by the Forest Guardians turned out to be costly for the organization and Sam Hitt in particular. They suffered greatly in the court of public opinion. For his extreme views, Hitt was ousted from the Southwest Forest Alliance, a regional organization of fifty-five conservation groups throughout New Mexico and Arizona, in a unanimous vote by the board in April 1997.[75] Manifest hostility to Hitt and the Forest Guardians in the Hispano community (including unjustifiable death threats) evidently deterred Hitt and the Forest Guardians from taking legal action against Crockett Dumas when Dumas was most vulnerable after he marked trees for Cordova and his people to cut despite the injunction.

Importantly, some in the USFS view the policy as a failure because Dumas violated the federal injunction against cutting timber. Moreover, when Dumas violated the injunction, "it created a lot of resentment" and "animosity between that unit and the rest of the forest that still exists today."[76] To evaluate this alleged failure, it is worthwhile to recall the situation. Dumas was forced to choose between violating or conforming to the injunction in light of his own conscience and interests and two conflicting sources of authority: the injunction and the mission to protect the land and serve people. Conforming to the injunction would have risked a violent confrontation; members of the Hispano community would have succeeded and assumed sole responsibility for taking fuelwood illegally or they would have failed and continued to be deprived of fuelwood, an injustice from their standpoint at least. Conforming also would have undermined the trust of the Hispano community on which the CRRD policy depended. As Max Cordova recalled, "Dumas was either going to stand with the community or go against us." Dumas and Cordova acknowledged that Dumas violated the injunction when he marked the trees. But under such circumstances, Americans sometimes accept civil disobedience as an alternative to strict conformance with technical rules of law.

To be justified as an act of civil disobedience, a violation of the law must be nonviolent, on behalf of a higher interest, proportionate to the deprivations that would otherwise continue, and done in the open. "When people act openly in a way that makes punishment simple, they implicitly declare that they seek no personal advantage from their action and are willing to pay the appropriate penalty." In addition, "By acting openly, the violators demonstrate the depth of their convictions, showing that they take their claims [of a higher interest] very seriously. They also signal their respect for their fellow citizens and for the law." Acting openly distinguishes civil disobedience from criminal behavior but also makes civil disobedience a risky alternative to conformance with the law. The severity of punishment depends on whether the attentive publics and public officials accept, after the fact, that a violation of the law was warranted by a higher interest. "*Pure* appeals to justice are rare; civil disobedience usually involves calculated elements of pressure."[77] Acceptance can take the passive form of letting the violation stand without prosecution or other severe punishments.

Dumas accepted the risk of civil disobedience when he marked the trees, and the community accepted his violation of the injunction. Many no doubt accepted the violation as environmental justice for the Hispano community or because they supported Dumas, the CRRD policy, or the common interest mission they served. Some probably let the violation stand to avoid challenging the community consensus. In any case, marking the trees was an act of civil disobedience. The act was nonviolent. It was proportionate. It corrected an injustice imposed on specific members of a community in need of firewood but did not attempt to challenge the injunction as a whole or throughout the region. Importantly, the act was done in the open. It was no secret to those who cut the trees Dumas marked, their families and friends, Dumas's superiors and others in the USFS, or even the Forest Guardians. These and other participants had opportunities to approach Judge Muecke and demand prosecution, and perhaps they did. They had opportunities to take their case to the news media and the court of public opinion, and perhaps they tried. But Dumas was not prosecuted or otherwise significantly punished.

Former Southwest Regional Forester Bill Hurst summarized the facts of the case and the community consensus: "That ranger broke the law. He was a lawbreaker. The law said you couldn't cut. That was a superior, federal judge [who] said that. [Dumas] violated the [order of the] federal judge. I think if they wanted to, they could have prosecuted him but if I had been the ranger I would have done the same thing he did. We can't let people go without wood. . . . The other rangers obeyed the judge's orders, as they were supposed to, but the rightness of the thing was so obvious that I don't think even the federal judge would have prosecuted him."[78] Thus once again, "the law" in practice adapts to differences and changes in social process though civil disobedience. This is also an example of legal reasoning, by which legal rules adapt to decisions case by case.[79]

## Understanding Outcomes

What accounts for these successes, and for the failure to sustain the policy? Such explanations are particularly relevant to field officials and others interested in practicing adaptive governance. Scientific management, as socialized into personnel in the USFS and institutionalized into national law and policy, did not change enough to explain the direction and magnitude of changes observed in the CRRD in the 1990s. Evidently, within the remnants of scientific management, there was something unique about the CRRD that fostered interpersonal relationships and policy innovations sufficient to advance the common interest, as formulated in the mission. Consider the specific participants, their perspectives, the situations in which they interacted, and the resources and strategies they used, all of which interacted to shape outcomes. There is no single-factor explanation for what happened.

Crockett Dumas was a catalyst, leader, and sometimes follower in the evolution of the CRRD policy. Importantly, a strong cast of followers and leaders supported Dumas as well. What often is construed too narrowly as leadership is actually a leader–follower relationship, in which one who leads in some circumstances follows in others.[80] Dumas, Cordova, Mascarenas, Kramer, and the CRRD staff all played important parts in these leader–follower relationships.

Dumas certainly was an exceptional forest ranger in his desire to learn about the community through horseback diplomacy, as were other people on his staff. For instance, several CRRD employees were key to horseback diplomacy's success, including Henry Lopez, Adolfo Lopez, Wilbert Rodriquez, and Ben Kuykendall. Altogether thirty-eight out of forty-two employees in the district participated in the outreach efforts during the initial 2- to 3-month effort in 1991. Horseback diplomacy called for the CRRD employees to go above and beyond the call of duty because they needed to visit with residents after work hours. The employees invested their own time to do the outreach, even if they were paid hourly. Likewise, Carson National Forest staff, such as Carveth Kramer, were amenable to innovative thinking to address the problems in the forest. Dumas needed to work with people in the USFS and outside the agency; otherwise, his efforts would have been in vain. Dumas's arrival coincided with two other events that supported change. In 1987, Max Cordova was inducted as the new leader of the Truchas Land Grant, and throughout the late 1980s the environmental community in the region grew in strength. Altogether, the arrival of Dumas, coupled with the new leadership of Cordova in the presence of an increasingly effective environmental community, created an opportunity for transformation.

In terms of perspectives, these participants were predisposed to change the status quo. Discontents (including the perception of missed opportunities) are necessary for change, which does not happen among the complacent or contented. Dumas increasingly was frustrated that he could not do his job: to protect the land and serve the people. His employees wanted to do their jobs and get critics off their back. They also wanted to be appreciated in the community. But community opposition effectively paralyzed Dumas and the CRRD employees, creating an incentive to search for an alternative approach to managing the forest. "If you keep running into a brick wall, take two steps over to the side and find the door," Dumas advises. Cordova and Mascarenas were frustrated with years of USFS policies that failed to serve their community and were interested in addressing these failings. Importantly, Cordova represented a new generation of leadership on the land grants, which meant a new perspective on how to accomplish their goals. Cordova's generation is more knowledgeable and sophisticated about the workings of government: "We understand the issue, we understand the language, we understand the system and we are trying to correct the centuries of injustice using the system and the knowledge that we have."[81] In addition to the predisposition for change among the Hispano community, moderate environmentalists increasingly were concerned about the health of the forest and the people and willing to take action to protect these values.

The overall situation was structured according to the many remnants of scientific management culture, laws, and regulations institutionalized in the USFS. Within this formal structure, most of the important interactions between Dumas and others were one on one and, to a lesser extent, group meetings. Dumas used various interpersonal strategies in these situations to channel the discontents among the various participants into constructive action through the CRRD policy. These included listening to understand their points of view, avoiding problems not ripe for solution, avoiding meetings until there was agreement on a concrete problem, finding ways to say "yes" and avoiding saying "no," and following up words with deeds as quickly as possible.

Consider some of the details. Horseback diplomacy provided a means to listen and interact one on one with community residents in their homes. Engaging in a strategy of horseback diplomacy and general community outreach, as suggested by Carolyn Bye and promoted by Dumas, district employees listened, communicated, and built trust with community residents and learned about problems with the location, timing, and number of permits issued by the USFS for cutting of firewood, vigas, and latillas. Their efforts produced new alternatives to serve the diverse needs of the communities, such as forest restoration, stewardship blocks, and grassbanks. Changing the situations where interaction took place allowed the staff and Dumas to change the perception of the ranger as a "ranger-god," supposedly in complete and total control, and to "change our management style from an authoritarian and autocratic situation to one that engages people."[82] Open and respectful two-way communication that better engaged Hispano communities and environmentalists led to a transformation in how USFS staff were viewed. "All of a sudden the employees are wearing the white hats," recalled Dumas.

In addition to horseback diplomacy, Dumas used other strategies to build interpersonal relationships. He was willing to accept risks when necessary and did not get sidetracked on problems that were not ripe for solution. He did not like meetings until people could agree on the facts of the issue at hand. In other words, he didn't accept intractable problems. This stemmed from his own personal experience: "Until we learned what was really true on the ground it didn't make any sense to proceed."[83] Until different parties broke away from predetermined beliefs that were not based on on-the-ground experience, it was difficult to make headway in solving a problem. He engaged in practice-based management by taking people out in the field to witness concrete problems and conditions. If downed fences on a grazing allotment were the issue, then everyone was invited to visit the site together to agree on the factual basis of the issue. Likewise, if there was contention over accessible dead and downed timber for the spotted owl, he advocated fieldtrips so everyone could see the situation for themselves. Those who were reluctant to engage in these field sessions were left vulnerable to criticism. Some, such as the Forest Guardians, preferred to engage their adversaries in a courtroom.

For many in the USFS the ability to protect the land and serve the people is constrained by the framework of laws and regulations and the scientific management culture institutionalized in the USFS, which make action difficult. Nonetheless, Dumas strove to find situations in which he could say "yes" to the requests brought to him. In this way he gained his power by accommodating people instead of depriving them. Dumas began by saying "yes" to personal use timber permits and gained the trust of Hispano communities. Ironically, in this manner the injunction stemming from the Forest Guardians lawsuit probably did more to strengthen the CRRD policy than harm it. Sam Hitt and the Forest Guardians wielded power by saying "no" to harvesting timber for firewood. Dumas gained credibility and increased legitimacy in the community by saying, "yes, I will mark the trees for you to cut" and in effect upholding the CRRD policy. This highlights another strategy of Dumas: taking advantage when other people said "no." For instance, when the Forest Guardians went after grazing permits as part of their effort to protect the spotted owl, they activated grazing interests to reach out to Dumas, who took advantage of the situation to open a dialogue and work on grazing issues. Trust was built when he followed the talk with action, and friendship flowed from the relationships.

Dumas used a second set of strategies and resources to keep the bureaucracy, law, and Forest Guardians off his back in the larger and more formal arenas of interaction. He was guided by the overall mission to protect the land and serve the people but was flexible and pragmatic in its implementation. His strategies included not getting diverted by time-consuming planning exercises, adapting formal plans to what already worked in practice, conforming diligently to rules governing the use of federal funds and property, and laying low while building broader community support through small-scale projects.

"My job is to deal with reality, not planning," proclaimed Dumas in reference to the national forest management plans mandated by the USFS. Dumas's reality meant consolidating support among the Hispano communities and environmentalists through smaller actions. As this strategy proved its effectiveness, he codified his actions in a small-scale functional plan, as suggested by Kramer and the core team. Dumas saw the need for his plan to be short and action oriented, in contrast to the more conventional, larger-scale plans with a 10- to 15-year horizon mandated under the National Forest Management Act. Thus Dumas put into practice Kramer's idea of smaller-scale planning on a shorter timeframe that could be adapted to changing conditions and incorporated knowledge and information from the relevant community members who were the ultimate users of the plan. "Our goal was to move from a dump truck to a sports car in terms of planning."[84] His sports cars were the small forest restoration, stewardship blocks, and grazing allotment restoration projects, which were adapted easily to the inevitably changing conditions in the district. In contrast to the long-term, unwieldy dump truck model of planning that incorporates large-volume commodity timber sales, the smaller projects can fail gracefully if they do fail and do not pose large and long-term consequences for forest and community health. Dumas recognized that if he had political support he could be free of the larger, more formal planning process and be more flexible to change his plan at any time. "You have to keep working and engaging; there's always something else coming in."[85]

Dumas also tried to avoid drawing too much attention to himself, at least initially. Smaller-scale projects were the key to avoiding appeals and litigation in the CRRD. The smaller projects around and supporting communities were less likely to be subjected to the rigors of a full-blown Environmental Impact State-ment (EIS) process. The EIS process usually is a lengthy and costly procedure to assess significant actions on the land from a proposed project and is preceded by an Environmental Assessment (EA), a less comprehensive, less open, and more streamlined version of the EIS. An EA determines whether a full-blown EIS is conducted. With an EIS, opportunities for public comment and listing in the *Federal Register* ensure that it will receive attention by concerned parties. Be-cause many projects were bogged down in appeals, a premium was placed on finding projects that could move through the EIS process without litigation. Unlike large timber sales that cover thousands of acres, small timber projects of a hundred acres or so are more likely to avoid a complete EIS process. In these cases an EA may be sufficient, or they may be "categorically excluded" from the EIS process, or "CatExed." Categorical exclusions are issued when the effects of a given action are limited, are known, and occur in a site-specific locale. In the cases in which an EIS or EA was necessary, the CRRD became more thorough in their procedures to ensure that the documents were not subject to success-ful appeals. According to Kramer, "Litigation strategies have changed the NEPA process. Instead of focusing on the analysis, you focus on the process. You spend more of your time trying to make it survivable in the courts. The litigators have been elevated above the NEPA process. They want judges to make the decisions. [NEPA] is subsumed under judicial decision in the courts."[86] In the past decade, the USFS has attempted to prepare "bullet-proof" EISs in an effort to avoid ap-peals. This entails doing comprehensive analysis to ensure that all procedures and content are done correctly.

As the CRRD undertook projects on a smaller scale, they could avoid an EIS process by receiving a CatEx. In this way, they received less attention and were less likely to be subjected to scrutiny by others both inside and outside the USFS. Among the projects that did need EISs or EAs, there was greater pressure to do more complete and comprehensive analysis and follow exact procedures. Laying low by pursuing the smaller-scale projects had the threefold benefit of involving fewer environmental problems, lessening the external scrutiny on the projects, and gaining well-earned support from the locals. If someone wanted to appeal a proposed project, the appellant could do so, but the CRRD had many other proj-ects throughout the district that were supported by the local communities.[87]

Finally, Dumas used a strategy that allowed him to interpret the law and other rules according to the mission and to use the power base to cut red tape. He did this in many cases, except where federal funds and property were in-volved. "Don't touch any money or property, but get the job done and you can skirt some rules. Be a good manager, keep people happy. But don't be stupid."[88] The basic approach was to advance the mission when he was strong enough to withstand scrutiny or unwanted attention from superiors or outsiders. Dumas chose to work through people in the local community who were widely scattered in small, separate groups and with his employees. He avoided his conventional-minded superiors, discounted the bureaucracy, and maneuvered within the gray areas of the law when they interfered with his mission. He built trust with his local communities and then was supported when he ventured into making changes more broadly. If he had taken on the bureaucracy or the law without first consolidating his support locally, he would have incurred unnecessary risks and left himself vulnerable.

This strategy paid great dividends. For instance, neither Dumas's supervisor, nor the regional office, nor Washington ever came down hard on him for violating the injunction, even though they knew that technically he was wrong. Dumas did not always have the support of his forest supervisor or others in the regional office, but he was not left vulnerable because of the support he had consolidated in the local community. Dumas acted similarly in other cases in which he used categorical exclusions and the new planning processes. The regional office informed him in 1996 that he was on his own if anyone took action for his violation of the injunction. The support base included outsiders who admired his innovations, including David Gergen, a senior advisor to President Clinton. Dumas was ready and able to call on Gergen if necessary, whom he met through the Ford award. Ironically, the success of this overall strategy partially undermined the policy. He lost his low profile when Gore and the Ford Foundation granted their awards, leading to infighting and jealousy among the people in the district.

The outcome of the interactions of the various people, their perspectives, in different situations using different strategies and resources was a highly personalized, not institutionalized, community-based initiative.[89] This accounts in part for both the success and the subsequent atrophy of the CRRD policy. The failure to sustain the policy is a consequence of changing perceptions in and around the CRRD, Dumas's decision to leave the district, and the broader USFS policies that are unsupportive of adaptive governance in practice.

A downside to having a highly personalized policy that revolved around Dumas was its vulnerability to personnel transfers. Although some of the specific changes such as stewardship blocks, personal timber permits, and grazing improvements have persisted, the outreach and personal relationships that allowed them to occur have been lost. The consequence is an inability to make further progress on issues facing the community and a risk of dissipating the progress made under the CRRD policy. As recalled by Cordova, "[Dumas] has this mentality that the mountain doesn't come to Mohammed, Mohammed goes to the mountain. He told staff to get out of their trucks and see what people want."[90] But if Mohammed leaves, then the policy also is vulnerable to change. "Every person on the administrative staff at the Camino Real District has been replaced since Crockett left. Without Henry Lopez there would be no continuity whatsoever."[91] Without Dumas, there was no one else who knew the policy so well, knew how to practice it, or was as well motivated to do so. The transfer of USFS personnel before their substantive gains and procedures were consolidated is an obstacle in the transition toward adaptive governance. If trust, respect, and relationships provide the flexible means to work adaptively in a rigid bureaucratic setting, then transfers that inhibit the use of trust, respect, and relationships are counterproductive.

The transfer policy is embedded deep in the USFS culture and is part of a broader set of organizational pathologies that prohibit the agency from more effectively protecting the land and serving the people. For all its rhetoric about working with communities, the broader culture of the USFS is not hospitable to working with "outsiders," even if they are the communities where the agency works and include the people the agency is supposed to serve. Community outreach strategies are built through the trust that is gained through contact with locals. Countless hours of understanding, education, patience, and trust are vested in these relationships that are irreplaceable once one of the parties is transferred elsewhere. Personnel policies treat district rangers (and other staff) as if they were interchangeable and their relationships with communities were strictly impersonal. But transfers are part of climbing the professional ladder within the agency. In USFS culture, "If you stay on a district that long it means that there is something wrong with you—that you are not moving up the [government] ladder, advancing your career." Nonetheless, "[Transfers] disrupt the continuity of all the projects and of course [the USFS] don't want any of these guys getting cozy with the community people."[92] Other cases in which USFS employees worked closely with communities have resulted in transfers to new assignments that are seen as punishment within the agency culture or have generated other tensions.

The long-term effects of this resistance to change in the USFS culture partially accounts for failure of the Vallecitos Sustained Yield Unit and the Northern New Mexico Policy and now poses a threat to the CRRD policy. With the Vallecitos and Northern New Mexico Policy examples, the agency clarified that common interest solutions must better serve the local populations, but the policies succumbed to the politics of bureaucratic inertia, entrenched organizational resistance, and a history of serving industrial interests over local needs. The failure has been less one of vision than one of the ability to execute the vision effectively over time. The institutional bias for large projects over small projects typified the need for bureaucratic efficiency in the agency. Each permit or timber sale entailed the same amount of paperwork. Thus one large timber sale or grazing permit meant that less paperwork was processed and tracked than did multiple small permits or small timber sales involving the same volume of timber. To operate efficiently, the USFS preferred routinized tasks that produced a standardized flow of goods, meaning timber and grazing allotments. The current challenge is to change this culture to one that is more supportive of alternative managerial efforts, such as horseback diplomacy, nonroutine tasks, small projects, and stewardship blocks, that allow rangers to advance their mission to protect the land and serve the people. Until there is greater tolerance in the USFS as a whole, rangers such as Crockett Dumas, who seek to serve the common interest in their districts, will be at risk in a broader culture that favors bureaucratic and single-interest politics.

## Diffusing the CRRD Policy

Using money from the Ford Foundation award, the people in the CRRD pulled together a conference in April 2001 to foster understanding about the CRRD policy and to diffuse the CRRD model for adaptation elsewhere. Diffusion of the CRRD policy is important so other communities interested in effecting change can learn from the Camino Real's successes and failures. A recurrent theme in the conference was the contextual nature of the CRRD policy and how it would have to be adapted appropriately for other areas and situations. According to Jake Kosek, an organizer of the conference, "The model needs to be a conception that is both coherent enough to be workable in the future while being elastic enough to adapt to the different places, cultures, and circumstances in which the many different people here live and work."[93] Jan-Willem Jansens, who runs a community forestry nonprofit in the region, observed that relationships between the communities and the agency are very important, but it is also important to "realize the enormous diversity in the communities, and that boilerplate blueprint approaches really don't work. We have to have models, but the models should be examples for inspiration of other groups."[94] Carol Holland, an 8-year CRRD employee, added a cautionary note: "These concepts are transferable, but ... the implementation is gonna be real different. Things that work here in Northern New Mexico ... will not work somewhere else. You're going to have to take the ideas, take the concepts and recreate them."[95] With these practical insights in mind, it is important to remember that the transition to the CRRD policy happened over a period of years as attitudes and incentives changed. Personal relationships appear to be the cornerstone in the CRRD policy and ultimately are limited by people who have the trust of locals within their own districts. That may be one reason why other districts in the Carson have not adopted similar approaches.[96]

Kosek offered four lessons from the CRRD policy that others might want to consider in their own search for common interest solutions under the practice of adaptive governance. First, transparency and trust are key, and they rely on communication that comes through everyday actions. Second, boldness matters, and people need to think outside their everyday practices. Success does not lie in hiding behind papers and defending procedures, laws, and habits. Third, the table is not always round or flat. Not everyone has an equal voice or equal resources, and these inequities must be taken into account in the search for the common interest. Finally, history and context cannot be ignored. The unique cultural attachment to the land in northern New Mexico creates a distinctive setting in which issues over land use and land management play out. To ignore this history and context means denying the day-to-day reality in which many people live.[97]

The current CRRD policy is an improvement over the status quo policy in serving the common interest through adaptive governance. The policy will continue to evolve over time and is in danger of slipping back to the status quo. Atrophying personal relationships and lack of outreach to local communities reduce the ability of the district to identify with and understand the people the district is supposed to serve. This undermines the ability of land mangers to use laws and rules flexibly and compromises the capacity to interpret how to use such laws and rules in a given context to care for the land and serve the people. As has been demonstrated in past attempts to forge policy in the common interest in the Carson National Forest, the remnants of scientific management pressure USFS officials to engage in large-volume timber sales, ignore the needs of locals, and subordinate the health of the forest to the interests of the bureaucracy and timber industry. The challenge now in CRRD is to remain vigilant of the threats to adaptive governance in the common interest.

## Adaptive Governance in the CRRD

The CRRD policy illustrates how a flexible and pragmatic response to the dynamic challenges of governance can be practiced even under the most challenging conditions. Great animosity, conflict, and violence have plagued land management in the Carson National Forest and CRRD for decades. And yet this divisiveness was overcome in a short period of time when Crockett Dumas, his colleagues, and friends worked to forge a common interest path, pioneering practices of adaptive governance. Consider how science, policy, and decision processes were used in developing and implementing the CRRD policy.

Assumptions about science in the CRRD underscored the dynamic nature of a changing environment. Dumas engaged in practiced-based science by taking people out in the field to witness concrete problems and conditions in their own context. Instead of relying on abstract scientific studies or experts alone, he invited everyone to visit a site together to agree on the factual basis of the issue. The science and practice of forest restoration were uncertain. But forest restoration produced improvements in habitats for various animals, increased water supply, and led to more diverse and healthy vegetation. It gained a following because people witnessed these changes and could relate the new vegetative management practices to these beneficial consequences. Additionally, multiple methods were used to confirm what was happening in the forest. People who inhabited the lands in and around the Camino Real knew that it was not suitable habitat for the Mexican spotted owl because they had never seen them there. This evidence was supported by two separate and more conventionally scientific studies by state and federal agencies.

The goals for the CRRD policy were multiple and clearly integrated. Improving permitting, grazing, and forest health and providing work to local communities all were equally important in achieving the overarching mission: to care for the land and serve the people. The policy evolved over time in response to the problems articulated by local communities. In contrast to giving expert knowledge priority, horseback diplomacy and outreach validated community knowledge in action-oriented projects and in the contextual plans crafted for the region. The joint knowledge generated through outreach efforts provided direction and prioritization for specific projects, continued into the evaluation of these projects. Uncertainty was incorporated into the plans and policies and adapted to unanticipated factors when they arose. In moving from a dump truck to sports car mode of planning, Dumas could adapt his plan agilely when conditions changed.

Decisions were not prescribed from above and delegated but rather emerged from multilateral outreach processes such as horseback diplomacy and group meetings. Dumas's decision-making style worked to accomplish a broad mission with discretion to adapt to changing conditions along the way. Personnel in the CRRD were encouraged to interact with the community and personalize relationships, and this resulted in the practice of politics in its best and most constructive sense. Dumas and his employees corroborated the concerns initially expressed by Mascarenas and Cordova and acted on them in a timely manner. By following words with action, Dumas and others in the CRRD built trust and support for subsequent decisions. This reserve of trust and support allowed Dumas to use laws, regulations, and rules flexibly. He could interpret how to use them appropriately in given contexts to advance his mission, and he had the support necessary to do so without leaving himself vulnerable. Law, rules, and regulations in this sense were not mechanically applied in depersonalized situations. Rather, when Dumas violated the injunction on woodcutting, used categorical exclusions, and tried new planning techniques, he adapted the law, rules, and regulations to specific contexts that advanced his mission and served the common good.

Public officials and others might harvest experience from this case study and apply it to adaptive governance of public lands elsewhere. Dumas and his other leaders and followers were able to craft relationships through listening and trust that provided a foundation for greater action within the inflexible bureaucracy of the USFS. Because there is no shortage of discontent among diverse people who value public lands, similar situations may be ripe for practicing adaptive governance to further the common good. If the motivation for change exists, then understanding how adaptive governance worked in this context can be helpful to others.

NOTES

1. Interviews with Carveth Kramer, Carson National Forest planner, Taos, N.M. (May 26, 2001) and Crockett Dumas, Boulder, Colo. (December 2–3, 2001).

2. This is our label for the collection of policies. Those who crafted and participated in them did not have one specific name for the policies as a whole.

3. For more comprehensive coverage of the history of the land grants and settlement by Hispano populations see Clark S. Knowlton, "Causes of Land Loss Among the Spanish Americans in Northern New Mexico," *Rocky Mountain Social Science Journal* 1 (1963), pp. 201–211; Clark S. Knowlton, "Reies L. Tijerina and the Alianza Federal de Mercedes: Seekers of Justice," *Wisconsin Sociologist* 2(4) (1985), pp. 133–144; Clyde Eastman, "Community Land Grants: The Legacy," *Social Science Journal* 28(1) (1991), pp. 101–117; Carol Raish, "Environmentalism, the Forest Service and the Hispano Communities of Northern New Mexico," *Society and Natural Resources* 13 (2000), pp. 489–508.

4. Ernest Atencio, *La Vida Floresta: Environmental Justice Meets Traditional Forestry in Northern New Mexico* (Santa Fe, N.M.: Sierra Club, 2001); Carl Wilmsen, *Fighting for the Forest: Sustainability and Social Justice in Vallecitos, New Mexico* (UMI Dissertation Information Service: Ph.D. dissertation in geography, Clark University, 1997).

5. William Hurst, "Evolution of Forest Service Policy for Managing the National Forest Land in Northern New Mexico" (paper presented before R-3 Forest Officers at a Northern New Mexico Policy Discussion Forum, March 28, 2001); William Hurst, "Region 3 Policy on Managing National Forest Land in Northern New Mexico" (Memo, March 6, 1972); Patricia Bell Blawis, *Tijerina and the Land Grants: Mexican Americans in Struggle for Their Heritage* (New York: International Publishers, 1971); Knowlton, "Reies L. Tijerina."

6. Hurst, "Region 3 Policy."

7. Ernest Atencio, *Of Land and Culture: Environmental Justice and Public Lands Ranch-*

*ing in Northern New Mexico* (Report by the Quivira Coalition and the Santa Fe Group of the Sierra Club, January 2001); U.S. Forest Service, "Applying the Northern New Mexico Policy" (brochure compiled by the Carson National Forest Supervisor's Office, February 1997).

8. Interview with Max Cordova, Truchas, N.M. (May 21, 2001).

9. Atencio, *La Vida Floresta*.

10. Telephone interview with Carveth Kramer (September 19, 2002).

11. Steve Marshall, "Application for Innovations in American Government 1998 Awards Program Semi-Finalist Application/Application #379, Northern New Mexico Collaborative Stewardship Program" (USDA–Forest Service Cooperative Forestry, April 28, 1998).

12. Cordova interview.

13. Quote from Marshall, "Application for Innovations"; and Zoe Miller, "The Northern New Mexico Collaborative Stewardship Program: Fitting an Agency-Led Initiative into the Model of Collaborative Government" (term project for Governance and Natural Resources, a seminar at the University of Colorado at Boulder, December 1999).

14. Kirsten Lundberg, "Collaborative Stewardship," in John D. Donahue, ed., *Making Washington Work: Tales of Innovation in the Federal Government* (Washington, D.C.: Brookings Institution, 1999), pp. 128–144.

15. Dumas interview.

16. Cordova interview.

17. Marshall, "Application for Innovations."

18. Quotes from interview with Kay Matthews and Mark Schiller, El Valle, N.M. (May 22, 2001), and Kramer interview, May 26, 2001.

19. Cordova interview.

20. Kramer interview, May 26, 2001.

21. Cordova interview.

22. Atencio, *La Vida Floresta*.

23. Kramer interview, May 26, 2001.

24. Camino Real Ranger District, "Existing and Desired Conditions and How to Get There: East Entranas" Version 1 (Peñasco, N.M.: USDA, USFS, South West Region, Carson National Forest, July 1996), on file with authors.

25. Lundberg, "Collaborative Stewardship."

26. Telephone interview with Crockett Dumas, (October 31, 2002).

27. Dumas interview, October 31, 2002.

28. Keith Easthouse, "U.S. Agency Wants 4.8 Million Acres for Owl Habitat," *The Santa Fe New Mexican* (December 1, 1994), p. B1.

29. Mike Taugher, "Judge Bars Federal Forest Logging," *Albuquerque Journal* (August 25, 1995), p. A1; Mike Taugher, "Scientist: Logging Ban Poses Fire Risk," *Albuquerque Journal* (August 30, 1995), p. A1.

30. Cathy Robbins, "An Unabashed Moralist Bows Out," *High Country News* (April 23, 2001).

31. Keith Easthouse, "Judge Halts Southwest Timber Sales," *The Santa Fe New Mexican* (August 25, 1995), p. A1; Keith Easthouse, "The Gathering Animosity Curbs on Firewood

Gathering and the Forest Service's Seemingly Broken Promises Put Hispano Villagers and Mostly Anglo Environmentalists on Opposing Sides," *The Santa Fe New Mexican* (December 11, 1995), p. A1.

32. Doug McClellan, "Factions Raise Squawk About Owl Protection," *Albuquerque Journal* (March 23, 1995), p. A1.

33. George Johnson, "In New Mexico an Order on Elusive Owl Leaves Residents Angry, Cold," *The New York Times* (November 26, 1995), p. A16.

34. Easthouse, "The Gathering Animosity"; Peter Eichstaedt, "Sides in Woodcutting Fight Trade Blame," *Albuquerque Journal* (December 29, 1995), p. A1.

35. U.S. FWS, *Biological Opinion on the Effects to the Mexican Spotted Owl from the Forest-Wide Dead and Down Personal Use Fuelwood Program on the Carson National Forest* (Albuquerque, N.M.: FWS, September 21, 1995), on file with authors; Easthouse, "The Gathering Animosity."

36. Eichstaedt, "Sides in Woodcutting Fight," p. A1.

37. Kramer interview, May 26, 2001.

38. Johnson, "In New Mexico an Order on Elusive Owl."

39. Ibid.; Keith Easthouse, "Community Leader: Firewood Ban Hurts Truchas Families," *The Santa Fe New Mexican* (November 24, 1995), p. A1.

40. Keith Easthouse, "Protesters Plan to Hang Two Activists in Effigy," *The Santa Fe New Mexican* (November 21, 1995), p. B4.

41. Keith Easthouse, "Residents Send Petition to Carson About Environmental 'Extremists,'" *The Santa Fe New Mexican* (December 2, 1995), p. A4.

42. Cordova interview.

43. John Hill, "Feds Will Allow Wood Gathering," *Albuquerque Tribune* (October 31, 1996), p. B8; A. Stiny, "Wood Dispute Burns Out," *The Santa Fe New Mexican* (November 1, 1996), p. A1.

44. Peter Eichstaedt, "Donated Wood 'Drop in Bucket,'" *Albuquerque Journal* (December 21, 1995), p. A1.

45. Doug Brown, "Ranchers Unite, Bash 'Radical' Environmentalists," *Albuquerque Tribune* (December 21, 1995), p. A1.

46. Associated Press, "Judge Orders Agreement on Owls," *The Santa Fe New Mexican* (October 3, 1996), p. B4; and Keith Easthouse, "Judge Lifts Ban on Southwest Logging. Loggers Are Relieved, but Environmentalists Vow to Continue Fight Against Cutting in Old Growth Forests," *The Santa Fe New Mexican* (December 5, 1996), p. A1.

47. Estevan Lopez, transcript from "Collaborative Stewardship at Work" conference, Taos, N.M., April 27–28, 2001. Sponsored by Carson National Forest and Camino Real Ranger District.

48. Steve Miranda, transcript from "Collaborative Stewardship at Work" conference.

49. Cordova interview.

50. Ibid.

51. Matthews and Schiller interview.

52. Interview with Steve Miranda, Peñasco, N.M. (May 22, 2001).

53. Mark Schiller, "Santa Barbara Rehabilitation Project: Show Us the Work," *La Jicarita News* 7(3) (2002).

54. Cordova interview.

55. Dumas interview, October 31, 2002.

56. Interview with Joanie Berde by Ghita Levenstein (December 8, 2000); phone interview with Joanie Berde by Ghita Levenstein (December 11, 2000).

57. Atencio, *Of Land and Culture,* p. 34.

58. Marshall, "Application for Innovations."

59. Atencio, *Of Land and Culture,* p. 34.

60. Atencio, *La Vida Floresta.*

61. Large businesses are defined as having 50 employees or more, a small business employs fewer than 10 people, and a medium-sized business employs 10–49 people.

62. Marshall, "Application for Innovations."

63. Greg Gunderson, "Distribution of Timber Sales on Northern New Mexico National Forests 1992–1999," SCFRC Working Paper 4 (Santa Fe, N.M.: Forest Trust, November 2001).

64. Jan-Willem Jansens, quote from transcript of "Collaborative Stewardship at Work" conference.

65. Cordova interview.

66. Max Cordova as quoted in Atencio, *La Vida Floresta.*

67. Marshall, "Application for Innovations," p. 6.

68. J. Kissinger, "Carson NF Ranger District Wins $100,000," *Forest Service Today* (November 1998).

69. Quote from Lou Baker, *U.S. Forest Service Policy in Northern New Mexico* (MIT master's thesis, 1996), p. 38.

70. Dumas interview, December 2–3, 2001.

71. Marshall, "Application for Innovations."

72. National Partnership for Reinventing Government, "Criteria for Vice President Gore's Hammer Awards." Accessed November 10, 2004, at http://govinfo.library.unt.edu/npr/library/awards/hammer/criteria/html.

73. E. Lynn Burkett, "Northern New Mexico Collaborative Stewardship," 1998. Accessed December 8, 2000, at http://www.ksg.harvard.edu/innovations. On file with authors.

74. Interview with Sam Hitt via e-mail conducted by Babs Brockway (November 30, 2000); transcript on file with authors.

75. Keith Easthouse, "Southwest Forest Alliance Takes a Hitt," *High Country News* (April 28, 1997).

76. Kramer interview, September 19, 2002.

77. The quotations in this paragraph are from Kent Greenawalt, "Civil Disobedience," in Edward Craig, gen. ed., *Routledge Encyclopedia of Philosophy* (London: Routledge, 1998), vol. 2, pp. 366–369, at p. 367.

78. Quoted in Baker, *U.S. Forest Service Policy,* p. 39.

79. Edward H. Levi, *An Introduction to Legal Reasoning* (Chicago: University of Chicago Press, 1948).

80. See Garry Wills, "What Makes a Good Leader?" *Atlantic Monthly* (April 1994), pp. 63–64; Harold D. Lasswell, "Conflict and Leadership: The Process of Decision and the Nature of Authority," in Anthony de Reuck and Julie Knight, eds., *Conflict in Society* (London: J. & A. Churchill, Ltd., 1966), pp. 210–228.

81. Cordova interview.

82. Dumas interview, December 2–3, 2001.

83. Telephone interview with Crockett Dumas by Toddi Steelman (August 5, 2002).

84. Ibid.

85. Ibid.

86. Kramer interview, May 26, 2001.

87. Marshall, "Application for Innovations."

88. Ibid.

89. A community-based initiative is composed of participants representing different interests who interact directly with one another over a period of time, in an effort to resolve an issue in the place where they live. See Ronald D. Brunner, Christine H. Colburn, Christina M. Cromley, Roberta A. Klein, and Elizabeth A. Olson, *Finding Common Ground: Governance and Natural Resources in the American West* (New Haven, Conn.: Yale University Press, 2002).

90. Cordova interview.

91. Matthews and Schiller interview.

92. Ibid.

93. Jake Kosek, transcript from "Collaborative Stewardship at Work" conference, p. 5.

94. Jansens, transcript from "Collaborative Stewardship at Work" conference.

95. Carol Holland, transcript from "Collaborative Stewardship at Work" conference.

96. Henry Lopez, transcript from "Collaborative Stewardship at Work" conference.

97. Kosek, transcript from "Collaborative Stewardship at Work" conference.

# 4. Grassbanks: Diffusion and Adaptation from the Radical Center

CHRISTINE M. EDWARDS

DESPITE PERSISTENT CONTROVERSIES over grazing practices in the American West, representatives of groups that often are polarized came together for a conference on "Grassbanks in the West: Challenges and Opportunities" on a rainy day in November 2000 in Santa Fe, New Mexico. Nearly two hundred ranchers, environmentalists, scientists, public land managers, and other government officials from eight western states were interested in learning more about the possibility of adapting a recent policy innovation, the grassbank, in their own communities. At the two-day conference they heard first hand from pioneers of the original Gray Ranch Grassbank™,[1] set up in 1994 in the Malpai Borderlands area of southern Arizona and New Mexico. They also heard from Bill deBuys and others who adapted the grassbank innovation to public rangeland, establishing the Valle Grande Grass Bank in northern New Mexico. By the time of the conference, additional adaptations diffused from these self-described radical centers were under way in at least five other communities in the American West. The innovation continues to be adapted elsewhere, thanks to the conference in Santa Fe and to a number of other networks that diffuse information and enthusiasm about grassbanks (figure 4.1).

The original grassbank innovation was simple in concept. Local ranchers in the Malpai Borderlands exchanged conservation easements on their private ranches for grazing privileges at the Gray Ranch, a large ranch owned by a local foundation and operated in coordination with a nonprofit organization of local ranchers called the Malpai Borderlands Group (MBG). This policy innovation helped reduce subdivision and fragmentation of the land, made it possible to reintroduce fire to improve the rangeland, and helped preserve the livelihood and lifestyle of the ranchers. Thus it advanced the common interest of the borderland community, including shared ecological, economic, and cultural interests. The concept was adapted to different circumstances in northern New Mexico. Local U.S. Forest Service (USFS) districts made commitments to restore

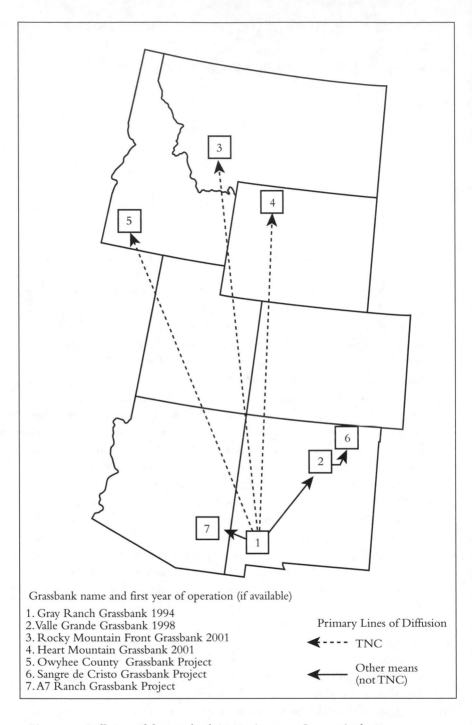

Grassbank name and first year of operation (if available)

1. Gray Ranch Grassbank 1994
2. Valle Grande Grassbank 1998
3. Rocky Mountain Front Grassbank 2001
4. Heart Mountain Grassbank 2001
5. Owyhee County  Grassbank Project
6. Sangre de Cristo Grassbank Project
7. A7 Ranch Grassbank Project

Primary Lines of Diffusion

◄ - - - - TNC

◄───── Other means
(not TNC)

Figure 4.1. Diffusion of the grassbank innovation. TNC, Source: Author.

damaged grazing allotments on public lands in exchange for grazing privileges on the Valle Grande Grass Bank, a grazing allotment in the Santa Fe National Forest established and overseen by a partnership of public and private organizations. Local ranchers who held grazing permits on the damaged allotments made commitments to transport their cattle to the Valle Grande each year while the USFS completed the restoration projects. The pioneers at the conference in Santa Fe recognized that there are many different ways to use a grassbank as a tool to advance the common interest, and the grassbank concept continues to evolve as it is adapted to new circumstances.

The diffusion and adaptation of successful innovations by community-based initiatives are neglected topics in natural resource policy.[2] The innovations alone have attracted nearly all the attention of researchers; a case in point is the Gray Ranch Grassbank innovation by the MBG. But all three processes—innovation, diffusion, and adaptation—must work together to realize the full potential of community-based initiatives to advance common interests at the local level. "Without successful innovations somewhere, good models for guidance elsewhere are lacking. Without adequate diffusion, the models are unavailable to those who might use them. And without adaptation, the models available make little difference in practice."[3] Thus to expand the significance of a successful innovation beyond one community, initiatives in other local communities must have the opportunity to build on it. This horizontal diffusion and adaptation, from one community to others, also provides the practice-based experience necessary for vertical diffusion and adaptation: the adaptation of state or national policies and programs to support what works on the ground. Thus vertical diffusion and adaptation can integrate the common interests of local and larger communities without ignoring important differences and changes on the ground.[4] The diffusion and adaptation of successful innovations are an important part of adaptive governance.

The purpose of this chapter is to clarify and illustrate adaptive governance through the diffusion and adaptation of grassbanks from the original innovation at the Gray Ranch and later from the Valle Grande. To various degrees, the diffusion and adaptation of grassbanks have advanced the common interest of the communities involved beyond the contemporary "range wars," the stereotyped, heated, and unproductive debates over grazing that serve as the baseline for appraising grassbanks and the default alternative. Thus grassbanks can serve as a model for the diffusion and adaptation of other innovations in the emergence of adaptive governance. Identifying and addressing malfunctions in these processes can allow them to function more smoothly in the common interest. The first section of this chapter examines the Gray Ranch innovation in the context of contemporary range wars. The second and third sections consider grassbank adaptations at the Valle Grande Ranch and in five other communities. The remaining sections describe the overlapping networks involved in the diffusion and adaptation of grassbanks and appraise the outcomes and processes from a common interest standpoint. The conclusion summarizes the implications for adaptive governance.


## Gray Ranch Innovation in Context

The diffusion and adaptation of grassbanks occur in the context of conflicting values and divergent expectations about grazing on public and private lands that have polarized ranchers, environmentalists, and public land managers throughout the West. In the last four decades, recreation has replaced livestock grazing as the predominant use of public lands. Livestock grazing is now the second most common use of public lands, with more than 270 million acres of federal land open to grazing.[5] As conflicts between nonextractive and extractive resource users have grown, so has the heated and passionate debate over grazing. However, debate typically has avoided consideration of what can and should be done to solve a particular problem. Each side, fearful of losing what little ground it retains, is often guilty of name-calling and finger-pointing. Some people roll all grazing issues into a dichotomous choice for or against grazing in general and polarize and perpetuate the debate with generalizations.[6] But not all ranchers are "welfare parasites," as Edward Abby suggests, and not all ranchers are "ultimate environmentalists," as Julie Jo Quick suggests.[7] It is incorrect to point to an overgrazed area and claim that all grazing is bad and equally incorrect to point to a healthy grazing allotment and claim that all grazing is good. The truth is that a variety of problems in addition to overgrazing must be addressed if an effective solution to the range wars is to be found, and that solution depends on the local context.

Decades of overgrazing, mismanagement, and drought have damaged some ecosystems in the West.[8] But the ecosystems of the West are not the only systems that have been damaged and threatened by these events. Rural communities and small family ranchers in the West are in danger of losing their livelihoods, lifestyles, and culture. These economic, social, and ecological systems are interdependent.[9] Simply pointing the finger of blame at ranchers and public land managers for the overgrazing and mismanagement of the ecosystem ignores two additional problems that may pose even greater threats to these systems: the artificial suppression of fire and the loss of unfragmented ranches.

The loss of the natural fire regime in western rangelands and the subsequent encroachment of woody plant species such as sagebrush and juniper have contributed to the loss of grassland available for livestock operations.[10] As a result, ranchers have been forced either to reduce herd sizes and reduce their incomes or to increase livestock grazing on the remaining grassland to maintain their incomes. They have been forced to choose between their own livelihood and the health of the land. In addition to the loss of grasslands, ranches in the West are also disappearing. They are being sold to developers and carved into small "ranchettes" and suburban developments to accommodate growing populations in western states.[11] The population boom and the increase in nonresident buyers of vacation homes are driving up land prices for ranchers interested in adding land to make their livestock operations more economically viable. Inheritance taxes and stagnant beef prices make it increasingly difficult for ranching families to stay in business, and many ranchers are being forced to sell. When this happens, rural communities lose the economic foundations on which they were built, and families lose the land and livelihood that has been part of their family for generations. At the same time, open, expansive, and contiguous landscapes are fragmented, and ecological processes are disturbed and degraded.[12]

Unlike others engaged in the grazing debate, some people in the Malpai Borderlands did not believe that choices had to be made between ecological, economic, and social systems. Instead, in an effort to find integrative solutions to the multiple problems facing their community, they developed an innovative policy solution known as a grassbank. Their journey began in January 1990, when The Nature Conservancy (TNC) purchased the 320,000-acre Gray Ranch in the heart of the Malpai Borderlands, much to the chagrin of the surrounding ranching communities. To TNC, preserving this area was the epitome of their work and mission. The Gray Ranch ecosystem was one of exceptional species diversity and beauty. By owning the ranch, TNC could guarantee that this magnificent landscape would be saved from ecological degradation. To the local ranchers, the Gray Ranch and the Malpai Borderlands as a whole were magnificent because of the long ranching tradition they supported. "Ranching livelihoods depend upon and maintain the open character of this huge landscape" according to the MBG.[13] At the Gray Ranch, cattle grazing had been maintained at low levels of intensity historically, allowing fine fuels to accumulate. Fires could burn naturally on these fine fuels and were not suppressed when they did start.[14] The result was a functioning ecological landscape that everyone wanted to preserve.

With its $18-million price tag, however, TNC could not afford to keep the ranch itself. They began looking for a buyer who shared TNC's commitment to protecting the ranch's ecological integrity, and the federal government seemed the most likely candidate. However, the threat of government takeover of the Gray Ranch was unacceptable to some members of the local community, who feared an end to cattle ranching and the influx of an estimated 65,000 visitors a year. Their lobbying campaign blocked the sale of Gray Ranch to all prospective federal agencies and a private buyer, but the community offered TNC an alternative.[15]

With encouragement from the ranching community, local rancher Drum Hadley and his family used their inheritance to create the Animas Foundation in 1992. The foundation's mission was to "conserve undeveloped wildlands and rangelands of the Southwest"; the first order of business was to purchase the Gray Ranch from TNC. "We want to preserve the Gray Ranch as a working cattle ranch and its traditions of grazing livelihoods while at the same time promoting the health and biological diversity of the lands which sustain them," said Hadley, great-great-grandson of August Busch.[16] On February 22, 1993, after 3 years of ownership, TNC sold the Gray Ranch to the Animas Foundation. According to TNC's project director, John Cook, "In the end ... we sold to an institution that has agreed to own the ranch forever, to never let it be developed, and to continue a very extensive monitoring program in perpetuity to ensure that the Conservancy's goals are being met."[17]

Around the time the Animas Foundation was formed, Hadley and other local ranchers began meeting to discuss the changing attitude toward ranching in the West and the future of the resource on which their livelihoods depended. According to Bill McDonald, "It seemed as though the 'dig in your heels' approach was doomed to fail, so we decided to embark on a different approach—to reach out to our critics and find common ground."[18] By 1994, the meetings led to the creation of the MBG, which included ranchers, environmentalists, scientists, land agency officials, and other concerned members of the community.[19] The mission of MBG reflects their common interest in ecological, economic, and cultural sustainability: "Our goal is to restore and maintain the natural processes that create and protect a healthy, unfragmented landscape to support a diverse, flourishing community of human, plant, and animal life in our borderlands region. Together, we will accomplish this by working to encourage profitable ranching and other traditional livelihoods, which will sustain the open space nature of our land for generations to come."[20]

The top priority for MBG was the reintroduction of fire into this landscape, and so they crafted a regional prescribed burn policy as their first order of business. With the addition of the 320,000-acre Gray Ranch, nearly a million acres of land in the borderlands were owned by MBG participants or managed by MBG participants as grazing allotments. Even so, because of the extensive mosaic of public land holdings in the borderlands, MBG's prescribed burn policy ultimately had to be approved by nine different government entities. "Despite widespread acceptance of the need to reintroduce fire into the natural ecosystems of the Southwest, the maze of conflicting and overlapping regulations seemed even to the agencies to be a gridlock too tough to overcome," recalls MBG Co–Executive Director Bill McDonald.[21] However, the strength and commitment of MBG was enough to overcome the agency gridlock. The group received the necessary approval from all entities involved in just 8 months, an accomplishment that would have been impossible only a few years earlier, without MBG.[22]

Support for the grassbank innovation was based on both ecological and economic conditions. Many ranchers in the area had been hard hit by drought and were looking for some sort of relief. Others wanted to reintroduce fire on their property to improve poor range conditions but needed a place to take their cattle before and after the burn.[23] Typically, one growing season without grazing is needed before a burn in order to accumulate the fine fuels needed to carry the fire; otherwise these fine fuels would be consumed by the cattle. After the burn takes place, one or two additional growing seasons are needed for the forage to regenerate. A pasture in poor condition is not economically beneficial for a rancher, but not having a herd for 3 to 4 years while a pasture burns and regenerates is not economically feasible for most ranchers. Together, MBG and the Animas Foundation had the necessary resources and vision to try a new approach to conservation and grazing. The Gray Ranch Grassbank, the first of its kind, granted grazing privileges on the Gray Ranch to ranchers in exchange for a land use easement on their property to preclude future subdivision and development. These easements were conveyed to MBG, which in turn used funds raised from individuals and grant-making institutions to pay the Animas Foundation for the grass used by the cattle while they were on the Gray Ranch. The amount of grazing permitted on the grassbank "was determined by the value of the easement conveyed, based on an appraisal of development value at the time of conveyance."[24]

The Gray Ranch Grassbank is a success according to many of the people most directly involved. It provided much-needed relief to ranchers facing persistent drought and allowed ranchers to reintroduce fire without selling their base herd. It helped preserve the ranching lifestyle and livelihood while also preventing further subdivision and development of the open spaces of the Malpai Borderlands. Many of the grassbank participants were pleased with the results. "This has been a great opportunity to ensure that my ranch will continue to be a ranch from now on," said Ed Elbrock, a Gray Ranch grassbanker; "at least the land is open space and not cut up and chopped up and houses built on it and all. I know people have to live somewhere, but we need open spaces too."[25]

By 2001, MBG held land use easements on 35,000 acres, including four easements from grassbank participants.[26] Bill McDonald attributes this success primarily but not exclusively to local landowners, who continue to be the driving force behind MBG's work. The participation, support, and dedication of the local community, coupled with the "enthusiastic participation of agency personnel" and input and expertise from MBG's Science Advisory Committee, has created a unique and effective organization that is strong and growing nearly a decade after it first began. "In a political climate where the traditional position on this issue of land use is usually at one end of the spectrum or the other, we find ourselves in the 'radical center,'" says McDonald.[27]

Although the Gray Ranch Grassbank had many benefits, Bill McDonald admits that this design is limited in one important respect: It takes a substantial amount of capital, even at a modest level of participation. For example, in the 2000 fiscal year, MBG received a $75,000 grant from the National Fish and Wildlife Foundation and provided an additional $250,000 in matching funds to purchase two easements on a total of 10,500 acres in southwestern New Mexico and southeastern Arizona.[28] "Clearly, this model has limited application for the long term," McDonald said.[29] Nevertheless, the work of MBG and the Animas Foundation has received a great deal of support and recognition from people outside the organizations. Between 1994 and 2001, the organizations and their leaders received more than sixteen awards including the Distinguished Achievement Award from the Society for Conservation Biology in 1996, the 1998 Governor's Award from the State of Arizona, and a "genius grant" awarded to Bill McDonald by the John D. and Catherine T. MacArthur Foundation in 1998.

It seems reasonable to conclude that the diverse participants in the Gray Ranch policy process were able to identify the valid and appropriate interests of the borderland community, to integrate them into a grassbank policy that advanced their common interest, and to implement that policy successfully in practice. The grassbank policy reduced subdivision and fragmentation of the land, reintroduced fire to improve the rangeland, and helped preserve the lifestyle and livelihood of local ranchers. The wholesale adoption of the Gray Ranch grassbank policy innovation does not seem feasible in most western communities, however. Purchasing the Gray Ranch and the conservation easements from participating ranchers was exceptionally expensive, and not every community will be lucky enough to have an heir of August Busch as an ally. Fortunately, several other communities recognized that the underlying concept of the grassbank—the quid pro quo, the benefits for the grass being exchanged—was a valuable concept and found ways to adapt this policy innovation to address the problems, values, and needs in their own communities.

## The Valle Grande Grass Bank Adaptation

The ranchers in the areas now encompassed by the Santa Fe and Carson national forests in northern New Mexico have a long and arduous history, as noted in chapter 3. Most are of Hispanic decent, and many have family roots in the area that can be traced back hundreds of years. Most operate small-scale ranches, as their ancestors did for generations, and most are tied as tightly to the tradition and the culture of ranching as they are to the meager income it brings. These families live in three of the poorest counties in the nation, in the poorest state in the nation, and none are getting rich from ranching.[30] Many run cattle in order to send their children to college or to buy food for their families. Most have other jobs to help make ends meet.

Their grandparents were the first to receive grazing permits from the newly formed USFS for lands that had once belonged to them as Spanish or Mexican land grants. In their own lifetimes, they have seen a barrage of lawsuits from environmental groups, increased pressure to eliminate all grazing from public lands, and a decrease in the herd size permitted on their grazing allotments.[31] They have also seen the influx of "outsiders" who have chosen the exquisite landscape of northern New Mexico as their new home but who often fail to recognize the culture and history of the people who have lived and worked on that very same land for generations. Ranchers in northern New Mexico today feel a great deal of distrust and resentment toward the USFS and the environmental community. The ranching tradition and culture are endangered. According to Courtney White, executive director of the Quivira Coalition in Santa Fe, New Mexico, "The traditional Hispanic ranchers feel like their backs are to the wall."[32] But things began to change for local ranchers in northern New Mexico in the 1990s.

By the summer of 1996, word of the MBG's efforts was spreading through the USFS and the environmental community in New Mexico. That summer, Jerry Elson and Bill deBuys toured the Gray Ranch to learn more about the grass-bank policy innovation. Elson was on the range staff for the Santa Fe National Forest at the time and had been looking for three swing allotments in the Santa Fe Forest to assist the local public grazing allotment permittees.[33] DeBuys, a well-known historian and conservationist in the Southwest, was also a repre-sentative of the Conservation Fund. He agreed with his friend Elson that grass banking presented a new opportunity for the ranching community in northern New Mexico. They knew the Gray Ranch Grassbank model had to be adapted if it was to meet the unique needs of the northern New Mexico ranching community, but both thought the idea had the potential to help the Hispanic ranchers, promote healthy ecosystems, and restore degraded USFS lands.

Upon his return to the district office, Elson learned that a local rancher wanted to sell his 240-acre Triple S Ranch and relinquish control of the associ-ated 36,000-acre grazing permit on the Valle Grande allotment in the Santa Fe National Forest.[34] Federal regulations would not allow the USFS to purchase the ranch and grazing permit itself, so Elson contacted deBuys to see whether he

and the Conservation Fund would take the lead on starting a grassbank on public lands. The fund agreed to pursue the purchase of the Triple S Ranch and the
acquisition of the Valle Grande grazing permit as a site for the grassbank. However, $500,000 to $700,000 would be needed to purchase the ranch and cover
operating costs of the grassbank. The job of fundraising was left to deBuys.

That summer, deBuys secured funds from the McCune Charitable Foundation and the Ford Foundation to conduct a grassbank feasibility study in
conjunction with the USFS. In November 1996, the Conservation Fund and the
Santa Fe National Forest released the Valle Grande Grass Bank concept paper, a
detailed description of the first grassbank adaptation. The concept paper states,
"The lands to be benefited by the Valle Grande grass bank would be other allotments within the Santa Fe National Forest. The goal would be to improve national forest lands so that they can more sustainably support continued livestock
grazing—at current levels—while also providing expanded habitat for both game
and non-game wildlife."[35] (Later the lands were expanded to include allotments
in the neighboring Carson National Forest.) The arrangement outlined in the
concept paper required a commitment from the rancher to transport his cattle
from his grazing allotment to the grassbank and a commitment from the USFS to
improve the rancher's home grazing allotments while the cattle were gone.

Unlike in the Gray Ranch Grassbank, easements would not be exchanged
for use of the grassbank because "permittees in northern New Mexico rarely
own significant expanses of deeded land, and as a result, the exchange of land
use easements under this plan would have little conservation value." Instead,
"transfers [of cattle to the grass bank] lasting several grazing seasons would permit substantial restoration of riparian areas, use of prescribed fire in uplands, removal of small diameter timber, and other land treatments intended to increase
and improve wildlife habitat and range productivity."[36] In other words, the USFS
would commit to particular restoration projects on a permittee's allotment in
exchange for grassbank grazing privileges elsewhere for the permittee's cattle.

The completion of the Valle Grande Grass Bank concept paper was an important first step in establishing the grassbank, but three issues remained to be
resolved for the project to move forward. First, the Triple S Ranch had to be
purchased and additional funds secured to operate the grassbank. Second, the
USFS had to agree to issue the grazing permit for the Valle Grande allotment
to the Conservation Fund and agree to place the permit in a special use status
in order for the allotment to be used as a grassbank. And third, the grassbank
project needed support in the local ranching community.

Although purchasing the Triple S Ranch would qualify the Conservation
Fund to be the sole grazing permittee of the Valle Grande grazing allotment,
owning the property did not guarantee that the USFS would issue the graz-

ing permit. To qualify for a grazing permit, USFS regulations require that a permittee own livestock and "validate" the grazing allotment by stocking the land with cattle owned by the permittee at 90 percent of the allowable level within the first year.[37] As outlined in the grassbank concept paper, the Conservation Fund would not own livestock, and the Valle Grande grazing allotment would be stocked with the grassbank participant's cattle. With these USFS regulations in effect, the Conservation Fund would need to have the grazing permit for the Valle Grande placed in a special status known as "non-use for resource protection and restoration" in order for the grassbank to move forward. This special permit status would allow the fund to stock the Valle Grande allotment with other rancher's cattle, and the fund would not be required to own livestock.

While Elson and deBuys were dealing with the permit issues, they were also working to gain support for the grassbank idea in the ranching community. The New Mexico Cattle Growers Association and the Farm Bureau immediately voiced opposition when approached with the idea and asked the local USFS not to issue the grazing permit to the Conservation Fund. Even with the intentions of the Conservation Fund detailed in the concept paper, concerns that the fund would retire the grazing permit as a conservation measure were predominant. When pressure on the USFS did not yield the desired results, the Cattle Growers and the Farm Bureau took their concerns to the lieutenant governor of New Mexico. Under pressure from his constituents, Lieutenant Governor David Bradley began to pressure the USFS to deny the grazing permit.

Not all ranchers opposed the idea, however. The Northern New Mexico Stockman's Association, a regional organization of predominantly Hispanic ranchers, represents the interests of public land permittees in the Santa Fe and Carson national forests. Many of its members supported the grassbank idea, although not without doubts and misgivings. In the words of deBuys, "The association held no special love for environmentalists, but its leaders recognized that the future of its members depended not just on defending their rights but on advancing their interests. Among those interests is the restoration of rangeland through the reintroduction of wildland fire, and the Stockman's Association recognized that the grassbank could help this happen."[38] However, much of the grassbank proposal depended on the support and commitment of the USFS and an environmental group. After years of conflict, lawsuits, and disappointment, the Stockman's Association was distrustful of this proposed partnership. Palemon Martinez, secretary–treasurer for the Stockman's Association, was one of the most vocal supporters and promoters of the grassbank idea in the association. But he noted that "there [were] suspicions, and I can understand why, considering the 400-year transformation of land tenure issues."[39]

Owen Lopez of the McCune Charitable Foundation approached Martinez with the idea and helped arrange a meeting between the Stockman's Association and deBuys in February 1997. The meeting was very stiff and tense at first, and Martinez admits that the whole project was headed down the drain at one point. The ranchers had many questions and concerns about the project, including the fate of the allotment if the Conservation Fund elected to sell the Triple S Ranch in the future. The association members did not want to see the ranch sold to another organization that would retire the grazing permit. Over the course of the next several meetings, a written Q&A briefing was developed to answer all of the Stockman's Association questions. According to deBuys, answering these questions in writing was the most important building block of trust between the parties involved.[40] The project gained enough support from the Stockman's Association to move forward, and representatives from the Conservation Fund, the USFS, the New Mexico State University (NMSU) Cooperative Extension, and the Northern New Mexico Stockman's Association met to further clarify the project's goals and to draft a memorandum of understanding (MOU).

The goals agreed on in the MOU were to improve the ecological health of the rangeland, to strengthen the economic and environmental foundation of northern New Mexico's ranching tradition, and to create a public land grassbank model that could be exported to other areas with similar needs. (Thus the MOU is a clear statement of the partners' commitment to a common interest solution to public land grazing problems.) The MOU outlines the roles each partner was expected to play in reaching these goals. The Stockman's Association would act as the liaison, organizer, and facilitator of permittee participation. The NMSU Cooperative Extension was responsible for pasture production and use monitoring on the grassbank and home allotments and for community outreach and education. The USFS was responsible for completing the restoration treatments, such as prescribed burns, in a timely fashion. And the Conservation Fund was responsible for raising the funds needed to operate the grassbank and complete the restoration projects.[41] The partners also created a steering committee to coordinate and evaluate the project, with representatives from all four partners and from each of the grazing allotments participating in the project. Among other duties, the steering committee would review allotment applications submitted by potential grassbank participants and recommend allotments and participants to the Santa Fe National Forest supervisor, who has the final say over grassbank participants. The permittees and their allotments would be selected to participate in the grassbank based on the quality, completeness, and likelihood of accomplishment of land treatments proposed in the application.[42]

The partners strongly believed that in addition to NMSU Cooperative Extension's monitoring program, a long-term, comprehensive monitoring program would be needed to assess the effects of the land treatments. "Monitoring is the only way to know whether what you've done has actually worked," said Will Barnes, chief investigator for the Valle Grande Grass Bank monitoring program. "Monitoring allows you to get past the 'blame game' and to the issue of finding real solutions to management problems."[43] Scientists from the Jornada Experimental Range developed and implemented an extensive monitoring program on the Valle Grande allotment and the grassbank participants' home allotments. By 2001, nine monitoring plots had been established for each of the seven sites that had undergone treatment such as thinning or burning.[44]

As part of the MOU, the working group also finalized the "assignable right of first refusal" agreement, a concept that had been discussed in earlier meetings with deBuys and the Stockman's Association. The document states that the Stockman's Association has exclusive rights to purchase the Valle Grande allotment base property for a period of 120 days after the Conservation Fund announces its intention to sell the property. It also states that if the Stockman's Association does not purchase the property, the Conservation Fund will "make every reasonable effort to ensure that the property will remain a livestock ranching operation."[45] According to deBuys, the assignable right of first refusal was a "threshold condition for the endorsement of the project by the Stockman's Association" and was agreed in principle before the MOU was completed.[46]

While the partners were working out the details of the Valle Grande Grass Bank, forest supervisor Leonard Atencio was still under a great deal of pressure to deny the Conservation Fund a grazing permit for the Valle Grande allotment. Atencio would not yield. By the summer of 1997, deBuys had secured sufficient funds from a variety of foundations and individuals, including the National Fish and Wildlife Foundation, the Thaw Charitable Trust, the Wyss Foundation, the New Cycle Foundation, and the Ford Foundation, to purchase the Triple S Ranch and operate the grassbank.[47] Finally, in August 1997, the Conservation Fund purchased the Triple S Ranch, renaming it the Valle Grande Ranch. The day after the purchase was completed, deBuys met with the editorial boards of the *Santa Fe New Mexican* and the *Albuquerque Journal* to discuss the new grassbank project. Within the next few weeks, both papers had published editorials giving the Valle Grande Grass Bank partnership and project high praise.[48] Soon after the editorials were published, the lieutenant governor backed down, opposition from the ranching community receded into the background, and Atencio issued the grazing permit under the special "non-use for resource protection and restoration" status to the Conservation Fund.

With the permit and partnerships now in place, the Valle Grande Grass Bank faced yet another challenge. National Environmental Policy Act (NEPA) regulations required the USFS to complete and approve an Environmental Assessment

(EA) for the Valle Grande grazing allotment before cattle could be allowed on the land. When the EA was finally completed, the Forest Guardians, an environmental group well known for their lawsuits, appealed it immediately. According to deBuys, the appeal was fraught with errors, including a claim that the EA failed to consult with the state of Arizona as to the effects of grazing on non–point source pollution—even though the allotment was in New Mexico, and no pollution from its watershed reaches Arizona. DeBuys observed, "Clearly, the Guardians' protest was a badly handled exercise in word processing. Just as clearly, the Guardians response to the EA, like the Cattle Growers and Farm Bureau to the project, was generic and unspecific.... The episode drove home for me the way in which knee-jerk dissension limits us."[49] The Guardians' appeal was rejected and the EA was approved; cattle would finally be allowed on the Valle Grande Grass Bank.

Finding ranchers to use the grassbank was not an effortless task, but the endorsement and active participation of the Stockman's Association made it much easier. The first cattle to arrive at the Valle Grande Grass Bank in March 1998 belonged to Jerry White, a highly respected rancher from the neighboring grazing allotment. Jerry's willingness to try the new grassbank and the Stockman's Association endorsement of it created an important sense of legitimacy for the project in the community.[50] By the end of that summer the grassbank supported 264 head of cattle from three grazing allotments. In June 1998, the Quivira Coalition, in association with the Camino Real Ranger District of the Carson National Forest and the Rio Pueblo/Rio Embudo Watershed Coalition, sponsored a workshop in Peñasco, New Mexico titled "Grazing and Fire in Northern New Mexico." Several members of the Santa Barbara Grazing Association attended this meeting, as did Bill deBuys. At the workshop, deBuys spoke with some of the ranchers about the Valle Grande Grass Bank and asked them to consider participating in the project; "a week later the ranchers of the Santa Barbara allotment had agreed to try the grass bank" starting in the 1999 summer grazing season.[51] By January 1999, the Valle Grande Steering Committee had received applications from permittees on seven different grazing allotments (including an application from the permittees on the Santa Barbara allotment), with these application requests totaling three times the amount of grazing available at the grassbank. In the several years after the summer of 1998, the number of cattle at the Valle Grande Grass Bank remained above 260 head, and permittees from five different allotments in the Santa Fe and Carson national forests brought their cattle to the Valle Grande Grass Bank. The USFS in turn completed several restoration and treatment projects on the home allotments. In 1999, 3,300 acres were burned, 900 acres of trees were thinned, and 80 acres of aspen groves were restored on the home allotments of grassbank participants.[52]

Not everything went as planned, however. In December 1999, a review of the project conducted by the Conservation Fund stated, "Actual accomplishments were much less than expected by grass bank partners."[53] In fact, only about one-third of the anticipated restoration work was completed. In 1999, the USFS made a commitment to burn 10,000 acres and thin 2,200 acres. The actual accomplishments of 3,300 acres burned and 900 acres thinned fell far short of the original commitment. In March 2002, an editorial in *La Jicarita News* accused the USFS and the New Mexico Environment Department of using the Santa Barbara grazing allotment restoration project to "line their own pockets and generate favorable publicity" without having to "actually hold themselves accountable for meeting project goals." According to editor Mark Schiller, the original grassbank application accepted by the forest supervisor in 1998 committed the USFS to thin and burn a combined 3,000 acres on the Santa Barbara grazing allotment by 2001. In October 1999, the USFS amended the Santa Barbara allotment project plan and reduced the number of acres to be treated by 2001 from 3,000 to 800. By October 2001, the USFS had thinned 383 and burned 150 acres of land on the Santa Barbara allotment, but they were still 267 acres short of the amended goal.[54] By December 2003, however, the USFS had thinned 1,289 acres of the Santa Barbara allotment and burned 286 acres. In a letter sent to Bill deBuys that month, district ranger Cecilia Seesholtz reiterated the Forest Service's commitment to the grassbank project, stating, "We will continue to burn additional acres within the allotment, weather permitting, over the next several years."[55]

The USFS blamed their shortfall on a lack of resources and staff, high levels of personnel turnover, wildfires in the area, and not having the necessary EAs in place before filing a grassbank application. In some cases, the USFS had not completed the necessary EA before the grassbank application was selected by the steering committee and approved by the forest supervisor. The treatments on the allotments were then delayed while the EA was completed and approved. In other cases, the USFS personnel who had written the original grassbank application and made commitments to particular land treatments were transferred before the treatments were completed.[56] The USFS also had to back away from a planned prescribed burn on a grassbank participant's allotment after the 2000 Cerro Grande wildfires diverted resources and personnel.[57]

Regardless of the reasons given by the USFS, George Maestas, a member of the Santa Barbara Grazing Association, expressed concern with the results. "The permittees based their decision to participate in this project on the idea that enough new forage would be created so that with careful management we would be able to maintain or increase the number of permits granted on this allotment."[58] For the permittees, participation in the Valle Grande Grass Bank is worthwhile only if the USFS improves their home allotments. Participants pay $1.50 per animal unit month (AUM) to the Conservation Fund to cover the cost of salt and fuel to pump water on the grassbank, plus the associated costs of transporting their cattle to and from the grassbank each season. In addition, they continue to pay the annual grazing fees of $1.36 per AUM on their home allotments, even when their cattle are at the grassbank.[59] Thus ranchers who participate bear a greater financial burden than ranchers who do not.

The partner organizations recognize that permittees' concerns about improvements in home allotments must be addressed if the program is to achieve its goals. Despite shortcomings and unmet expectations, permittees including Maestas continued to support the grassbank program into 2002, even though it was proceeding more slowly than expected. The trust and commitment that were built between the participants and partners certainly helped sustain the program. At the same time, many permittees recognize that a substantial number of acres on their allotments have been treated only because of their participation in the grassbank program.[60]

The Valle Grande Grass Bank advanced the common interest of the community in developing a policy accepted by the Conservation Fund, the USFS, the Stockman's Association, and the NMSU Cooperative Extension. This partnership represents the valid and appropriate ecological, economic, and cultural interests of this community and built much-needed communication and trust in the community. The Forest Guardians' claims and those of the New Mexico Cattle Growers Association and the Farm Bureau were appropriately discounted or ignored in the decision process. Each group sought to impose its own interests at the expense of the community as a whole. The partners' expectations that the grassbank policy would advance their common interest was formalized by the MOU. However, the policy in practice has not met some of those expectations or realized the goals of the Valle Grande Grass Bank. If the USFS cannot complete the land treatments it has committed to, rangeland conditions will not improve to the extent partners expect. The participating permittees will have increased their grazing costs to support a program that has not delivered the rangeland improvements they expected and may be left once again with the feeling that the USFS has broken its promise. For the Valle Grande Grass Bank to corroborate the expectations of the partners and advance the common interest of the community in practice, the USFS will have to find a way to fulfill its commitments.

The Valle Grade Grass Bank is an important and unique grassbank model. It is unique as the first grassbank adaptation and as an innovation itself, the first grassbank to use a public land allotment. It is important as an early adaptation because the success of early adapters often is a critical factor in sustaining the processes of diffusion and adaptation.[61] Others are not likely to adapt an innovation perceived as a failure. But each successful adaptation of an innovation expands the range of models from which potential adapters might choose.

## Additional Adaptations

Additional grassbank adaptations have been initiated elsewhere in the American West. Compared with the Valle Grande Grass Bank, they are new adaptations, and there is less experience available for appraisals. Nevertheless, similarities and differences between the following examples are significant because they illuminate the workings of the diffusion and adaptation processes, both in connection with grassbank policies and in general.

### Rocky Mountain Front Grassbank, Montana

The Rocky Mountain Front stretches from Montana to Canada and encompasses more than 2 million acres of land at the mountain–prairie interface along the east side of the Rocky Mountains. The front includes a variety of unique ecosystems that are often supported and buffered by large private ranches. Subdivision and development are becoming more common and threatening to the ranching tradition and unfragmented ecosystems along the front. Early in 1999, TNC of Montana created the Rocky Mountain Front Advisory Committee (RMFAC), a fifteen-member committee of ranchers, conservationists, agency personnel, and scientists, to develop conservation initiatives along the front in Montana.

In the spring of 1999, members of the RMFAC toured the Gray Ranch to see the original grassbank first hand. The committee members saw a great deal of potential in the grassbank idea but did not think it was feasible to obtain a private ranch the size of the Gray Ranch along the front in Montana. The resources needed to purchase a large ranch simply were not available. Instead, TNC of Montana and the RMFAC took the lead in adapting the grassbank policy innovation to land ownership patterns in their area. Committee members wanted to improve grassland health by enabling ranchers to rest their land and preserve unfragmented grasslands through the use of conservation easements. To achieve these goals, they envisioned a private grassbank model that would use a series of small private ranches along the front. This "string of pearls" would serve as a cumulative grassbank for ranchers in the area.[62]

In the summer of 2001, TNC of Montana and the RMFAC launched a 320-acre grassbank pilot project. The arrangement involved two adjacent private landowners who were willing to let their properties serve as a grassbank in exchange for natural resource information, land management, and grassland monitoring. The grassbank lessee was Wayne Gollehon, a local rancher and member of the RMFAC. He grazed seventy head of cattle on the two properties for a total of 35 days and provided in exchange approximately $400 in maintenance and repair on the two grassbank properties. The U.S. Fish and Wildlife Service covered an additional $2,000 in maintenance and repair costs on the grassbank properties. The Nature Conservancy and the Natural Resources Conservation Service initiated a monitoring program on the grassbank before the cattle arrived and agreed to continue monitoring the land after the cattle were removed. This grassbank arrangement allowed Gollehon to rest a pasture on his home ranch that had been burned the previous year and allowed the private owners to benefit from maintenance and repair work on their properties and to use their grassland resource in a sustainable manner.[63]

The Nature Conservancy of Montana, the RMFAC, and all grassbank participants considered this mini-grassbank pilot project an initial success. Although the grassbank did not increase the amount of land under easement, it did allow the grassbank lessee Gollehon to rest his home ranch after a prescribed burn. In addition, long-term monitoring plots on the burned and unburned areas of the home ranch were established, and TNC established monitoring plots on the grassbank properties. Gollehon calculated that it cost him $9 per head the year he used the grassbank, a figure that is $6 to $11 less than the average cost per head in that region. Even with its initial success, TNC of Montana believed that it would take up to 2 years to fully establish the grassbank pilot project and perhaps longer to work out the details that would allow them to increase the scale and scope of the project.[64]

The grassbank project they envisioned was motivated in part by the expectation that TNC of Montana can recruit through their Conservation Buyer Program nonresident recreation buyers who will allow grazing on the property and might also allow TNC of Montana to purchase a conservation easement on the property. (A nonresident recreation buyer is a person who purchases a second home for recreation and does not intend to graze cattle on the property.) The RMFAC wanted priority use of the new grassbanks to be given to ranchers who placed easements on their property. However, many ranchers in the area have already placed easements on their property, so use of the new grassbanks probably will be granted to ranchers who agree to rest and monitor their home ranches. The Nature Conservancy of Montana did not plan to exchange home ranch restoration commitments for use of a grassbank, as they do at the Valle Grande, but would encourage better land management practices. They wanted their string of grassbanks to be self-sustaining and planned to charge participating ranchers a fee for use of the grassbanks to cover the maintenance and repair costs. Costs that are not covered by these fees would have to be covered by TNC of Montana, the grassbank lessee, or the U.S. Fish and Wildlife Service.[65]

The members of the RMFAC who developed and signed off on the grassbank project represented a diverse set of interests. In addition, the RMFAC and TNC of Montana did not expect significant public opposition to the grassbank pilot project.[66] This indicates progress in advancing the common interest. However, this grassbank adaptation had not yet been implemented at full scale, and the details of the larger project envisioned had not been worked out. Time will tell whether the envisioned policy will generate further progress. It remains to be seen whether TNC of Montana will have the funds necessary to purchase conservation easements or whether they can recruit nonresident recreation buyers to participate in the grassbank program. It remains to be seen whether rest alone will improve the health of the grasslands; rangeland managers disagree on this point. In addition, it is not clear yet what TNC of Montana and the RMFAC might do if rest alone does not improve rangeland health.

## Heart Mountain Grassbank, Wyoming

The Heart Mountain Ranch in the western part of central Wyoming encompasses more than 15,000 acres of grassland, including a mix of Bureau of Land Management (BLM) and state grazing allotments, and 600 acres of productive irrigated farmland. TNC of Wyoming purchased the ranch in 1999 to protect its biological diversity and cultural importance from development. In this area, large private ranchers "form a buffer along the perimeter of national forest lands and provide essential habitat for migrating ungulates, the wide-ranging carnivores of the Greater Yellowstone Ecosystem, and many other species." Increasingly, these ranchers are becoming vulnerable to development and fragmentation. To address these threats to the community, in February 2001 TNC of Wyoming began contacting representatives from the BLM, Shoshone National Forest, Wyoming Game and Fish, Wapiti Ridge Coordinated Resource Management Group, Park County Commissioners, local ranchers, and the Rocky Mountain Elk Foundation to solicit ideas, feedback, and direction for a new grassbank at the Heart Mountain Ranch.[67]

It turned out that the situation facing public land ranchers in Wyoming was similar to that of ranchers in northern New Mexico. Through conversations with community members, TNC discovered that public land allotments needed to be restored and local ranchers needed a place to take their cattle while the restoration treatments were completed. In addition, the Shoshone National Forest had recently completed an extensive fuel reduction burn plan. The plan included twenty-two different prescribed burns, ranging in size from

100 to 8,300 acres, that would take place on the public lands over the next 5 to 10 years. Public land permittees would be required to remove their cattle from the affected allotments for 2 to 4 years to allow the buildup of fine fuels and to accommodate unpredictable weather conditions that could delay the burn schedule. Many of the ranchers expressed a great deal of animosity toward this USFS plan. They were concerned that they would have to sell their base herds or portions of their private ranches to support themselves while their cattle were forced off their public land allotments.[68]

Using the irrigated farmland on the Heart Mountain Ranch, TNC of Wyoming launched the Heart Mountain Grassbank in 2001 in an effort to restore public rangelands and to protect and promote the livelihoods of the local ranchers. The Heart Mountain Grassbank combined elements of the Gray Ranch and Valle Grande grassbank models. Although the Heart Ranch included both public grazing allotments and private land, the portion used as a grassbank was privately owned, just as it was at the Gray Ranch. And like the Valle Grande Grass Bank, the Heart Mountain Grassbank was originally designed to assist public land ranchers in the area through the exchange of grazing privileges on the grassbank for commitment to restoration treatments on home allotments. The Heart Mountain Grassbank is now open to the best conservation projects on any land, whether public or private.[69]

In the spring of 2001, three local ranching families were selected by the BLM, the USFS, and TNC of Wyoming to participate in the Heart Mountain Grassbank trial. Two families brought cattle from their public land grazing allotments that were scheduled for fuel reduction burns in the summer of 2001. The other family brought cattle from a BLM grazing allotment that was critical elk winter range and in need of rest and regeneration. Grassbank participants in 2001 were charged $5 per AUM for use of the grassbank, a cost well below the market value at that time of $9 to $11 per AUM on private land. Only half of the available AUMs at the grassbank were used in the 2001 trial. Because of unfavorable weather conditions in the summer of 2001, the USFS was not able to complete the scheduled burn on the two grazing allotments. The grassbank participants from these two allotments were not discouraged by the delay, however. They planned to bring their cattle back to the Heart Mountain Grassbank in the spring of 2002 to allow the USFS to conduct the burn that summer. At that time, TNC of Wyoming was seeking funding to fully implement the grassbank project. Priority participants would be the permittees on allotments scheduled to be burned between 2002 and 2005, as outlined in the Shoshone National Forest fuel reduction burn plan.[70]

The Nature Conservancy of Wyoming involved a network of people with diverse interests in the development and implementation of this grassbank policy adaptation. Through individual conversations, workshops, and meetings with community leaders, ranchers, and agency personnel, TNC of Wyoming was able to clarify the common interest of this community. The Heart Mountain Grassbank has received a great deal of support and praise from the community. For example, an article published in the *Casper Star Tribune* featured a former Wyoming Stockgrowers Association president who praised TNC for coming up with a solution that helps both ranchers and the environment.[71] However, more time is needed to determine whether this grassbank adaptation will advance the common interest in practice. Like that of the Valle Grande Grass Bank, the success of the Heart Mountain Grassbank in practice depends on timely completion of the USFS fuel reduction burn plan. The Valle Grande Grass Bank experience suggests that dependence on the USFS may be a weakness of this kind of grassbank model.

## Owyhee County Grassbank Project, Idaho

Owyhee County is located in the southwest corner of Idaho near the Oregon–Nevada border. Eighty-four percent of the county's 4.9 million acres of land are federally owned, and most are managed by the BLM. Conflicts between ranchers, environmentalists, and agency personnel had grown heated by the end of the 1990s, as the BLM threatened to reduce the number of AUMs on public lands by 35 percent and environmentalists called for an end to public land grazing.[72] The exclusion of fire had allowed juniper to expand eight to ten times beyond its historical range in the region. In addition to the loss of grasslands to juniper, overgrazing and drought had damaged the health of the rangeland.

In 1999, a group of ranchers from Owyhee County traveled to the Malpai Borderlands to learn more about MBG and the Gray Ranch Grassbank. They were tired of lawsuits and deadlock. They did not want to be forced off their grazing allotments, but they did not have the tools or flexibility to implement changes. Around the same time, BLM officials approached TNC of Idaho for help. They also were looking for an opportunity to reduce conflict and improve range conditions but did not know what to do. Upon their return from the Gray Ranch, the Owyhee County ranchers formed the Owyhee Borderland Trust, Inc. (OBT), a nonprofit organization of ranchers modeled after the MBG. They wanted to develop a grassbank program for the county as a way to promote the long-term stability of rural communities. In May 2000 they approached TNC of Idaho with the idea. The partnership that developed between OBT and TNC of Idaho drew both attention and skepticism from the ranching and environmental communities.[73] However, the OBT and TNC of Idaho saw a great deal of potential in their partnership and their plans for a grassbank. They believed the grassbank project could be incorporated into TNC's large-scale effort to protect millions of acres of habitat throughout Idaho, an effort that had gained widespread support in the state because of TNC's commitment to building partnerships with private landowners and government agencies.[74]

The OBT and TNC of Idaho envisioned a grassbank similar in some ways to the Valle Grande Grass Bank. Grazing rights would be exchanged for commitments from the BLM to reintroduce fire on the home allotments, although OBT and TNC of Idaho wanted to avoid the capital intensive investment that the Conservation Fund had to make.[75] This design would help improve rangeland conditions and help prevent the reduction of AUMs. The grassbank partners recognized that the successful implementation of this program would require the support of the entire community, including environmentalists, ranchers, and agency personnel. There must be support in the community for the reintroduction of fire, and the community must believe that the BLM has the capacity to carry out the fires and meet applicable regulatory requirements. Lou Lunte, TNC coordinator for this grassbank project, observed that the BLM was already stretched thin in its ability to complete EAs. A vocal minority of environmentalists who oppose any grazing of public lands could file a suit against the BLM under NEPA in an effort to delay and derail the grassbank project.[76] The OBT and TNC of Idaho would need to gain support for the grassbank program from other community members, but with the long history of distrust and conflict between ranchers, environmentalists, and agency personnel, they knew it could be a difficult task.

By July 2001, however, OBT and TNC of Idaho were not the only groups interested in exploring alternatives that would incorporate conservation and ranching interests. The Owyhee County Commission began to develop the Owyhee Initiative, a legislative initiative to protect the economic interests and the cultural, historic, and natural resources of the area.[77] The creation and use of grassbanks throughout the county were included as a recommendation for the initiative. The OBT and TNC of Idaho both had members on the Owyhee Initiative steering committee and were encouraged by the initiative. However, they decided to pursue a grassbank independent of the Owyhee Initiative if the opportunity arose and continued to look for a site that could be used as a grassbank and build support for the idea in the community.

An appraisal will have to wait until more details of the policy have been clarified and until conflicting interests in the community have been explored and addressed. However, the OBT and TNC of Idaho appeared to be on track to advance the common interest. Their partnership integrated some of their different interests, and through the Owyhee Initiative the grassbank idea gained support and approval of county commissioners, the Idaho Cattleman's Association, the BLM, and local soil and water conservation districts. The antigrazing environmentalists' interest is not compatible with the interests of the community as a whole. However, the OBT and TNC of Idaho recognized that the antigrazing environmental interest group could delay or derail the process and must be dealt with in some way if the grassbank is to move forward.

### Sangre de Cristo Grassbank Project, New Mexico

In the Sangre de Cristo Mountains, near Taos, New Mexico, the BLM faces many of the same problems as the Carson and Santa Fe national forests nearby. The encroachment of woody plant species, the exclusion of natural fire processes, and overgrazing have led to an overall degradation of the public lands for which they are responsible. The BLM was familiar with the work at the Valle Grande Grass Bank. So when several allotments in the Sangre range became available they decided to create a grassbank project of their own in an effort to help restore the ecological integrity and economic potential of the rangeland.[78]

From the beginning, the BLM strongly believed that ranchers needed to be the driving force behind this grassbank project if it was to be sustainable over the long term. A nonprofit organization such as the Conservation Fund or TNC was not involved during the inception of this grassbank project, and the BLM did not pursue a nonprofit organization as a primary partner. Although the Quivira Coalition helped the BLM organize several educational workshops and meetings with members of the local community to gain support for the grassbank, the Quivira Coalition was not involved in any greater capacity. Instead of having a nonprofit organization secure grants or special funding for the grassbank project, the BLM planned to issue the grazing permit for the grassbank to a rancher or group of ranchers who would then manage and maintain the grassbank themselves. In exchange for managing, improving, and maintaining the grassbank, grassbank permittees would be able to run a partial herd of their own cattle on the grassbank and to use the grassbank permit title as collateral to secure loans.[79]

The main goals of the Sangre de Cristo Grassbank project were to restore public rangeland and to encourage the ranching tradition in an effort to discourage subdivision and development. Like the Valle Grande Grass Bank, the Sangre de Cristo Grassbank would exchange grazing privileges on the grassbank for restoration treatments on public grazing lands. Eventually, the BLM wanted to involve the USFS in the project, but they wanted to get the project off the ground first. To do that, the BLM needed to restore the ecological integrity of the grazing allotments that would serve as the grassbank. These allotments had not been grazed in more than 20 years, and thick sagebrush groves had taken over the land. Burning and restoring the grassbank allotments was expected to take 2 to 4 years to complete. Three ranchers in the area had already joined together to apply for the BLM grassbank permit, and each had applied for a $50,000 grant from the Natural Resources Conservation Service to fund the initial restoration work on the grassbank.[80]

Although the BLM and the local ranchers involved in this project certainly represented some of the interests in this community, they did not by themselves represent the broad range of community interests. Furthermore, although three ranchers applied for the grassbank and the BLM supported the policy, there was little information on how other members of the community felt about this project. At that time, there had been no public opposition to the project. This may indicate that there was tacit support for the grassbank project from other members of the community or that other members of the community had not yet formed an opinion, perhaps because they did not know about the project. In addition, every other grassbank project reviewed so far has involved a conservation organization. Among other things, these organizations play a key role in representing conservation interests in the community and providing much-needed financial support. Their absence could help the Sangre de Cristo Grassbank gain support among ranchers who are suspicious of conservation organizations, but it could also leave local environmentalists suspicious and un-supportive of the grassbank.

## A7 Ranch Grassbank Project, Arizona

In 1999, the city of Tucson purchased the 7,300-acre A7 Ranch near the Cata-lina mountain range in southern Arizona in an effort to preserve open space and prevent subdivision. At the time, 471 acres of farmland located on the A7 Ranch were under easement, but the remaining acres were not. The mayor's council directed the new manager for the A7 Ranch, Bart McGuire, to find a way for the city to recover the $2.5 million spent on the ranch. The one stipulation the council imposed was that the portions of the ranch could be sold only under easement.[81]

McGuire, who lived in proximity to the Malpai Borderlands and had heard about the grassbank innovation, believed the A7 Ranch could be used as a grass-bank to improve watershed and grassland conditions in the area and recover the purchasing cost. In 2000, McGuire invited representatives from the USFS, the Southwest Center for Biological Diversity, the BLM, TNC, local ranchers, Arizona Game and Fish, and the University of Arizona to oversee the develop-ment and operation of the grassbank. This steering committee was charged with working out the details of a grassbank on the A7 intended to increase produc-tive grasslands, remove or reduce woody plant species on the rangeland, and reestablish instream flows in the surrounding streams and rivers. The committee agreed that the grassbank would be made available to local ranching families who were experiencing hardship from fire or drought as well as those making commitments to restoration projects on their home ranges.

McGuire also proposed a new idea to recover the purchasing cost of the A7 Ranch: "What I eventually want to do is sell development rights on some parts of the A7 Ranch, maintaining control of the property as a working cattle ranch, and develop a foundation funded by the sale of development rights. The interest on those funds would run the ranch indefinitely."[82] Transferring developing rights is an alternative to buying the land as a means of protecting land.[83] In the case of the A7 Ranch, land developers who purchased development rights on A7 property would be allowed to develop land within the city of Tucson, and land on the A7 Ranch would be protected from future development.

### Other Adaptations

Several other communities throughout the West are also considering or creating grassbanks as a tool to advance their common interest. The Nature Conservancy has several new grassbank projects in addition to the ones mentioned earlier, including the Matador Ranch Grassbank in Montana (created in 2003) and the Vina Plains Grassbank in California (created in 2002). In New Mexico, the Galisteo Watershed Restoration Project is interested in incorporating a grassbank into their watershed restoration plan as a tool to improve watershed conditions. In Sacramento, California, Wildlands, Inc., a wetland mitigation company, is exploring the possibility of creating small grassbanks to manage the company's properties and to assist local ranchers. In the Navajo Nation, near Window Rock, Arizona, the Navajo Environmental Protection Agency believes a grassbank could greatly benefit the tribal ranchers. Several other national forests in Region 3, including Kaibab, Coronado, and Tonto national forests in Arizona and the Gila National Forest in New Mexico, have expressed interest in establishing a grassbank like the Valle Grande. However, they are having trouble securing vacant grazing allotments and finding outside organizations that are willing to purchase the permits. As events continue to unfold in these and other places, there will be much more experience available for appraising grassbank adaptations and improving on present knowledge of the diffusion and adaptation processes.

## Overlapping Networks

What diffusion and adaptation networks are behind the Valle Grande Grass Bank and additional adaptations of the original innovation? At least three different kinds of overlapping networks are worth distinguishing in the cases just summarized: news media, conferences and tours, and institutions actively involved in grass banking, including the Quivira Coalition, TNC, and the USFS. Each network can be understood as a communication process, linking appraisals of experience in one community with planning for adapting grassbanks to another. Therefore it is appropriate to consider the basic components of a communication process: Who says what to whom, how, and with what effects?[84] Each network can be distinguished primarily by its structure (who communicates, how, and to whom), but each is specialized to communicating distinctive kinds of information and generating distinctive effects. This section reviews each network in turn. The next section offers appraisals.

First, consider the news media. The Gray Ranch Grassbank and the Valle Grande Grass Bank have both have been covered intermittently in national and local newspapers, magazines, and newsletters, agency publications, and scientific journals. The diversity of news sources, media, and audiences is indicated in an informal sample in box 4.1, including some sources already cited in this chapter.

Scanning over the sample, it is clear that diverse news media connect grassbank practitioners, reporters, and opinion and editorial writers with general and specialized audiences of different sizes and geographic scope. The practitioners include Bill deBuys and Courtney White as writers and as key sources for news stories and editorials. Both were quoted in the long story by Sandra Blakeslee, for example, along with Palemon Martinez, Ellie Towns, and others. Judging from the diversity of media represented, the audiences are quite diverse. At one extreme are large national audiences of the *News Hour with Jim Lehrer* on PBS, programs on CBS, and *The New York Times.* At the other extreme are local and regional audiences measured in thousands or tens of thousands rather than millions. *La Jicarita News* is the quarterly publication of the Rio Pueblo/Rio Embudo Watershed Protection Coalition of Northern New Mexico and has perhaps the smallest audience. In between are regional audiences, which have access to grass banking through the *Santa Fe New Mexican* and the *Albuquerque Journal,* the state's largest newspapers, and the *Denver Post.* Two of the regional media are specialized: *High Country News,* published biweekly in Paonia, Colorado, as "A Paper for People Who Care About the West"; and *Range,* published in Carson City, Nevada, and billed as "The Cowboy Spirit on America's Outback." Other channels reaching specialized audiences include *Clearing the Waters,* the New Mexico Environmental Department newsletter; *FS Today,* the USFS newsletter; and *BioScience,* a journal of the American Institute of Biological Sciences.

In terms of content, the coverage of the Gray Ranch has been overwhelmingly positive. The articles typically provide a definition of *grassbank,* information on who was involved in this and other grassbanks, and what the grassbank projects hoped to accomplish. The coverage also tracks the evolution of the Valle Grande Grass Bank. There was a cluster of positive news and opinion in

*Box 4.1. Grassbank Networks: News Media*

"Range Wars on the Arizona–New Mexico Border," *News Hour with Jim Lehrer* (PBS, February 13, 1996).

"Grassland Helpers," *CBS This Morning* (August 11, 1997).

"Group to Set Up 'Grass Bank,'" *Santa Fe New Mexican* (August 26, 1997).

"Up to the Minute," CBS Network (September 5, 1997).

"Grass Bank Project Is Good—and Timely," editorial, *Santa Fe New Mexican* (August 31, 1997).

"Grass Bank an Experiment in Cooperation," *Albuquerque Journal* (September 7, 1997).

"Ranchers and Environmentalists Search for Common Ground," *Santa Fe New Mexican* (June 6, 1998).

"Coalition Seeks Common Ground," *Albuquerque Journal* (June 7, 1998).

"A Great Beginning for 'Grass Bank,'" editorial, *Santa Fe New Mexican* (June 14, 1998).

"Rowe Mesa's Valle Grande Grass Bank Open for Business," editorial, *Albuquerque Journal* (June 14, 1998).

Melanie Greer Deason, "What Do Cows, Turtles, and Javelina Have in Common?" *NMED Clearing the Waters* 4 (December 1998).

Courtney White, "The Quivira Coalition and the New Ranch," *Range* (Winter 1999).

William deBuys, "Needed: A Larger Cast for the Rangeland Drama," *Denver Post* (April 4, 1999).

William deBuys, "Growing Credit at the Grass Bank," *Range* (Summer 1999).

Dolores Maese, "Grass Bank Gives Option to Ranchers," *FS Today* (October 1999).

Bill deBuys, "In Search of a Politics of Union," *High Country News* 32 (April 10, 2000).

Mark Schiller, "Santa Barbara Grazing Allotment Rehabilitation: A Progress Report," *La Jicarita News* 5 (November 2000).

Associated Press, "'Grassbank' Concept Has Spread from Origin in N.M.'s Bootheel," *Livestock Weekly* (December 7, 2000).

Sandra Blakeslee, "On Remote Mesa, Ranchers and Environmentalists Seek a Middle Ground," *New York Times* (December 26, 2000).

Sandra Blakeslee, "'Grass Bank' Solution Pays Off for Ranchers, Environmentalists," *Denver Post* (December 30, 2000).

Mari Jensen, "Can Cows and Conservation Mix?" *BioScience* 51 (February 2001).

W. Maxwell, "Banking on the Land," *Taos News* (May 3–9, 2001)

"Valle Grande Grass Bank Water Quality Improvement Project: Success Breeds More Success," *Section 319 Success Stories* 3 (February 2002).

Mark Schiller, "Santa Barbara Rehabilitation Project: Show Us the Work," *La Jicarita News* 7 (March 2002).

August and September 1997, around the time the Valle Grande MOU was signed. This was followed by intermittent coverage through an editorial in *La Jicarita News* in March 2002 titled "Show Us the Work." Compared with an editorial in November 2000 by the same author, Mark Schiller, the title signals growing skepticism and concern about USFS cutbacks in the rehabilitation of Santa Barbara grazing allotments.

*La Jicarita* has featured articles and updates on Santa Barbara home grazing allotment restoration projects, in addition to editorials. It has perhaps the most extensive coverage. Mark Schiller and Kay Matthews, cofounders of the watershed coalition and publishers of *La Jicarita,* believe the newsletter not only communicates important information to the local community but also helps keep the USFS focused on its commitments to the community.[85] Lacking details on other effects of news stories and editorials on the Gray Ranch and Valle Grande grassbanks, it seems probable that the coverage signaled an innovation and adaptation of interest to some people in the diverse audiences of these media. But even those interested were not likely to be convinced to proceed on that basis alone because the information in these articles is insufficient for that purpose. Any serious effort to create another grassbank probably needed more complete and specific information to evaluate the grassbank alternative.[86]

Second, consider conferences and tours as a more specialized kind of network. These events communicated information and advice on grassbanks to those already interested enough to commit the time and additional resources needed to attend. Research for this chapter turned up the conferences shown in box 4.2. The different times and places of these conferences expand opportunities for participation by those interested in following up an introduction to grassbanks. In addition, numerous individuals and small groups have toured the sites of the original innovation and the first adaptation.

The first comprehensive and concentrated source of detailed information on grassbanks for potential adapters was "Grassbanks in the West: Challenges and Opportunities," the conference in Santa Fe featured at the beginning of this chapter. The conference was sponsored by the Quivira Coalition, the Conservation Fund, the MBG, the Northern New Mexico Stockman's Association, the USFS, and the NMSU Cooperative Extension. Panelists who provided information and advice included some of the key practitioners responsible for establishing and operating the Gray Ranch and Valle Grande grassbanks: Drum Hadley, Bill McDonald, Bill deBuys, Leonard Atencio, Palemon Martinez, Bruce Runnels, and Ellie Towns and Ann Bartuska from the USFS. In addition, conference participants included ranchers, environmentalists, scientists, public land managers, and government officials from across the American West, including Califor-

Box 4.2. *Grassbank Networks: Conferences*

"Farming and Ranching for the Future," Taos, N.M. (March 1999).

"Culture, Ecology, and Economics of Ranching West of the 100th Meridian," Fort Collins, Colo. (May 2000), organized by Richard Knight and Wendell Gilgert of the Department of Fisheries & Wildlife Biology, Colorado State University, and Ed Marston of *High Country News.*

"Grassbanks in the West: Challenges and Opportunities," Santa Fe, N.M. (November 17–18, 2000), sponsored by the Quivira Coalition, the Conservation Fund, the MBG, the Northern New Mexico Stockman's Association, the USFS, and the NMSU Cooperative Extension.

"The New Ranch^sm Conference," Las Cruces, N.M. (March 10, 2001), sponsored by the Quivira Coalition.

5th Annual USEPA Region 6 Non–Point Source Pollution Watershed Conference," Angel Fire, N.M. (May 2002), sponsored by the New Mexico Mining Association, New Mexico Watershed Coalition, USEPA Region 6, and New Mexico Environmental Department.

"National Cowboy Poetry Gathering," Elko, Nev. (January 2002), sponsored by the Western Folklife Center.

"Building in Leopold's Legacy: Conservation for a New Century," Madison, Wisc. (October 2002), presented by the Wisconsin Academy of Sciences, Arts, and Letters.

"Grassbank Symposium," Salt Lake City, Utah (January 24, 2004), sponsored by the Society of Range Management.

nia, Nevada, Arizona, New Mexico, Texas, Colorado, Utah, and Montana. Some of them represented colleagues in public or private organizations back home, augmenting the effective audience for the information and advice discussed at the conference. The Forest Guardians and Southwest Biodiversity Center were unable to attend according to one report. The executive director of the New Mexico Cattle Growers' Association did not attend either. She explained, "We don't oppose grass banks as a tool per se. . . . But we don't want anyone to tell us how to run our business."[87]

The conference provided both basic and detailed information on grassbanks. For example, workshop topics included

- Definition of a grassbank and how and why it could be an effective tool in meeting both economic and ecological goals
- How a grassbank project is organized and structured and what components are essential to success

- Challenges grassbank projects face, including raising funds, developing strong partnerships, and following federal rules and regulations
- The importance of establishing and maintaining a monitoring program to assess progress

Several clear and consistent messages were delivered throughout the conference. Drum Hadley and Bill deBuys stressed that a grassbank involves the exchange of "real goods"—restoration commitments, land use easements, or something else of value—for grazing privileges on a grassbank. Exchange is essential·for achieving both economic and ecological goals. Bruce Runnels of TNC and deBuys spoke about the important role grassbanks play in fostering cooperation and partnerships in a community of place. "Ultimately, the future of these western landscapes depends on the people who work and live in these landscapes," Runnels said. A grassbank, by design, is not something an individual or an organization can do alone. Cooperation and partnerships are essential. The Valle Grande partnership crossed the boundaries of interest groups traditionally in conflict, and gained political power for that reason: "We are able to attract more money, have more influence, and get a lot more done," deBuys noted. But deBuys also noted that starting and maintaining a grassbank takes a great deal of commitment and resources including time, labor, and money. Conference speakers expected and encouraged adaptations of the grassbank policy, noting that grassbanks in practice may change across space and time depending on the mixture of goals set by those participating.[88] Although this conference included an opportunity for participants to tour the Valle Grande adaptation and see it first hand, the tour was canceled because of inclement weather.

Certain general characteristics of conferences and tours probably augmented the effects of this conference. It provided valuable opportunities for two-way conversations between innovators and potential adapters of grassbanks. Some of these opportunities were formally structured in the question-and-answer periods after each workshop presentation; others came up informally during breaks, meals, and discussions in the evening. Such discussions go well beyond the influence of the news media by allowing potential adapters to get informed feedback on specific questions and problems relevant to their own circumstances back home. Both two-way conversations in person and first-hand observations tend to have more effect than mediated information alone. There is some evidence that this conference spurred additional grassbank initiatives after November 2000.[89] However, all six of the grassbank adaptations featured in this chapter were already under way by then. Three of the six followed tours of the Gray Ranch by Jerry Elson and Bill deBuys in the summer of 1996, the RMFAC in the spring of 1999, and a group of ranchers from Owyhee County, Idaho, in 1999. The conference helped clarify and reassess the experience of the Gray Ranch, Valle Grande, and other grassbanks under way in November 2000.

Third, consider the institutions actively involved in the diffusion and adaptation of grassbanks, beginning with the Quivira Coalition. It took the lead in organizing the workshop in Peñasco and the "Grassbanks in the West" conference. It organized several tours and workshops at the Gray Ranch and Valle Grande grassbanks, and it helped the BLM with the Sangre de Cristo grassbank. Tony Benson, a rancher from Taos, New Mexico, who applied to operate that grassbank, first learned about grass banking through the Quivira Coalition.[90]

The origins of the organization can be traced back to 1995, when Courtney White first saw rancher Jim Winder at an executive board meeting of the New Mexico chapter of the Sierra Club. White was shocked: "What in the world is a *rancher* doing on the Board of Directors?" he recalls asking himself. The two men began to talk, and before long White accepted an invitation to visit Winder's ranch near Nutt, New Mexico. White confessed, "What I saw on Jim's ranch was everything I wanted as an environmentalist—healthy grasslands, wildlife, healthy riparian areas."[91] What he saw also changed his mind about ranching and prompted action. Winder and White, together with Barbara Johnson, another former Sierra Club leader, formed a new organization called the Quivira Coalition on June 11, 1997, in Santa Fe, New Mexico. The word *quivira* was used during the Spanish colonial era to designate unknown territory beyond the frontier. It is also a term for an elusive golden dream. The goal of the Quivira Coalition reflects its origins and name. It seeks "to teach ranchers, environmentalists, public land managers, and other members of the public that ecologically healthy rangelands and economically robust ranches can be compatible." For this goal the coalition works to "define the core issues of the grazing conflict and to articulate a new position based on the common interest and common sense."[92] The position is called the New Ranch[sm] and includes grass banking and a variety of other ranching techniques.

The Quivira Coalition has a mailing list of more than 1,500 people and an active board of directors that includes public land managers, ranchers, scientists, and environmentalists. From workshops to conferences, ranch tours to lectures, a quarterly newsletter, other publications, and demonstration projects, the Quivira Coalition makes a point of getting its message and program across, focusing on anyone predisposed to listen. "We don't want to sit around a table with disputing ranchers and environmentalists trying to get them to agree that the sky is blue. We don't want to agree on the lowest common denominator. Instead, we have a program that we think works. We stand outside the traditional battle field, wave our hands, and say 'come over here, join us in a third position, join us in what we call 'the radical center.'" White believes the Quivira Coalition has developed a message that is consistent and powerful. "We don't change the core of our message when we talk to environmentalists versus when we talk to ranchers. There are some slight modifications, but the core message remains the same." He recognizes that not all solutions will work in all places but believes that getting information to the people who want it is the first step. The Quivira Coalition firmly believes that "seeing is believing" and organizes more than a dozen hands-on workshops and field trips a year to ranches and demonstration projects throughout New Mexico. White hopes that other ranchers and environmentalists have an experience similar to his when he visited Winder's ranch and that they too see the possibility of common interest solutions.[93]

The Quivira Coalition's work and accomplishments have been recognized. The organization received the Piñon Award from the Santa Fe Community Foundation for "outstanding service to the environment" and the Merit Award from the New Mexico Chapter of the Soil and Water Society for their work. The Environmental Protection Agency has also bestowed the Environmental Excellence Award on the coalition for work with the Rio Puerco Management Committee on Non–Point Source Pollution. And in 2000, the New Mexico Community Foundation presented the coalition with an award as the Outstanding 1999–2000 Grantee Organization.[94]

The Nature Conservancy, a much older and larger organization than the Quivira Coalition, has also begun to institutionalize the diffusion and adaptation of grassbanks as part of a more comprehensive program. TNC's core mission since its founding in 1951 has been to "preserve the plants, animals and natural communities that represent the diversity of life on Earth by protecting the lands and waters they need to survive" through land purchases, easements, partnerships, and other tools.[95] But its experience at the Gray Ranch changed the way TNC does business. Officials at higher levels in the TNC hierarchy are now promoting grassbanks as another conservation tool for the organization, according to Bruce Runnels, director of its Rocky Mountain Division. Runnels believes that "grassbanks foster win–win situations. . . . We see the grassbank as a very high-potential and high-leverage tool. It has the potential to reap benefits and be adapted across a wide area of the west."[96] That leverage is particularly obvious at the Heart Mountain Grassbank in Wyoming, where 600 acres of irrigated farmland can support cattle from 40,000 to 50,000 acres of public rangeland while that rangeland undergoes restoration treatments.[97] The breadth of the potential is suggested by other grassbank adaptations initiated by TNC in Montana, Idaho, California, and Oregon.[98]

Information about grassbanks was diffused directly from the Gray Ranch to other TNC personnel involved in the Heart Mountain, Rocky Mountain Front, and Owyhee County adaptations. For example, Lou Lunte, the TNC coordinator in Owyhee County, had not even heard of the Valle Grande Grass Bank when the Owyhee Borderland Trust and TNC of Idaho began developing their grassbank.[99] They were simply adapting the Gray Ranch model to meet particular needs and circumstances in their own community. In these adaptations, information about new projects, problems, and innovations traveled quickly among personnel in the Rocky Mountain Region of TNC. Some of this information moved vertically from higher-level officials such as Bruce Runnels to TNC personnel on the ground. Some moved horizontally between personnel on the ground in various states included in the region. From there it spread further into the local communities in partnerships with TNC.

The diffusion and adaptation of grassbank information was also institutionalized through various networks developed by TNC. One was the Aridlands Grazing Network, established in April 2001 to provide "a forum for ongoing support for the development and implementation of conservation strategies in the context of aridland ranching."[100] Grass banking was included as one of the conservation strategies. Lou Lunte was a member of the network, and the Owyhee County Canyonlands was one of the four focal landscapes of the network. This network aimed to foster cross-site learning among TNC personnel while advancing ecological management practices on the landscapes of highest priority to the organization. The Nature Conservancy also created the Grassbank Working Group in 2001 to deepen TNC's understanding of whether and how grassbanks can produce lasting conservation results on a large scale.[101] Although now dissolved, this network included Laura Bell from the Heart Mountain Grassbank, Lisa Bay and David Carr from the Rocky Mountain Front Grassbank, and other TNC personnel from western states. Among other things, the Grassbank Working Group was developing an initial screening test that could be used to assess whether a grassbank would be an effective conservation tool in different communities. According to Steph Gripne, a grassbank researcher at the University of Montana, the TNC is now deeply involved in the National Grassbanking Network, a new network of grassbank participants and practitioners.[102] Although the two TNC networks did not extend beyond TNC personnel, they had great potential to multiply the significance of the original Gray Ranch Grassbank through diffusion within TNC and adaptations in partnership with local communities.

Finally, consider the USFS, an even older and larger organization than TNC. Forest Service personnel allowed the diffusion of grassbanks across upper and lower levels of the agency's hierarchy. Recall that after a visit to the Gray Ranch, range staff Jerry Elson of the USFS and Bill deBuys took the lead in adapting the original grassbank to the Valle Grande. This initiative could not have proceeded without the support of personnel in the Santa Fe and later other national forests.

Elson recommended it to his peers at the same level and up the line to his superior, Leonard Atencio, who recommended it down the line to rangers in the districts that would be involved in implementing the project. (Recall that this kind of vertical diffusion also occurred in TNC.) Following this innovation in the Santa Fe National Forest, USFS personnel in several other forests expressed interest in establishing grassbanks, including the Kaibab, Coronado, and Tonto national forests in Arizona and the Gila National Forest in New Mexico.

In addition, the USFS itself had taken at least one step at the national level to facilitate the diffusion of grassbanks. In February 2001, the associate deputy chief of the National Forest System, Sally Collins, issued an interim directive to all USFS personnel. The directive "establishes an exception to the base property and livestock ownership requirements necessary to qualify for a term grazing permit when the applicant agrees to operate the allotment(s) as a grassbank."[103] Four years earlier, deBuys's Conservation Fund had to apply for grazing permit under the special "non-use" status, exposing it to more opponents. This interim directive eliminated a requirement that frustrated, delayed, and could have blocked the Valle Grande Grass Bank and was a small step toward institutionalizing support for grassbanks in the USFS. Additional steps are critical not only because they would help institutionalize the processes of diffusing and adapting grassbanks but also because grassbanks involving public lands cannot be realized without the active support of officials in public land management agencies.

Support and analyses from higher-level officials at the "Grassbanks in the West" conference suggest that these additional steps are possible. Forest Supervisor Leonard Atencio told conference participants that he did not see any significant regulatory or institutional obstacles to prohibit the USFS from participating in grassbank programs. The biggest problems were in the perspectives of other USFS personnel: "We went to every level of our organization when we were starting the Valle Grande Grass Bank and they would say 'you can't do this, you can't do that.' But a lot of it was fear of the unknown and different interpretations of the regulations." Ellie Towns, then regional forester for the southwestern region, agreed with Atencio. "There is no way that 10 inches of public land laws aren't going to conflict with each other. The legislature left the resolution of those conflicts to the agencies." Within this latitude for interpretations of applicable law, both Atencio and Towns viewed the grassbank as a promising new approach to multiple use in public land management in the USFS. Atencio recognized that a grassbank was the right choice in the case of the Valle Grande but is not the right tool for every situation. Towns agreed that a grassbank is worth considering: "It's an idea that has potential—if it's not going to make us any worse off then we should try it." Ann Bartuska, who oversaw forest and rangeland management for the USFS at the national level, also expressed her support for the grassbank policy at the conference.[104]

Considered in light of the literature on diffusion, there appears to be nothing strikingly new in these three kinds of diffusion and adaptation networks, apart from the historical details. However, one observation is worth making: The classic diffusion model is missing here. According to Everett Rogers, it "dominated the thinking of scholars, policy makers, and change agencies" for decades. "In this model, an innovation originates from some expert source (often an R&D organization). This source then diffuses the innovation as a uniform package to potential adoptors who accept or reject the innovation. The individual adoptor of the innovation is a passive accepter." The classic model emerged from the technological successes of agricultural extension services, which provided the basic paradigm for diffusion research. It is clearly a remnant of scientific management. However, Rogers and others "gradually became aware of diffusion systems that did not operate at all like centralized diffusion systems. Instead . . . innovations often bubbled up from the operational levels of a system, with the inventing done by certain lead-users. Then the ideas spread horizontally via peer networks, with a high degree of re-invention occurring as the innovations are modified by users to fit their particular conditions. Such decentralized diffusion systems usually are not run by technical experts. Instead, decision making . . . is widely shared, with adoptors making many decisions."[105] Adapters, not passive adopters, served as their own agents of change.

The diffusion and adaptation of grassbanks are decentralized, in accord for the most part with the recently recognized alternative to the classic model. The sources of grassbank innovations represented different interests in local communities, not remote technical experts. The basic grassbank innovation was modified extensively as it was diffused horizontally and adapted to different conditions, not adopted without modification. The important decisions were shared by partners in each community and distributed across communities, not centralized. The most interesting departure from Rogers's model of a decentralized diffusion system, as summarized in this chapter, is the vertical diffusion and adaptation of grassbanks from the bottom up. This is represented by the Forest Service's national interim directive and to a lesser extent by verbal and other forms of support for grassbanks above the district level. The interim directive was not in accord with the remnants of scientific management. It was a small step to facilitate access to grazing permits by grassbank initiatives anywhere in the national forest system but not to impose them uniformly across the system from the top down. This is adaptive governance. Grassbank adaptations can serve as a working model for the diffusion and adaptation of other successful innovations in the transition to adaptive governance.

## Substantive and Process Appraisals

An appraisal of processes cannot be completed without an appraisal of substantive outcomes of those processes and vice versa.[106] This section offers first an appraisal of the substantive outcomes of the processes of diffusion and adaptation from the radical centers, the Gray Ranch and the Valle Grande, and then turns to an appraisal of the processes themselves. In each appraisal, normative criteria direct attention to what was important in the descriptions of the individual adaptations and in the networks by which they are interconnected. The practical implications of these appraisals are developed at the end of this section.

The appropriate criterion for an appraisal of substantive outcomes is the common interest, for reasons summarized in chapter 1. Overall, based on the evidence reviewed here, grassbank adaptations have advanced the common interest of local communities, as represented by people from diverse interest groups who are predisposed to come together to find common ground on grazing issues. Some of these people are officials who represent the communities where they live as well as the public land management agencies in which they work. What varies is the degree of progress beyond contemporary range wars, the historical baseline for appraisal and the default alternative to grassbanks. In a case such as the A7 near Tucson, representatives of diverse local interests were still in the planning phase. In other cases such as the Valle Grande, representatives of ecological, economic, ranching, and other interests had already signed off on a plan that each representative expected to serve its particular interests. (From a common interest standpoint, it matters little that the radical center in the Valle Grande Grass Bank did not include the Forest Guardians at one extreme or the New Mexico Stock Growers Association at the other.[107]) It remains to be seen whether the expectations of those who signed off on the Valle Grande and other grassbanks will be realized in practice and advance the common interest. From what has been seen so far there are grounds for both skepticism and optimism. None of the adaptations has gone as far as the Gray Ranch Grass Bank in advancing the common interest.

Limited progress in advancing the common interest can be explained in part by the limited time the grassbank adaptations have been in operation. It takes time to develop and implement a grassbank adapted to new conditions, and none of the adaptations has been in operation as long as the original Gray Ranch Grassbank. Other familiar factors are also at work, as suggested by the most significant grounds for pessimism in this chapter: the Forest Service's failure to fulfill its responsibility to rehabilitate grazing allotments under the Valle Grande Grass Bank MOU. This is reminiscent of the Forest Service's failure to implement nearly all of the Community Stability Proposal of the Quincy Library Group, as mandated by an act of Congress in 1998.[108] A formal agreement, even an act of Congress, is not sufficient to ensure progress when funds and trained, committed personnel are in short supply on the ground or priorities for using them lie elsewhere. Innovations such as the Community Stability Proposal are subject to the same impediments as grassbank adaptations. Thus there appears to be nothing distinctive about the limited progress of grassbank initiatives.

Similarly, the progress that has been made in advancing the common interest through grassbank initiatives can be explained in part by factors familiar from other community-based initiatives. The Gray Ranch Grassbank is similar to the Quincy Library Group in that both resource management plans were much more innovative rather than adaptive because there were no suitable precedents or models to build on at the outset.[109] What is distinctive about the grassbank adaptations is that each grassbank after the Gray Ranch was encouraged and informed by the diffusion and adaptation of relevant models. The diffusion and adaptation processes were facilitated by tours of the Gray Ranch and the Valle Grande grassbanks, which served as models adapted in at least five additional communities. The "Grassbanks in the West" conference also facilitated the diffusion and adaptation of the original innovation because it clarified the experience of the Gray Ranch and Valle Grande grassbank participants and made these experiences available to another wave of communities. These potential adapters did not have to plunge into unexplored territory on their own. They were encouraged by knowledge of the progress made by the original grassbank and the first adaptation and were informed by practice-based knowledge for meeting challenges and realizing opportunities.

Criteria have not been standardized for appraising diffusion and adaptation as communication processes, linking appraisals of experience in one decision process with planning in others. Appropriate criteria consistent with the common interest are proposed here and distinguished according to the structure of communication networks, their content, and their effects.[110] These criteria are then applied to the evidence available on the three kinds of networks involved in grass banking, as summarized in the previous section. Overall, the processes of diffusion and adaptation of the original grassbank innovation have functioned well up to this point, but there are some areas of possible concern.

The first set of criteria directs attention to the structure of the communication networks to be appraised and more specifically to who communicates, how, and to whom. Multiple sources of information to distribute control over the diffusion of information are preferred over a few. This criterion reflects the value placed on a marketplace of ideas in the American political tradition, that is, minimizing concentrations of control and the possibility of censorship by the few at the expense of the many.[111] To accommodate different kinds of information and diverse audience needs, multiple media with different specializations are preferred over a few homogeneous media. Not everyone needs the same kinds and amounts of information; it would be inefficient and an imposition to insist that they do. This criterion reflects the practical need to conserve the limited time and attention of audience members. Finally, the structure of communication should be open to diverse audiences potentially interested in the content and accessible to them, rather than effectively closed to many. This criterion implies that audience members can and should choose what information is of interest to them and what is not. They will ignore the latter.

In terms of control, the evidence in this case indicates that many different sources participated in the diffusion of information about grassbanks through different networks and different kinds of networks. These included the various authors and publishers in print media, speakers and producers in electronic media, the organizers of conferences and tours and their invited speakers, and personnel in the Quivira Coalition, TNC, and the USFS. One interpretation is that control over the diffusion of information was widely dispersed, with each network and each kind of network compensating to some extent for any concentrations of control in the others. Another interpretation is that the available information nevertheless often came from a handful of the people centrally involved in the original grassbank and the first adaptation—people such as Bill McDonald, Bill deBuys, Courtney White, and Bruce Runnels. They were often the primary sources for others and proponents of grassbanks as well. But independent, third-party sources of information were also involved. For example, *New York Times* reporter Sandra Blakeslee interviewed skeptics as well as proponents of grassbanks, and Mark Schiller drew attention to cutbacks in the rehabilitation of Santa Barbara grazing allotments to pressure the USFS to fulfill its commitments under the Valle Grande MOU. Pending more evidence, a case can be made for each interpretation.

In terms of media or channels of communication, the evidence suggests sufficient diversity and specialization among the different kinds of networks. Geographically, various networks covered grassbanks in the Malpai Borderlands and northern New Mexico at least, for audiences at these geographic scales as well as for the American West and the nation as a whole. Functionally, specialized coverage and audiences included grazing, ranching, forestry, water quality, science, and policy, as well as general audiences. Moreover, different audiences appear to have had multiple channels from which to select information according to their needs, ranging from an introduction to grassbanks, question-and-answer sessions to evaluate this alternative, and site visits for first-hand observation of operational details and results. In addition, research in TNC and elsewhere clarifies the circumstances under which a grassbank might work and how to make it work. All of these kinds of information are relevant to decisions to initiate planning for another grassbank. Again, each network and each kind of network compensated to some extent for the limitations of the others, including limited coverage, limited audiences, and limited kinds of information.

In terms of audiences, the evidence suggests that the various grassbank networks are open and accessible to most of the people potentially interested in them. People introduced to grassbanks through the news media are likely to spread the news to friends, neighbors, and colleagues if they are interested, especially if they are interested enough to follow up with participation in a conference or tour. The multiplier effect of word of mouth in reaching people potentially interested in grass banking is unknown and probably unknowable but could be as significant as news media in providing an introduction to grassbanks. Moreover, an introduction to grassbanks probably is sufficient for most audiences. There are ample opportunities among the various kinds of networks to follow up the initial introduction or not, depending on the degree of interest. Either outcome represents a choice of the audience member, not a structural flaw in grassbank diffusion and adaptation processes.

A second set of criteria directs attention to the content of information distributed through the networks. There is a preference for dependability: "Statements of fact that are made available to other members of the decision process are dependable; and if there is doubt, an indication is given of probable credibility." Without dependable information, policymakers tend to proceed on unrealistic expectations. There is a preference for selectivity and comprehensiveness in that the flow of information available is relevant to the problem at hand and addresses the logical components of a proposed solution to that problem. Without comprehensive information, policymakers tend to overlook or misconstrue considerations necessary for ameliorating their problem. Without appropriately selective information, they are left in the dark regarding their problem. Finally, there is a preference for creativity: "New and realistic objectives and strategies are compared with older and less realistic alternatives."[112] Without new alternatives to consider, policymakers tend to default to business-as-usual alternatives even if they are obsolete. Where these criteria are met, the odds are greater that policymakers can develop a policy that succeeds.

The most dependable information on grassbanks was available through major conferences such as "Grassbanks in the West," tours of the Gray Ranch and Valle Grande, and the institutions actively involved in grass banking. These information sources allow potential adapters more time to address questions of fact and more opportunities to resolve them by cross-checking facts, asking questions, and making first-hand observations in some cases. However, these opportunities can be compromised through promotion of grassbanks by the best-informed sources, who are understandably proud of their accomplishments as grassbank pioneers. For example, it is unclear whether their cautions regarding financial constraints, unfulfilled USFS commitments, and other challenges were lost amid many other specific factors and general enthusiasm. The opportunities for more dependable information also can be compromised by premature acceptance of claims of success by potential adapters, who understandably hope to find a way to move beyond contemporary range wars back home. The Heart Mountain Grassbank, for example, is based in part on the Valle Grande Grass Bank, which includes the USFS as a partner. But the USFS did not fulfill its commitments to rehabilitate grazing allotments under the Valle Grande MOU and did not implement prescribed burns in a timely fashion as a partner in Heart Mountain.

Early information on grassbanks was based largely on practice in the Gray Ranch and the Valle Grande. A review suggests that although practice-based information from the best-informed sources does not ensure comprehensiveness and selectivity, it certainly helps compared with science-based alternatives. Practitioners such as Bill McDonald and Bill deBuys risked failure if they overlooked important factors in a particular context of innovation or adaptation. They also needed some understanding of how the many important factors involved in a particular context interacted to shape outcomes. Potential adapters also face the risk of overlooking something important, and they must integrate a large number of factors to succeed in their own unique contexts. They need models that have been successfully implemented in practice, such as the Gray Ranch, to draw their attention to otherwise overlooked factors and to understand the interactions. In contrast, scientific and technical information tends to be less comprehensive or selective. Such information often addresses a few factors but seldom covers the many other factors and interactions that are important to practitioners. Scientists and technical experts cannot know much about the particular context without investing large amounts of time there, and they are seldom trained or otherwise predisposed to appreciate or cope with the human factors, including politics.

Creativity will improve when there are more models, adapted to different contexts, available in the flow of grassbank information. For example, when more fully implemented, the Rocky Mountain Front Grassbank will clarify the viability of the "string of pearls" concept, an adaptation to another land use pattern and to financial constraints. Similarly, the grassbanks envisioned for Owyhee County and the Sangre de Cristo Mountains might clarify whether the BLM is more reliable than the USFS in fulfilling rehabilitation commitments. To the extent that these and other grassbanks turn out to be successful in practice, they can provide potential adapters with newer models, adapted to somewhat different circumstances, to compare with the original Gray Ranch model and the first adaptation at Valle Grande.

The final criterion directs attention to the effects of the information diffused. The preference is to expand the effective range of informed choice for potential adapters. This criterion is an alternative to what is found in the literature. Success there is defined in part as how many adopt an innovation and how quickly.[113] The implied preference is control from the top down. The supporting expectations apparently are that central experts are the innovators, that their innovations are adopted without modification, and that such innovations are uniformly relevant across a jurisdiction or another defined set of circumstances. These expectations and preferences clearly are remnants of scientific management. In the alternative criterion, the expressed preference is to inform and empower people on the ground to make their own choices and decisions. The supporting expectations are consistent with observations on the grassbanks examined here: Circumstances differ from one community to the next, so that there is no one-size-fits-all solution; an innovation is adapted to those circumstances by people on the ground; and the adapters are the experts on their own unique circumstances and more responsible decision makers as well. They cannot avoid responsibility for the direct consequences of any decisions they make, short of leaving the community permanently. These expectations and preferences are clearly consistent with the concept and emerging practice of adaptive governance as developed in this book.

The diffusion of the grassbank innovation clearly has expanded the effective range of informed policy choices for potential adapters. Thanks to the diffusion and adaptation of information about the Gray Ranch, the Valle Grande, and possibly other grassbanks, communities no longer have to choose between a healthy ecosystem and a healthy socioeconomic system. Successful grassbank models represent a third set of choices and an opportunity to move the debate past contemporary range wars and down to specific grazing issues that are much easier to resolve. The communities that have already taken advantage of the opportunity to make more informed choices and decisions are located in or around the Santa Fe National Forest in New Mexico, the Rocky Mountain Front in Montana, Heart Mountain in Wyoming, Owyhee County in Idaho, the Sangre de Cristo Mountains near Taos, and the A7 Ranch in Arizona.

Overall, the grassbank diffusion and adaptation processes have functioned well so far. There are no glaring malfunctions, although there are some areas of possible concern. Both the lack of glaring malfunctions and areas of possible concern can be explained in general by the quasi-evolutionary nature of the overlapping networks engaged in the diffusion and adaptation of grassbank information.

The overlapping networks engaged in the diffusion and adaptation of grassbanks were not created and managed by a single, central authority. Instead, each emerged from a distinctive confluence of interests served by grassbanks and has been reinforced by progress in meeting their needs. For example, TNC learned in the Malpai Borderlands that grassbanks were a new promising tool in support of its traditional mission and found other communities interested in grassbanks as well. After touring the Gray Ranch, Jerry Elson and Bill deBuys understood that a grassbank could serve their interests in northern New Mexico, and they collaborated with others in setting up the Valle Grande Grass Bank. After his insight that his environmental aspirations and ranching could be compatible, Courtney White incorporated what he learned from existing grassbanks into the New Ranch toolbox. These people and others brought their interests together in the "Grassbanks in the West" conference. In the conference and related events before and after, people in the news media found material for stories, editorials, and opinion pieces and audiences for them.

Diffusion and adaptation are evolutionary processes in that they rely on diversity in the actions taken and in the selection of what works to exploit opportunities and meet challenges as they arise. They are quasi-evolutionary processes in that the actions taken and the selection of what works are goal directed, not random. In view of the quasi-evolutionary nature of these processes, it is not difficult to understand how a possible overreliance on a handful of sources could arise. The early grassbank participants are the best informed about and most committed to grassbanks. They are obvious sources of information who are willing to talk about their experiences. It is not difficult to understand a possible underemphasis on challenges and overemphasis on opportunities, backed by premature claims of success. However, progress justifies enthusiasm up to a point, and there is a demand for alternatives to contemporary range wars. Finally, it is not difficult to understand an unmet need for more grassbank models with more practical experience and adapted to different circumstances. It takes time to coordinate people and resources within and across the various networks. There is no single, central authority attempting to direct action or force progress or willing to invest resources for that purpose.

At the same time, this quasi-evolutionary process accounts for the absence of any glaring malfunctions. People have been willing to persist in making grassbanks work because interim progress has been sufficient to justify the effort in terms of their own interests. From a larger standpoint, they have established overlapping networks for diffusion and adaptation and distributed information that is on the whole dependable, comprehensive and selective, and creative; that information has had the effect of encouraging and informing other grassbank adaptations. All of this has been accomplished cheaply, efficiently, and in accord with the multiuse missions of the public land management agencies involved.

The practical implication of these substantive and procedural appraisals is to allow diffusion and adaptation to continue working as quasi-evolutionary process and to identify and address any procedural malfunctions and substantive problems as they arise. More specifically, this means welcoming additional news media, conferences and tours, and institutions that diffuse and adapt advice about grass banking. This means encouraging an open marketplace of ideas regarding grassbanks. For this purpose it would be appropriate for supporters to recruit some devil's advocates to increase the constructive criticism of grassbanks available through established and new networks. Constructive criticism accepts the goals of grassbanks and strives to improve action alternatives for making them work. This also means persisting in efforts to implement in practice more grassbanks in more diverse circumstances and communicating what is learned on the ground. Finally, for both substantive and procedural reasons, this means allowing the time and providing the other resources necessary for community-based initiatives involved in grassbanks to succeed or fail on their own merits. The default alternative to the diffusion and adaptation of grassbanks is the perpetuation of the deadlocked range wars.

In conclusion, the experience of grassbanks can be taken as a working model for understanding and shaping the diffusion and adaptation of other policy innovations and as an opportunity to move beyond the equivalent of range wars in other areas of natural resource policy. It is no longer necessary to presume that innovations are solely the responsibility of central experts, to be diffused and adopted without modification, uniformly across a range of circumstances. These were the presumptions behind the establishment of the Committee of Scientists by the USFS in 1997 to ensure that the agency's new planning regulations were scientifically based (see chapter 1). The Quivira Coalition, TNC, and even the USFS have shown how to multiply the effects of successful innovations by diffusing and adapting them horizontally to other communities. Similarly, the Rocky Mountain Division of TNC and the USFS at the national level have taken large and small steps, respectively, to facilitate and support grassbanks by adapting higher-level policies to differences and changes on the ground. It is not possible to predict the future of grassbanks or other policy innovations. It is possible to understand the processes of diffusion and adaptation, to allow them to function in the common interest, and to intervene selectively to address malfunctions as they arise. The diffusion and adaptation of successful innovations are an essential part of a possible transition to adaptive governance.

NOTES

1. "Grassbank" is a registered trademark of Grassbank, Inc.

2. On innovations in natural resource policy, see Barb Cestero, *Beyond the Hundredth Meeting: A Field Guide to Collaborative Conservation on the West's Public Lands* (Tucson, Ariz.: Sonoran Institute, 1999); Philip Brick, Donald Snow, and Sarah Van de Wetering, eds., *Across the Great Divide: Exploration in Collaborative Conservation in the American West* (Washington, D.C.: Island Press, 2001), which includes a chapter on the Malpai Borderlands; and Ronald D. Brunner, Christine H. Colburn, Christina Cromley, Roberta A. Klein, and Elizabeth A. Olson, *Finding Common Ground: Governance and Natural Resources in the American West* (New Haven, Conn.: Yale University Press, 2002). Focusing on the diffusion and adaptation of grassbanks in parallel with this case study are Claire Harper of Duke University and Steph Gripne of the University of Montana. Beyond the natural resource area, diffusion has attracted a lot of attention. The standard text, now in its 4th edition, is Everett Rogers, *Diffusion of Innovations* (New York: Free Press, 1995).

3. Ronald D. Brunner and Christine H. Colburn, "Harvesting Experience," in Brunner et al., *Finding Common Ground*, ch. 6, p. 231.

4. Chapters 5 and 6 of this volume focus on working examples of vertical diffusion and adaptation at the state and federal levels, respectively.

5. George Cameron Coggins, Charles F. Wilkinson, and John D. Leshy, *Federal Public Land and Resources Law* (New York: Foundation Press, 2001), p. 17.

6. Dan Dagget, *Beyond the Rangeland Conflict: Toward a West That Works* (Flagstaff, Ariz.: Good Stewards Project, 1998).

7. Edward Abby. "Free Speech: The Cowboy and His Cow," in *One Life at a Time Please* (New York.: Henry Holt & Company, 1985), p. 12.

8. Lynn Jacobs, *The Waste of the West* (Tucson, Ariz.: Lynn Jacobs, 1991), and Coggins et al., *Federal Public Land and Resources Law*.

9. Consider Aldo Leopold's land ethic: "The individual is a member of a community of interdependent part . . . which include soils, waters, plants, and animals, or collectively: the land." From his *A Sand Country Almanac with Essays on Conservation from Round River* (New York: Oxford University Press, 1949), p. 239.

10. Craig Allen has shown that the loss of grasslands to woody species was almost 1% per year between the 1930s and 1980s in the Jemez Mountains in northern New Mexico. Ray Turner supports this finding through the use of comparative photography throughout the Southwest. See "Valle Grande Grass Bank, Innovation in Landscape-Scale Land Rehabilitation in the American West: A History and Project Description," accessed at http://www.conservationfund.org/conservation/sustain; and Dagget, *Beyond the Rangeland Conflict*.

11. According to the 2000 census, New Mexico's population grew by 20% in the 1990s, Arizona's by 40%, and Colorado's by 30.6%, each well above the nation's overall growth of 13.1%. U.S. Census Bureau, *Census 2000,* accessed at http://quickfacts.census.gov/qfd/states/35000.html.

12. Eric Schlosser, *Fast Food Nation* (New York: Perennial, 2002), p. 144; M. Jensen, "Can

Cows and Conservation Mix?" *BioScience* 51 (2001), p. 85; and Luther Propst, *Preserving Working Ranches in the West* (Tucson, Ariz.: The Sonoran Institute, 1997), p. 7.

13. Malpai Borderlands Group, promotional pamphlet, on file with the author.

14. Dagget, *Beyond the Rangeland Conflict*.

15. Ibid.

16. Quoted in "Hotline," *High Country News* 25 (April 5, 1993).

17. Quoted in Dagget, *Beyond the Rangeland Conflict,* p. 21.

18. Bill McDonald, "The Malpai Borderlands Group: Ecosystem Management in Action," in *The Future of Arid Grasslands: Identifying Issues, Seeking Solutions* (Fort Collins, Colo.: USDA Forest Service Proceedings RMRS-P-3, 1996), p. 290.

19. MBG project cooperators include the state land departments of Arizona and New Mexico, the Coronado National Forest, the USFS, the U.S. Fish and Wildlife Service, the Natural Resources Conservation Service in Arizona and New Mexico, the BLM, the Hidalgo Soil and Water Conservation District, the Whitewater Draw Natural Resource Conservation District, the game and fish departments in Arizona and New Mexico, the Desert Laboratory of the University of Arizona, The Nature Conservancy, and the Animas Foundation. Ibid., p. 291.

20. Ibid., p. 290.

21. MBG, "Fire," accessed at http://www.malpaiborderlandsgroup.org.

22. Ibid.

23. Bill Miller, presentation at the "Grassbanks in the West: Challenges and Opportunities" conference (Santa Fe, N.M., November 17–18, 2000). Conference audiotapes on file with author.

24. Bill McDonald, testimony before the U.S. Senate Committee on Finance (June 12, 2001), accessed at http://www.senate.gov/~finance/061201bmtest.pdf. See also "Sharing Common-Sense Solutions to the Rangeland Conflict," *Quivira Coalition Newsletter* 4(3) (2001); and Ben Brown, "Grassland Management by the Animas Foundation," in *The Future of Arid Grasslands: Identifying Issues, Seeking Solutions* (Fort Collins, Colo.: USDA Forest Service Proceedings RMRS-P-3, 1996).

25. MBG, "Grassbank," accessed at http://www.malpaiborderlandsgroup.org.

26. According to McDonald's June 12, 2001, testimony for the U.S. Senate Committee on Finance, the four easements were acquired by trading grazing rights on the Gray Ranch Grassbank. The grassbank easements "contain an escape clause should the government grazing policies make the goals of the easement unattainable. Thus, ranchers who can't continue ranching as a livelihood because of changed regulations of the industry would not be further penalized with loss of other economic use of their land." Three other easements were purchased outright for cash, with the purchase price "agreed to by the MBG and the landowner and based on the appraisal of the current development value of the particular ranch."

27. McDonald, "The Malpai Borderlands Group," p. 295.

28. National Fish and Wildlife Foundation, "National Fish and Wildlife Foundation Grants in Fiscal Year 2000: New Mexico," accessed at http://www.nfwf.org/programs/grant_NM.htm.

29. McDonald, "The Malpai Borderlands Group," p. 291. From 1994 to 1997, MBG raised $1,393,856 in contributions, gifts, and grants. In the 1998 fiscal year, MBG had $860,295 in net assets or fund balances and raised $298,668 in contributions, gifts, and grants. The MBG relies heavily on TNC as a source for funding but has also received grants for conservation easements from a variety of other private foundations including the Norcross Wildlife Foundation, the J. M. Kaplan Fund, and the National Fish and Wildlife Foundation. See J. Z. Walley, "Follow the Money," *Paragon Powerhouse* (2000), accessed at http://www.nmagriculture.org/Part%204.htm.

30. The average per capita income in the northern New Mexico counties of Taos, Rio Arriba, and Mora is $14,279. The average per capita income in the state of New Mexico is $20,288, and the U.S. average per capita income is $25,924. U.S. Census Bureau, *Census 2002,* accessed at http://www.census.gov.

31. Edmund Gomez, personal interview, Alcalde, N.M. (June 28, 2001).

32. Quoted in W. Maxwell, "Banking on the Land," *Taos News* (May 3–9, 2001). For more on the ranching tradition and culture in northern New Mexico, see Ernest Atencio, *Of Land and Culture: Environmental Justice and Public Lands Ranching in Northern New Mexico* (Santa Fe, N.M.: The Quivira Coalition, 2001).

33. A swing allotment is a public land grazing allotment that is temporarily stocked with cattle from another public land grazing allotment. Swing allotments typically are used for the purpose of fire or drought relief. Unlike in a grassbank, no exchange or commitment is required of the ranchers who use the swing allotment.

34. The ranch was a "base property," a parcel of land to which an individual can obtain fee title and access to the public grazing land allotments associated with the base property. Under the Taylor Grazing Act, an individual must own a base property in order to be eligible for grazing permits on public lands. This system of ownership and access was established by the Homestead Act, related land disposition acts, and the Taylor Grazing Act. Coggins et al., *Federal Public Land and Resources Law.*

35. *Valle Grande Concept Paper* (1996), p. 2, on file with the author.

36. Ibid., pp. 2 and 1.

37. Bill deBuys, presentation at the Valle Grande Grass Bank tour, June 30, 2001.

38. Bill deBuys, "In Search of a Politics of Union," *High Country News* 32 (April 10, 2000).

39. Palemon Martinez, at the "Grassbanks in the West" conference.

40. Owen Lopez, Palemon Martinez, and Bill deBuys, at the "Grassbanks in the West" conference.

41. Valle Grande Grass Bank, *Memorandum of Understanding* (1999), on file with the author.

42. Valle Grande Grass Bank, *Review of Allotment Improvement and Rehabilitation Projects* (December 1999), on file with the author.

43. Will Barnes, at the "Grassbanks in the West" conference.

44. Six monitoring plots were established in a treatment site, and three control plots were established outside a treatment site. At each monitoring plot, three 100-meter transects project from a central point. Baseline data on species composition, percentage bare ground, percent-

age canopy coverage, floral ratios (i.e., grass to tree), and soil stability will be collected and photographs taken along each transect before a treatment. Data will be collected and photographs taken immediately after a treatment, a year after treatment, and every 3 years after that. Sustainable Communities, "Valle Grande Grass Bank: Need for Monitoring," *The Conservation Fund,* accessed at http://www.conservationfund.org/conservation/sustain; and Will Barnes, at the "Grassbanks in the West" conference.

45. Valle Grande Grass Bank, *Memorandum of Understanding, Attachment C: Assignable Right of First Refusal,* p. 2.

46. Bill deBuys, personal communication, June 3, 2004.

47. According to deBuys, ibid., the funding from the Ford Foundation was granted for the operation of the grassbank, not the purchase of the Triple S. However, the Ford Foundation's support of the operational side of the project greatly assisted in the raising of purchase funds because it created a sense of project legitimacy.

48. Ibid. The editorials are "'Grass Bank' Project Is Good—and Timely," *Santa Fe New Mexican* (August 31, 1997), and "Grass Bank an Experiment in Cooperation," *Albuquerque Journal* (September 7, 1997).

49. deBuys, "In Search of a Politics of Union."

50. Bill deBuys, personal communication, June 3, 2004.

51. Courtney White, "The Quivira Coalition and the New Ranch," *Range* (Winter 1999), p. 13.

52. Valle Grande Grass Bank, *Review of Allotment Improvement and Rehabilitation Projects;* and the Conservation Fund, *Valle Grande Grass Bank: Innovation in Landscape Rehabilitation and Sustainable Ranching in the American West,* informational brochure on file with the author.

53. Valle Grande Grass Bank, *Review of Allotment Improvement and Rehabilitation Projects,* p. 2.

54. Mark Schiller, "Santa Barbara Rehabilitation Project: Show Us the Work," *La Jicarita News* 7 (March 2002).

55. Bill deBuys, personal communication, June 3, 2004.

56. Charlie Jankiewicz, presentation at the Valle Grande Grass Bank tour, June 30, 2001.

57. Bill deBuys, personal communication, June 3, 2004.

58. Quoted in Mark Schiller, "Santa Barbara Grazing Allotment Rehabilitation: A Progress Report," *La Jicarita News* 5 (November 2000), p. 3.

59. Bill deBuys, at the "Grassbanks in the West" conference.

60. Schiller, "Santa Barbara Grazing Allotment Rehabilitation."

61. Rogers, *Diffusion of Innovations,* p. 244; and Harold D. Lasswell, Daniel Lerner, and Ithiel deSola Pool, *The Comparative Study of Symbols: An Introduction* (Stanford, Calif.: Stanford University Press, 1952), p. 4.

62. David Carr and Lisa Bay, "A Case Study of the Rocky Mountain Front Grassbank" (The Nature Conservancy of Montana, 2001), unpublished report on file with the author.

63. Lisa Bay, excerpts from TNC of Montana's progress report to the GM Foundation, on file with author.

64. Carr and Bay, "A Case Study of the Rocky Mountain Front Grassbank"; and Claire

Harper, "The Grassbank Movement, 2001: A Status Report of Grassbank Initiatives in the West," unpublished paper on file with the author.

65. Harper, "The Grassbank Movement."

66. Ibid.

67. Laura Bell, "A Case Study of the Heart Mountain Grassbank" (2001), unpublished report on file with the author. Bell is the Heart Mountain Ranch project director.

68. Ibid.

69. Steph Gripne, personal communication, May 24, 2004.

70. Bell, "A Case Study"; and Laura Bell, "Heart Mountain Ranch: Business Plan" (2001), unpublished report on file with the author.

71. Bell, "A Case Study."

72. Stephen Lyons, "Owyhee County: Portrait of a Changing Economy," *University of Idaho Magazine* (Winter 2000).

73. "Ranchers Hope to Improve Rangeland," *Idaho Falls Post Register* (May 11, 2000); and Lou Lunte, telephone interview (March 15, 2002).

74. "Conservation Group Acting on Grand Scale," *Associated Press State and Local Wire* (April 25, 2001), dateline Boise, Idaho.

75. Steph Gripne, personal communication, May 24, 2004.

76. Lou Lunte, telephone interview (March 15, 2002).

77. "County Takes Bold Step of Gathering Interests for Management Plan," *Associated Press State and Local Wire* (July 27, 2001), dateline Boise, Idaho.

78. Harper, "The Grassbank Movement."

79. Tony Benson, personal interview, Valle Grande Grass Bank tour (June 30, 2001).

80. Harper, "The Grassbank Movement."

81. Bart McGuire, at the "Grassbanks in the West" conference.

82. Ibid.

83. "Transfer of Development Right Facts Sheet," Ohio State University Cooperative Extension Service, accessed at http://ohioonline.osu.edu/cd-fact/1264.htm. With a transfer of development rights, developers pay to develop one parcel of land and protect another. In essence, Tucson sacrificed some land it owns for development in the city to protect other land, the A7. With a conservation easement, an individual or group basically buys the right to protect the land.

84. Harold D. Lasswell, "The Structure and Function of Communication in Society," in Wilbur Schramm, ed., *Mass Communications,* 2nd ed. (Chicago: University of Illinois Press, 1960), pp. 117–130.

85. Mark Schiller, telephone interview (April 27, 2001).

86. Rogers, *Diffusion of Innovations,* pp. 195–196.

87. Sandra Blakeslee, "On Remote Mesa, Ranchers and Environmentalists Seek a Middle Ground," *New York Times* (December 26, 2000), p. F4.

88. Runnels and deBuys at the "Grassbanks in the West" conference.

89. Claire Harper, telephone interview (July 12, 2001), on the influence of the conference. On the expected effects of two-way communication, see Rogers, *Diffusion of Innovations,* p. 194. See also Harold D. Lasswell and Abraham Kaplan, *Power and Society* (New Haven, Conn.:

Yale University Press, 1950), pp. 113–114. On controversial issues, information alone is not likely to change predispositions unless supported by other factors, including direct, first-hand experience.

90. Tony Benson, personal interview, Valle Grande Grass Bank tour (June 30, 2001).

91. Courtney White, personal interview, Santa Fe, N.M. (June 26, 2001).

92. "The Quivira Coalition: Sharing Common-Sense Solutions to the Rangeland Conflict," at the Quivira Coalition Web site, http://www.quiviracoalition.org.

93. Courtney White, personal interview, Santa Fe, N.M. (June 26, 2001).

94. "The Quivira Coalition: Sharing Common-Sense Solutions to the Rangeland Conflict."

95. The Nature Conservancy mission statement, accessed at http://www.nature.org.

96. Bruce Runnels, at the "Grassbanks in the West" conference.

97. Bob Budd, personal interview, Loveland, Colo. (April 18, 2002).

98. Claire Harper, "The Grassbank Movement." See also Hal Herring and Steph Gripne, "Fair Trade: Ranchers Bank on Conservation," at TNC's Compatible Ventures Web site, http://compatibleventures.us/grassbank.html.

99. Claire Harper, "The Grassbank Movement."

100. The Nature Conservancy, "Developing a Conceptual Scientific Framework for Conservation in the Arid West," proceedings of the Aridlands Grazing Network, Workshop 1, Medano-Zapata Ranch, Colo., April 11–13, 2001.

101. The Nature Conservancy, "Grassbank Working Group Meeting Proceeding," Denver, Colo., July 19–20, 2001.

102. Steph Gripne, personal communication, May 24, 2004.

103. USDA Forest Service, *Interim Directive No. 2230-2001-1. Grazing and Livestock Use Permit System* (Washington, D.C.: USDA Forest Service, February 16, 2001).

104. All quotations in this paragraph are from the "Grassbanks in the West" conference.

105. Rogers, *Diffusion of Innovations,* pp. 364–365. For an example of diffusion in a centralized system, see Bryce Ryan and Neal C. Gross, "The Diffusion of Hybrid Seed Corn in Two Iowa Communities," *Rural Sociology* 8 (1943), pp. 15–24. For an example of diffusion in a decentralized system see Lorraine Sherry, "The Boulder Valley Internet Project: Lessons Learned," *T.H.E. Journal* 25 (September 1997), pp. 68–72.

106. Harold D. Lasswell, *A Pre-View of Policy Sciences* (New York: Elsevier, 1971), p. 76.

107. The Guardians' interest in preventing grazing on public lands and the Stock Growers' interest in total control of grazing are special interests, achievable only a great cost to the community as a whole if they are achievable at all. The common interest does not necessarily entail unanimity.

108. See Christine H. Colburn, "Forest Management and the Quincy Library Group," in Brunner et al., *Finding Common Ground,* ch. 5, pp. 159–200.

109. See ch. 1 and Brunner et al., *Finding Common Ground.*

110. Appropriate criteria consistent with the common interest are available for each phase of decision process and the decision process as a whole in Lasswell, *A Pre-View of Policy Sciences,* pp. 85–97. The criteria for the appraisal and intelligence (or planning) phases are adapted here.

111. Commission on Freedom of the Press, *A Free and Responsible Press* (Chicago: University of Chicago Press, 1947).

112. The quotations are from Lasswell, *A Pre-View of Policy Sciences,* pp. 86 and 88, respectively. Comprehensiveness and selectivity are also specified and elaborated in the same source.

113. Rogers, *Diffusion of Innovations,* pp. 100–106.

## 5. The Oregon Plan: A New Way of Doing Business

LINDY COE-JUELL

IN 1992, BARBARA ROBERTS, then governor of Oregon, brought together fishers, timber owners, biologists, farmers, and bureaucrats to consider how to reverse the declines of coastal salmon. Out of that meeting came a focus on coho salmon restoration through voluntary local watershed groups funded by a patchwork of state and federal grants. Formerly unemployed fishers were soon restoring habitat for runs of coastal fish that once provided their livelihoods. Mary Lou Soscia, manager of this state Watershed Health Program, understood its significance: "The old way of doing business was that people at offices wrote plans and said, 'This is the way it's going to be.' We continued to see a major decline in natural resources. The new way of doing business is that the government works in partnership with people at the community level." A spokesperson for the National Marine Fisheries Service (NMFS), Brian Gorman, agreed and looked ahead: "The notion that the federal government is going to come riding in on a white charger and say, 'Trust us, we know what we are doing,' I think that era is passing." Legacies of that era in Oregon included "hard feelings ... over the heavy hand of the federal government forcing logging cutbacks on federal as well as private land to save the northern spotted owl from extinction."[1]

In 1995, newly elected Governor John Kitzhaber made a strong personal and political commitment to the approach taken in the state Watershed Health Program. This commitment was based on his personal inspection of the watershed councils and their work up and down the coast and prompted by fear of the heavy hand of the federal government: NMFS was expected sometime soon to list the coho salmon as threatened under the Endangered Species Act (ESA). Kitzhaber promoted, modified, and expanded the approach taken in the state program and named it the Oregon Plan for Salmon and Watersheds. Under his leadership, the Oregon Plan accomplished enough to support the expectations of Mary Lou Soscia and Brian Gorman, as quoted earlier. They saw a significant change under way in 1995, a change that can be understood here as part of a possible transition from scientific management to adaptive governance. The establishment of the Oregon Plan, especially the state's embrace and resulting contributions of community-based initiatives, is worth examining in that context, even though the political and fiscal environments in Oregon continue to evolve, as does the plan itself.

The purpose of this chapter is to clarify and illustrate adaptive governance through the Oregon Plan for Salmon and Watersheds. The Oregon Plan is another model for adapting natural resource policy decisions to real people, to differences and changes in local contexts, and to twenty-first–century realities. It is a distinctive model, showing how authorities at the state level can actively encourage and support the work of community-based initiatives, organized as local watershed councils (figure 5.1), without controlling how from the top down. It is also a means of expanding the significance of successful innovations. The plan facilitated the diffusion and adaptation of innovative working solutions to habitat restoration and fish recovery problems across watersheds and modest adaptations of state government practices to the achievements and needs of the watershed councils. The Oregon Plan also offers another example of innovative leaders using demands created by the ESA to advance the common interest rather than forcing change based on a single interest. This chapter begins with the biological and historical context of the Oregon Plan. It then turns to the origins, implementation, and appraisals of the plan, focusing on the embrace of a network of community-based initiatives, which sets the Oregon Plan apart from previous salmon recovery efforts in the state and perhaps the country. It concludes with a summary of experience under the Oregon Plan as an example of adaptive governance.

## Biological and Historical Context

The biology of salmon is necessary to understand their historical abundance and swift decline, the failure of past recovery efforts, and the need for a different approach: the Oregon Plan. The chinook, coho, sockeye, chum, and pink salmon are the five salmon species that inhabit the waters of the Pacific Northwest. Along with the steelhead trout, these are anadromous fish, which means they are hatched in freshwater, spend part of their lives in the ocean, and return to freshwater to spawn in the same streams and river reaches where their lives began. Gravel beds provide a safe place for newly hatched salmon to hide from predators and hunt for insects. Side channels, beaver ponds, and fallen trees provide resting areas during periods of high flow. Salmon spend 1 or 2 years maturing in their freshwater homes before descending with the river currents to the ocean. The journey downstream is completed primarily at night, the safest time for small fish to travel. By day, stones and large tree branches provide cover from larger fish, birds, and many other predators. This carefully staged migration from stream to ocean can take up to 4 months to complete.

Different salmon species use different ocean ranges. For example, the Oregon coastal coho stay close to home, usually within a few hundred miles of the coast. By contrast, chinook salmon travel thousands of miles to the Gulf of Alaska. The chinook's navigational feat is still not understood, although sensitivity to the sun, stars, or the earth's magnetic field may be involved. Most salmon species use the ocean as a bountiful feeding ground for 1 to 2 years and in turn serve as food for tuna, sea lions, whales, and other ocean species.[2] The inland range of salmon also is collectively enormous and varies by species. Chinook salmon travel hundreds of miles up the Columbia River and its tributaries to graveled sites in the high reaches of the watershed to spawn. They are powerful and driven enough to leap waterfalls 10 to 15 feet high. Pink and chum salmon prefer to spawn in estuary habitats and the low reaches of creeks, staying close to the saltwater. Steelhead trout seek out streams near the river headwater, and sockeye salmon spawn near lakes where their juveniles grow. The Oregon coho do not travel as far inland as the chinook or steelhead. The coho searches for clean gravel in small upper tributaries. After spawning, the salmon die and pass their nutrients on to the ecosystem. Their eggs begin the life circle anew. Steelhead may make one or two more trips to spawn in freshwater before they die.[3]

The different species have diverse inland and ocean ranges that help protect them from catastrophic events. Their age structures (i.e., when they mature and spawn), length of residence in freshwater, and timing of returns to freshwater also help protect them. Because they use different habitats over space or time, some part of a diverse population probably can survive a flood or drought. Thus different species and populations survived natural variations and disturbances over the last 2 million years. They also became bound to different complex environments as they coevolved with those environments. Some disturbances were beneficial if not essential for continued survival. For example, landslides that temporarily destroyed river habitats also replenished the gravel supplies that salmon need for spawning and moved large trees, branches, and boulders into the stream, making the habitat more complex and safer for young salmon. Floods that swept young salmon downstream too early also cleaned silt from the spawning gravel beds. Historically, salmon returned to their freshwater homes in the Pacific Northwest in incredible abundance. However, salmon populations have been decimated by the direct and indirect impacts of countless human activities since the westward migration of European Americans in the late nineteenth century.

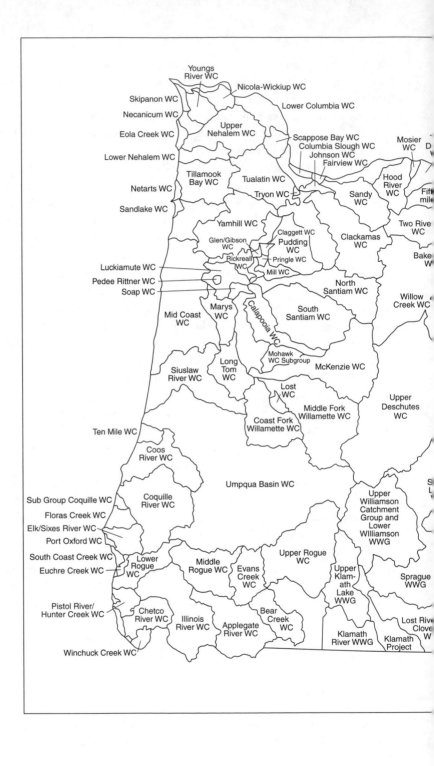

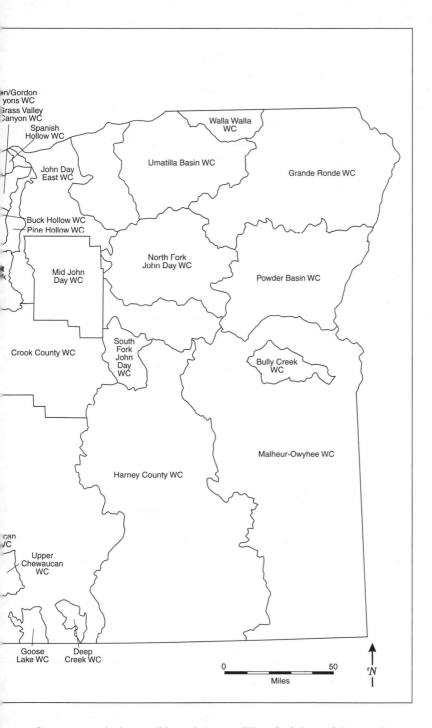

re 5.1. Oregon watershed council boundaries. wc, Watershed Council. Source: Or-
Watershed Enhancement Board, June 2001.

At that time observers exaggerated the abundance, claiming that salmon were so thick during spawning runs that one could walk across the water on their backs. On the Columbia River the returning stocks consistently numbered between 10 and 15 million fish annually. The current average annual return is around 1 million salmon, and of those 80 percent are estimated to be hatchery fish.[4] Commercial fishing and canning was the first industry to diminish what seemed an inexhaustible resource, precipitating the current population crisis. With harpoons, hooks, gillnets, traps, and fish wheels, salmon were caught in record numbers in the late 1800s. Dam building in the 1930s was the next major blow for the salmon of the Columbia River. The vast network of private and federal dams covering the basin imposed many barriers to salmon migration, reduced natural sediment transfer, and otherwise greatly altered the natural ecosystem. These dams are widely recognized as the single most significant cause of salmon decline in that basin. But it is difficult to hold one single activity above all others in other basins as the primary cause of the decline of salmon population, and the causes vary over time and space. A different combination of human activities has damaged or blocked access to the salmon's habitat in each major watershed.[5]

Oregon's coho salmon population also has experienced a significant decline. Based on fish catches from the 1890s, historic coho populations have been estimated at 1.25 million. In recent years that population dipped to fewer than 50,000. The decline of Oregon's coastal coho has been caused in large part by a large number of uncoordinated, incremental human activities.[6] Outside the Columbia River Basin in Oregon, there are as many as 3,600 smaller dams that provide water for municipal and industrial purposes as well as irrigation and livestock. Although small, the dams can still block fish passage upstream, and the reservoirs slow downstream migration.[7] Logging, ranching, mining, and farming have all deposited silt and chemicals into the water. Early logging removed trees from riversides and coastlines, eliminating shaded areas and increasing water temperature. Livestock grazing near streams trample the vegetation that is an important source of nutrients for aquatic insects that salmon feed on. Irrigation withdrawals have left streams so shallow that water temperatures increase to lethal levels for juvenile salmon or simply have made the streams impassable. Runoff from urban areas carries pollution in the form of petroleum products, lawn and garden chemicals, sewage, and sediment into the adjacent watersheds. Natural variations and disturbances sometimes compound the damage caused by these human factors. Researchers believe that a warming trend in the Pacific from 1976 to 1999 made conditions worse for the coho. Warmer conditions have been correlated with declines in krill and other zooplankton, which make up a large portion of the salmon's diet. That helps explain the crash of a salmon fishery off the Oregon coast after 1976.[8]

Simplification of a complex natural environment is the connection between these many human factors contributing to salmon decline. Human development has destroyed parts of the complex environments that coevolved with the salmon, and human management through hatchery production has reduced the salmon's genetic diversity. Some biologists argue that saving the salmon will entail restoring natural complexity in all parts of the watershed.[9] That argument places effective responsibility for salmon restoration in the hands of many landowners and citizens as well as professional managers at the state and federal level. Furthermore, the unique attributes of different populations and different ecosystems across Oregon make the problem of salmon decline place based. The problem is somewhat different for each local watershed community and ultimately presents a unique challenge to each community.

Generally, this is a hard problem for the people of the Pacific Northwest because they revere both the salmon and the way of life that led to salmon decline. Pacific salmon have been a cultural icon for many human generations from early Native Americans to the present population. Salmon were a central part of the Native American experience for both sustenance and spiritual connection. For more recent immigrants the salmon's abundance and amazing life journey have symbolized the land's natural bounty and the determined, fervent spirit of the American West. People with different lifestyles and political interests do disagree over who should be responsible for salmon recovery and how to do it. Still, as one citizen of Scappoose Bay, a small town north of Portland, puts it, "No one is against the salmon."[10] It is fair to say that the people of the Pacific Northwest have a common interest in protecting and recovering the salmon. It is also fair to say that through past efforts, managers have not secured that common interest for the public.

In the last 130 years, dozens of plans or programs for salmon management have been prepared and implemented to varying degrees in Oregon. However, all have failed to halt the salmon decline.[11] A brief review of the most prominent past management efforts clarifies why. In the early years of European American settlement of the Pacific Northwest, the natural resource policy of the United States government was very much hands off to encourage settlement of the American West, the overriding policy objective. The fledgling governments of Oregon and Washington passed few restrictions, if any, regulating the explosive growth of the salmon fishing industry. A combination of the natural abundance of salmon, the lack of regulatory constraints, and new canning technology allowed a "frenzied free-for-all of salmon harvesting."[12] In 1883, just 15 years after the first cases of chinook were canned, the harvest from the Columbia River peaked and then declined. But even before the harvest peaked, the resource was recognized to be vulnerable. In response to the growing problem of overfishing, the territories of Oregon and Washington introduced gear restrictions and began regulating the duration of the fishing season between 1871 and 1878.[13] But these early regulations were ineffective because they were rarely enforced and widely ignored.

Under pressure from business and political leaders who wanted to sustain the fishing industry, the Oregon legislature requested advice from the U.S. Fish Commission. In 1875, Spencer Baird, the U.S. fish commissioner, reported that excessive fishing, dams, and altered habitat were the three most significant threats to the Columbia River salmon industry. Instead of addressing the identified threats, Baird recommended artificial propagation of salmon in Oregon to make them so plentiful that protective regulation would be unnecessary. In 1877, the commission opened a salmon hatchery on Oregon's Clackamas River. However, there were no apparent effects on the size of the salmon runs, and the hatchery was soon abandoned. Baird's recommendation was the first of many that relied on hatchery production, revealing one reason for failure to recover the salmon populations. The historical recovery plans focused on managing the resource to conserve it but paid little attention to managing the humans or human behaviors that were causing the salmon populations to plummet.[14] By the early 1900s, the fishing and canning industry was crippled under the weight of its own success.

In 1908, President Theodore Roosevelt lamented the decimation of fisheries on the Columbia River by fishers "naturally" catching all that they could while the U.S. government failed to intervene and the Washington and Oregon state legislatures could not agree on joint action. Under Roosevelt's leadership, management for conservation and a sustainable harvest replaced the "frenzied free-for-all" that had dominated western development. In that spirit, Oregon and Washington eventually agreed to the Columbia River Compact of 1918, which outlawed destructive techniques such as fish wheels and commissioned a system of hatcheries to sustain salmon runs for long-term consumption.[15] Through the Great Depression and two world wars, the country continued to rely on the vision of Progressive conservationists. Salmon populations were augmented with hatchery production, and wildlife managers continued to pursue efficiency in production. The unintended consequence was a decline in the salmon populations' genetic diversity. Several studies conducted by Oregon and Washington state wildlife management agencies in the 1930s and 1940s acknowledged the importance of addressing problems such as stream pollution, habitat loss, and impacts on salmon food sources. Other state and federally funded studies convinced many biologists of the "home stream theory," which held that salmon species were composed of diverse local populations adapted to their home stream environments.[16] Despite biologists' skepticism about hatcheries, decision makers continued to rely on this technological fix as the primary management tool.

In 1943, the Washington State Senate recognized that the 1918 Columbia River Compact was not preventing further decline of salmon populations. The Senate commissioned a study that identified overfishing of some runs, habitat loss and degradation, and institutional problems as the three major causes of the decline of salmon in the Columbia Basin. Recommendations for a tristate fishery commission were never implemented, perhaps because of the prospect of further development of hydroelectric dams on the Columbia. In 1946, Oregon, Washington, and the U.S. Fish and Wildlife Service developed a cooperative program, the Lower Columbia Fisheries Development Program, to mitigate the impacts of the proposed hydroelectric dams. The focus of this plan was to concentrate salmon production below the dams, clean up pollution, transplant stocks from above dams, and expand hatchery production. This program continued for many years. By 1986, hatchery production clearly was the dominant component, with 79 percent of the program's budget dedicated to hatchery operation and maintenance.

After the ocean warmed significantly in 1976 and Oregon's coho salmon declined sharply, the Oregon Department of Fish and Wildlife (ODFW) released a plan for the production and management of the coho. The plan's ten management policies were still focused on hatchery production, but natural production also was recognized as an important element. The plan fell short of expectations to increase salmon numbers and was curtailed after a few years. Harry Wagner, the former chief of fisheries for the ODFW, said the department suffered from two major flaws in implementing the plan. It assumed that ocean conditions would soon change, improving the survival of coho, and it did not encourage adequate public involvement.

Several interacting factors account for the failure of these historical salmon recovery plans. The plans focused on a single goal or target, increasing the number of salmon, and discounted the other values at stake. The plans relied primarily on a single technological fix, hatchery production, to increase the number of salmon. The plans largely ignored the adverse, unintended consequences of that fix and discounted alternatives that might have modified the multitude of human activities largely responsible for the decline of salmon populations. Finally, the development and implementation of such plans depended on the knowledge and authority of management experts, who made the important decisions. Management experts did not encourage public involvement, as Wagner noted in connection with one of the later plans. They did not perceive a significant need for local knowledge or public support. Overall, there is nothing unique about this pattern except the historical details. C. S. Holling attributed failures in twenty-three other managed ecosystems to management of a target variable by technological fix.[17] The pattern is also another example of scientific management as defined in chapter 1.

In the 1960s a series of dramatic events sparked public outrage over involuntary exposure to environmental pollution, prompting the rise of modern environmentalism.[18] This led to national legislative landmarks to clean up air and water and to the ESA of 1973. The stated purpose of the ESA is to provide means whereby endangered and threatened species and their ecosystems may be conserved. Under the act, *conserve* means to use all methods and procedures necessary to bring endangered and threatened species to the point where they no longer need protection.[19] Neither Congress nor the public anticipated the intense controversies and high costs of attempts to implement the ESA. In the Pacific Northwest, for example, protection for the spotted owl forced a precipitous drop in timber production from federal lands beginning in the late 1980s. The costs were manifest in widespread unemployment in timber-dependent areas of the region and in resentment of the heavy hand of the federal government. To date, the NMFS, now called the National Oceanic and Atmospheric Administration (NOAA) Fisheries, has listed four of the five Pacific salmon species (and sixteen of the thirty-six populations within the species) as threatened or endangered. It has also listed ten of the fifteen populations of steelhead trout. Overall, by 1999 salmon had disappeared from 40 percent of their original habitat in the Pacific Northwest, prompting the salmon crisis.[20]

## An Innovative Approach

An innovative approach began to mature into something new and significant, the Oregon Plan, under the leadership of John Kitzhaber. Roy Hemmingway, his first advisor for salmon and energy issues, recalls that the Columbia River salmon issue was particularly inflamed when Kitzhaber became governor of Oregon in 1995. "Like many new Governors, he wanted to get involved, roll up his sleeves and solve the problem," Hemmingway said. However, Hemmingway advised that the salmon issue in the Columbia River Basin, with so many jurisdictions, was too complex for the governor to make a difference during his time in office.[21] But the salmon crisis remained a high priority for Kitzhaber. The NMFS was considering listing Oregon's coho salmon as a threatened species. Kitzhaber knew that many timber-dependent communities in Oregon had been torn apart, economically and socially, after the spotted owl listings several years before. When people in his hometown of Eugene, Oregon, lost work, he was personally touched. He believed that a state-led program would be more flexible and better suited for recovering salmon than the regulations accompanying a federal listing. Moreover, having grown up in southern Oregon, Kitzhaber brought to the salmon crisis his love of fly-fishing and rafting on Oregon's rivers.[22]

Right away Kitzhaber began seeking input on how Oregon could address salmon decline. Just weeks into his term Kitzhaber visited several local watershed groups in southwestern Oregon. These watershed groups, called watershed councils, had been partially funded by the Oregon Legislature through a program for model watershed councils. The legislature began providing some funds to watershed councils in 1993 as a part of an initiative called the Watershed Health Program, which was prompted by the success of several locally initiated watershed councils, including the Applegate Partnership. Under the 1993 program, the state had provided some funding to approximately twenty watershed associations but was not really involved in a coordinated fashion.[23]

Most of the watershed councils had attracted a diverse cross-section of the local communities, including ranchers, farmers, timber industry representatives, and other landowners. This forum for local involvement promoted by the Watershed Health Program proved to be very popular in these communities. For example, one watershed council, the Coos Watershed Association, hired displaced fishers to help identify fish passage problems and rebuild the streams they once fished. Loggers in small family operations and large commercial timber companies got involved by volunteering their lands for restoration projects. Representatives from natural resource agencies such as the Bureau of Land Management also got involved, providing support to both the Coos and Coquille watershed associations from the beginning.[24]

Charlie Waterman, president of the Coquille Watershed Association (CWA), thinks that the focus on local control encouraged many people to participate in these early councils. "[Some people] were pretty upset at the federal government and suspicious. They figured the government always had more power at the table than they did. But once we got there, they could see that the landowners had as much power as the state and federal agencies did," he recalled. Local control over decisions about salmon restoration was the aspect of the watershed groups that community members really seemed to appreciate, especially with the NMFS considering a coho salmon listing. Joan Mahaffy, a rancher in the Coos watershed, expressed sentiment shared by many, saying, "We could control our destiny by recognizing the problem and deciding what to do to fix it, instead of having the federal government tell us what to do."[25]

The small scope of the Watershed Health Program supported the beginning vision for a new kind of state-funded program in Oregon. Kitzhaber was very excited by what he saw in the communities he visited. Roy Hemmingway remembers that the governor was particularly impressed by two characteristics of the community groups he visited. First, the groups had significant support from the community and were actually making changes on the ground. Hemmingway recalls the governor saying, "There are thousands of members of the Coquille Watershed Association. They have salmon spawning in a place where they just put in some boulders. It is unbelievable." Second, Kitzhaber was impressed that the groups were avoiding the kind of acrimony that had caused stalemate on the Columbia River.[26]

After his visits to the watershed councils in the spring of 1995, the governor and his advisors began considering how to structure a plan that would involve communities as well as key state and federal stakeholders in an effective and appropriate way. The effort was placed on a fast track because in July 1995 the NMFS announced a proposal to list two populations of Oregon coho salmon as threatened under the ESA. The governor wanted to avoid a federal listing, and from that point developing a state led alternative became a priority for his administration.[27]

In October 1995, Kitzhaber publicly announced the planning effort to restore the coastal coho salmon populations. Recognizing that many state-initiated restoration plans had been implemented in the past with poor results, Kitzhaber believed that he needed the support of the entire state government as well as federal agencies, the Oregon public, and private interests to address the multifaceted causes of salmon decline. He brought together an outreach team that worked with key state agency representatives and the NMFS to develop an action plan to address management practices and environmental factors that were affecting salmon populations. Determined to gain state agency buy-in to the plan, Kitzhaber brought agency directors together biweekly for several months to report progress on incorporating salmon-sensitive measures into their programs and coordinating with each other. Jay Nicholas, principal author for the state-led plan, recalls that the governor made a huge commitment in winning agency support for the effort in 1996. He also applied some pressure through budget approval. As Nicholas observed, "He was vetoing so much in his first term that he became known as Dr. No."[28]

Most government programs are centrally organized, with ideas to address a problem coming from the political center while implementation is delegated to the localities, according to Roy Hemmingway. Kitzhaber's idea was different. The state agencies were to be responsible for helping to restore salmon, but the core of this plan was to support community-based action such as conducting watershed assessments, assessing factors affecting coho salmon, and implementing restoration projects with partial state funding. In Kitzhaber's mind, the biggest problem with the ESA was its inability to address natural resource issues on private lands. In fact, invoking the ESA against private landowners, especially those who might affect aquatic species, is difficult. Section 9 of the ESA prohibits anyone, including individual landowners, from "taking" listed species. As defined in the act, *to take* means to "harass, harm, pursue," and court decisions have extended it to destruction of a listed species' habitat. However, federal agencies face difficulties in enforcing this provision of the law with respect to listed fishes' habitat because proving who is responsible for harm is difficult. Multiple factors and multiple resource users have degraded most river basins. Furthermore, in Oregon, more than 65 percent of coho salmon habitat borders on private land.[29]

Given this limitation of the ESA, Kitzhaber wanted to create an approach that would encourage the private landowners to participate. Regulations might prevent actions that harm salmon but probably would not encourage actions to restore salmon. Kitzhaber and his advisors wrote that addressing the cultural system as well as the natural system was necessary to successfully address the salmon problems. In his opinion, grassroots support for restoration was crucial. "This whole thing is about how people in Oregon acquire a deeper level of understanding that how they live their lives affects the environment in which they live. It's about changing the culture."[30] Hemmingway understood this perspective, "You don't recover salmon with orders from Salem [Oregon's capital]. You don't recover them with orders from D.C. either. People on the ground have to want to do it. You can't make them do it. You get it done through long, hard work, stream reach by stream reach and gravel bar by gravel bar."[31]

In the spring of 1996, outreach and planning teams continued working to draft a plan that would provide an ecologically sound basis for avoiding a federal listing and incorporate the idea of local planning at its core. Kitzhaber submitted a draft titled the Oregon Coastal Salmon Restoration Initiative (OCSRI) to the NMFS in August 1996. The key elements of the OCSRI consisted of cooperative agency plans, community-based action, and a plan to monitor and adapt actions based on lessons learned from experience. The NMFS was interested in reviewing the plan and making recommendations for improvement to the state and so postponed a final listing decision to April 25, 1997.[32] This signaled that the NMFS might not list the salmon in lieu of a sound state-led initiative. However, Kitzhaber still needed public support, funding, and key private interests' buy-in to be successful in implementing the plan "stream reach by stream reach."

In September and October 1996, Kitzhaber took the OCSRI to the public with a series of meetings up and down the Oregon coast. His planning teams received extensive feedback from the public, established watershed groups, environmental groups, and private landowners. Members of the CWA recall commenting on several drafts. Kitzhaber was hoping that the plan would sell the idea of maintaining local responsibility and authority for salmon recovery. It was the design that had been so popular in the first watershed groups. This approach was appealing to Oregonians, who share a legacy with other western states of desiring state control and minimum federal interference. But in order to have credibility with the NMFS deadline fast approaching, Kitzhaber needed substantial state funding. The Oregon legislature at that time had a Republican majority that was wary of environmental policies.[33] Their support for the OCSRI was uncertain until the governor won a critical partner, the timber industry.

In February 1997, the timber industry joined the effort to implement the governor's plan by agreeing to provide $13 million through a 2-year tax on themselves that would be renewed contingent on NMFS deciding not to list the coho salmon. Ray Wilkeson is the legislative director for the Oregon Forest Industries Council (OFIC), an organization that represents most of the large and midsize forest land–owning companies in Oregon. At the time Kitzhaber approached the OFIC, Wilkeson recalls that the spotted owl ESA listing was fresh on the minds of the organization's members. According to Wilkeson, the OFIC was very concerned that a coho salmon listing could affect private timber industries the way logging on public lands had been affected after the spotted owl decision. The OFIC had developed trust for Kitzhaber during his 14-year stint as a state legislator. Wilkeson and others at the OFIC believed that Kitzhaber was environmentally concerned but also an advocate for his industry-based constituents. Wilkeson said, "Kitzhaber told us that if we were willing to do our part to solve the problem with voluntary efforts, he would help keep the federal bureaucrats out of our hair. It was a win for us and the fish." In general, the timber industry believed it would be better off implementing changes to recover the fish voluntarily and maintaining a positive image in the public's eye than it would be under an ESA listing.[34]

In March 1997, following the timber industry's decision, the state legislature agreed to provide the $30 million that authors of the plan thought would be necessary to begin to weave a web of community-based watershed groups across the state and to implement other key elements of the plan. In December 1997, shortly after the legislature decided to fund the OCSRI, the governor released a supplement to the OCSRI that expanded the scope of restoration to include declining steelhead populations.[35] The governor hoped that new partners would join the effort to improve the steelhead's inland habitat, helping to realize his vision of a statewide network of grassroots restoration activities. With the steelhead expansion, the governor and the media began referring to the initiative as the Oregon Plan for Salmon and Watersheds, or the Oregon Plan for short.

In April 1997 Oregon entered into a memorandum of agreement (MOA) with the NMFS under which the state agreed to continue existing measures under the OCSRI. The state also agreed to work with the NMFS to improve other land use policies that affect the salmon, including revising Oregon's Forest Practices Act. In turn, the NMFS promised to guide the state toward actions that would make a listing unnecessary. Kitzhaber was on the verge of avoiding an ESA listing. On May 6, 1997, in an unprecedented decision, the NMFS found that the Oregon population of coho salmon did not warrant listing. This was the first time the federal government had relied on a state's conservation plan as an alternative to listing. However, this situation was short-lived as environmental groups immediately filed suit.[36]

Several of Oregon's most respected environmental groups and national organizations, including the Oregon Natural Resources Council (ONRC), the Pacific Rivers Council, the National Audubon Society, and the Sierra Club, led the suit, claiming that a decision not to list based on the voluntary efforts of the OCSRI was arbitrary. Doug Heicken, an attorney with the ONRC, explained that his organization was completely supportive of Kitzhaber's efforts to recover the coho salmon. "The conflict emerged because [the governor's office] wanted their plan to be the only solution for restoration rather than having the ESA as an accountability mechanism." Environmentalists also believed that a listing would hasten agreements or new regulations for timber and agriculture practices. Mary Scurlock of the Pacific Rivers Council, an environmental group that had been involved in forming the Oregon Plan, observed, "Things were moving incredibly slowly. Early on, there was this pie-in-the-sky idea that [the state and the NMFS] would hold hands and develop proposals together. That fell apart pretty quickly." On June 2, 1998, U.S. Magistrate Janice Stewart, of the U.S. District Court for Oregon, ruled with the environmental groups, ordering the NMFS to reconsider its decision without taking into account any parts of the Oregon Plan that were not enforceable measures. Under court order, the NMFS listed the Oregon coastal coho salmon as threatened under the ESA on October 2, 1998.[37]

At the time of the listing, the number of active watershed councils across Oregon had grown to around eighty. With help from partial state funding, the watershed councils and other groups had completed more than 1,200 stream improvement projects including stream fencing, culvert replacement, and road repairs to aid salmon passage. The plan had won the support of the state legislature and the timber industry but would lose millions from the timber tax that was contingent on avoiding an ESA listing. Oregonians expressed their frustration, believing the plan would be crippled if landowners and the timber industry withdrew their support. It was reported that "key participants in the program talk bravely of soldiering on, regardless of ESA, but can timber companies justify spending millions on Oregon's approach while also fighting the command-and-control rulings of ESA?" Kitzhaber was also understandably disappointed. He had always believed the strength of the Oregon Plan was the willingness of individuals and companies to change practices on their own land. "The whole plan is based on getting people to the table, giving them ownership, and then helping them go further than they have to go. . . . [The plan] takes about 50 to 60 percent of the woods out of production in the Coast Range, the feds could never get that kind of a cutback."[38]

Despite Oregon Plan supporters' initial fears, the timber industry remained supportive of the Oregon Plan. The timber tax was annulled in November 1998, but commercial foresters remained committed to assessing and renovating a vast network of roads that affect water quality in addition to performing other instream improvement projects and culvert replacements. This commitment was significant. Industry officials estimated that the efforts would cost companies $100 million over the next 10 years. The public also remained supportive of the Oregon Plan. In November 1998, voters approved Ballot Measure 66, dedicating 7.5 percent of net lottery proceeds to salmon restoration under the Oregon Plan. Measure 66 was passed to give the Oregon Plan a stable source of funding through 2014.[39]

Kitzhaber also pressed on, fueled by personal commitment and belief in the concept of local responsibility at the heart of the Oregon Plan. "The Oregon Plan has thousands of landowners working together to make changes in their management practices to improve habitat for salmon. It is those actions that count in species recovery," he insisted. In January 1999, the governor signed an executive order reaffirming the state's intent to play the leading role in protecting coho salmon and extending the effort to all watersheds and fisheries statewide. With the order, Kitzhaber directed state agencies to take actions to restore salmon and to mitigate actions that could reduce the likelihood of salmon recovery. State agencies were also given the directive to work cooperatively with landowners undertaking restoration activities. The comprehensive directives to state agencies in the executive order again stressed the idea that a successful restoration effort would require the entire state government and many individuals to take responsibility for the impact of their actions on salmon habitat.[40]

Later in 1999, legislation was passed to authorize Measure 66 and to create the Oregon Watershed Enhancement Board (OWEB). The OWEB is the state agency charged with supporting the Oregon Plan. The board is made up of six voting members from all regions of the state, including a tribal representative and members of five state natural resource agency boards and commissions. Five nonvoting representatives from federal natural resource agencies and the Oregon State University Extension Service also sit on the OWEB. These board members are responsible for coordinating the broad goals of the Oregon Plan, which include establishing a shared priority among state and federal government agencies for watershed and salmon recovery, encouraging local initiatives for implementing restoration efforts, and monitoring progress.

Promoting local partnerships to support watershed restoration efforts is a fundamental part of the OWEB's charge. OWEB grants are made available for five different types of activities: watershed restoration, assessment and monitoring, education, land and water acquisition, and watershed council support. Regional technical advisory committees review grant applications, evaluate the projects, and make recommendations regarding funding. The OWEB awards grants to the watershed councils on a competitive basis to fund council coordinators and watershed enhancement projects. The grants are not restricted to watershed councils; funds may also be given to landowners or soil and conservation districts that submit plans for watershed projects.[41] The OWEB decides which projects to fund on an annual cycle. The OWEB has two important policies regarding grant awards. The first mandates that the majority of the grant will go to project supplies and implementation, requiring administration costs to be 10 percent or less of the total grant amount. Second, matching funds in the amount of 25 percent of the total OWEB grant sought must be secured from other sources.[42]

Oregon's 1995 state legislature passed a bill that provided simple guidance on establishing watershed councils. The two primary guidelines are that the watershed council be a local, voluntary group and that the council should represent a balance of interested people within the watershed. These guidelines give a lot of flexibility to the interested groups in deciding how to structure their councils, although members in several recently formed watershed councils report basing their structure on successful established groups, so tried-and-true structures are diffused across watersheds. The 1995 legislation also made clear that the establishment of a watershed council should be a local government decision. Often the county board of commissioners recognizes a council as an official group. However, other city or county government bodies can also recognize the councils.[43]

The first supporters of the Oregon Plan came to the table because they wanted to maintain local control over salmon restoration in the face of a possible ESA listing. The timber industry and individual landowners were concerned about federal imposition under a listing, which provided motivation for taking action. However, even after the coho and other Oregon salmon species were listed, many people remained supportive of the Oregon Plan. Kitzhaber's leadership and vision further helped to bring people across Oregon to the table to improve habitat conditions for salmon through a new way of approaching salmon recovery.

One final point to address in the historical context of the plan is the prospect for the Oregon Plan under different state leadership. Many people interviewed for this study were concerned about what would happen once Kitzhaber's final term was over in January 2003. In March 2003, Oregon's new governor, Ted Kulongoski, pledged to oppose any attempt to roll back the state's existing environmental programs in his first speech on the environment. However, Oregon is currently facing a recession and budget crisis. Since he has taken office, Kulongoski has focused almost exclusively on economic problems and job creation. Oregon's legislature is focused on finding money for the state's education and health care systems, and some think that Oregon Plan funds will be redirected to those purposes. Considering the current budget crisis, Governor Kulongoski will face tough decisions regarding environmental legislation, decisions he may want to delay. Hinting at that strategy, the head of Kulongoski's natural resource team said the governor would wait until the 2005 legislative session to push his own environmental agenda.[44]

## Appraisals

This section considers the claims of supporters and several criticisms of the Oregon Plan, from people who are well informed on the subject. It concludes with an evaluation of these claims and further observations. Generally, the appraisals focus on the role of the watershed councils, although the Oregon Plan includes executive orders, laws, and coordinated agency efforts at the state level and is connected with regional and national decision-making structures, all of which have evolved and will continue to evolve. However, the watershed councils are the critical part of the plan that sets it apart from previous salmon recovery efforts in the state and make it relevant to adaptive governance.

### Supporters' Claims

Supporters of the Oregon Plan claim that the program has motivated broad public support for habitat restoration and salmon recovery and cite evidence to that effect. Louise Solliday, who was the director of Kitzhaber's Natural Resource Office, pointed to the growing number of watershed councils under the Oregon Plan. In 1995, before the development and implementation of the plan, there were about twenty watershed councils across the state. In the fall of 2001, the number of councils stood at more than ninety. Solliday believes that the development of the plan sparked public interest and motivated tangible public commitment to salmon recovery. Jennifer Hampel, council coordinator for the CWA, pointed to more evidence of public support for the Oregon Plan and habitat restoration at the local level. "We have people on a waiting list.

We are not that big of a watershed and are in a rural and pretty conservative area. But we still have people calling everyday wanting to do projects with us. I always point that out as one of the biggest successes."[45] Solliday also cited the legislature's continuing support of the Oregon Plan as further evidence that the public and their elected representatives support the approach to salmon recovery taken by the Oregon Plan.

The evidence cited by supporters is relevant to the Oregon Plan's goals and strategies as described by Kitzhaber and outlined in the OCSRI. According to the latter, "A basic tenet of the OCSRI is that all Oregon citizens share responsibility for the changes to the natural systems that have hurt the salmon and, likewise, share responsibility for restoration. . . . Government, alone, cannot conserve and restore salmon across the landscape. . . . The bulk of the work to conserve and restore watersheds will be done by local people."[46]

According to supporters, the watershed councils are primarily responsible for motivating so much public involvement in the Oregon Plan. The watershed councils have educated communities about their own watersheds, gaining public understanding and support at that level. Dave Sahagian, coordinator of the Scappoose Bay watershed council, believes "that the most important thing that we have done is to raise the community's conscience about the watershed. Before the council existed, people just kind of took the streams for granted and didn't know about the conditions." Ted Lorenson, a manager with the Oregon Department of Forestry (ODF), said research and education by the watershed councils on practices that harm salmon are easier for people to accept than some other approaches. For example, he said that some forest landowners he works with had old culverts that were blocking passage on their land and were willing to make changes because they were working with watershed councils, while they might have been hesitant to make similar changes suggested by an agency. Tom Paul of the Oregon Water Resources Department (OWRD) agreed that the watershed councils have been highly effective from an educational standpoint. He believes that the watershed councils are able to facilitate education because they are local groups with close ties to the community.[47]

Several council coordinators reported that people in their watersheds believe habitat restoration is the right thing to do. Supporters believe this commitment has been fostered by education through the Oregon Plan and is another reason why so many people have gotten involved with watershed councils. For example, Dana Erickson, a council coordinator in midstate Oregon, reported, "A lot of the farmers that I work with say it is the right thing to do. They want to do what they can on their own place. They don't want any pollution leaving their place and possibly contributing to pollution downstream. Water quality is a really easy thing for people to understand. It doesn't have to be all about the fish all the time, there are basic health concerns and pride in ownership that are obvious."[48] Holly Coccoli elaborated on citizens' attachments to their own lands. A council coordinator in northern Oregon, she said that some people get involved because they have heard that the council can help them to make improvements to their land such as preventing erosion. She also said that others are simply interested in learning about their community's natural resources, not because they own big tracts of land. "They like to hear what the latest fish runs are, or learn about the natural resources in our community from knowledgeable people like state biologists."[49]

According to supporters, the strategy of working in areas of possible agreement is another reason why the watershed councils have motivated broad public support. Roy Hemmingway said that he and Governor Kitzhaber understood in 1995 from their first meetings with people from Applegate and the Coquille that this strategy had been very important to the establishment and endurance of those early councils. People in the Applegate community "discovered that we know that we don't agree on this 20%, so let's not keep talking about that. Let's talk about the 80% that we can agree to. There are certain practices, things that we can do, investments we can make in the watershed that will help everyone." Dana Erickson, coordinator with the Long Tom Watershed Council, agreed that concentrating on common ground has allowed her council to keep moving forward. Erickson said many people who hold divergent opinions on natural resource practices, from pesticide use to the size of riparian buffers, nevertheless come to the watershed council meetings and are involved in restoration projects. She acknowledges disagreement on the fringes, "but everyone agrees that they want good water quality in the Long Tom and everyone agrees it should be monitored."[50]

Another major claim of supporters is that many restoration projects and changes in management practices that benefit the salmon have been implemented and probably would not have been implemented without the Oregon Plan and public support. Louise Solliday talked about the effects of one such project. "There are places where watershed councils have put large wood in the streams to create pools and riffles and they can tell you that smolt [juvenile salmon] counts in that area are way up over the last five years." Another positive change attributed to the Oregon Plan is the elimination of push-up dams that were common across the state not too long ago. Roy Hemmingway explained that push-up dams are created by forming a mud and gravel barrier with a back hoe to divert water. These structures were a cost-effective way to irrigate crops or provide water for livestock but blocked salmon migration. Hemmingway reported that the practice of making push-up dams is fast disappearing in Oregon because of the educational efforts of the watershed councils.[51]

The testimony and examples given by supporters highlight the success of the Oregon Plan in motivating citizens to make changes "stream reach by stream reach." The cumulative long-term effects on salmon recovery remain to be seen. Meanwhile, it is also important to address criticisms of the plan.

## Criticisms of the Oregon Plan

On a personal level, most of the people who criticized aspects of the Oregon Plan reported that they were enthusiastic about the public involvement motivated by the Oregon Plan and were themselves active participants in local councils or even working with the OWEB. They nevertheless criticized some aspects of the plan in a professional capacity. In doing so, they typically focused on aspects that failed to meet expectations grounded in the remnants of scientific management and revealed some discomfort with the Oregon Plan's departures from that traditional approach.

One of the most common criticisms is that restoration work under the Oregon Plan is not prioritized, planned, or implemented in a manner that benefits salmon to the greatest degree possible because these tasks have been devolved to the watershed councils. Michael Tehan, director of NOAA Fisheries' Oregon State Habitat Office in Portland, said that although the local planning process promotes education and ownership of projects, a strategic vision for guiding people to take the right actions in the right places has been a missing link in the Oregon Plan. Joe Whitworth, executive director of Oregon Trout, agreed that a lot of restoration projects have been implemented, "but if they are happening helter skelter, what is it buying?" Tehan claims the basic problem is that the biological needs of the salmon demand planning on a larger geographic scale than local watersheds. Furthermore, Tehan said that NOAA Fisheries already has a recovery planning process to analyze salmon populations to identify what the recovery goals and population viability criteria should be, and to deal with other technical issues. He said that ideally, the next step after these technical issues are resolved would be involving local groups to "spearhead the actual implementation part . . . so it is not a federal top down plan that sits on a shelf somewhere."[52]

Some people have been more directly skeptical of the voluntary approach of the Oregon Plan. They believed for various reasons that a voluntary approach means ineffective project implementation at the local level. In January 2000, the Pacific Rivers Council and Trout Unlimited released a report titled "Maximizing the Effectiveness of Watershed Councils," claiming that "within watersheds, geographical targeting of projects to ecological priorities is limited by the available pool of volunteers. This dynamic limits the implementation of even the most technically sound plans."[53] Some people are concerned that local council participants lack the expertise necessary for effective planning. According to Tehan, "One of the problems that we've seen is that [the watershed councils] have a lot of good intentions, but they don't always have access to the technical assistance that they need." According to Whitworth, " There is a lot of local input" to watershed councils, but "a number of council members are out of their depth in conceiving of how a watershed functions and how lost function can be repaired. When they get out of their depth they lose focus of what councils were set up to do."

A related criticism from environmentalists and federal agency representatives was that the Oregon Plan relies too heavily on the watershed councils to improve environmental conditions for the salmon. These people believed that the state needs to expand its approach to include tougher regulations for natural resource use and that too much emphasis has been given to voluntary recovery actions. Several of these people based their expectations for salmon recovery on the demands of the ESA. For example, Michael Tehan said,

> In my mind there has been too much attention focused on the voluntary participation part of the Oregon Plan. While that is good from the standpoint of trying to encourage people to be involved on their own terms, the problem is that it falls short in some areas that need more regulatory muscle to accomplish the objective. . . . What we [NOAA Fisheries] are saying is that under the ESA, we need to avoid jeopardy in the short term and work toward long-term recovery. We don't have any way of offering legal assurances under the ESA in terms of take if someone just plans to do better than they are today. If you are not meeting a certain level of protection, then it may not be good enough for us to issue take permits.[54]

Other people lamented the fact that watershed councils lack the formal power to stop bad practices and demanded application of regulatory powers under the ESA and strengthened state legislation. Doug Heicken, an attorney for the ONRC, one of the environmental groups that led the suit to force NMFS to list the coho salmon in 1998, offered this perspective:

> Through the Oregon Plan, watershed councils are doing good things, which is great. But they are not stopping bad things. There are still lots of bad things going on and that is why we need regulation through the ESA or through changes in the [state] Forest Practices Act so that the progressive good restorative actions of the councils are complemented by regulatory powers that stop the bad. Watershed councils don't have power, they are only good at finding solutions that everyone can agree to. . . . The focus has to be really narrow for councils to contribute.[55]

Several people who criticized the reach of state laws said that buffers (where logging is prohibited) around streams should be increased and that logging on steep, unstable slopes should be prevented to reduce erosion. Sybil Ackerman, a conservation director with the Audubon Society of Portland, said that her group had been very active in trying to convince the state to increase standards under the state's Forest Practices Act. The most recent action at that time (March 2002) was a suit against the state of Oregon filed by a consortium of environmental groups including the Audubon Society of Portland alleging that state standards were too low to improve salmon habitat. Ackerman also spoke to the role watershed councils should play. "It seems to me that [watershed councils] are very on the ground in terms of looking at restoration projects in their area. Those are positive things. What we are engaged in is sort of the broad-based changes to all forest practices. We are working on setting a standard from which the councils could then work."[56]

Dave Powers, a regional director for the EPA, summarized and elaborated the reasons why he believes the Oregon Plan cannot make enough progress to offset the harm done by poor management practices. First, he acknowledges that the voluntary nature of the watershed councils has both positive and negative aspects. On the positive side, watershed councils attract people who would not normally be interested in restoration. On the negative side, forestry and agricultural management regulations are so weak in Oregon that some watershed councils become vehicles for local industries to protect the status quo or become co-opted by groups with narrow interests other than recovery. Moreover, in his view some watershed councils have better plans, have sought appropriate technical help, and are more effective than others. More generally, Powers believes that the watershed councils would be more effective if the state had a stronger regulatory framework. The Pacific Rivers and Trout Unlimited report mentioned earlier also claims that watershed councils are inherently limited in what they can accomplish because of existing land use policies. The authors explain that necessary changes in land use practices, such as industrial forest practices, cannot be accomplished through council actions. Instead, policy changes are needed at the appropriate level of government.[57]

## Appraising the Claims

The main claims of the supporters are not disputed in these criticisms, which focus on what the Oregon Plan allegedly has not or cannot accomplish. The growing number of watershed councils and habitat improvement projects implemented by them substantiate the main claims that the Oregon Plan has motivated broad public support for salmon recovery and on-the-ground action to restore habitat. Given scientific uncertainty about this complex recovery problem, implementing recovery actions is not necessarily equivalent to recovery. But it may be the best concerned citizens and their government can do in the short run. Certainly, garnering public support for making changes to recover salmon should be recognized as an improvement over previous salmon management plans. As demonstrated by past failed plans, mobilizing broad public support is a necessary first step for the state of Oregon to gain traction on the issue of salmon decline.

It is also credible that education facilitated by the watershed councils has been essential in building and maintaining public support. Importantly, funding for council coordinators under the Oregon Plan has allowed the state to foster a network of community-based initiatives that facilitates local education about watersheds and salmon. From the information available, including interviews with stakeholders and participants across the state, it is clear that council coordinators are also essential in maintaining the day-to-day operations of the councils, allowing localized self-scrutiny and building trust among community members. For example, Dave Powers, regional director with the state's Environmental Protection Office, said that the funding provided by the state for council coordinators sets the Oregon Plan apart from other community-based initiatives in surrounding states in a positive and significant manner.[58] However, the Oregon Plan has experienced high turnover rates for these critical people, which could present a problem in developing and maintaining trust in the local communities.

A closer look at the work of coordinators is warranted by their importance in the Oregon Plan and potentially elsewhere. Most coordinators perform a variety of jobs that breathe life into the watershed councils. The coordinators are hired to do the administrative and organizational jobs that several professionals might be hired to do in another situation. They usually run a small office, keep records, and balance the budget. They organize volunteers and direct any office staff they are lucky enough to have. They coordinate council meetings and manage landowner agreements. Beyond these administrative tasks, many coordinators write the grant applications that fund the council and its activities and work with technical experts to plan projects. But perhaps most important to the Oregon Plan is the coordinators' role in facilitating education and building relationships. As appraisals in this chapter have shown, many people believe that the watershed councils in Oregon have had great success in educating community members about watershed health problems and salmon decline and in encouraging people to take action. The credit for the councils' success belongs largely to the council coordinators who work to establish the relationships and trust that lead to action.

The coordinators interviewed for this study all said in some way that they believe their role is to help the council realize goals that its members hold in common—in other words, to advance the common interest of the community. For example, Holly Coccoli, coordinator for the Hood River watershed council, believes the council exists to help its members, including various groups from the Warm Spring tribe to the agricultural community, solve problems they agree should be addressed. A council's work is controlled by its members' goals.[59] But in order to reach the point at which members are willing to share their problems and goals, a base of trust in other members and the process and must be built. The coordinators are able to build trust among the various interests in the watershed because they are also a part of the community. Unlike employees of natural resource agencies, the coordinator is not perceived as a regulator coming from the outside, trying to impose directives that were not locally generated.

Like other coordinators, Dave Sahagian invites landowners in his community to participate in the planning process. His council gives the landowner some insight into best management practices. Then it is up to the landowner to initiate a project. Landowners appreciate the invitation to participate. Coordinators noted that people were willing to undertake restoration activities because they felt that the project belonged to them too. Once trust is established in the councils, coordinators can help establish trust between local citizens and agency personnel as well. For example, in planning a project with a landowner, Dana Erickson suggested that she could bring a fish biologist with her when she came out to look at the stream. The landowner agreed even though he had refused to allow another agency fish biologist on his land a few weeks earlier. Erickson also said that it is easier for the landowners to do restoration through the councils than through agency programs.[60] Councils can be more flexible, and they can borrow expertise from the agencies. Landowners prefer to work with councils because landowners can skip the paperwork often involved in working directly with state agency programs.

Erickson views her role with the Long Tom watershed council as a "convener" of interests, which depends on listening to and telling stories. She described part of a conversation with a farmer about water quality and his distrust of the Oregon Department of Environmental Quality (DEQ). She said, "I know that you hate the DEQ, but I know a woman who went through school with the desire to help clean water the same way you do. Now she works in this agency in a cubicle with fluorescent lights overhead and her job is about regulation and people hate her. She doesn't understand exactly how that meshes with just wanting to help clean the water." At the next council meeting that farmer welcomed the DEQ representative as a member of the group. Erickson also tells people stories about the farmers. She said, "Other people think that they farm right down to the creek. But I've walked those creeks and they look great.

I don't hesitate to share my experiences with others."[61] She is the hub, the one person everyone can trust. The experiences of Erickson and other council coordinators reveal that most people want to be a part of the council at first because they want control over natural resources in their watershed. But council coordinators agreed that over time the personal relationships and respect for the common interest keep people motivated and interested.

With trust and respect for the council's purpose, the coordinator is also in a good position to initiate self-scrutiny by council members. Holly Coccoli explained that the DEQ is not a popular agency in her watershed because it regulates. But the growers in her council volunteered to allow the DEQ to monitor water on their property, partly out of self-interest: "No one wants a toxic or expensive chemical getting into the water. It is not done on purpose," Coccoli said. Erickson has had a similar experience. The members of her council wanted to start a water monitoring program. For the program, the council established ten subbasins within the larger basin that they believed should be monitored. They measured pollution levels and temperature at the confluences of all the subbasins. Previously, the DEQ had monitored the same area, the entire Long Tom River Basin, with just a few data points. The DEQ's program made it difficult for a farmer to know whether his or her activities were causing problems because the data points were so far from their land. Because the council provided more data points, the farmers are able to understand where problems are generated, sometimes on their own land. Erickson also realizes that it is more difficult for people to admit responsibility for a problem at big meetings. So she meets with people in their living rooms with a giant aerial map and the data. She says that after she shares the monitoring data, even the most conservative landowners have been willing to make changes and talk to their neighbors.[62]

The watershed council coordinators clearly play an important role in the community-based initiatives encouraged by the Oregon Plan. However, the turnover rate for council coordinators was fairly high in 2002. The average time a coordinator stayed with a council was only about 18 months. Because coordinators need time to build relationships and trust within the communities, the turnover rate is arguably too high. According to coordinators, the high turnover rate results from burnout: There is too much to do, with little compensation. Some coordinators raised funds to supplement their own salaries, but others did not feel comfortable doing that. The OWEB recently removed the cap on their annual salaries at $27,000. It is too early to tell whether that will significantly lower the turnover rate, although coordinators on average are staying in their jobs longer than they did in 2002. The coordinators remain qualified for much higher-paying jobs, but most also remain very committed to their jobs and find it gratifying to help restore watersheds and salmon.

Returning to the main criticisms of the Oregon Plan, many are framed by remnants of scientific management. As a whole, these criticisms assert or imply that salmon recovery in Oregon requires a statewide, centralized plan to identify the best priorities; that it should be designed and managed by experts from the top down; and that compliance with the plan should be enforced against challengers by the federal and state governments under the ESA and a strengthened state Forest Practices Act. It is not surprising that the Oregon Plan fails to meet these criteria: it was not designed to. The Oregon Plan was designed and justified as an innovative approach because previous plans also framed by remnants of scientific management had failed to achieve the primary goal of salmon recovery. The criticisms discount what the Oregon Plan has achieved beyond the status quo in 1995 and focus on what the Oregon Plan has failed to achieve according to criteria discredited by the test of experience over previous decades. But there is more to be said about specific criticisms.

Statewide biological priorities might be the scientific ideal for salmon restoration, but there is no evidence that such ideals are practical or politically feasible. Michael Tehan acknowledged, "We probably aren't sophisticated enough to say where the priority areas are for salmon recovery, I think that will come with recovery plans." The multiplicity of factors contributing to the salmon's decline defy any definitive identification of policy priorities on large scales. The biological diversity of salmon and the many scattered, often unrelated actions that led to their swift decline support the case for devolution and decentralization of planning over exclusive reliance on centralization, the structure of previous failed programs for salmon recovery. That case is also supported by council coordinators who emphasize the need to manage at the local watershed level. For example, Jennifer Hampel of the CWA observed, "The Coquille and Coos watersheds are right next door to each other. We both have watershed councils, but our members want to be kept local and separate. Our issues are completely different. They have estuary issues that we don't have and we have agricultural issues that they don't have."[63] The structure of the Oregon Plan is better adapted to differences and changes on the ground, where recovery actions must take place.

Furthermore, it is not politically prudent or realistic to wait for a central planning authority to become "sophisticated enough to say where the priority areas are for salmon recovery." The Oregon Plan and its predecessor have been supporting individuals and communities that have been willing and able to plan and implement restoration actions for more than a decade. This includes the owners of private lands that include 65 percent of coho habitat in Oregon. Experience shows that the landowners are likely to resist efforts by federal authorities to impose science-based priorities in a centralized plan that ignores their interests. That heavy-handed approach forces landowners with a personal interest in salmon recovery and clean water to become opponents in order to protect their other interests in forestry, agriculture, and the like. The Oregon Plan is better adapted to tapping into existing public support for salmon recovery and action and building on that support.

Public support is also a base for more sophisticated planning by the watershed councils in support of recovery actions. Jennifer Hampel explained how project planning in the CWA has matured over time. At first the CWA approached project implementation in a very opportunistic manner. They did restoration projects wherever they found a willing landowner. She pointed to a map of the Coquille watershed that was randomly covered with colored pins representing places the CWA had completed projects. Hampel said that the CWA took a lot of criticism from seemingly every corner, from agencies to environmental groups who believed their approach was too scattered to make an impact. However, she said the CWA's initial approach established contacts and gained supporters throughout the watershed.[64] More recently, the CWA has been able to identify the most probable priority areas in the watershed with help from state agencies and biologists. Because of their initial scattered approach, they now have contacts who are willing to approach their neighbors and build the support necessary to implement projects in a concentrated area.

Recall that there were several criticisms of the Oregon Plan's reliance on volunteers. In their report, Pacific Rivers and Trout Unlimited considered the pool of available volunteers under the Oregon Plan "limited" with respect to an implied standard, a larger pool they would consider satisfactory. Ironically, the existing pool is an improvement over the baseline before the Oregon Plan and an asset that would have been unused if salmon recovery had been left to paid personnel, including technical experts. Realistically, who else is available to do the work? A related criticism considers the scientific and technical expertise in the councils inadequate. However, according to every coordinator interviewed, the councils have been able to access more than adequate scientific and technical help from state biologists and others. Furthermore, the councils are the experts on their friends and neighbors, whose participation and support are necessary to implement small-scale technical alternatives that build further public support with results. For example, long-time resident Paul Heikkila recalled that the first project sponsored by the CWA removed a culvert that blocked a salmon stream running right through the middle of town. "Opening the creek was a great attention-getter in town, and young salmon were spotted upstream in a matter of months."[65] Watershed councils have found landowners willing to implement such projects on their own property because local people, who know their personalities and quirks, guide council decisions.

Although people who criticized aspects of the Oregon Plan acknowledge that it has contributed to restoration of salmon habitat, they also believe the plan is not tough enough to prevent damage in the first place. However, the Oregon Plan has already demonstrated that tougher regulations and their enforcement are not necessary for progress, at least in habitat restoration. (No one really knows what full recovery requires, and no one can know empirically until full recovery occurs.) The stalemate over strengthening the Forest Practices Act calls into question the political feasibility of tougher regulations and their enforcement at the state level. Even if they were politically feasible, there is a good chance they would limit progress to predefined standards. For example, if a more conservative standard for stream buffers could be prescribed and enforced, landowners could be forced to go that distance but out of resentment could also decide to go no further. Meanwhile, different interests still have recourse to the courts to toughen and enforce standards for natural resource use. However, if advocates of salmon recovery win the battle for tougher standards, they might lose the war for salmon recovery by alienating the many people already involved in restoration activities and by forcing them into opposition. Tougher standards are not equivalent to recovery but could unwittingly displace recovery as the primary goal.

At the federal level, it is difficult to imagine tougher standards than the ESA. Recall that the ESA has been interpreted to require all methods and procedures necessary to conserve endangered and threatened species and bring populations to the point where they no longer need protection. NOAA Fisheries is legally bound to implement the ESA; Michael Tehan noted that anything less than the ESA standard is really not "good enough for us." But experience shows that heavy-handed implementation of the ESA, without regard for the other interests at stake, creates opposition to recovery and the ESA and does not necessarily contribute to recovery. The protests and civil disobedience over the implementation of the ESA in the Klamath Basin in 2001 are a case in point (see chapter 1). Federal officials in the Upper Colorado River Basin were much more constructive when they used the ESA to bring diverse interests to the table, to negotiate their differences in the 15-Mile Reach (see chapter 2). As with most laws and policies, the practical outcome of the ESA depends on leadership, interpretation of the constraints, and the approach to implementation. The Oregon Plan and Kitzhaber's vision and leadership represent a success in bringing popular support to species recovery. A review of the track record of species recovery warrants further innovation in the implementation of the ESA. By 2000, almost 1,200 species in the United States and another 600 species worldwide had been listed as endangered or threatened under the ESA. Since the ESA was passed in 1973, only about thirty species have been delisted.[66]

It is worth noting that the goal of the Oregon Plan is similar to and motivated in part by the ESA. As stated in the OCSRI, the goal is "to restore our coastal salmon populations and fisheries to productive and sustainable levels that will provide substantial environmental, cultural, and economic benefits."[67] However, the approach of the Oregon Plan is different from the ESA's. It encourages people to identify priorities for recovery actions according to their unique local circumstances, implement them, monitor them, and adapt them to their experience. Neal Coenen, Kitzhaber's salmon policy advisor, considers the Oregon Plan a success and attributes it to people who have taken action because they believe that restoring salmon and watershed health is the right thing to do. This could not have been accomplished through regulation alone in his view.[68]

A final criticism is that some councils work better than others and, at the extreme end, that some have been co-opted to validate the status quo. However, no specific cases of co-optation were cited. Nonetheless, it must be true that among ninety watershed councils, some have better restoration plans, have sought more appropriate help, and have been more effective in restoration than others. But there is no good reason to demand that they proceed uniformly on a standardized basis according to the aspirations of scientific management. Standardization would serve special interests in control, not the common interest in recovery at costs acceptable to other community interests. Diversity is an asset, not a liability, in a quasi-evolutionary process: The rate of progress in such processes depends on implementing a number of innovations at the same time, selecting the ones that work well, deleting or modifying the ones that do not, and building on the successes further through innovation. The budget crisis in the state is an opportunity to identify and select out any council that is co-opted or otherwise ineffective. The OWEB would be well advised to fund the most effective councils if it must choose between them.

## The State's Contribution

The watershed councils and their coordinators have done most of the work to make progress under the Oregon Plan, but their work is not unusual in the larger context of other community-based initiatives. What is unique about the Oregon Plan is state support of their work, enabling the councils and coordinators to make more progress than they would have on their own. The details of the state's contribution are important for completing an appraisal of the Oregon Plan and facilitating possible diffusion and adaptation of this innovative approach to other states.

Under the Oregon Plan, the state has provided financial support. According to council coordinators and others involved in the Oregon Plan, an initial grant from the OWEB often is the boost that gets an organization rolling and initiates cumulative progress. For example, with assistance from the OWEB, the Scappoose Bay watershed council, as one of its first activities, completed a watershed assessment. A watershed assessment is a study that examines the history of the watershed, describes its features, and evaluates resources in the watershed. Through the assessment the council discovered many barriers to fish passage that could be removed by replacing old, poorly designed culverts, dams, and tide gates. On the basis of the assessment, the council obtained another grant from the OWEB, $450,000, to hire an engineer to design the culvert replacements and to implement the project. With support from the OWEB on the barrier removal project, several other organizations pitched in to help. Olympic Resource Management, one of the biggest timber companies in the area, dedicated $200,000 to the effort. The county road department volunteered $200,000, and a small city in the watershed, St. Helen, contributed $15,000.[69]

Technical assistance is another aspect of the state's contribution that has been critical in the many accomplishments of the watershed councils. In conducting watershed assessments and planning restoration projects, the councils get ample assistance from technical experts through five regional teams. Each team is staffed by representatives from the regional offices of state agencies who review grant applications for the OWEB, help coordinate interagency actions, and provide technical assistance to the watershed councils. A regional team may also have federal representatives from the Bureau of Land Management (BLM) or U.S. Fish and Wildlife Service. However, their participation is flexible, not fixed, because federal representatives volunteer their time.[70] Most of the councils draw on their regional team for help in designing projects, but like most other council activities this varies across councils. Some have more and some have less contact with personnel from different regional offices of the agencies.

Jennifer Hampel seeks technical help from state and federal agencies in designing most projects and in reviewing every project the CWA completes. For example, the ODF provided a lot of help in designing riparian planting projects. More generally, agency representatives on the board of the CWA provide a lot of help on current state law and on best practices for various restoration tasks. The local BLM office also was a tremendous help. In 2000, the BLM provided engineering services on a culvert replacement project free of charge. Hampel estimated that hiring a private engineer for that project would have cost the council $20,000. On the project review end, the CWA has a project committee with people from different state and federal agencies—the "ologists," they are called—who help review and rank the projects in terms of biological priority.[71]

Dave Sahagian reported that his council has drawn on technical assistance from natural resource agencies in the area, including the ODF, the ODFW, and the BLM. Dana Erickson also said that local agency personnel lend a lot of help to the Long Tom for planning restoration projects. She described a recent council meeting in which a landowner talked about culverts on his land that had been a problem for years by causing flooding and blocking fish passage during high flows. During the meeting, the landowner sketched a diagram of the culvert, and the next day Erickson faxed it to a contact in the ODF. The ODF contact was interested in helping and within days brought in an Army Corps of Engineers employee. A replacement project was soon implemented, thanks to the landowner's willingness, the council's contacts, and technical support from several agencies.[72]

The state's contribution also includes resources for the diffusion and adaptation of innovative solutions to problems of salmon decline across watersheds. One resource is a list with contact information for all watershed councils working in the state. The OWEB updates the list twice a year and sends it to the watershed councils. According to several council coordinators, this low-tech method has been effective in transferring important knowledge and advice. A good example is a story told by Jennifer Hampel about finding a solution to the problem of blackberry encroachment on riparian plantings.[73] Hampel's council, the CWA, has completed a number of riparian fencing projects to keep livestock from causing sedimentation by trampling the banks of salmon streams. In these projects the council often planted trees to further stabilize the banks. But CWA crews noticed that a nonnative type of blackberry often responded so intensely after sites were disturbed to plant trees that the trees were overwhelmed and died. Their first response was to cut the blackberries away from the trees as they grew. However, by the time the council work crew completed 100 miles of fencing, they realized that they could not keep up by cutting the blackberries, and the newly planted trees were in danger of dying. One option was to use a herbicide to kill the blackberry bushes, but a portion of the council firmly opposed that option. They needed a better alternative.

Hampel called several other councils on the list to see whether they had dealt with a similar problem. It turned out that one of the councils had been doing a lot of site preparation before planting trees. But in contrast to CWA, their technique had been to root out the entire blackberry bush, all the way to the bulb, to keep it from spreading after the site was disturbed. Hampel wanted to adapt this technique to solve her problem, but it was much more labor intensive than what CWA had been doing. She needed more funds to pay for the extra work. So she wrote a proposal and got a grant from the OWEB to try the new technique. It controlled blackberry encroachment, justifying the extra work and expense. This was pragmatic solution for a council that did not want to use herbicides. The story demonstrates that council members and crews are the people close enough to the ground to detect unexpected problems as they occur. It also demonstrates how they are able to develop and share innovative solutions to restoration problems. This informal, bottom–up style of problem solving is an important part of the Oregon Plan.

In addition to the list of contact information, the OWEB provides other resources for the diffusion of information across watersheds. One is an online network for council coordinators sponsored by the OWEB. Using the network, a council coordinator can send out a question on a project such as a culvert replacement. All other council coordinators get the question on the network. Often one of them has dealt with a similar question or problem before and can provide advice based on that experience. The OWEB also sponsors a conference that brings watershed council coordinators together every 2 years. This is an opportunity to share information more intensively and extensively, face to face, over a few days.

The state's contribution includes some modest changes in state and federal practices under the Oregon Plan, in addition to direct support for the work of watershed councils. This is perhaps the beginning of change from the bottom up, or vertical diffusion and adaptation. It is initiated as agency personnel see an advantage in working with the councils and each other through the Oregon Plan. Field personnel in the state natural resource agencies were the most excited about working with councils and local communities, according to Neal Coenen in the fall of 2001. Some agencies had secured funding for additional personnel to help the councils, but most personnel worked with councils on a voluntary basis. Similarly, EPA management had a "gentlemen's agreement" with staff to encourage those who wanted to work with watershed councils, according to Dave Powers of the EPA. The EPA management made it known that they considered working with watershed councils a good learning experience but did not free up additional time for them to work with the councils. The BLM reportedly had a progressive director who dedicated staff to working with watershed councils.[74]

Ted Lorenson of the ODF observed that the Oregon Plan prompted his department to step back and think about who its customers are. The department's field personnel traditionally have been organized into two groups. One group took care of regulatory issues, and the other helped landowners implement best practices and use the department's incentive programs. In some offices, field personnel have had to play both roles because of funding and distance constraints. A few of them reported that responsibility for both kinds of work allows them to be more useful to their communities and watershed councils. Because of this experience, the ODF was considering how to merge programs, in part for the benefit of local communities and watershed councils, now recognized as customers.[75]

Tom Paul of the OWRD observed that the watershed councils might enable his department to find ways to reduce consumption by educating water users, although the department's resources limit what they have been able to do. Paul also noted that his department was working more cooperatively with the ODFW under the Oregon Plan.[76] One of his agency's responsibilities under the Oregon Plan was to work with the ODFW to identify the most important places for increasing instream flows to help salmon. The agencies did create a list, and the OWRD has focused their activity on those priority places.

A possibly unexpected result of the Oregon Plan has been greater inter-agency communication and coordination, involving state agencies in addition to the OWRD and ODFW. A water quality modeler with the Oregon DEQ, Mike Wiltsey, reported a huge increase in the amount of collaboration between the DEQ and other agencies, particularly the Oregon Department of Agriculture. He said that the culture under the Oregon Plan has changed so that the agencies are encouraged to exchange information. The state conducted at least three annual workshops for agency personnel working on the Oregon Plan to get together to discuss issues across agencies.[77]

Wiltsey also reported an example of public involvement under the Oregon Plan helping the DEQ to meet its own goals. The DEQ is responsible for monitoring and improving water quality in the state. As required by the Clean Water Act, streams that fall below a certain level of water quality must have a total maximum daily load (TMDL) analysis completed by the DEQ. In the late 1990s, a group of environmental interests sued Oregon to force the DEQ to expedite its TMDL process. As a result of that suit, the DEQ is now working under what Wiltsey viewed as a very ambitious timeframe to complete TMDLs on all streams in the state's ninety-one subbasins by 2007. Many DEQ staffers were uncertain they could meet the goal. The DEQ's TMDL process intersects with the work of many watershed councils in the state because improving water quality for salmon habitat and community well-being is paramount for many of the councils. Part of the DEQ's responsibility under the Oregon Plan was to work as closely as possible with local initiatives in regulating water quality. At first, that expectation seemed as if it would be a tough tradeoff between getting the DEQ's work done and working with the local initiatives.

One of the first TMDL processes involving a local initiative proved to be very helpful to the DEQ. The Umitilla subbasin is located in the northeastern part of the state upstream from where the Umitilla River flows into the Columbia River. Here the water quality problems are caused primarily by non–point source pollution, mainly from agricultural runoff, exacerbated by a lack of riparian shade. A watershed council from the Umitilla subbasin formed a technical committee with representatives from local offices of other state agencies, county officials, and citizens from the town of Pennalton. The DEQ worked very closely with this technical committee to collect data and develop a plan for identifying pollution problems, culminating in a TMDL and a water quality management plan to decrease pollution levels. Collaborating on data collection and sharing information with the technical committee was fairly time-consuming, according to Wiltsey. But he considered that time spent up front worthwhile in the end. The members of the local initiative were much more comfortable hearing from the technical advisory group than from the DEQ. As the TMDLs are finalized, communities have a process to petition the DEQ for changes. Because the technical committee had been so closely involved, people in the Umitilla Basin were comfortable approving the TMDL and did not need to petition the DEQ for changes.

Wiltsey believes that working with local initiatives and watershed councils will help the DEQ meet its TMDL target. Some staff at the DEQ are enthusiastic and see opportunities for the department in working with watershed councils and other local initiatives, whereas others are not. However, he believes more agency staff will begin to appreciate opportunities for collaborating with local groups as the DEQ continues to work with local groups in completing some of the TMDL processes.

Stepping back from the state's contributions, the bottom line of this appraisal is that the Oregon Plan has made some progress in salmon recovery at acceptable cost to other interests since it was established in 1995. This progress is most impressive in comparison with Oregon's failed salmon recovery programs of the past. The Oregon Plan has fostered more public understanding and support for salmon recovery. It has implemented a large number of small projects to restore salmon habit. And it has been able to build on these successes.

Whether its past and projected progress are sufficient to recover the salmon remains to be seen. As Louise Solliday noted, recovering any species is a long, hard process that takes decades, and evaluating overall progress in salmon recovery is difficult. Annual salmon returns are not sufficient because so many variables, including ocean conditions, interact to cause changes in salmon returns each year. Thus it is difficult to isolate the effects of the Oregon Plan or any other factor. Despite the difficulty of isolating the impact of recovery actions implemented under the Oregon Plan, it enjoys the support of informed citizens, many of whom can see for themselves results on the ground, such as smolts upstream from a culvert that once blocked their migration in the middle of town until the CWA removed that culvert. The OWEB has found that such anecdotal evidence is more effective than salmon population numbers in maintaining the support of the public and public officials. Legislators and other government officials support the plan because their constituents can see progress on the ground, even if they have not been able to measure it.[78] Satisfied constituents are a surrogate indicator for salmon recovery in the common interest and are worth something in a democracy.

In conclusion, it is worthwhile to review experience under the Oregon Plan as an example of adaptive governance and as a departure from scientific management. First, the plan is an adaptation to real people who have multiple interests and are capable of learning, not the cardboard caricatures whose interests are fixed and limited to support or opposition to salmon recovery. Under the failed plans of the past, people in favor of clean water and salmon recovery were forced into political opposition to defend their other interests in forestry, agriculture, and the like. Under the Oregon Plan, those interests have been integrated with habitat restoration to advance salmon recovery and the common interest, building public support at the same time. Furthermore, the adaptive governance demonstrated by the Oregon Plan provides an example of uniting interests and public support for species recovery efforts rather than dividing interests and creating roadblocks to implementing recovery actions.

Second, the plan is an adaptation to differences and changes on the ground. People in the watershed councils and their work crews are close enough to the ground to detect unexpected problems such as blackberry encroachment in riparian areas and to find solutions to them. They are also able to capitalize on opportunities, taking into account the differences from one watershed to the next. Under the Oregon Plan, people on the ground have made progress addressing the multiple biological and human factors that affect policy problems and solutions in each watershed. Salmon recovery in Oregon is not one problem but many different problems in different places.

Third, the decentralized structure of decision making under the plan is adapted to the uniqueness of problems, opportunities, and solutions in each watershed. Some experts under the spell of scientific management still aspire to control recovery actions uniformly from the top down. Under the Oregon Plan, state financial, technical, and other resources have supported recovery actions but not attempted to control them. The decentralized structure facilitates the diffusion and adaptation of experience across watersheds and has begun to modify practices in state government, when and where agency officials realize the advantages of cooperating with watershed councils and with each other. In short, the Oregon Plan is a model of adaptive governance worthy of consideration by other states.

NOTES

1. Jeff Barnard, "Grass-Roots Effort to Save Salmon in Oregon; Protection Could Hinge on Local Solutions," *Los Angeles Times* (October 29, 1995), p. 4 of the Metro section, is the source of all quotations in this paragraph.

2. See Roy Hemmingway, "Salmon and the Northwest," *Open Spaces Quarterly* 1 (1998), pp. 2–11, for a description of the migration routes of Pacific salmon and habitat use. For a

description of salmon ocean navigation see John Daniel, "Swimming Among the Ruins," in *Oregon Salmon* (Portland: Oregon Trout, 2001), pp. 7–10.

3. For a discussion of the life history and characteristics of Pacific salmon and steelhead, see R. .J. Childerhouse and Marj Trim, *Pacific Salmon and Steelhead Trout* (Seattle: University of Washington Press, 1979). See also Charles F. Wilkinson, "The River Was Crowded with Salmon," *Crossing the Next Meridian* (Washington, D.C.: Island Press, 1992), ch. 5, for a detailed description of the salmon life journey.

4.. See Wilkinson, "The River Was Crowded," p. 184, for the river metaphor. See Hemmingway, "Salmon and the Northwest," p. 7, for numbers of returning Columbia River salmon.

5. For example, early hydraulic mining and more recent irrigation withdrawals have reduced salmon populations in the Sacramento–San Joaquin Basin.

6. See Northwest Power Planning Council, Derek Poon, and John Garcia, *A Comparative Analysis of Anadromous Salmonid Stocks and Possible Cause(s) for Their Decline*. Unpublished report prepared for the Northwest Power Planning Council, Portland, Ore. (June 1982), p. 176, table 24.

7.. For a description of the Pacific salmon historic interaction with the ecosystem and causes of their decline see Oregon Forest Resources Institute, *Saving the Salmon* (Portland: OFRI, 1998), and Oregon State University Extension Service, *A Snapshot of Salmon in Oregon* (Corvallis: Oregon State University, 1998).

8. See State of Oregon, *Oregon Coastal Salmon Restoration Initiative, Executive Summary* (OCSRI) (Salem: State of Oregon, 1997), p. 4, cited hereafter as the OCSRI, for Oregon coho salmon population numbers. See Katie Greene, "Coastal Cool-Down," *Science* 295 (March 8, 2002), p. 1823, for a description of temperature changes in the Pacific Ocean. Oceanographers believe that temperatures in the North Pacific flip from warm to cool every 20 to 30 years in a phenomenon called the Pacific Decadal Oscillation.

9. Jim Lichatowich, *Salmon Without Rivers* (Washington, D.C.: Island Press, 1999), p. 63.

10. Quote from author's interview (March 1, 2002) in Scappoose Bay with Dave Sahagian, watershed council coordinator for the Scappoose Bay Watershed Council.

11. OCSRI, ch. 5.

12. Wilkinson, "The River Was Crowded," p. 188.

13. See Wilkinson, "The River Was Crowded," pp. 190–192, for a description of early state actions to improve salmon populations.

14. See OCSRI, ch. 5, for a description of historical programs for salmon restoration in Oregon.

15. See *Oregon Salmon,* pp. 33–41, for a historical perspective on the evolution of salmon politics in Oregon.

16. Chapter 5 of the OCSRI cites several studies from the 1930s and 1940s that explored the home stream theory and other salmon characteristics.

17. Lance H. Gunderson, C. S. Holling, and Stephen S. Light, eds., *Barriers and Bridges to the Renewal of Ecosystems and Institutions* (New York: Columbia University Press, 1995), pp. 6–9.

18. Richard N. L. Andrews, *Managing the Environment, Managing Ourselves: A History of American Environmental Policy* (New Haven, Conn.: Yale University Press, 1999), especially ch. 11.

19. ESA of 1973, 16 U.S.C. §§ 1531–1532 (2002).

20. As defined by the NMFS, species determined by the NMFS to be in imminent danger

of extinction throughout all of a significant portion of their range are listed as endangered. Species determined by the NMFS likely to become endangered in the foreseeable future are listed as threatened. Definitions of listed species and the number of salmon species listed were accessed online at http://www.nwr.noaa.gov/1salmon/salmesa. On the salmon crisis see Lichatowich, *Salmon Without Rivers*.

21. Author's interview (November 5, 2001) in Salem with Roy Hemmingway, Governor Kitzhaber's first salmon policy advisor and Oregon plan manager in Salem, Ore.

22. See "Protecting the Coho," *High Country News* (September 18, 1995), for the long-anticipated federal announcement. See Carlotta Collette, "Oregon's Plan for Salmon and Watersheds: The Basics of Building a Recovery Plan," in Philip Brick, Donald Snow, and Sarah Van De Wetering, eds., *Across the Great Divide* (Washington, D.C.: Island Press, 2001), pp. 140–149, for a description of Kitzhaber's reaction to the spotted owl and the ESA and his visits to the model watershed councils.

23. OCSRI, ch. 17A, pp. 1–2. Also author's interview (November 5, 2001) in Salem with Louise Solliday, at that time head of the governor's Natural Resource Office.

24. Jon Christensen, "Bringing Salmon Back," *American Forest* 103 (Winter 1998), pp. 16–20.

25. Ibid., p. 17.

26. Hemmingway interview.

27. See "Proposed Threatened Status for Three Contiguous ESUs of Coho Salmon Ranging from Oregon Through Central California," 60 *Federal Register* 38011 (proposed July 25, 1995), for the NMFS proposed listing.

28. See Hemmingway, "Salmon and the Northwest," p. 11; and OCSRI, p. 4. Quote from author's interview (November 5, 2001) in Salem with Jay Nicholas, science and policy advisor for the Oregon Watershed Enhancement Board in Salem. The "Dr. No" nickname refers in part to Kitzhaber's medical degree and practice of emergency medicine for 13 years in Roseburg, Ore.

29. See Hemmingway, "Salmon and the Northwest," p. 11, for a discussion of the administration's ideas for the structure of the state-led plan. See "Governor's Statement on Coastal Coho Decision," *State of Oregon Press Release* (1998), accessed online at http://www.oregonplan.org/PR-06-04-98.html for Kitzhaber's opinion on the ESA and the Oregon coho listing. See Jennie L. Bricker and David E. Filippi, "Endangered Species Act Enforcement and Western Water Law," *Environmental Law* 30 (2000), p. 735, for a description of Section 9 of the ESA and of the difficulties federal agencies face in enforcing the provision.

30. See Carlotta Collette, "The Oregon Way," *High Country News* (October 26, 1998), p. 11, for the Kitzhaber quote.

31. See OCSRI, pp. 6–9, for the administration's view on addressing the cultural system. See Collette, "The Oregon Way," p. 9, for the Hemmingway quote.

32. See the OCSRI, p. 1, for a brief history of the NMFS's decisions regarding the plan and listing of the coho.

33. Collette, "The Oregon Way," p. 145.

34. See Hemmingway, "Salmon and the Northwest," p. 11, for the timber tax agreement. Wilkeson's views from author's interview (February 27, 2002) in Salem with Ray Wilkeson, legislative director for Oregon Forest Industries Council in Salem.

35. State of Oregon, Executive Order No. EO 99-01, *The Oregon Plan for Salmon and Watersheds* (Salem: State of Oregon, 1999), hereafter cited as 1999 Executive Order.

36. See the 1999 Executive Order for a brief history of the Oregon Plan, including NMFS actions.

37. The Heicken quote is from the author's interview (February 25, 2002) in Eugene with Doug Heicken, attorney with the Oregon Natural Resources Council in Eugene. Scurlock quoted in Michelle Nijhuis, "Salmon Plan Can't Stand Alone," *High Country News* (August 17, 1998). See 1999 Executive Order for listing details.

38. See Bob Applegate, "Governor Releases State of Salmon Report," Oregon State press release, accessed online at http://www.oregon-plan.org/PR-05-20-98.html for watershed council accomplishments. See "ESA Listing Muddies Oregon Plan," opinion piece, *The Columbian* (August 9, 1998), for the supporter's quote. See Collette, "The Oregon Way," for the Kitzhaber quote.

39. Timber industry's commitment from Wilkeson interview. See Oregon State, *The Oregon Plan for Salmon and Watersheds; Annual Progress Report 2001,* for passage of Measure 66. Section 16 of Oregon's 1997 House Bill 3700 required that the timber tax be terminated the first day of the month after a listing of coastal coho.

40. See Applegate, "Governor Releases State of Salmon Report," for Kitzhaber quote; 1999 Executive Order.

41. Funding for the OWEB comes from the state legislature and lottery receipts. Legislatively approved funding for watershed restoration projects has grown substantially in recent years. The 1995–1997 biennium budget was $5.5 million, the 1997–1999 budget was $20 million, and the 1999–2001 budget was $32 million. See Oregon State, *The Oregon Plan for Salmon and Watersheds; Annual Progress Report 2001.*

42. See the Watershed Enhancement Board Web site for program policies, accessed online at http://www.oweb.state.or.us.

43. See the OCSRI, ch. 17A, p. 3, for a summary of the requirements for a watershed under the 1995 state legislation.

44. See "Kulongoski Delivers Speech on Environment," *Associated Press and Local Wire* (March 25, 2003), and Michelle Cole, "Cost of 'Green' Initiatives May Color Lawmakers' Decisions," *The Oregonian* (April 18, 2003).

45. The quote is from the author's interview (November 7, 2001) in Coquille with Jennifer Hampel, council coordinator for the Coquille Watershed Council in Coquille, Ore. Other material is from the Solliday interview.

46. OCSRI executive summary, pp. 1, 3.

47. Author's interview (March 1, 2002) in Scappoose Bay with Dave Sahagian, council coordinator for the Scappoose Bay Watershed Council in Scappoose Bay, Ore. Author's interview (February 27, 2002) in Salem with Ted Lorenson of the Department of Forestry in Salem, Ore. Author's interview (February 26, 2002) in Salem with Tom Paul of the Water Resources Department in Salem, Ore.

48. Author's interview (February 25, 2002) in Eugene with Dana Erickson, council coordinator for the Long Tom Watershed Council in Eugene, Ore.

49. Author's interview (November 6, 2001) in Hood River with Holly Coccoli, council coordinator with the Hood River Watershed Council in Hood River, Ore.

50. Hemmingway interview; Erickson interview.

51. The quote is from the Solliday interview; see also the Hemmingway interview.

52. Author's interview (February 27, 2002) in Portland with Michael Tehan, director of the Oregon State Branch of NMFS in Portland. Also author's interview (March 1, 2002) in Portland with Joe Whitworth, executive director of Oregon Trout in Portland.

53. See Mary Scurlock and Jeff Curtis, *Maximizing the Effectiveness of Watershed Councils: Policy Recommendations from Pacific Rivers and Trout Unlimited* (2000), p. 5. Accessed online at http://www.pacrivers.org/alerts/watershed.html.

54. Tehan interview.

55. Heicken interview.

56. Author's interview (February 28, 2002) in Portland with Sybil Ackerman, conservation director for the Audubon Society of Portland, Ore.

57. Author's telephone interview (April 11, 2002) with Dave Powers, regional director for rangelands and forests with the Ecosystems and Communities Office of the EPA in Portland, Ore. See also p. 4 of the *Pacific Rivers and Trout Unlimited* report.

58. Powers interview.

59. Coccoli interview.

60. Sahagian and Erickson interviews.

61. Erickson interview.

62. Coccoli and Erickson interviews.

63. Quotes are from the Tehan and Hampel interviews.

64. Hampel interview.

65. Quote from Collette, "Oregon's Plan for Salmon and Watersheds," p. 143.

66. Holly Doremus and Joel E. Pagel, "Why Listing May Be Forever: Perspectives on Delisting Under the U.S. Endangered Species Act," *Conservation Biology* 15 (2001), p. 1260.

67. OCSRI, front cover.

68. Author's interview (November 8, 2001) in Salem, Ore., with Neal Coenen, salmon policy advisor to Gov. Kitzhaber in his last term. Also, Hampel and Sahagian interviews.

69. Sahagian interview.

70. Coenen interview.

71. Hampel interview.

72. Sahagian and Erickson interviews.

73. Hampel interview.

74. Coenen and Powers interviews.

75. Lorenson interview.

76. Paul interview.

77. Author's interview (March 1, 2002) in Portland with Mike Wiltsey, water quality modeler in the Science and Data Department of the Oregon Department of Environmental Quality in Portland.

78. Author's interview (November 5, 2001) in Salem with Ken Bierly, deputy director for the Oregon Watershed Enhancement Board in Salem, Ore.; Nicholas and Solliday interviews.

# 6. Community-Based Forestry Goes to Washington

CHRISTINA M. CROMLEY

ON JUNE 24, 2002, senators Bingaman (D–N.M.) and Craig (R–Idaho) introduced the Community Based Forest and Public Lands Restoration Act (S. 2672). The cosponsors were senators Cantwell (D–Wash.), Domenici (R–N.M.), Feinstein (D–Calif.), Murray (D–Wash.), Smith (D–Ore.), and Wyden (D–Ore.). The bill directs the Agriculture and Interior departments to invest in ecosystem restoration and maintenance activities using community-based approaches. At a June 2002 hearing on the bill, Senator Bingaman explained that over the past several years, "two important facts [have become] clear. First, forests and adjacent communities depend on one another for their long-term sustainability. Second, our national forests and public lands are in desperate need of restoration to establish healthy, fire-adaptive ecosystems and to improve water quality and quantity."[1] The bill passed in the Senate Energy and Natural Resources Committee but has yet to move to the full Senate and the House. It nevertheless integrates almost a decade of efforts by practitioners of community-based forestry and national policymakers on behalf of healthy forests and healthy communities. It also demonstrates the bipartisan support and influence of this small grassroots movement.

Before going to Washington, D.C., practitioners of community-based forestry began working together to clarify a common vision including priorities. First, they relied on open, inclusive, and transparent processes to find common ground on the overriding goal: stewardship of the land and its communities. They continue to rely on such processes to encourage the meaningful engagement of diverse interests in forest activities at the community level. In addition, they rely on monitoring and evaluation to improve stewardship decisions and practices. Finally, they mobilize investments in stewardship. These became the four cornerstones of community-based forestry: process, stewardship, monitoring, and investment.

One of the leaders of the movement, Lynn Jungwirth, characterized its significance for members of the Communities Committee of the 7th American

Forest Congress. "It has been said that history is littered with odd happenings that were allowed to fade away into nothing instead of being seized on as a new beginning. The Forest Congress, the work of community-based groups, and the programs and the projects you, [our members], are now developing are wonderful and encouraging 'odd happenings'" that may turn out to be a new beginning.[2] These odd happenings help distinguish the community-based forestry movement: loggers working side by side with environmentalists and businesspeople; community members and scientists working together, with each group recognizing the unique expertise of the other; people integrating public and private investments for stewardship in and around their own communities; and Democrats and Republicans introducing bipartisan legislation. It is no surprise that community-based forestry has been called the "we movement."[3]

This chapter is intended to clarify and illustrate adaptive governance at the national level by harvesting experience from community-based forestry. The movement can serve as a model for other groups of community-based initiatives that need Washington's help to achieve their objectives. This chapter focuses on the movement as a loosely organized effort affecting national legislation in support of community-based forestry in rural communities around public lands. However, the movement also is concerned with forestry policies in urban communities and on private lands, and its strength and vitality depend primarily on the practice of community-based forestry. Nevertheless, practitioners of community-based forestry have found it worthwhile to go to Washington as an important part of advancing common interests in their communities, as formulated in the four cornerstones. There are certain challenges they could not adequately address in their communities alone. Foremost among these are inflexible officials in government agencies, unbending representatives of national interest groups, and prohibitive federal laws and regulations. Community practitioners must identify and work with officials and interest group representatives interested in improving stewardship of the land.

The first section of this chapter reviews the organization of the community-based forestry movement from its origins on the ground to its presence in Washington. The second section describes national programs and legislation the movement has influenced. The third provides an interim appraisal of accomplishments and remaining challenges, together with a few recommendations for meeting those challenges. The conclusion summarizes this case as an example of adaptive governance. Before proceeding, it is important for readers to know that in 2001 and 2002 the author was director of forest policy for American Forests in Washington and in that position was closely associated with many of the people and some of the events considered here.

## Organization of the Movement

Community forestry began out of necessity. Forest policies and practices from the late 1800s throughout the 1900s left national forests and their resources in what many consider an unhealthy condition. Traditional timber harvesting removed the biggest, most valuable trees, thereby lessening the economic value of the forest and altering its species and habitat. A fire suppression policy for 80 years prevented low-intensity fires from burning small trees and downed wood, leaving many western forests overstocked with fuel. Too many trees increase the risk of catastrophic fire and result in over populated, unhealthy stands that facilitate the spread of diseases and insects. In response to declining forest conditions and pressure from environmental advocates, Congress passed several pieces of environmental legislation in the 1970s to protect forests from further degradation. But misguided timber management practices and the use of environmental legislation by environmentalists to sue land management agencies often had adverse, unintended impacts on the health of communities and the forests that surround them.

The impacts of these practices have been felt in places such as Hayfork, in Trinity County, California, where Lynn Jungwirth lives. She runs the Watershed Research and Training Center, a nonprofit organization that retrains loggers to do restoration work on the land. More than 30 percent of employment in Trinity County depended on the timber industry until the late 1980s.[4] Timber harvests from federal lands dropped from 7.2 million board feet in 1989 to 2.4 million board feet by 1993, a 66.7 percent drop in timber harvests.[5] By 1996, the last large sawmill in Hayfork closed permanently. With the loss of the timber industry, it is difficult for residents in these rural communities to find living-wage jobs. This trend continues today. In August 2003, the *Spokane Spokesman Review* ran a story on Bill Jenkins, a former sawyer in Naples, Idaho. Jenkins lost his job when the Louisiana–Pacific Corporation closed its Bonner's Ferry Mill in Boundary County. At $7 an hour, the remaining local jobs pay half of what Jenkins earned at the mill, and unemployment in Boundary County reached 13 percent in July 2003. He may have to move to find work, an option he is reluctant to pursue.[6]

Practitioners working independently began organizing at the local level to overcome similar environmental, economic, and social problems. For example, in 1998 a $5-million renovation of La Fonda, Santa Fe's oldest hotel, was made possible when Forest Trust Lumber in northern New Mexico linked local businesses producing specialty woods and standard lumber to urban markets. In northern California, local foresters were doing market research to determine the feasibility of selling fine-grained lumber cut from trees that grew in dense thickets, suppressing their growth. Hundreds of similar efforts were occurring nationwide at the time.[7] Back in Naples, Idaho, Mayor Darrell Kerby and Chuck Roady, a forester who worked for the former owner of Bonner's Ferry Mill, were working with other community members in 2003 on the possibility of retooling the mill to produce a different line of products. Roady said, "When a community is down and out, you pretty much have to be an opportunistic group."[8]

Working opportunistically at the local level often is not enough, however, as practitioners engaged in the community forestry movement have learned. The Quincy Library Group (QLG) was one of the first and perhaps the most famous community group to go to Washington for help. The QLG began organizing in Quincy, California, late in 1992. Bill Coates, a former Plumas County supervisor, and Tom Nelson, a Sierra Pacific Industries forester, invited Michael Jackson, a local environmental attorney and no friend of the timber industry, to work together to save the local community. The QLG soon included business owners, school officials, timber union leaders, and many others. They developed a Community Stability Proposal to protect wilderness areas, scenic river corridors, and riparian areas; to reduce the threat of catastrophic wildfires; and to sustain the community economically. The proposal included thinning densely forested areas and selecting individual trees and groups of trees to supply timber for local sawmills. After local Forest Service officials declined to implement the proposal, members of the QLG decided to go to Congress. They worked with their delegations to pass the Herger–Feinstein Quincy Library Group Forest Recovery Act. The bill was first introduced in the House in February 1997 and passed in October 1998 as a rider to the fiscal year 1999 Interior Appropriations Bill. The act directed the Forest Service to conduct a 5-year pilot project based on the QLG's Community Stability Proposal.[9] As of April 2004, the Forest Service had developed, in conjunction with QLG, a fiscal year 2004 Program of Work and fiscal years 2005 to 2009 Implementation Plan. The Quincy case illustrates the need for practitioners to seek help from members of Congress and the ability of local Forest Service officials to defy the will of Congress and their own neighbors. When they went to Washington, the diverse interests integrated in the QLG focused on advancing their local common interest.

In contrast, the community-based forestry movement has been involved in legislation benefiting communities and forests generally. One of the first attempts to expand beyond a local issue to integrate the interests of multiple community groups was the Roundtable on Communities of Place, Partnerships and Forest Health that met October 6–7, 1995, in Blairsden, California. The roundtable came to be called the Blairsden meeting. It was convened by the Lead Partnership Group (LPG), then a consortium of nine community-based, bioregional, and watershed groups including QLG. (As of June 2004 the LPG included roughly twenty groups.) The LPG was assisted by Forest Community Research, a local group, and American Forests, a national nonprofit conservation organization. These organizers sought to encourage "dialogue with national interest groups to discuss perspectives, to reduce mistrust of and opposition to local needs, and to demonstrate that community and partnership groups are not interested in local control or home rule."[10] In addition to LPG members, roundtable participants included representatives from five environmental organizations, seven "bridge groups" that connect local practitioners and policymakers in Washington, eight timber industry and private land groups, and two Forest Service employees. The interests of LPG members at that time collectively covered 13.5 million acres in northern California and southern Oregon.[11] Their missions range from identifying cultural issues in forestry to providing restoration training for displaced forest workers. They consist of representatives from the timber industry, environmental groups, and others interested in expanding the role of community- or place-based decision making.

Three challenges arose during the Blairsden meeting that remain challenges today in the community forestry movement. First, organizers had to develop common ground within their own groups. Second, they had to engage representatives of national interest groups in the meeting and on issues. Third, they had to communicate effectively with such representatives on complex subjects. Organizers addressed these challenges by identifying and developing papers on five practical issues: fire and fuels, forest restoration, reinvestment, social and economic monitoring, and stewardship contracting. Organizers say these were "difficult issues in which to find common ground." The papers identified both agreement and disagreement among participants. The roundtable did not focus on the papers, but preparing the papers "[sensitized] LPG members to their differences and commonalities so that they could later convey a sense of mutual understanding and respect for differences to the national groups. . . . [Without them] the groups would not have achieved the collective voice that they did."[12] "Our power has been in ideas," according to Gerry Gray, vice president for policy at American Forests.[13]

Organizers also helped national interest groups understand the complexity and diversity of issues covered by community groups. They reported that "participants acknowledged the [community] groups' difficult work, respected them for their efforts, and wondered whether these group processes might not be adapted effectively elsewhere."[14] National groups also recognized that they had the power to sway the perceptions and votes of federal decision makers on community-based forestry issues—in effect, a veto over community involvement in national-level decisions.[15] Among these groups were the American Forest and

Paper Association, the National Hardwood Association, the Sierra Club, The Nature Conservancy, and the National Wildlife Federation.

In 1996, about a year after Blairsden, the Seventh American Forest Congress convened in Washington, D.C. This was the second major event in the empowerment of community-based forestry at the national level. The theme of the Congress was "many voices, a common vision." Several ballrooms and breakout rooms at the Sheraton were abuzz with discussions between environmentalists, Native Americans, consultants, loggers, restoration workers, students, academics, policy and community leaders, and others. Voices were raised and tears shed. Environmentalists believing that the community movement was a front for the timber industry carried signs saying "many voices, a *corporate* vision." One forester and Yale professor responded to a sign carrier, "Young man, I think you're wrong."[16] Despite the emotions and dissenting views, participants identified a common vision and guiding principles. In this process, they built relationships, gained understanding of other perspectives, and recognized an appreciation for collaboration. One active participant in and observer of community forestry said of participants in the Congress, "Their lives, their communities, and their forests have never been the same."[17]

One of the most significant outcomes of the Forest Congress was creation of the Communities Committee, one of the few active committees remaining from the Congress. According to Carol Daly, current president of the committee, it is "clearly the leading voice for communities' ideas about forestry. For a long time, communities weren't present at the table when important decisions were being made about the future of the nation's forests. Now we are heard and we're making a difference."[18] The Communities Committee began as an informal group but applied for 501(c)(3) status in January 2003 and has since received it. This allows the committee to create "a distinct identity and voice of [their] own."[19] Previously, the informal status of the committee required that members work through groups such as American Forests to take official policy positions.

Local and regional groups are the core of community forestry, but the Communities Committee gave them a collective voice. With the Forest Congress, participation by national partners in community forestry began to solidify. For example, Gray recalled that "around the time of the Forest Congress, we at American Forests were working on better defining our niche in forest policy."[20] He and Maia Enzer, then director of the Policy Center, asked community leaders how they could be most helpful. Practitioners identified the need for a bridge group in Washington, D.C. In response, Gray says they "developed partnerships with a number of community leaders and visionaries who work with us to bring the lessons and voices of community foresters into the Washington, D.C. policy environment."[21]

One of the first and most novel attempts to link practitioners to national-level policymakers occurred on May 22, 1997. Senator Larry Craig (R–Id.), then chair of the Senate Subcommittee on Forest and Public Land Management of the Energy and Natural Resources Committee, asked the Communities Committee to help organize a workshop on community-based forestry. The workshop departed from a traditional congressional hearing, in which committee members sit above witnesses much like a judge in a courtroom, hear testimony from those witnesses, and ask questions in a formal proceeding. The physical setting and procedures express the traditional relationship between Washington powerhouses and witnesses.[22] In contrast, Senator Craig and his staff member Mark Rey worked with the Communities Committee through Enzer and Gray at American Forests to use the interactive format of a workshop.[23] Senator Craig and congressional staff sat at a table with workshop panelists, including six members of the Communities Committee, a grassroots activist from Plumas County, California, and representatives from the Timber Producers Association of Michigan and Wisconsin, Inc., the California and Nevada office of the Wilderness Society, the American Farm Bureau, and the Pilchuck Audubon Society. The six community panelists included were Lynn Jungwirth, Jonathan Kusel of Forest Community Research, Carol Daly, Wendy Hinrichs Sanders of the Lake States Forest Alliance, Dan'l Markham of the Willipa Alliance, and Jack Shipley of the Applegate Watershed Protection Association. Observers sat beyond the immediate roundtable but also participated in the discussion.

Community panelists reviewed the four cornerstones of community forestry and discussed the interdependence of economic, ecological, and social needs. Jungwirth, for example, emphasized that "community based forestry is not about subverting environmental laws. Community forestry is about a meaningful role for a local voice, local knowledge, [and] local experience in a decision-making process about natural resources. It is not about local control."[24] She added, "Community-based forestry is about changing the role of forest industry to support stewardship which depends on a high-skill, in-place workforce that knows the landscape. It is not about no forest products production from public lands."[25] Criticisms of community forestry also arose. Louis Blumberg of the Wilderness Society called community-based forestry "an untested and risky model of decision making" that could cause resource damage.[26] The interactive format allowed rich discussion about these differences of opinion. When Craig asked what attempts were being made to integrate community-based interests with national interests and whether they were successful, panelists advised him that multiparty monitoring of resource management might be the most promising method of integration. When he asked how federal land management agencies can incorporate community-based interests better, panelists responded that earlier engagement of communities and more open sharing of information by the agency were critical.[27]

About a year later, on June 23–28, 1998, Gray and Enzer held a workshop on community-based forestry in Bend, Oregon. The Bend workshop was the third event that helped practitioners at the national, regional, and local levels articulate a shared understanding of community-based forestry. A seventeen-member steering committee included practitioners, scientists, agency officials, and interest group representatives who identified topics and participants. The steering committee developed six working groups to provide "a conceptual framework" for community-based forestry. Working groups used a collaborative process to develop, in 3 days on site, draft papers on complex topics that integrated diverse interests and values. Four topics discussed in Bend became the cornerstones of community-based forestry: process, stewardship, monitoring, and investment. Organizers consider the process successful. They described the central dynamic as "the work groups' ability to build trust and open rapport among their members, a critical factor as they grappled with complex and controversial issues." Gray and Enzer compared the week to final exams week, filled with a range of emotions from joy and relaxation to frustration and anger. They also said, "It is impossible to convey the energy and emotion of the workshop, or the participants' enthusiasm for sharing ideas and experiences about community-based ecosystem management."[28]

Maia Enzer of Sustainable Northwest in Portland, Oregon, worked with partners to organize the fourth major event, a regional meeting on December 12–14, 2001, in Portland. The official name was "Working Together to Facilitate Change: 2001 Pacific Northwest Community Forestry Public Lands Policy Organizing Meeting." This meeting helped practitioners assess the current situation and plan for the future. (Community-based practitioners not only preach monitoring, they also practice it.) It was different from the meetings described earlier in that it was the first to focus on linking regional organizing to the national community forestry movement. One goal was developing and prioritizing messages for key national policy issues. Another was exploring ways for groups in northern California, the Pacific Northwest, and the northern Rockies to affect national policy and dialogue with decision makers, interest groups, and the media. Still another was creating an "asset map" of participants' capacity for affecting policy and identifying their needs and gaps in Washington.

Organizers included staff of Sustainable Northwest, the Watershed Research and Training Center in Hayfork, California, and Wallowa Resources in Wallowa County, Oregon. The Portland meeting was sponsored in part by the Surdna and Packard foundations.[29] The meeting lasted 2 days and included thirty-five people from twenty community-based forestry groups. National groups included American Forests, the Communities Committee, the National Network of Forest Practitioners (NNFP), and the Pinchot Institute. Regional groups came from Oregon, Washington, Idaho, northern California, and Montana. Only three of thirty-eight invitees declined to attend, indicating the demand for an organizational meeting like this and a collaborative relationship between the participating organizations.[30]

Before and during the meeting, groups identified twelve policy issues. Given a lack of resources to deal with all of the issues and overlaps between them, groups focused on four issue areas: adequate appropriations and funding, contracting and procurement practices, collaboration with communities, and the National Environmental Policy Act (NEPA) and the Endangered Species Act (ESA). For each issue area, a group clarified problems, desired outcomes, key messages, and strategies.

First, participants expressed concern over lack of consistent, adequate, and long-term funding for and investment in ecosystem restoration and maintenance. They agreed to continue focusing on the budget and appropriations processes, advocating investment in the key programs of the Forest Service and Bureau of Land Management (BLM) that help deliver federal funds to practitioners. The budget and appropriations processes are opportunities to fund specific programs on an annual basis. But over the years these processes also allow community-based groups to build and maintain relationships with each other and with environmentalists, resource agencies, members of Congress, and others.[31]

Second, because agencies use contracts to achieve work on the ground, contracting provides a vehicle for practitioners and resource agencies to advance stewardship of the land and communities. However, participants agreed that "the current [contracting] system was designed to fit industrial forestry and is not a good fit for restoration and maintenance." They identified a need for "new tools for new times." The tools actually exist, but barriers prevent their implementation. Organizers wrote that "there was broad concern over the lack of agency capacity to utilize fully existing and special authorities for the purposes of restoration and maintenance in a way that provides high skills, high wage jobs for local and small/micro businesses."[32] Participants also agreed to continue supporting stewardship contracting authorities and monitoring provisions in the legislation described in this chapter. They understood that advocating these programs might require more information on agency use of special authorities and how their use affects the environment, communities, and the mobile workforce.

Third, participants affirmed collaborative processes. They expressed a desire to continue collaborating with interest groups, including environmental, industrial, labor, and academic groups, while being mindful of both the positive and negative political implications of such collaboration. However, they noted that the "ability—and willingness—of federal land management agencies to work with communities and external interests"[33] is inconsistent. Some officials collaborate, and some do not, at various levels. Participants in the Portland meeting considered two potential solutions: multiparty monitoring and performance indicators. The institutionalization of multiparty monitoring, they believed, can facilitate collaboration by integrating traditional science with practice-based, local knowledge. In addition, performance indicators provide a means to institutionalize collaboration by forcing agencies to "link the collaborative process to the production of tangible, measurable results." They recognized that "collaboration re-engages people in the democratic process" and recommended that "if you treasure what you measure, measure collaboration."[34]

Finally, participants talked at length about the NEPA and the ESA, with a focus on the NEPA and process issues. Overall, "community groups want to ensure the law promotes stewardship, rather than prevents it." Practitioners agreed with the NEPA's intent but expressed concerns over its implementation and use in litigation. These concerns included the time, costs, and lack of agency capacity to complete NEPA analyses, the inability of the NEPA process to improve stewardship restoration projects, and the effects of litigation on communities and the land. One participant suggested that the NEPA "needs to be reinvented as a vehicle for restoration." Participants also emphasized their desire to engage with policymakers in rethinking the NEPA, saying, "We want to be part of improving the NEPA *process* to *add value to decisions—not just reduce [the] time it takes to complete.*"[35]

In addition, Portland meeting participants discussed the potential to engage the media more fully to institutionalize community forestry practices and build understanding of them. Real stories and real-life examples are assets in working with the media, participants believed. However, the potential is limited because "the media responds to conflict, controversy, timeliness and sexiness"; "these characteristics rarely reflect community forestry and sustainable development issues."[36] Unlike the media focused on conflict, practitioners of community forestry seek common ground.

According to organizers, "the success of this [Portland] meeting can be attributed to the small, focused and adaptive group of participants who fully engaged in the process offering their immeasurable expertise and insights."[37] One participant, Melanie Parker of Northwest Connections, "noted that the coalition must be construed on the concept of 'we'—to be powerful and significant, it must be broadly inclusive of local business leaders, environmentalists, industry, recreation interests and others." A major part of the enduring strategy is to share lessons on the ground with policymakers in Washington.

## National Legislation and Programs

Organization of the community-based forestry movement is an essential part of its capacity to influence legislation and programs in Washington, D.C. This influence includes new as well as existing programs in which the recurrent themes are the four cornerstones: process, stewardship, monitoring, and investment. Of the many different pieces of new and existing legislation that practitioners have influenced, the most important for community-based forestry are Economic Action Programs (EAPs), stewardship contracting, the National Fire Plan, and the Community-Based Forest and Public Lands Restoration Bill. They are considered in this section. In addition, practitioners sought to secure benefits for communities and their environments in selected provisions of the newer Healthy Forests Restoration Act of 2003 and their implementation.

### Economic Action Programs

The Forest Service's EAP is a vital source of technical and financial assistance for practitioners of community-based forestry. The EAP was created under several pieces of legislation and internal Forest Service policy and guidance in the early 1990s. Its goal is to help forest-dependent communities and businesses become sustainable and self-sufficient. The Washington office of the Forest Service coordinates and oversees the EAP, and officials at the forest and regional levels administer the program. The EAP grants average $35,000 and are awarded to eligible communities, counties, and tribes dependent on natural resources to develop strategic plans and implement natural resource–based projects to diversify rural economies. Eligible projects include community action plans, technology transfer to businesses and communities, market or feasibility studies, natural resource–based business cooperatives, community development staff to perform activities in a community action plan, natural resource–based art and craft industries, and projects that fill gaps left by other programs. Once communities build their capacity, they can apply for larger U.S. Department of Agriculture (USDA) Rural Development grants, on the order of $1 million, that are used to improve infrastructure.[38]

The EAP allows regions to select diverse projects based on local context and needs. This decentralized and flexible structure is vital to its success. For example, a $32,000 EAP grant helped the community in Seward, Alaska, conduct a feasibility study and designs for the Alaska Sealife Center. The center now employs almost seventy people full time and hosts more than 300,000 visitors annually. In Neopit, Wisconsin, the EAP helped the Menominee Nation Tribal Forestry Enterprise stay in business. The enterprise has been profitable for several years

and was recognized nationally and internationally for sustainable forestry practices.[39] The EAP's cost-share funds helped the Camino Real Ranger District in
the Carson National Forest in northern New Mexico collaborate with local
communities to address a suffering economy, deteriorating natural resources,
and continuous appeals and lawsuits. The work in Camino Real won the Innovations in American Government award sponsored by the Ford Foundation
and administered by the Kennedy School of Government (see chapter 3).

One of the most important effects of the program is leveraging federal dollars. In a letter to Congress requesting continued funding for the EAP, Nancy
Farr of the Partnership for a Sustainable Methow in northern Washington said
that an EAP grant of $193,249 helped her community secure $442,797 in matching funds. Such leveraging "carries the value of the initial EAP dollars far into
the future."[40] In another example, the Forest Service invested $45,000 of EAP
funds to develop value-added wood products in western Pennsylvania. This
seed money led to a private investment of $120 million and created 160 manu-
facturing jobs.[41] In 1998, the Forest Service helped more than 2,800 natural
resource–based rural communities strengthen and diversify their economies.
More than six hundred of those communities developed strategic plans that
prescribed means for building skills to address social, environmental, and economic changes.

The Forest Service is formally accountable for the EAP through annual appropriations, self-initiated assessments, and congressional oversight including
several hearings. In hearings on the EAP before the Senate Energy and Natural Resources Committee on June 30, 1999, Michael Rains of Cooperative
Forestry in the Forest Service used the results of EAP funding provided to the
Camino Real Ranger District as an illustration of the program's success.[42] More
generally, witnesses acknowledged challenges, but their overwhelming message
was the remarkable success and approval of the EAP. Nevertheless, the program
repeatedly is burdened by internal strife and budget cuts and by obscurity in
the Forest Service. In 1997, when invited by Senator Bingaman to champion
the EAP at a budget hearing, former chief Michael Dombeck instead presented
statistics on private forest land ownership, as if he were unfamiliar with the
EAP. According to one observer of the hearing, "If Dombeck is familiar with
the Economic Action Programs administered throughout rural America by his
own agency, he doesn't tell the Senate Budget Committee."[43] In 1999, several
members of Congress took the nation's prosperity at the time as a justification
to eliminate the EAP.[44]

The president's proposed fiscal year 2003 budget attempted to eliminate the
EAP. Diane Snyder of Wallowa Resources in Oregon remarked, "The administration says that it wants benefits to go to communities, but they are taking away

the best mechanisms we have to do just that."[45] Even environmental groups, many of them suspicious of the Forest Service and community-based groups, support the EAP. Peter Nelson, policy director for Biodiversity Northwest, said, "The EAP helps rural communities build the infrastructure they will need to transition from a commodity-based economy to one based on stewardship," adding that "it doesn't make sense to end the program at this point."[46] Agricultural groups also benefit from the EAP. Ellen Stein, executive director of Community Agriculture Alliance in Colorado, said that "if EAP funds are not restored, other worthy projects will also be losing an important funding source that builds community capacity, strengthens community resilience, and supports community economic diversification."[47] These comments all come from letters written to members of Congress in an effort to restore the funding eliminated from the president's proposed budget.

The EAP has received additional funding under the National Fire Plan in recent appropriations bills. National Fire Plan community assistance activities fall into four categories: fire suppression and prevention, hazardous fuel reduction, restoration, and assistance with hazardous fuel use. The multiple uses for these funds are intended to help link fire fighting, hazardous fuel reduction, and use of small-diameter trees for subsistence and business purposes. For example, EAP funds can be used to develop community fire plans that help to improve fire suppression coordination and direct hazardous fuel reduction money to areas of highest need. In fiscal year 2002, the Forest Service received a total of $38.1 million, including $25.7 million for the EAP itself and another $12.4 million to be used in the EAP under the National Fire Plan for rural development through forestry activities aimed at reducing the risk of destructive wildfire in national forests. In fiscal year 2003, the Forest Service received $26.3 million for the EAP and $5 million for the EAP under the National Fire Plan, for a total of $31.3 million. In fiscal year 2004, they received $25.6 million, although the president's budget proposal included nothing for the EAP. The president's budget proposal for fiscal year 2005 once again eliminated funding for the EAP, requiring communities to continue to fight for funding for a program that has proven results year after year.

## Stewardship Contracting

Recall that participants in the Portland meeting identified the need for "new tools for new times." The stewardship contracting program addresses the need for new tools by providing innovative contracting mechanisms more in line with the Forest Service's and the communities' new goals. Experiments with stewardship contracting began in the 1970s and 1980s when people recognized the need for changes in the way the Forest Service contracted for work. Contracting laws and regulations in the Forest Service arose from its historical focus on producing timber.[48] This focus required timber contracts to sell timber and service contracts to purchase goods and services such as disposing of brush buildup from timber sales and planting trees. The old system of timber contracts and service contracts remained in place even as the agency was shifting away from timber production to restoration and maintenance of healthy ecosystems.

In the mid-1990s, community groups and the Forest Service began considering changes to existing contracting laws. It was about this time that the Flathead Forestry Project (FFP) in Montana worked with contractors who wanted to focus on "what's left on the land, not what's taken off of it."[49] The FFP also worked with the Forest Service and other community groups to develop innovative contracting mechanisms, including some mechanisms that required new legislative authority and some that did not. Meanwhile, the Forest Service asked national organizations for assistance to help identify how to use the current system to promote stewardship and to identify contracting mechanisms requiring new legislation. In October 1996, a scoping session facilitated by the Pinchot Institute led to innovative ideas for contracting mechanisms. Participants included the FFP, the Watershed Research and Training Center, the Ponderosa Pine Partnership, the NNFP, the National Association of State Foresters, the Society of American Foresters, and American Forests. They urged the agency to find ways to manage vegetation to maintain and restore ecosystems and presented ideas based on earlier agency experiments with service contracts in the 1980s and early 1990s. They also urged the Forest Service to collaborate with nonfederal entities when developing new mechanisms and when testing the new tools as a pilot project.[50] Many of the innovative ideas identified in the Pinchot workshop entailed legislative changes.

Community-based practitioners were involved in writing and supporting passage of the initial legislation, Section 347 of the fiscal year 1999 Omnibus Appropriations Act (P.L. 105-277), to bring about changes to existing contracting laws. This section granted the Forest Service new authorities to contract with private and public entities to achieve land management goals on national forests and to meet the needs of local and rural communities. It included five contracting mechanisms. First, exchange of goods for services allows the agency to combine or "bundle" a timber sale with a service contract.[51] Contractors can accept some or all of the forest products from work done on Forest Service land in payment for their services. Second, receipt retention allows the agency to reinvest portions of the profit from selling commercial products in local stewardship projects rather than returning revenues to the general treasury. Third, designation by description or prescription (also called "end results contracting") allows a contractor to develop the method to achieve an end result described by the agency. Otherwise, the agency must mark every tree to be cut or left on a treatment area. Fourth, best-value contracting allows the agency to consider factors such as past performance and technical approach when choosing a contractor. When not applying stewardship legislation, the agency must award timber sales to the highest bidder. Finally, multiyear contract legislation extends the allowable period for a stewardship contract from 5 to 10 years.

The stewardship contracting program has been growing. The initial legislation granted authority to implement up to twenty-eight demonstration projects. Interior Appropriations Acts for fiscal years 2001 and 2002 each authorized an additional twenty-eight projects, for a total of eighty-four. In addition, the fiscal year 2003 Interior Appropriations Act (P.L. 108-007) authorized the stewardship contracting program through 2013, extended the authorities to the BLM, and removed any limits on the number of projects that could use stewardship contracting authorities. This expansion of the program came as a rider in the appropriations bill without hearings, open discussion, or even awareness of the rider among stakeholders until just before passage of the bill. The expansion of the program for fiscal year 2003 also required program-level monitoring only. In contrast, the initial legislation in 1999 required both program- and project-level monitoring. In particular, section 347(g) required the Forest Service to report annually to the appropriation committees of the U.S. House and Senate. It directed the agency to provide project-level information in these reports and to establish a multiparty monitoring and evaluation process, a key component of stewardship contracting.

Congress directed the agency to establish a multiparty monitoring and evaluation process to assess each demonstration project, to test the potential for greater collaboration between agency officials and staff and external stakeholders, to assess the potential of new authorities to facilitate effective implementation, and to assess the potential of stewardship contracting to meet the needs of local communities. Multiparty monitoring and evaluation are not equivalent to scientific research projects, which are designed to test hypotheses that can lead to generalized results and often take much longer to complete. Multiparty monitoring is designed to provide more timely feedback on whether ecological, economic, and administrative goals are being achieved in a specific place. It is a practice-based approach to improving restoration decisions.[52] For practitioners, multiparty monitoring is the primary oversight mechanism for these projects. It is designed to capture lessons learned and to build relationships based on credibility and trust by engaging diverse groups to work together.

In July 2000, the Forest Service awarded a contract to the Pinchot Institute to oversee the multiparty monitoring process. The institute worked closely with the agency and its local, regional, and national partners, many of whom were involved in the October 1996 workshop, to establish a framework for monitoring. The framework includes local, regional, and national monitoring teams. Local teams consist of interested stakeholders, local or national. To help on the regional level, Pinchot subcontracted with four organizations: the Flathead Economic Policy Center in the West, the Montezuma County Federal Lands Program in the Southwest, the Watershed Center in the Pacific Northwest, and the Pinchot Institute itself for the East. The subcontractors provide guidance to local teams to ensure consistency in collecting and reporting data, distribute funds for monitoring, provide technical assistance to and gather lessons learned from local groups, and assist in the monitoring process. The national team consists of representatives from the regional teams and national organizations. In addition, American Forests subcontracted with the Pinchot Institute for outreach to national groups that might not be aware of or involved in stewardship contracting.

The local, regional, and national teams coordinate with each other in the monitoring process. All participants have formally equal standing. A national framework has been developed for consistency, but monitoring proceeds from the bottom up. Local teams develop site-specific monitoring methods to reflect site-specific conditions, to build trust, and to show respect for local expertise and involvement. The regional teams, also multiparty, interact with local teams to synthesize and analyze data. They also assess the success of the projects on a regional scale and the administrative effects of the program on the agency. The national team assesses the program from a national level, covering issues such as forest policy; links to local, regional, and national interests; and improvements in agency accountability. The national team collaborates with the regional and local teams to identify lessons learned and to assess whether the authorities meet legislated objectives. Thus local citizens participate at all levels to capture their expertise and experience within the community and to build trust.

As of September 30, 2003, the Forest Service had completed nine pilot projects and had initiated work on sixty-eight.[53] They have multiple goals that include wildlife habitat and forest health improvement; improvement in forest structure; watershed restoration; environmental education; reduction of threats from wildfire, insects, and disease; improvement in recreational opportunities and viewsheds; local community development; and development of innovative markets and processing of byproducts of restoration.[54] The Forest Service had completed treatment on about 13,800 acres and plans to treat about 158,000 additional acres.[55]

Like many other aspects of community forestry, however, the story of stewardship contracting is perhaps best told from projects on the ground. One project that has met with success and won approval by participants and national-level policymakers is Grassy Flats. This stewardship demonstration program in northern California involves thinning 272 acres of the Trinity National Forest, maintaining a 305-acre plantation, building a shaded fuelbreak on 211 acres, and eliminating more than 4 miles of road. The collaborative team that helped design and monitor the project includes agency employees, a mill owner, local residents, and environmental advocates.[56] In the spring of 2000, congressional staff visited Grassy Flats on a community-run field tour. The Forest Service coordinator of the Hayfork Adaptive Management Area, Andrei V. Rykoff, noted on the tour that "it's a new thing for us. We're talking about what the land needs and trying to treat all of those needs at the same time." Kira Finkler, then a staff member of the Senate Energy and Natural Resources Committee who attended the tour, commented, "This is such a breath of fresh air—a bigger idea than traditional either/or politics. We can have healthy communities and healthy forests. . . . If the people say that's what they want, a bigger piece of the pie will go to natural resources." Mark Rey, then a staff member of the Senate Energy and Natural Resources Committee, was enthusiastic about the stewardship work and cooperation between the agency and local contractors.[57]

The monitoring has helped to engage stakeholders at the local and national levels and has generated some data on the usefulness of contracting mechanisms. Numerous projects reported that combining activities into one contract helps increase efficiency by reducing the number of contracts to prepare, advertise, and award. Project coordinators report that combined contracts for multiple goods and services allow more comprehensive ecosystem treatments, fewer entries onto a site and thus fewer adverse impacts on the land, and the creation of opportunities for multiskilled workers to work longer periods of time on projects closer to home. According to Brian Cottom of the Greater Flagstaff Forests Partnership and a participant in two stewardship projects, the program gives "rural practitioners ways to continue to work in the woods, and [it] allows the Forest Service to use practitioners as tools to achieve its land management goals."[58] Although numbers are lacking on the actual amounts of time and money spent on stewardship contracting, the U.S. General Accounting Office reported in June 2004 that projects generally used preaward and postaward financial controls such as mechanisms to ensure completion of specific work tasks before contractors were paid.[59]

Monitoring also shows that stewardship contracting demonstration projects often experience roadblocks, litigation, and delays. Agency planning and implementation processes have been particularly frustrating for practitioners. In July 2002, Andrea Bedell Loucks of the Pinchot Institute told a House Agriculture Subcommittee that only thirty-one stewardship contracting projects awarded between 1999 and 2001 had completed assessments under the National NEPA, of the projects being monitored. (At the time of the hearing, only fifty-six of the eighty-four projects authorized were being monitored.) Of those that had completed the NEPA, thirteen faced appeals or litigation. It was unclear whether the litigation was related in any way to the projects' status as stewardship projects. Dan Oakerland, project leader for the Monroe Mountain project in southern Utah, said their project "is two years beyond schedule due to delays in the NEPA process."[60] In addition, although statistical data are lacking, anecdotal data suggest that the process was slower than a typical contracting process because the Forest Service and its clientele were learning a whole new way of doing contracting. Contracting officials had to interpret new authorities. Contractors might have been reluctant to bid on a new type of contract; some projects received no bids. In addition, some contractors might have been unable to hire enough subcontractors to handle combined contracts for goods and services with many different types of work. These difficulties might be ameliorated as the participants learn how to do stewardship contracting. Meanwhile, the delays are frustrating to all involved.

Congress occasionally holds oversight hearings on the program. For example, the House Agriculture Subcommittee on Department Operations, Oversight, Nutrition and Forestry held a hearing on July 18, 2002. The appraisals there also were mixed. Few groups objected to the purposes of the legislation. However, the exemptions and new authorities in the law were controversial. Environmental groups were most concerned about goods for services and designation by description. Goods for services, they said, creates "perverse incentives" to log more trees than necessary so the agency can generate funds for services. Designation by description, they said, lacks adequate control to ensure that contractors are not taking more wood than necessary to fulfill the treatment prescription. Such controversy has led community groups to express support for the program and at the same time caution against premature expansion. The hearing showed that participants believe that "we just don't have enough information yet to know how well the stewardship contracting process works in practice."[61] But representatives of community groups also are pleased with the results so far. Lynn Jungwirth, for example, said that "the new authorities provide more flexibility to do complex restoration in a manner which provides benefit to rural communities."[62]

Carol Daly, chair of the Communities Committee and president of the Flathead Economic Policy Center in Montana, also expressed concern to the House subcommittee over institutional barriers within the agency. Daly noted problems with inconsistent project-level management, information flows, and investment and budgeting, as well as insufficient training and support for personnel involved in the stewardship program. She also noted agency resistance at various locations and across organizational levels to collaborate with external partners, disincentives, and a lack of rewards to collaborate. For example, she quoted an assistant district ranger who collaborated with a community "tirelessly" for 3 years on a stewardship program. He gave up a chance for promotion to stay with the project and said, "I've probably hurt my career at this point, but I didn't feel I could leave at this stage." She said, "He shouldn't have had to make that choice." She recommended that "effective collaboration and innovation should be encouraged, evaluated, and rewarded on par with work on achievement of other, more traditional, performance targets."[63] Daly also recommended that personnel receive training and resources for collaborative processes and that timber sale and service contracting officers be taught how to work together.[64]

In addition to multiparty monitoring and congressional oversight hearings, the U.S. General Accounting Office, the investigative arm of Congress, completed a study in June 2004 on the status of contracting projects; the extent to which agencies have contracting and financial controls in place; the steps agencies have taken to involve communities in designing, implementing, and evaluating stewardship contracting projects; and each agency's plans for future stewardship contracting activities. They found that the Forest Service generally used preaward and postaward controls, accounted for retained receipts, and incorporated procedures to ensure that contractors completed work before receiving payment. However, they found that the Forest Service provided limited guidance on soliciting and incorporating multiparty involvement in stewardship projects and "may have missed valuable opportunities to strengthen their projects."[65]

Practitioners of community-based forestry have struggled to keep the stewardship contacting program at a smaller scale until it is "debugged." In 2001, a provision was added to the 2002 Farm Bill in the House that would have given the Forest Service blanket authority to use stewardship contracting mechanisms nationwide rather than on a limited number of projects. Many practitioners feared that the premature expansion of the program would undermine the trust they built with the environmental community through the small scale of the program and multiparty monitoring. Senate staff opened the process on a bipartisan basis to develop a provision that satisfied all parties. A revised version of the stewardship contracting provision was developed and included in the Senate version of the bill, but the provision was dropped altogether in the final bill. As noted earlier, the fiscal year 2003 Interior Appropriations Bill expanded the program through a closed process. Practitioners and their national partners were concerned over the lack of public debate and transparency.

The permanent expansion of the program despite the misgivings of practitioners gives the appearance, whether true or not, that the environmental community is right in its claims that stewardship contracting is merely a method for the Forest Service to return to logging for profit. For example, the American Lands Alliance claims, "The Bush Administration's aggressive attempt to gut environmental laws and protections signals their willingness to give away trees and free management reign to private timber interests landscape wide."[66] Mike Leahy at Defenders of Wildlife acknowledges that "stewardship contracting can make sense" if it is applied comprehensively at the watershed level, if best-value contracts are used to achieve desired end results, and if ecological disturbance is minimized. "However," he continues, "like previous Forest Service reinvention schemes, it appears that stewardship contracting is being co-opted to promote and entrench logging rather than restore forests and help communities as promised."[67] In addition, the concerns first expressed in the debate over expansion in the Farm Bill remain. They center on whether communities have learned enough about how the projects work to achieve the goals of restoration, promote community benefit, and build a more collaborative and practice-based approach to stewardship. The long-term effects of the expansion remain to be seen.

## National Fire Plan

In 2000, wildfires burned 8.4 million acres of forested land in the United States, almost twice the 10-year average. The rise in destructive wildfire is expensive: Costs for fire suppression were approximately $1.4 billion in 2000, $900 million in 2001, $1.7 billion in 2002, and $1.3 billion in 2003.[68] The situation is likely to remain the same or worsen in the near future. Many western forests are fires waiting to happen because of fire suppression policies over the decades. These policies allowed small trees to create a dense thicket of fuel that burns intensely when fire strikes and fallen dead trees to catch on the limbs of standing live trees, creating a ladder for fires to climb to the crown of the forest. The result is a buildup of hazardous fuels. Other factors such as weather, wind, and drought affect the intensity of wildfires, but the main factor that humans can address is the buildup of hazardous fuels. Congress recognized the need to reduce this buildup and saw it as an opportunity to provide training and work to local communities. A program started in 2001 under the National Fire Plan addresses fire risk and community needs.

In 2001, Congress allocated $1.9 billion to the National Fire Plan to help address the wildfire problem. Title IV of the fiscal year 2001 Interior Appropriations Bill (P.L. 106-291) allows the USDA Forest Service to expend $240 million of the $1.9 billion total for wildland emergency management and community-based forest restoration efforts. Similar language was contained in the fiscal year 2002 and 2003 Interior Appropriations Bills, although funding varied: The USDA received $209 million in 2002, $236.6 million in 2003, and $250.3 million in 2004 for hazardous fuel reduction, including activities that benefit community-based forest restoration efforts. As part of this broader effort, Congress provided funding to build, maintain, and provide work for a restoration workforce in local communities, a workforce that can help reduce fuel buildup in the forests surrounding their communities. The bill links restoration work with community benefit by providing expanded authority to facilitate public–private partnerships. Existing Forest Service processes, including the NEPA, administrative funding priorities, and lack of monitoring, present potential barriers to meeting the goals of the authorities under the National Fire Plan. However, this response to destructive wildfires in the West is "the first time there's been a written edict from Congress to benefit local economies from restoration work and to get some commercial return from public land," according to Diane Snyder of Wallowa Resources in Oregon.[69]

The bill seeks to provide employment and training opportunities in rural communities and includes provisions recognizing the importance of planning and monitoring. To provide employment and training opportunities, Congress gave the Forest Service and the Department of the Interior authority to use grants, contracts, or cooperative agreements to conduct hazardous fuel reduction work. These are three mechanisms agencies use to get work done with nonfederal labor. Whereas grants and cooperative agreements can be used with noncommercial organizations such as nonprofit groups, existing contracting laws allow contracts to be used for the most part with businesses only. Because many community-based groups are not in traditional businesses, Congress waived prohibitive contracting laws—when conducting hazardous fuel reduction work—to allow the Forest Service and the Department of the Interior to award contracts to a variety of community organizations, including nonprofits, Youth Conservation Corps crews, or other entities that will hire or train a significant percentage of local people. This clearly indicates congressional direction to the agencies to expand competition for fire-plan related activities to nonprofits, states, and other entities not typically permitted to partner with the Forest Service in contractual relationships. The result could be improved stewardship and increased investment in community and forest health, depending on implementation.

The Appropriations Bill goes further by specifically stating that the Forest Service can use such criteria as the "ability of an entity to enhance local and small business employment opportunities in rural communities." The bill's conference report also directs the agencies to give preference to local workers and youth groups when developing hazardous fuel reduction projects. These provisions encourage the Forest Service both to work with many different types of community groups and to consider potential community benefit when planning and conducting hazardous fuel reduction activities. To emphasize monitoring, the bill allows grants, contracts, and cooperative agreements to be used for monitoring activities. This provision recognizes that monitoring can be done by nonfederal entities. To emphasize collaboration and planning, the conference report for the bill directed the agency to work with the Western Governors' Association to develop a 10-year collaborative state–federal strategy for fuel reduction and forest restoration on lands at risk of destructive wildfire. Federal agencies, tribal and local governments, and stakeholders were identified as appropriate parties to participate in the development of such a plan. Lynn Jungwirth participated with numerous other stakeholders, including representatives from several government and state agencies, the Wilderness Society, the National Association of Counties, the National Cattleman's Beef Association, and the American Forest Resource Council, in the development of the Western Governors' Association's *10-Year Comprehensive Strategy Implementation Plan*.[70]

The Forest Service must report to Congress on its activities conducted with this funding to show that it is using the money as Congress intended. In addition to many congressional hearings, a number of community groups and researchers nationwide have been monitoring the implementation of the National Fire Plan. Both quantitative data and qualitative reports from specific communities indicate that the legislation has led to progress in many communities and regions. The Ecosystem Workforce Program at the University of Oregon reports that in Oregon and Washington "the Forest Service used the local preference language of the Title IV authority, which led to local contractors capturing proportionately more of the ecosystem management Fire Plan contracts than was the case with contracts funded through normal channels."[71] They also report that hiring by the Forest Service for permanent positions to implement the National Fire Plan seemed to benefit rural community residents: One-half to two-thirds of employees hired to implement the National Fire Plan did not have to relocate. In addition, these jobs paid above the median wage for the poorest rural communities and paid above minimum wage for contract fire suppression crews. Data on BLM implementation were not conclusive. This may be the only study completed of the aggregate effects of the legislation.

Specific communities have reported both progress and remaining concerns over implementation of the Title IV language. The rural fire district in Frenchtown, Montana, used $50,000 in National Fire Plan funding to hire a ten-person crew to help residents thin dense thickets of trees around a hundred homes. The homeowners donated $100 each to the project. As fire chief Scott Waldron explained, "We want them to be part of this work, not just have someone doing the work for them."[72] In Wallowa County, Oregon, residents used National Fire Plan money to build a 400-foot community fuel break adjacent to the Wallowa–Whitman National Forest. This fuel break will help improve safety around a 1.4 million–acre wooded area vulnerable to wildfire.[73] In Catron County, New Mexico, the Catron County Citizen's group began working with the USDA Forest Service to develop a plan for thinning hazardous fuels from the Gila National Forest and other forest land in the county. The county purchased the Stone Container mill in New Mexico to process the logs. Bob Moore, director of the Catron County Citizen's group, expects that local workers can thin approximately 2,000 acres, or about 5 to 10 million board feet, per year in the county. So much work needs to be done that it would take 50 years for loggers to do a first thinning.[74] Overall in the Southwest, contracts under $25,000 are granted to local operators.[75]

However, community monitoring and congressional oversight have shown that written edicts do not always lead directly to achievements on the ground. Lynn Jungwirth, of the Watershed Training Center in Hayfork, California, said, "I'm afraid the economic benefits from the fuels reduction work may or may not be forthcoming. There's no money to do the planning. Costs are too onerous. The forest had a whole year to plan but they don't have any NEPA-ready projects. The analyses have driven up planning costs beyond reach. The system is totally broken." As Jungwirth indicates, much of the problem stems from difficulties in planning and insufficient attention to monitoring. Forest Service chief Dale Bosworth says, "I believe you can write an environmental analysis to death and not end up improving the quality of a decision." Nancy Farr with the Partnership for a Sustainable Methow in Oregon believes there is a problem not only with upfront planning but also with monitoring. She says there "hasn't been any focus on the types of treatments and ecological impacts. You shouldn't be thinking restoration if you're not paying attention to the effects of the work itself. The projects need to be monitored, with follow-up studies. That's not really on the table right now." But Diane Snyder points out that despite such setbacks, it is important not to get discouraged because "it takes more than one year."[76]

Another problem surfaced in 2002. The Forest Service expended all of its annual appropriations for firefighting by July, the height of the fire season. To pay for costs that continued to mount, Forest Service chief Dale Bosworth issued a directive on July 8 ordering forests to stop or defer payment (or "freeze spending") on projects unrelated to firefighting, including restoration and hazardous fuel reduction work. As a result of the loss of funds from this directive, according to Jungwirth, "communities all over the country that have worked persistently, creatively, and collaboratively with federal agencies to develop agreements and contracts to get the preventive work—the hazardous fuels reduction and forest restoration work—done will suffer."[77] It will also have a negative impact on ecosystems. For example, in Wallowa County, Oregon, activities that were halted because of the funding freeze included a forest stewardship project, stream restoration activities, seed collection activities for native plant restoration work, a community planning process, and a hazardous fuel reduction project that would have provided $125,000 to the community. Grant and Harney counties in Oregon lost $250,000 of expected funds for small-diameter thinning and fuel removal projects, including the loss of more than $100,000 from a National Fire Plan grant that was already awarded to purchase equipment.[78]

Members of Congress expressed strong concern about the Office of Management and Budget's (OMB's) refusal to ask for additional funding to pay back accounts from which the Forest Service borrowed to pay for firefighting. Eight members of the Senate Energy and Natural Resources Committee sent a letter on June 25, 2002, to Mitch Daniels, then director of the OMB. In the letter, they said that borrowing "is unacceptable" and that they are "strongly opposed to the business-as-usual practice of borrowing from other agency accounts to pay for firefighting" because the accounts are never repaid and the accounts borrowed from, including hazardous fuel reduction, are equally important.[79] However, the OMB's focus as an agency is on constraining expenditures.

According to Jungwirth, the funding issue shows "a fundamental disconnect between the direction the agency *says* it is going—towards community-collaborative and preventative measures—and what it is actually *doing*—directing funds away from collaborative, long-term efforts and toward reactive fire-suppression efforts. The current actions are perpetuating . . . long-term problems such as mistrust between the agency and the public and the policy gridlock that prevents work from being done on the ground."[80] The Western Governors' Association plan also highlights the tension between the old way of doing business—the Forest Service as insular and expert driven—and the direction from Congress to move toward a more collaborative, community-based process.

The mixed results are an opportunity to highlight places where the Forest Service and possibly federal legislation need further improvement. Unlike the EAP, which has more than a decade of experience to assess, expanded authorities under the National Fire Plan are only several years old. And because the work affects federal lands, it is subject to other national environmental laws such as the NEPA and ESA. Environmental analyses often take extended periods of time and result in administrative appeals and lawsuits. In short, the National Fire Plan provides an example of the legislative barriers highlighted in the Portland meeting discussed earlier. New tools and mechanisms exist to provide benefit to communities and the ecosystem, but numerous challenges arise in implementation. The challenges include varied priorities within the Forest Service, conflicting priorities among federal policymakers, and inconsistent application of policies across communities and years. Those affected most are communities and surrounding forests.

### Healthy Forests Restoration Act

The Healthy Forests Restoration Act (P.L. 108-148), enacted on December 3, 2003, warrants a brief discussion. Community practitioners and their national partners worked with Congress on several provisions in the hazardous fuel reduction provisions of the act contained in Title I. Senator Crapo (R–Id.) and his staff, for example, worked closely with practitioners and played a key role in ensuring that provisions important to communities were included in the final version of the act. In addition, community groups are working with the Forest Service to ensure that they implement the act in a "credible way."[81]

The first focus for community practitioners involves collaboration on community protection plans and defining the wildland–urban interface within those plans. The act defines a community protection plan as one developed in the context of collaborative agreements involving interested parties. These plans will prioritize areas in need of hazardous fuel reduction and will recommend methods for treatment to protect communities and essential infrastructure. They will also contain a definition of the wildland–urban interface for the particular community affected by the plan. Gerry Gray of American Forests views these plans and their inclusion of place-based definitions of wildland–urban interface as an opportunity to increase collaboration with diverse groups.[82]

Practitioners also plan to work with the Forest Service on multiparty monitoring provisions in the act.[83] These provisions were excluded from earlier versions of the bill in the Senate, and practitioners wrote to senators requesting that the provisions be added. They were included in the November 2003 version of the bill in the House and retained in the final version. These provisions require the Forest Service and BLM to establish a multiparty monitoring, evaluation, and accountability process when "significant interest is expressed in multi-party monitoring." The act requires participants in a multiparty monitoring process to determine the social and ecological effects of hazardous fuel reduction activities and for treatment of land deemed at risk of insect infestation. The act requires such monitoring to include diverse stakeholders including interested citizens and tribal representatives.

It is too soon to determine the impact of these provisions on communities. As with the EAP, the National Fire Plan, and stewardship contracting, the key will be how well the agency implements them. It is a sign of increasing community influence in national legislation, however, that the provisions were included in the act at all. Communities are working with the Forest Service and other partners to help ensure the emphasis on collaboration and multiparty monitoring in Title I of the Healthy Forests Restoration Act will help communities and the agency work together to improve community and forest health.

## Community-Based Forest and Public Lands Restoration Bill

On June 24, 2002, senators Bingaman (D–N.M.) and Craig (R–Id.) introduced bipartisan legislation aimed at restoring and maintaining degraded rural environments and degraded rural communities. The bill's drafters envision moving forest management from an era of resource extraction to one of restoration by directing the Agriculture and Interior departments to invest in ecosystem restoration and maintenance activities using community-based approaches.

The bill would develop consistent and long-term community-based restoration through a number of mechanisms. First, it would create "value-added centers" to help link research and learning to practices on the ground. These centers are intended to help communities develop effective restoration treatments and use the byproducts of restoration—such as small-diameter trees—in an economically viable manner. For example, small rural enterprises working with value-added centers might learn how to take traditionally low-value material such as small trees and add value by turning it into flooring, paneling, and kitchenware such as cutting boards and bowls. As the legislation is written, local nonprofit organizations, conservation groups, or community colleges would run the value-added centers in partnership with the Forest Service, giving nonfederal entities a central role in planning and providing technical assistance. "These value-added centers would be a perfect fit in communities like Cascade [Idaho]," observed Senator Craig. "Cascade has a ready made workforce of skilled forest workers and business people who are eager to undertake work designed to improve our public lands. This legislation would help communities like Cascade, it would help our federal land managers reestablish a close working relationship with them, and it would help cure our ailing public forests."[84]

Second, to make the restoration economically viable and beneficial to communities, the bill would provide innovative contracting mechanisms that direct how the work is contracted and who gets the work. For example, the bill authorizes the use of best-value contracting for doing restoration work such as decommissioning roads and cutting trees for restoration purposes such as habitat enhancement. Best-value contracting allows land management agencies, when awarding contracts, to consider noneconomic factors, including the ability of the contractor to meet the ecological objectives of the contract and their ability to provide local benefit and training opportunities. Third, the bill would require multiparty monitoring of projects and the program itself to improve account-ability, promote collaborative learning, and provide feedback mechanisms to encourage corrective action. Finally, the bill would direct the Forest Service on how to work with the centers to promote collaboration between federal and nonfederal entities.

Initial drafting of S. 2672 began in 2000. The bill was developed in a collab-orative, bipartisan fashion with senators Bingaman and Craig and their staff and with input from other congressional offices. Several community forestry leaders worked closely with congressional staff to draft the initial version of the bill. Once a draft was completed, staff were ready to share it with a broader audi-ence. Kira Finkler and Frank Galdics, both with the Senate Energy Committee, held a briefing with practitioners to discuss the bill. (This occurred during the 2002 Week in Washington, an annual event described later in this chapter.) American Forests worked with congressional staff to facilitate the distribution of the draft to a large network of partners and to facilitate the collection of feedback on it. After revisions by congressional staff and their members based on input from community practitioners and interest group representatives, the bill was introduced in June 2002 in the Senate Energy and Natural Resources Subcommittee on Public Lands and Forests. The committee held a hearing on the bill in late July to get more feedback. At the hearing, Senator Bingaman expressed concern that many rural communities will not survive without sup-port at the national level. Forest-dependent communities cannot restore public lands on their own, he said. S. 2672 provides "much needed new authority and programs to improve the partnership between federal agencies and communities in restoration efforts," he said.

Because of concerns raised by practitioners and others during the hearing and subsequent discussions about the bill, specific provisions may change before further action is taken on the bill in Congress. For example, some stakehold-ers raised concern that some provisions could limit competition by granting preferential treatment in awarding contracts to small operators. However, the bill's drafters have expressed a willingness to revise provisions to further clarify the common interest and increase broad-based support. Additional members of Congress may also join the collaborative effort, working with practitioners and the existing cosigners to rewrite portions of the bill and gain support for it.[85] The substance and process of the bill, including continued consideration of revisions to increase broad-based support, reflect the cumulative influence of community-based forestry over nearly a decade.

## An Appraisal with Recommendations

Appraisals of community-based forestry are important for the guidance of people in the movement over the years ahead and for other community-based movements that might be organized around other natural resources, such as water, endangered species, and grasslands. This appraisal considers first what the movement has accomplished in Washington and on the ground and then turns to the principal challenges that have blocked additional progress. It concludes with some recommendations.

### Accomplishments

The movement's major accomplishment in Washington has been to advance the common interest through national legislation. The advances have been modest so far but important in demonstrating the possibility of more to come. Stewardship of the kind sought by the movement is a common interest goal, integrating the interdependent needs of the land and its communities. But official common interest goals are nothing new in forestry. The Forest Service mission "to protect the land and serve the people," for example, predates the organization of the community-based forestry movement beginning with the Blairsden meeting in 1995. What the movement added was assistance for community-based initiatives, which are distinctive means of finding and implementing specific practices to advance the common interest in forestry. Thanks in part to the movement, legislation on stewardship contracting and the National Fire Plan provided more flexible new authorities to assist community-based forestry, and the EAP, despite continual battles over funding, has survived and continued to receive funding to advance community forestry activities. This series of legislative accomplishments entailed the integration of many valid and appropriate interests at the local community level and in Washington.

Those interests include bipartisan interests in support of the pending Community Based Forest Public Lands Restoration Act (S. 2672), which integrates the efforts of practitioners, their national partners, and both Democratic and Republican members of Congress and their staff. Such bipartisanship is not unprecedented in natural resource policy, but it is rare. Along with the bill itself, bipartisanship represents a political basis for additional advances. In addition, national interest groups have supported the bill or at least its common interest goals. For example, Mary Chapman, executive director of the Forest Steward's Guild, who had several suggestions for the bill, nevertheless wrote, "Providing the pathways and resources to enable nearby citizens and businesses taking an active role in public land stewardship is critical to long term success in achieving forest restoration goals. [This bill] contains important provisions in support of the ecological, social and economic elements needed to achieve these goals."[86] Steve Holmer, campaign coordinator for American Lands Alliance, supported the common interest goals of S. 2672, even though he had suggestions to improve the bill.[87] National environmental interest groups once highly skeptical of community-based forestry have reached out to help develop shared "restoration principles" and craft legislation. Timber interests in general are less interested in community-based forestry and proceed less openly in the legislative process.

Thus local and national interests have been integrated to some extent through pending and enacted national legislation, and the latter in turn has assisted the practice of community-based forestry, but not uniformly or consistently. Much remains to be done, both in Washington and in local communities. Nevertheless, compared with the period before 1995, when practitioners began to organize at the national level, the movement has advanced the common interest. No single factor accounts for the accomplishments to date. Instead, a variety of interacting factors, both within and outside the movement, explain what happened and provide guidance for the future.

Among the factors outside the movement, the most important are people open to departures from normal power-balancing politics in the Congress, the executive branch, and elsewhere in Washington. It is difficult to imagine how anything could have been accomplished without senators Bingaman, Craig, Wyden, and Crapo, their staff, and others like them. To craft legislation that works more effectively on the ground, people such as these appreciate the practice-based knowledge that practitioners bring to the legislative process. Against a background of spin, specific information about concrete achievements stands out as credible. To minimize the political costs of supporting such legislation, members of Congress appreciate knowing that representatives of ecological, social, and economic interests at the local community level have signed off on a particular legislative proposal. From a practical political standpoint, the option to please more constituents and displease few or none of them is an obvious choice. Policymakers recognize that the movement provides an intelligence service that improves legislation and saves time and effort that otherwise might be consumed in fruitless negotiations. They also distinguish this service from paid lobbyists who make demands based on the policy positions of the single-interest groups they represent rather than specific achievements. Recall former Senate staffer Kira Finkler's relief after seeing demonstrations of stewardship contracting: "This is such an incredible breath of fresh air—a bigger idea than traditional either/or politics."[88] Indeed, on at least one occasion, congressional staffers cautioned practitioners of community-based forestry not to jeopardize their reputation for credibility by attaching endorsements from single-interest groups to proposed legislation.

Policymakers open to community-based forestry have found it worthwhile to follow up after working relationships have been established with practitioners.[89] Senate Agricultural Committee staff, aware of practitioners' reputation as something other than a traditional interest group, called on practitioners of community-based forestry to help conflicting interest groups find common ground on a stewardship contracting provision in the 2002 Farm Bill. In addition, on wildfires and other issues of importance to communities, congressional staff often ask American Forests to identify witnesses among practitioners at the community level. To increase participation by practitioners, congressional staff have scheduled hearings during a training week in which practitioners come to town to learn about the legislative process. Congressional staff have also helped in training them to participate more effectively in the Washington arena. Staff have responded to requests to hold briefings on draft legislation, even though such requests generally are not fulfilled. For example, in 2002, Frank Gladics and Kira Finkler, then of the minority and majority staff for the Senate Energy and Natural Resources Committee, briefed practitioners on the draft Community Based Forest and Public Lands Restoration Bill and solicited their feedback on it. Such working relationships have been established and maintained through several congresses and a change in the White House since the movement began to be organized in 1995.

The working relationships established and the practice-based knowledge imparted to policymakers represent political capital that leaves practitioners of community-based forestry in a better position to take advantage of opportunities as they arise. For example, when a catastrophic wildfire season erupted in 2000, appropriators in Congress decided to address the problem by increasing funding significantly. Congressional staff working with those appropriators understood the core problem to be the buildup of hazardous fuels, not firefighting. They knew from practitioners that restoration workers are needed to reduce that buildup, and they worked with practitioners to change contracting mechanisms to allow the Forest Service to use grants, contracts, and cooperative agreements to train local restoration workforces and provide work for them.

People who have working relationships with practitioners and their national partners and a working knowledge of community-based forestry are scattered across the institutional landscape in Washington and beyond. Certainly some of the most receptive people can be found in the Senate Energy and Natural Resources Committee under the bipartisan leadership of senators Craig and Bingaman. The Senate Agriculture Committee also has worked with practitioners on community-based forestry, including Senator Crapo in his capacity as chair of the Senate Agriculture Subcommittee on Forestry, Conservation, and Rural Revitalization. On the other hand, people in the House Agriculture Committee were not particularly receptive to practitioners' concerns about forestry provisions in the 2002 Farm Bill, nor were people in the OMB receptive to participants' request to continue funding the EAPs in fiscal year 2002 or 2005, despite demonstrated results. Working relationships have been established with selected Forest Service officials and members of the Western Governors' Association, the National Association of Counties, Defenders of Wildlife, the American Forest and Paper Association, and others. In an open system of governance there are many possible points of access within and outside government. It takes persistence over time to find people who are open to improving legislation through integrative politics and practice-based knowledge, to impart that knowledge, and to establish working relationships based on credibility and trust.

How did practitioners of community-based forestry and their partners capitalize on these opportunities to realize some modest but important advances in stewardship through national legislation? An important factor is a shared vision and clear priorities based on the four cornerstones. Fundamentally, practitioners seek better stewardship of communities and the land, to be achieved through open, inclusive, and transparent processes, investments in people and natural resources, and continuous monitoring and corrective action. As a shared vision, the four cornerstones are the core of solidarity within the movement. As priorities, they are the basis of cooperation between practitioners, including the coordination of what is said to policymakers. These cornerstones are grounded in similarities between the experiences of practitioners in individual community-based initiatives such as the QLG. They have been gradually clarified and integrated into practices on the ground and in Washington through thousands of contacts, face-to-face and mediated, in a variety of settings. The settings include networks such as the LPG; key meetings such as Blairsden in 1995, Bend in 1998, and Portland in 2001; and organizations such as the Communities Committee of the Seventh American Forest Congress, the Pinchot Institute, the National Network of Practitioners, and American Forests.

Practitioners clarified and integrated the four cornerstones not only through thousands of contacts but also through programs to identify and train potential leaders among practitioners of community-based forestry to carry out the shared vision in Washington. For example, Carol Daly began working in community forestry in 1994 when two local contract loggers invited her to join their project. She is now president of the Communities Committee and the Flathead Economic Policy Center in Montana. Daly and her organization's work helped to "set the stage for the federal stewardship contracting demonstration program."[90] Similarly, working out of Hayfork, California, Lynn Jungwirth serves on numerous national policy committees, including a diverse panel convened by the Western Governors' Association to address wildfire issues. The panel developed *A Collaborative Approach for Reducing Wildland Fire Risks to Community and the Environment: A Ten-Year Comprehensive Strategy* and a companion implementation plan.[91] One of the three guiding principles in the approach taken by the panel is "collaboration among governments and broadly representative stakeholders."

The Week in Washington is the most direct training opportunity. Each year the NNFP, the Communities Committee, American Forests, the Pinchot Institute, and, more recently, the Aspen Institute collaborate to sponsor and organize this week. About twelve to twenty practitioners of urban and rural community forestry from around the country arrive in Washington, D.C., to learn about national policy and to educate policymakers. A mentoring program engages former participants in the Week in Washington to help train first-time participants. Often, practitioners who participated in the Week in Washington return to testify in Congress. Staff at American Forests help them write and practice delivering their testimony or prepare for visits to their delegations in Congress. For the first time in 2003, practitioners held a Western Week in Washington to focus on issues of particular concern in the West. The Community Based Forest and Public Lands Restoration bill was a focus of Western Week in 2004. Training also occurs at information and development sessions during annual meetings of the NNFP. Additional information to build practitioners' capacity to work with policymakers includes such resources as the "quick guides." Already in print are quick guides to federal appropriations, the budget process, and working with the media; how to conduct a congressional field tour and how to use wildfire and county payment legislation; and a "power map" of who's who on natural resource issues in Washington.

The shared vision and priorities based on the four cornerstones are expressed in a loose organizational structure. This structure in turn helps sustain solidarity and cooperation between practitioners on the ground and with their partners in Washington. The structure is not centrally controlled, so it allows the movement to adapt smoothly to new experience on the ground or in Washington. Practices consistent with the four cornerstones must be updated continuously as events unfold, even though the cornerstones stabilize the direction and operational priorities of the movement.

The national partners in community-based forestry are the core of the horizontal and vertical networks. They bring voices from the woods into the national policy dialogue and bring information from that dialogue and national policymakers to practitioners on the ground. The NNFP serves as a horizontal network linking community groups to capture and share lessons about collaboration and other community-based methods. The NNFP holds annual meetings to identify common issues and develop strategies to address those issues. It also publishes an electronic update, *Forest Community News*. The Aspen Institute formed a partnership with the Ford Foundation to run the Community-Based Forestry Demonstration Program, which provides assistance to and facilitates interaction between community groups nationwide. Michael Goergen, vice president of the Society of American Forests, works closely with community groups and professional foresters to identify common ground among them. They receive assistance on policy from the Communities Committee's Policy Task Group, which Goergen cochairs. Goergen also provides informal policy updates for practitioners. The Communities Committee coordinates the writing of a quarterly newsletter, *Communities and Forests*. It includes policy updates, upcoming meetings and workshops, profiles of community projects, member profiles, and other relevant information for practitioners. Other groups such as the Sonoran Institute and The Nature Conservancy also work on community-based issues but are not as closely linked with the network of national groups described here.

In Washington, national partners maintain face-to-face contact with policymakers, helping them identify and resolve policy and regulatory problems and promoting institutional reforms in the land management agencies. American Forests and the Communities Committee work mostly with legislators. The Pinchot Institute for Conservation works mostly with the Forest Service. These groups also hold forums to increase awareness among national interest groups and develop information for policymakers in Washington, D.C. In addition to bringing practitioners to Washington, these national and regional partners often bring congressional staff, other policymakers, and interest group representatives from Washington to the field. The Communities Committee sponsors at least one congressional field tour a year, in conjunction with national partners who, in years past, have included American Forests, the Pinchot Institute, the NNFP, and local and regional groups such as the Flathead Economic Policy Center in Montana, the Watershed Research and Training Center in California, and Sustainable Northwest in Oregon.

The basic strategy in this loose organizational structure helps build the movement's political capital in Washington and sustain it. This capital includes practice-based knowledge, internal solidarity and cooperation, and working relationships with policymakers based on credibility and trust. Part of the strategy is to rely on face-to-face contacts and direct experience on the ground, including tours and multiparty monitoring, whenever practical within the movement and outside. That helps maximize shared understandings and minimize tendencies to discount mediated information as mere propaganda. As Anne Dahl of the Swan Ecosystem Center in Montana put it, "When you participate in monitoring, you see the changes yourself, and you increase your understanding of land management issues."[92] According to Maia Enzer, direct contact with congressional staffers on field tours and in Washington works because "community forestry practitioners have a degree of integrity and honesty and a willingness to be self-critical that's not normally found in Washington D.C. That combination gives forest practitioners a lot of credibility in the national forest policy process."[93] Thus another part of the strategy is to provide an intelligence service useful to practitioners and policymakers for their own purposes. According to Gerry Gray, community-based forestry works in part "because it is not an advocacy program but a service that helps our community partners develop and articulate their own views on national policy."[94] Finally, the strategy is also collaborative and consensus based. As Carol Daly put it, "Our strength has always come from our collaborative and consensus-based approach, and it's important that we maintain that as much as possible."[95] In contrast to conventional strategies, it does not pit jobs against the environment, resort to litigation, or seek to impose more standardized rules and regulations from the top down.

The basic strategy does attempt to integrate ecological, social, and economic interests into better policies, rely on collaboration to find common ground, and adapt to differences and changes in contexts from the bottom up. For these purposes, it attempts to increase authorities for flexibility on the ground and to mobilize other resources from the top down. For leaders of the movement, the basic strategy is a matter of principles including honesty and integrity as well as expediency. It is expedient because the movement does not have the means to compete effectively with interest groups in more conventional ways, such as hiring lobbyists and litigators, placing full-page ads in major newspapers, or turning out enough voters to make a difference in close elections.

## Challenges

Despite its progress, much remains to be done to realize the potential of community-based forestry to advance the common interest in stewardship of the land including its human communities. The modest accomplishments to date are important as demonstrations of the possibility of more progress in the future. The major challenges ahead are exemplified by specific events in the recent past.

First, in connection with stewardship contracting, some people in or around Congress expanded authority for stewardship contracting mechanisms nationwide through the 2003 Interior Appropriations Act and did so in a rider at the eleventh hour, without an inclusive and transparent process. This served some special interests at the expense of the common interest. On procedural grounds, the program expansion arbitrarily excluded other interest groups that had opposed an earlier attempt to expand the program in the House version of the 2002 Farm Bill. On substantive grounds, expansion jeopardizes the success of the pilots because they depend on the cooperation and trust of multiple diverse groups at the local level and national levels. Environmental interest groups in particular accepted the pilot programs because they expected the pilots to remain small in numbers and in scale and to include multiparty monitoring to minimize the inevitable risks of innovation. On practical grounds, the expansion was premature at best given the mixed and incomplete appraisals available. It would have been much more reasonable to "debug" the stewardship contracting program first, as intended when the pilots were established. The common interest is better served by programs that work in practice and by open, inclusive, and transparent decision processes and by substantive consensus among diverse interest groups.[96]

Second, in connection with multiparty monitoring, some legislators, agency officials, and staff continue to view monitoring exclusively as a means of assessing programs for accountability from the top down. The most obvious example is deletion of specific authority and funds for multiparty monitoring of projects on the ground in the fiscal year 2003 Interior Appropriations Act. But multiparty monitoring of projects on the ground is fundamentally different from monitoring for accountability from the top down and essential in realizing the potential of community-based forestry to advance the common interest. Multiparty monitoring provides guidance for adapting each project to a specific, changing context. It also attracts buy-in and resources from multiple groups, builds working relationships, and generates practice-based knowledge for diffusion and adaptation to local and national groups. Practitioners understand that such "monitoring is critical to making better land management decisions, and all-party monitoring is promoted as a way to increase both the quality and public acceptability of those groups."[97] Not all community groups, or even all stewardship contracting pilot projects, practice multiparty monitoring. It nevertheless remains a cornerstone of the movement, and a priority within it. The implementation of multiparty monitoring provisions in the Healthy Forests Restoration Act may serve as a litmus test to determine whether mindsets about the purposes and practices of monitoring can change with persistence and successful examples. However, little attention has been given so far to these provisions.

In contrast, monitoring for program accountability from the top down relies primarily on aggregate measures of performance at the program level. Although aggregate data such as costs, mechanisms used, and time to plan and complete projects provide information on program performance, aggregate data without information on local contexts obscures significant differences between projects under the program.[98] The problems of aggregate measures can be ameliorated to some extent by information from multiparty monitoring in narrative form, including stories of success and failure that are easier to communicate to policymakers at the national level. They seldom have the time, even if they have the interest, to attend to the distinctive needs of more than a handful out of hundreds or thousands of communities dependent on natural resources. Because of time and cognitive constraints, much of the effective monitoring and evaluation of federal programs must be devolved to the community level. To the extent that multiparty monitoring helps diverse interests advance the common interest in different communities at the local level, it also helps busy national policymakers understand and advance the common interest at the national and local levels.

Third, there will continue to be challenges in the implementation of national legislation, especially obstruction from Forest Service officials at multiple levels compounded by insufficient and inconsistent funding for community-based programs and projects. For example, Forest Service chief Bosworth halted spending on all contracts not related to firefighting because of overruns in firefighting budgets in fiscal year 2002. The administration refused to ask Congress for funds to repay accounts from which money was "borrowed" to pay for firefighting, including accounts to pay for hazardous fuel reduction, a preventive measure that would have used grants, contracts, and cooperative agreements to implement local projects to advance the common interest in protecting lives, natural resources, and property. In addition, even projects authorized and mandated by act of Congress can be blocked in implementation at the local level. The QLG's modified Community Stability Proposal is an example. Similarly, Forest Service officials sometimes divert resources from planning, implementing, and monitoring community-based projects in which they are involved. The Valle Grande Grass Bank in the Santa Fe National Forest is a case in point (see chapter 4). Sometimes Forest Service officials divert resources from implementation of their own and community-based forestry projects to preliminary NEPA analyses, in attempts to avoid appeals and litigation by environmental interest groups. When adequate resources are provided, it often seems to be despite traditional culture and procedures in the Forest Service.

These barriers in implementation make it difficult to advance the common interest, despite its articulation in local projects and in national legislation supported by diverse interest groups. Although the integration of diverse interests in national legislation through collaboration represents progress, support based on their expectations is not enough. Advancing the common interest also depends on realizing those expectations to some extent through implementation. The importance of implementation is understood in the community-based forestry movement. Indeed, according to Jane Braxton-Little, many practitioners are "anxious to move beyond the collaboration they have established to project implementation. For them, the last seven years have simply laid the foundation for on-the-ground changes. There will be no guarantee of success, they say, until community-based forestry achieves widespread work in the woods and watersheds based on new principles."[99]

In short, as previewed in the movement's past, the main challenges for the movement to overcome in the future are tendencies

- To reject the slow process of "debugging" the stewardship contracting and other programs, project by project, in favor of premature expansion from the top down
- To reject multiparty monitoring on the ground, project by project, in favor of aggregate measures to monitor accountability from the top down
- To reject collaboration with other interests in implementation, in favor of asserting bureaucratic control at all levels, especially when goals conflict or resources are limited

These tendencies may be interpreted as defenses of the status quo and, more specifically, as remnants of scientific management. At least it is consistent with the remnants of scientific management to plan and monitor programs from the top down, to assert bureaucratic expertise and control in program implementation, and to exclude other interests in the decision process. It should come as no surprise that many people in Washington and beyond are steeped in practices of scientific management and often predisposed to defend them. These practices have been institutionalized and inculcated through education and socialization over many decades. No doubt some people are satisfied with them and perceive no need for alternatives. Others may be dissatisfied but unaware of the alternative practices in community-based forestry. Still others may be aware of these alternative practices but skeptical that they have worked or can work better.

Whereas the challenges represent the restriction of community-based forestry, the accomplishments represent the partial incorporation of those practices in a possible transition to adaptive governance.[100] At least it is consistent with adaptive governance to accept the slow process of "debugging" innovations through experience on the ground, to emphasize project-by-project multiparty monitoring for that purpose, and to collaborate with other interests in the decision process. It should come as no surprise that some people have accepted these innovative practices, at least tentatively. Receptivity to innovations has been growing and spreading with frustrations in national forest management for some time. For example, from ten hearings of a subcommittee of the Senate Energy and Natural Resources Committee, committee chair Senator Frank

Murkowski concluded in 1995 that "nobody is defending the status quo." He acknowledged "different views of what is broken, what needs fixing, and how to fix it. But I have been overwhelmed by the universal dissatisfaction with the current status."[101] Capitalizing on these opportunities, practitioners and partners in community-based forestry have found enough allies among policymakers to effect some modest but important changes in national legislation. Moreover, they have opened these niches in the landscape of scientific management in a rather short period of time, since the mid-1990s. This is an impressive accomplishment when one considers the limited resources and normal resistances to personal and institutional change.

## Recommendations

What should practitioners and partners in community-based forestry do in the next several years? The basic recommendation is to continue making incremental progress by relying primarily on the key practices responsible for the accomplishments so far. Relying primarily on the key practices makes sense because they have worked well enough in practice, and their potential for further progress is far from exhausted. Patience and persistence are necessary because there is no magic bullet or panacea for fundamental reform. This basic recommendation includes

- Training more people inside the movement to represent community-based forestry effectively in the legislative arena in Washington, based on the four cornerstones
- Finding more people outside the movement who are open to departures from the status quo and power-balancing politics and providing intelligence services for them
- Augmenting existing political capital, including more practice-based knowledge, internal cooperation and solidarity, and working relationships based on credibility and trust
- Relying mostly on face-to-face contacts and direct experience (in Washington, D.C., and on field tours) to communicate, collaborate, and find common ground effectively
- Maintaining a loose organizational structure that gives practitioners and partners the flexibility necessary to implement what is learned and to avoid bureaucratization

Of course the details are always subject to modification in light of experience. But by building on these key practices, with patience and persistence, the movement will be able to make the most of its opportunities to influence national legislation and programs to support community-based forestry on the ground. There are no satisfactory reasons for radical departures from the key practices or for giving up altogether.

Within this basic recommendation, the priority tasks are to address the three principal challenges described earlier. Thus the first task is to resist premature expansion from the top down that might leave programs more visible and more vulnerable to defenders of the status quo. Practitioners and partners should assess the overall success of community-based forestry by how well programs advance the common interest in practice at the national and local levels, not by the scale of programs or the amount of influence over legislation. The complementary task is to insist on practice-based knowledge as the key to a quasi-evolutionary approach to the development of national legislation and programs. This recognizes limitations to what we can know at the national level about innovations as complex as community-based forestry initiatives. Moreover, differences and changes in contexts necessitate reassessing and updating on a continuous basis what knowledge we do have. Thus despite knowledge limitations, we can improve national legislation and programs by harvesting practice-based knowledge continuously from many different projects and contexts at the same time.

A second task is to insist on multiparty monitoring to facilitate collaboration and consensus, to improve practices in projects on the ground, and to improve intelligence for national legislation on that basis. Concrete experience can be used to make the case. It is easy to show that multiparty monitoring on the ground facilitates collaboration and consensus. For example, according to Liz Johnson, leader of the Priest–Pend Orielle project in Idaho, "the diverse group involved in the project gives the project credibility for environmental groups, private landowners, as well as the Forest Service."[102] Her testimony can be supplemented by testimony from representatives of these groups and by case-specific details. It is also easy to illustrate the importance of learning through practice. For example, the Forest Service received only two bids, of insufficient quality, on a request for contractors to use designation-by-description contracting to design treatments for particular areas of the Flathead National Forest. Looking into the problem, their partners in the FFP discovered that contractors did not know how to specify desired future conditions of the treatment area at posttreatment intervals of 5 to 200 years and did not have time to learn because the request for a quote came at the busiest time of their year. With this information, the Forest Service reissued the request in modified form and received acceptable bids.[103]

Such information from experience on the ground should be available to improve intelligence for national legislation. But experience at the national level also can be used to draw attention to the limitations of the top-down accountability mindset that stands in the way of multiparty monitoring. For example, from the aggregate measures used to monitor the stewardship contracting pilot program for accountability, it was not known whether appeals or litigation under the NEPA in thirteen of thirty-one pilot projects that had completed NEPA assessments resulted from their status as pilot projects or from more systemic problems with the NEPA. Without more information from multiparty monitoring of each project on the ground, it is difficult to know how to improve the national program or the local pilot projects. More generally, aggregate measures of the number of communities helped by the EAP or the money this program leveraged are appropriate for assessing performance for one purpose of the program but not for all of its purposes. However, without context-specific information from monitoring on the ground, the aggregate measures alone shed little light on how to improve program effectiveness overall.

Still more generally, practitioners and their partners might distinguish between what is measurable and what is observable in making their case for multiparty monitoring on the ground. Collaboration and consensus are a case in point. The number of people who participate in a meeting or series of meetings is not a meaningful measure of collaboration unless they include the principal interests at stake, all those interests actually are represented in meetings, and their interests are taken into account by other participants. Similarly, the number of people who sign off on a proposal is not a meaningful measure of consensus unless they know what they have signed off on, they include those necessary to support implementation, and they support implementation. And finally, the significance of consensus and collaboration in some cases may depend on what did not happen and is therefore unobservable (an appeal or lawsuit avoided, for example). The various contingencies that matter in assessing collaboration and consensus are observable in any particular context, but it is not obvious that collaboration and consensus can be meaningfully measured across contexts.

A third task is to address obstacles to the implementation of national legislation in support of community-based forestry. The remnants of scientific management are well represented by many officials at all levels of the Forest Service. Not much can be done about them in the short run, except to work around them and to work with the exceptional people who are open to alternatives. For the longer run, it would be prudent for practitioners and partners to encourage the Forest Service to recruit more young people who are open to alternatives and to provide continuing education in the alternatives and other resources for all employees who are interested. For example, the Pinchot Institute has been working under contract with the Forest Service to develop collaborative stewardship in the agency. This is a good start, but it is only a start if the potential of adaptive governance as a whole is to be taken into account.

Funding for the implementation of national legislation in support of community-based forestry is not likely to come from large increases in the agency's base budget, as distinguished from funds to address crises. Since the wildfire crisis of 2000, for example, the Forest Service has benefited from significant increases in funds appropriated for wildfire purposes. Otherwise, past trends in the agency's base budget, competition with other national priorities including defense and homeland security, and projected increases in the cumulative federal debt all suggest the need to look elsewhere. More funding for the restoration of forests and forest-dependent communities might be freed up by reducing the number of appeals and lawsuits through collaboration, consensus, and NEPA reforms. Beyond that, the movement must continue to rely on funding and leveraged funding from private foundations. This has worked well in building the movement and can be expanded as practitioners develop regional organizations and increase the number of issues on which they work. Documenting successes through multiparty monitoring can help practitioners demonstrate that community-based forestry is a good investment.

Finally, given the uncertainties, reasonable people can differ over what should be done by and for community-based forestry over the next several years. One proposal under consideration is to establish a more formal national presence. Carol Daly summarized the issue.

As the movement comes of age, there is pressure from some participants to establish a more formal national presence. Advocates say an office and staff in Washington would give better access to the principles and people who articulate them to policy makers. Elevating the profile as a mainstream organization would also help recruit new members, including youth and minorities. Opponents call establishing a national presence the kiss of death. The strengths of community-based forestry are its ties to the land and communities it represents in national policy discussions. Without these, the movement is in danger of becoming just another interest group.[104]

Establishing a more formal national presence could be considered part of a trend toward more organization and outreach that includes emphases on regional organization and working with the media in the Portland meeting; 501(c)(3) status for the Communities Committee and its first media field tour in 2001; and the Week in Washington, which emphasized training for work with the media in 2002. Establishing a more formal national presence might help sustain progress.

Nevertheless, practitioners might proceed with caution for several reasons. First, the movement's progress in Washington depends in large part on the perception that community-based forestry is not just another interest group. Further progress could be inhibited by organization and promotion as a conventional group. Second, as recognized in the Portland meeting, news media tend to focus on conflict and controversy, take short-term views of issues, and oversimplify. In contrast, community-based forestry emphasizes collaboration and consensus, a long-term approach to enduring reforms in forest practices, and the complexities of adapting to new experience, interests, and issues on a continuing basis. And third, establishing a more formal national presence could divert limited time, attention, and other resources from integrating multiple interests within the movement and outside. Practitioners have identified this as the central task since the Blairsden meeting, and in this regard the loose organizational structure has served it well so far.

In conclusion, the experience of community-based forestry can be considered an example of adaptive governance at multiple levels of decision making. After nearly a decade in Washington, the work of practitioners and their partners is still based on stewardship efforts in diverse communities nationwide. In each community, this typically includes the collaboration of diverse interests to find a consensus on projects that advance their common interest and multiparty monitoring to improve those projects and strengthen working relationships. In Washington, selected policymakers appreciate knowing from practitioners and their partners what changes are needed to make national legislation and programs work more effectively. Knowing what is a matter of consensus on the ground also helps Washington policymakers gain support and minimize the political costs of needed changes. Changes in national legislation and programs have provided assistance to practitioners in various forms, including new authorities such as stewardship contracting, new or more stable funding, and technical support. Thus in the decision-making structure that evolved after community-based forestry went to Washington, localized policy initiatives from the bottom up are complemented by assistance from the top down. Clearly, both levels in the structure are important in adaptive governance.

The modest but important changes in national legislation and programs have helped integrate the interests at the national level with the interests of practitioners of community-based forestry nationwide. At the same time, the changes on balance have enhanced, not compromised, the capacity of practitioners on the ground to adapt to differences across communities nationwide and to changes over time. Thus policy processes and outcomes have advanced the common interest at the local and national levels. Policy processes and outcomes at both levels are based on shared practical experience and face-to-face negotiations.

They nevertheless can and already have to some extent integrated local knowledge with the best available science in developing projects and in the multiparty monitoring of these many concurrent field trials nationwide. Overall, this experience can be considered a model for community-based initiatives organized around other natural resources and in need of assistance from Washington, a model especially for practitioners and observers who are less impressed by the formidable challenges that lie ahead than by the modest progress and significant promise of community-based forestry.

NOTES

1. Christina Cromley, "Legislation for a New Era," *Communities and Forests* 6 (Fall 2000), p. 3.

2. Lynn Jungwirth, "Letter from the Chair," *Communities and Forests* 3 (Spring 1999), p. 2.

3. Jane Braxton-Little, "Coming of Age: Seven Years After the Seventh American Forest Congress," *Communities and Forests* 7 (Spring 2003), p. 1.

4. Cecilia Danks, Lisa J. Wilson, and Lynn Jungwirth, *Community-Based Socioeconomic Assessment and Monitoring of Activities Related to National Forest Management,* Part One (text and charts revised September 2002), available at http://www.thewatershedcenter.org.

5. GAO, *Private Timberlands: Private Timber Not Likely to Replace Declining Federal Harvests* (Washington, D.C.: U.S. GAO, February 1995).

6. Becky Kramer, "Mill's Closure Leaves Hole in County," *Spokane Spokesman Review* (August 13, 2003).

7. Jane Braxton-Little, "The Woods: Reclaiming the Neighborhood," *American Forests* 103 (Winter 1998), pp. 12–15.

8. Kramer, "Mill's Closure."

9. See Christine H. Colburn, "Forest Policy and the Quincy Library Group," in Ronald D. Brunner, Christine H. Colburn, Christina M. Cromley, Roberta A. Klein, and Elizabeth A. Olson, *Finding Common Ground: Governance and Natural Resources in the American West* (New Haven, Conn.: Yale University Press, 2002), ch. 5.

10. Jonathan Kusel, Gerry J. Gray, and Maia J. Enzer, eds., *Proceedings of the Lead Partnership Group Northern California/Southern Oregon Roundtable on Communities of Place, Partnerships, and Forest Health* (Washington, D.C.: American Forests/Forest Community Research, 1996), p. 4.

11. The groups included the Applegate Partnership; the Jefferson Center, the Feather River Coordinated Resource Management Group, the QLG, the Rogue Institute for Ecology and Conservation, the Shasta–Tehema Bioregional Council, the Siskiyou Bioregional Group, the Trinity Bioregional Group, and the Watershed Research and Training Center.

12. Kusel et al., *Proceedings,* p. iii.

13. Interview with Gerry Gray, American Forests, Washington, D.C. (August 23, 2002).

14. Kusel et al., *Proceedings,* pp. 5–6.

15. Ibid.

16. Author's observations and notes from the congress.

17. Braxton-Little, "Coming of Age," p. 1.

18. Carol Daly, "Strengthening Our Voice," *Communities and Forests* 7 (Spring 2003), p. 2.

19. Ibid.

20. Gerry Gray, "Member Profile," *Communities and Forests* 6 (Summer 2002), p. 4.

21. Ibid., p. 4.

22. "Making Our Mark in Washington D.C.," *Communities and Forests* 1 (Fall 1997), pp. 1–2.

23. Rey later became undersecretary for natural resources and the environment in the Department of Agriculture in the Bush administration.

24. "Making Our Mark," p. 2.

25. Tape of the workshop, archived at American Forests.

26. "Making Our Mark," p. 2.

27. "Making Our Mark." About 1998, the Communities Committee began reaching out to people who live in urban areas. According to Gray, the effort came in response to "a concern that our policy program wasn't reaching urbanites, and an interest in reaching out to those larger constituencies in order to shift forest policy," p. 2.

28. Gerry J. Gray and Maia J. Enzer, "Preface," in Gerry J. Gray, Maia J. Enzer, and Jonathan Kusel, eds., *Understanding Community-Based Forest Ecosystem Management* (Binghamton, N.Y.: Haworth Press, 2001), p. xxii.

29. Sustainable Northwest, Watershed Research and Training Center, and Wallowa Resources, *Working Together to Facilitate Change: 2001 Pacific Northwest Community Forestry Public Lands Organizing Meeting* (Portland, Ore.: December 12–14, 2001). For an electronic version, contact menzer@sustainablenorthwest.org.

30. In addition to the organizing groups, regional groups included Partnership for a Sustainable Methow in Twisp, Wash.; Flathead Economic Policy Center in Columbia Falls, Mont.; Columbia Pacific Resource and Conservation District in Aberdeen, Wash.; Grass Lakes Consulting in Olympia, Wash.; Northwest Connections in Swan Valley, Mont.; Framing Our Community in Elk City, Idaho; Ecosystem Workforce Program in Eugene, Ore.; Alliance of Forest Workers and Harvesters in Eugene, Ore.; Collaborative Learning Circle in Ashland, Ore.; Jefferson Sustainable Development Initiative in Ashland, Ore.; Lake County Resource Initiative in Lakeview, Ore.; the Lead Partnership Group/Forest Community Research in Taylorsville, Calif.; and the Sierra Economic Development Council in Auburn, Calif.

31. Sustainable Northwest et al., *Working Together,* p. 11.

32. Ibid., p. 9.

33. Ibid.

34. Ibid., p. 13.

35. Ibid., pp. 9, 13.

36. Ibid.

37. Ibid., p. 4.

38. Maia Enzer and Christina Cromley, "Economic Action Programs at Risk," *Communities and Forests* 6 (Spring 2002), p. 3.

39. "Statement of Michael Rains, director of Northeastern Area State and Private Forestry, U.S. Department of Agriculture, Forest Service, Before the Senate Energy and Natural

Resources Subcommittee on Forest and Public Land Management Concerning Economic Action Programs" (June 30, 1999).

40. Enzer and Cromley, "Economic Action Programs," p. 3.

41. "Statement of Michael Rains."

42. Ibid.

43. Jane Braxton-Little, 1999, "Stirring the Soup in Washington, D.C.," *Communities and Forests* 3 (Spring 1999), p. 3.

44. "Federal Programs," *Communities and Forests* 3 (Spring 1999), p. 3.

45. Enzer and Cromley, "Economic Action Programs," p. 2.

46. Ibid.

47. Ibid., p. 3.

48. On Forest Service contracting laws and regulations, see Title 36 of the Code of Federal Regulation and the National Forest Management Act (NFMA).

49. Carol Daly, "Member Profile," *Communities and Forests* 7 (Spring 2002), p. 3.

50. Mary Mitsos, "USFS Pilot Projects to Test New Management Methods," *Communities and Forests* 2 (Spring 1998), p. 6.

51. Although bundling can help small businesses win contracts for work in or around their own communities, it also can lead to contracts too big for all but large businesses operating on regional or larger scales.

52. This term was picked up in the Portland meeting to describe the approach already taken in community-based forestry. For more on the concept, see Ronald D. Brunner and Tim W. Clark, "A Practice-Based Approach to Ecosystem Management," *Conservation Biology* 11 (February 1997), pp. 48–58.

53. U.S. GAO, *Additional Guidance on Community Involvement Could Enhance Effectiveness of Stewardship Contracting* (Washington, D.C.: U.S. GAO, June 2004). In September 2004, the U.S. GAO changed its name to the U.S. Government Accountability Office.

54. Pinchot Institute for Conservation, *Implementation of Multi-Party Monitoring and Evaluation: The USDA Stewardship Contracting Pilot Program FY 2001* (Washington, D.C.: Pinchot Institute, January 2002).

55. U.S. GAO, *Additional Guidance.*

56. Alex Conley, "All-Party Monitoring Taking Off," *Communities and Forests* 3 (Fall 1999), pp. 1, 3.

57. Braxton-Little, "Congressional Staffers," pp. 1, 3.

58. Patricia Greenburg and Ann Moote, "Stewardship Contracting: The Jury's Still Out," *Communities and Forests* 6 (Fall 2002), p. 5.

59. U.S. GAO, *Additional Guidance.*

60. Greenburg and Moote, "Stewardship Contracting," p. 5.

61. "Statement of Carol Daly, president Flathead Economic Policy Center, Columbia Falls, MT for the U.S. House of Representatives, Committee on Agriculture Subcommittee on Department Operations, Oversight, Nutrition and Forestry, Hearing on the Forest Service's Present and Future Ability to Enter into Stewardship Contracts" (July 18, 2002).

62. "Testimony of Lynn Jungwirth, executive director, the Watershed Research and Training Center, Hayfork, California, U.S. House of Representatives, Committee on Agriculture

Subcommittee on Department Operations, Oversight, Nutrition and Forestry, U.S. Forest Service Stewardship Contracting Hearing" (July 18, 2002).

63. "Statement of Carol Daly."

64. For an update on training and collaboration issues, see U.S. GAO, *Additional Guidance.*

65. U.S. GAO, *Additional Guidance,* "Highlights" page.

66. *Stewardless Logging: Stewardship Contracting Becomes Permanent,* online at http://www. americanlands.org/permanent_stewardship_authority.htm.

67. *Funding for Forest Service—With Trees: Forest Service Seeks Unprecedented Autonomy, Financial Independence,* online at http://www.defenders.org/forests/steward.html.

68. Statistics are from the National Interagency Fire Center, online at http://www.nifc. gov/stats/wildlandfirestats.html.

69. Quoted in Mark Matthews, "When Fire Came to Town," *American Forests* 6 (Winter 2002), p. 25.

70. Western Governors' Association, *A Collaborative Approach for Reducing Wildland Fire Risks to Communities and the Environment: 10-Year Comprehensive Strategy Implementation Plan* (May 2002). The report is available at http://www.westgov.org/wga/initiatives/fire/implem_plan. pdf.

71. Cassandra Moseley, Nancy Toth, and Abe Cambier, *The Business and Employment Effects of the National Fire Plan in Oregon and Washington in 2001* (Eugene: Ecosystem Workforce Program, University of Oregon, December 2002), p. 15. The report is available at http://ewp. uoregon.edu. Additional research on the implementation of wildfire legislation, from a project directed by Toddi A. Steelman at North Carolina State University, may be found at http:// www.wildfirecommunities.ncsu.edu.

72. Matthews, "When Fire Came to Town," p. 28.

73. Jane Braxton-Little, "Building Fire Safety and Community Stability," *American Forests* 5 (Fall 2001), p. 35.

74. Matthews, "When Fire Came to Town."

75. Laura McCarthy and Gerry Gray, *Community Based Forestry and the National Fire Plan Briefing Paper* (April 2003), available at http://www.americanforests.org/downloads/fp/reports_pubs/hartzell_natl_fire_plan.pdf.

76. Jungwirth, Bosworth, Farr, and Snyder are quoted in Matthews, "When Fire Came to Town," pp. 27–29.

77. "Statement of Lynn Jungwirth, director, Watershed Center, Hayfork, California, Before the Senate Energy and Natural Resources Committee on Issues Related to Federal Emergency Funding for Wildfire Suppression" (July 16, 2002).

78. "Statement of Lynn Jungwirth," p. 5.

79. Senators Jon Kyl, Jeff Bingaman, Pete Domenici, Max Baucus, Tim Johnson, Maria Cantwell, Ben Nighthorse Campbell, and Barbara Boxer, letter addressed to Mr. Mitchell Daniels, Jr., director, Office of Management and Budget (June 25, 2002).

80. "Statement of Lynn Jungwirth," p. 6.

81. Phone conversation with Gerry Gray, American Forests (February 9, 2004).

82. Ibid.

83. Ibid.

84. Cromley, "Legislation for a New Era," p. 3.

85. Phone conversation with Gerry Gray.

86. From her letter (August 8, 2002) to Senator Bingaman in support of the bill. The Forest Steward's Guild is a national organization of foresters and other natural resource professionals managing 6 million acres of forestland across the country.

87. For a summary of Holmer's and other witnesses' comments at the July 25, 2002, hearing on S. 2672, see http://www.americanforests.org/downloads/fp/reports_pubs/sum_sub_commbasedrestoration.pdf.

88. Quoted in Braxton-Little, "Congressional Staffers," pp. 1, 3.

89. Interview with Lynn Jungwirth (August 23, 2002), Washington, D.C., by phone to Hayfork, Calif.

90. Daly, "Member Profile," p. 3.

91. The full document is available at http://www.westgov.org/wga/initiatives/fire/implem_plan.pdf.

92. Quoted in Alex Conley, "Monitoring Community Based Forestry," *Communities and Forests* 3 (Fall 1999), p. 3.

93. Maia Enzer, "Perspective: Community Foresters Play a Critical Role in National Forest Policy," *Communities and Forests* 4 (Fall 2000), p. 5.

94. Gerry Gray, "Member Profile," p. 4.

95. Daly, "Strengthening Our Voice," p. 2.

96. On common interest criteria, see the section on "The Common Interest" in Brunner et al., *Finding Common Ground,* pp. 8–18.

97. Conley, "Monitoring Community Based Forestry," p. 3.

98. Moreover, it is difficult to devise adequate measures of performance for established programs, quite apart from innovative programs such as stewardship contracting; in any case, the Congress and administration tend to make resource allocation decisions on other grounds. See, for example, the survey of local, state, federal, and international experience by the Congressional Budget Office, reported in *Using Performance Measures in the Federal Budget Process* (Washington, D.C.: Congressional Budget Office, 1993). Congress nevertheless enacted the Government Performance and Results Act of 1993. On difficulties with performance measures in the Forest Service, see U.S. GAO, *Forest Service: Little Progress on Performance Accountability Likely Unless Management Addresses Key Challenges,* GAO-03-353 (Washington, D.C.: GAO, 2003).

99. Braxton-Little, "Coming of Age," p. 4.

100. For hypotheses on the restriction and partial incorporation of innovations, see Harold D. Lasswell, Daniel Lerner, and Ithiel deSola Pool, *The Comparative Study of Symbols: An Introduction* (Stanford, Calif.: Stanford University Press, 1952), p. 5.

101. Quoted in Robert H. Nelson, *A Burning Issue: A Case for Abolishing the U.S. Forest Service* (Lanham, Md.: Rowman & Littlefield, 2000), p. 120.

102. Greenberg and Moote, "Stewardship Contracting," p. 5.

103. Carol Daly, personal communications on several occasions.

104. Braxton-Little, "Coming of Age," p. 6.

# 7. Toward Adaptive Governance

RONALD D. BRUNNER AND TODDI A. STEELMAN

THE PREVIOUS CHAPTERS have focused on clarifying and illustrating the emergence of adaptive governance in various forms and in various places: the 15-Mile Reach of the Colorado River in western Colorado, the Camino Real in northern New Mexico, the diffusion and adaptation of grassbanks across the American West, the Oregon Plan to recover salmon at the watershed level, and legislation in the nation's capitol to support community-based forestry. Here we turn from past experience in these and other relevant cases to future possibilities for natural resource policy, including the possibility of major reforms. The future cannot be predicted with confidence, especially as the time horizon extends beyond the next few months or years.[1] The longer the time horizon, the less predictions can exploit the momentum of recent trends, and the more predictions are exposed to events that cannot be reliably anticipated or controlled. Important among these events are new insights and learning by the people involved at all levels of natural resource policy and governance.

It is nevertheless prudent to project future possibilities based on the present understanding of past trends and the factors shaping them, to clarify what, if anything, might be done to realize a better approximation to priority goals. Projections and scenarios also provide a baseline for reassessing expectations in light of experience and therefore an opportunity to learn. For example, it would have been instructive if more officials and scientists involved in the Forest Service's Committee of Scientists at the outset in 1997 had made explicit their expectations about the impacts of the committee's report and recommendations (see chapter 1). The next section projects business–as–usual scenarios at the national and local levels. These scenarios are connected only loosely, but are based alike on remnants of scientific management overlaid with power balancing and bureaucratic politics. The section then turns to an evaluation of the two business–as–usual scenarios and concludes with consideration of the prospects for adaptive governance as an alternative to business as usual. Because adaptive governance is far from inevitable, the next section suggests a basic strategy—including substantive and procedural goals, action alternatives to realize the goals, and integrative politics—to bias outcomes in favor of a transition toward adaptive governance. The final section reviews pitfalls and potentials in a transition toward adaptive governance. The task overall is less to predict the future than to shape it to advance common interests.

## Scenarios

At the national level, a business-as-usual scenario can be extrapolated from historical trends in legislation and litigation over the last several decades and from the persistence of power-balancing politics. The iron triangle consisting of Forest Service officials, members of Congress, and their commodity constituents began to lose control over legislation directly affecting their interests with the Multiple Use Sustained Yield Act (MUSYA) of 1960 and the Wilderness Act of 1964. Politically, these acts signaled the rising power of environmental interest groups that did not trust the Forest Service and other agencies of the federal government to protect intrinsic values of natural resources. The MUSYA directed that national forests "shall be administered for outdoor recreation, range, timber, watershed and wildlife and fish purposes." "Since the act set no specific priorities among these uses it did not explicitly challenge the traditional priority of logging, but left this judgment to the discretion of the forest manager."[2] The Wilderness Act "represented a great turning point in the value symbolism of American life. . . . Instead of control over nature, a wilderness area represented the very opposite."[3] These acts also initiated an era of environmental legislation that peaked in the 1970s and 1980s, empowering environmental groups to advance their interests through litigation that challenged actions and inaction by government and businesses in court. In Richard Andrews's assessment, "such litigation was arguably the leading force driving environmental protection policy throughout the environmental era, though it was itself an additional drain on professional effort and resources" in federal agencies.[4]

But the advances of environmentalists stimulated efforts by others to block or reverse them. Beginning in 1981, the Reagan administration shifted the action from the courts and a Congress controlled by the Democratic party to the executive branch. The administration moved nonenvironmentalists into key positions in natural resource policy, eliminated some environmental regulations, and blocked federal enforcement of other regulations through cuts in agency budgets, among other means. This frontal assault catalyzed support for environmental interest groups and increased their membership. Beginning in 1995, during the Clinton administration, the 104th and 105th congresses controlled by the Republican party and led by Representative Newt Gingrich initiated another assault on environmental protection. Their strategy left environmental laws on the books but starved the agencies mandated to implement them by withholding funds and other resources. They included more than fifty riders in seven different appropriations bills in the 104th Congress alone to halt enforcement of environmental laws by the Environmental Protection Agency, Interior Department, and other federal agencies.[5] Nonetheless, proponents of environmental protection "succeeded once again in blocking major reversals of environmental policy ... but by the late 1990s they appeared far more effective simply at protecting the existing system of statutes and regulations than at mobilizing support for significant reforms or new initiatives."[6] Beginning in 2001, the Bush administration acted quietly to roll back environmental protections in multiple legislative and regulatory confrontations while wearing the green cloak of friends of the environment in public. For example, the "Clear Skies Initiative" and the "Healthy Forests Initiative" as publicly promoted appeared environmentally friendly, even though the initiatives themselves were questionable on environmental grounds. The disguise made it more difficult to mobilize public opinion on behalf of environmental protection. Neither the disguise nor attempts to legislate sound science in support of administration policy serves the common interest.[7]

In short, the trend overall resembles the movement of a pendulum, to borrow Andrews's metaphor, with smaller movements (or amplitude) over time, indicating temporary advantages for one side or the other and possible convergence toward a stalemate between them. Of course movements of the pendulum are subject to disruption from environmental disasters and external events, such as security crises, economic recessions, and federal budget deficits.

The underlying power-balancing dynamics are familiar in American politics. Each temporary advantage for one side tends to encourage expectations among its supporters that past gains are permanent and future gains are possible. For example, in 1999, after the Forest Service's Committee of Scientists affirmed ecological sustainability as the "guiding star" of forest management, one veteran environmentalist foresaw a permanent change. "No longer will the question be ... 'How much does environmental protection cost in forgone timber production?' The new question will be 'What is necessary to restore and preserve biological diversity across broad interownership landscapes?'"[8] But these perceived gains catalyze support to counter long-lasting change. The Healthy Forests Restoration Act (HFRA) of the Bush administration does not address the latter question. Rather, initial legislation sponsored by Representative Scott McInnis (R–Colo.) gave a traditional answer to the old question: increased timber production, especially of mature and old-growth forests, in the guise of hazardous fuel reduction. This invited environmental groups to lobby heavily against it and devise their own legislative alternatives.[9] Thus each temporary advantage tends to give the other side proportional opportunities and incentives to block or reverse it. Each side also can mobilize more public support when it is disadvantaged because public opinion is divided and most easily activated by an apparent disadvantage.[10]

At the local level, a business-as-usual scenario can be extrapolated from cases such as the Klamath Basin water crisis in 2001. The Klamath case is unusual because the controversy attracted national attention. It is not unusual in the temporary advantages gained by one side over the other. As noted in chapter 1, the pendulum swung in favor of endangered fish advocates in April 2001 when the Bureau of Reclamation withheld 500,000 acre-feet from irrigators under pressure from the National Marine Fisheries Service (NMFS), the U.S. Fish and Wildlife Service (FWS), and a court order. In late July 2001, the secretary of the interior announced the release of up to 75,000 acre-feet of water for irrigators. In the spring of 2002, the Bureau of Reclamation and the NMFS settled on a 10-year plan that dropped summertime flows in the lower Klamath River to as little as half the amount prescribed for salmon a year before. In September 2002, after 33,000 chinook and more than 100 federally protected coho went belly up in the lower Klamath River, fisheries and environmental interests filed suit to require higher summer flows for salmon. On July 17, 2003, "Judge Saundra Brown Armstrong of the U.S. District Court in Oakland ordered the National Marine Fisheries Service to come up with a new 10-year plan for the salmon, labeling parts of the existing plan as 'arbitrary and capricious.'"[11] The ruling left water allocation in place for the remainder of the growing season but not for subsequent seasons.

The underlying bureaucratic dynamics also are familiar from American politics. Public officials on the ground face institutionalized incentives to avoid risks by going by the book, the rules codified in law and regulations. The threat of lawsuits heightens those incentives; so do claims of inconsistency and other forms of controversy. These invite outside scrutiny and sometimes force unwanted disclosure of inside information. But no one knows for sure what "the book" is because applicable laws are interpreted differently. If the laws were definitive and above politics, there would be only one interpretation in the Klamath case, rather than the different interpretations advanced by the field offices of different federal agencies, the interior secretary and other high officials in the Bush administration, and various courts. Under these circumstances, power balancing dynamics kick in rather easily, and sound science provides no refuge for beleaguered or vulnerable field officials who must make a political decision. Similarly, if science were definitive and above politics, there would be no articles with titles such as "'Combat Biology' on the Klamath."[12] Expectations nevertheless persist that outcomes on the ground nationwide can and should be determined on a scientific basis and directed by laws and regulations from the top down. These remnants of scientific management surfaced, for example, in an endorsement of the Committee of Scientists' report for the Forest Service in 1999: "Clear standards must be written into regulations and upheld, or planning will continue to suffer from the problems caused by too much agency discretion. Meeting this challenge will represent a major victory for the agency by transforming the most current and respected scientific theories into on-the-ground management rules and regulations."[13] But the laws and regulations governing natural resources come in complementary opposites reflecting many but not all of the diverse interests in society.[14] This leaves a great deal of discretion to officials and others on the ground. They can use it to defend the status quo, the default outcome, or they can use it to advance the common interest, as they did in implementation of the Endangered Species Act (ESA) in the 15-Mile Reach.

## An Appraisal

Is business as usual satisfactory? Under either the national or the local scenario, one faction blocks the other, as envisioned in the constitutional separation of powers and the system of checks and balances. But the common interest is not limited to blocking action in an evolving society, with various interests rising and declining continuously, and attempting to adapt as events unfold. And the common interest is not served when more factions on each side become more entrenched in defending their positions, moving the system toward stalemate and gridlock.[15] Among the rising interests not served are the common interest in the restoration (not merely the protection) of interdependent ecosystems and socioeconomic systems in various places. In any frank accounting, the narrow interests of competing factions are not served by continuation of business as usual either. Each temporary advantage for advocates of ecosystems or communities comes at a greater cost in resources, and neither is satisfied with stalemate if their professed interests are taken seriously. Each professes to want more healthy ecosystems or more healthy socioeconomic systems, with little regard for the costs to other interest groups.

What sustains business as usual at the national and local levels, if neither the common interest nor the professed interests of factions are served by it? Perhaps the main factions are satisfied with business as usual despite their professed interests. In the balancing of power, some leaders and followers learn that pursuing more than a small temporary advantage is likely to cost more than they are willing or able to pay. Over time they become reconciled to defending or maintaining their policy positions and power, whatever their aspirations to improve the ecological or socioeconomic health of communities once might have been. Perhaps the main factions are unaware of any alternative to the balancing of power for dealing with other interests. Americans are socialized to be more competitive than collaborative, particularly when they go to Washington. (Community-based forestry is an exception.) And their attention tends to track controversies such as the one in the Klamath Basin more than working consensus solutions such as the one in the 15-Mile Reach. Finally, perhaps they are skeptical of collaborative and consensual alternatives to the balancing of power, even if they are aware of them. Skepticism is a virtue that becomes problematic when skeptics exempt failed alternatives from close scrutiny, focusing exclusively on flaws in innovations that threaten the status quo.

Business as usual in natural resource policy at the national or local level probably is not sustainable over the long run, even if it is adapted to the short-run narrow interests of participants. It builds up frustrations among lobbyists, legislators, and litigators, who are aware of many constraints manifest in the growing costs of smaller gains and stalemate, particularly in comparison to what they once hoped to accomplish. Consider the frustrations of one legislator, David Obey, in box 7.1. It also builds up frustrations among officials and citizens in local communities who suffer collateral damage in wars over natural resources in Washington or in court. These include the timber wars over spotted owls in the Northwest and Southwest, wars over grazing rights on public lands, and wars over endangered species protection in many locales. Some frustrations are internalized, as a loss of faith in the system, for example. Others are overtly expressed in words or in efforts to press harder to prevail in the power-balancing process. Pressing harder compounds frustrations over the long run rather than alleviating them. Some frustrations are expressed in civil disobedience, such as forcing open the Bureau of Reclamation's headgates in Klamath Falls or taking fuelwood from the Camino Real in violation of a region-wide federal injunction. Others are expressed in criminal disobedience, including shots fired at enemies, bombing of federal property by disaffected resource users, or arson in the name of the Environmental Liberation Front.

## An Alternative

Still other frustrations are worked out constructively in various ways exemplified in the chapters of this book. For example, in 1996, when the recovery program in the Upper Colorado Basin was about to blow up, public officials,

---

*Box 7.1. Frustrations with Business as Usual*

Mr. Chairman, I find myself very frustrated tonight. I feel like I am in Forestry Theology 1A. I am not a forest manager. I have a district with one of the largest national forests in the eastern region of the United States, and I have firsthand dealing with how the public and the Forest Service and the various legitimate interest groups that use forests have to work with each other . . . .

I get very frustrated being whipsawed between the users of forests who want to use it for economic purposes and the recreational users of forests, the environmentalists on the other side. The only way that you can get rational public policy in an area like the forest is to sit down and work out compromises.

Now, I have seen environmental groups who are willing to challenge every blessed timber sale that comes up. I think that is nuts. I think there is a legitimate reason to cut timber in forests. But I also see some people on the other side who have never met an environmentalist that they could tolerate, and they think the forest is there simply for economic exploitation. And I just want to say to both sides, it makes no sense to have one administration go in one direction and have another administration come in and go in another direction, depending upon what the electorate decides every 4 years. We get a yinging and a yanging in forest policy, and nobody knows what the rules are going to be more than a year ahead of time. Now, that drives everybody nuts. It should.

So it seems to me that rather than both sides being engaged in a theological debate every blessed year on this issue, sooner or later, for each and every forest in the country, the interested groups need to sit down with each other and work out reasonable compromises. I am so damned sick of theology on this floor, political theology invading every issue. And that goes for both sides on this issue. . . . .

And I think we have a right as legislators to go to groups on both sides of this issue and say, we have had it, fellows. Get together. Work it out. . . . . That is the only thing that serves the interests of the country.

*Source: Remarks of Rep. David Obey (D–Wis.), ranking member of the House Appropriations Committee, Congressional Record (June 16, 2004), pp. H4258–59.*

---

water users, and environmentalists reassessed their diverse interests and decided to work together to find a mutually satisfactory solution. In 1992, when Crockett Dumas was getting nowhere as "ranger god" in the Camino Real Ranger District (CRRD), he switched to horseback diplomacy to begin working with people in the community. In the mid-1990s, the grassbank innovation in the Malpai Borderlands of southern Arizona and New Mexico began to be diffused and adapted in other places where environmentalists, ranchers, and public officials were predisposed to find common ground. In 1995, impressed by the work of local watershed councils, the new governor of Oregon, John Kitzhaber, decided to augment state support for their salmon restoration work as a better way than failed programs and federal listing under the ESA. The record of ESA implementation still does not inspire confidence in recovery,[16] despite the burdens imposed on local communities and because of those burdens. In the mid-1990s, practitioners of community-based forestry organized to go to Washington, where they achieved small but significant gains in authorities, appropriations, and other resources to support their work on the ground. Thus adaptive governance emerges here and there in response to the many failures of power-balancing politics and the remnants of scientific management, exploiting opportunities for innovation. Clearly, not everyone is satisfied with defending business as usual.

But defenders of business as usual have ample means to discourage or block innovations in many places. For example, federal and state agencies organized as the Greater Yellowstone Interagency Brucellosis Committee systematically rejected innovative proposals from community-based initiatives while struggling unsuccessfully to reconcile differences among themselves for more than a decade. Local Forest Service officials rejected the innovative Community Stability Proposal of the Quincy Library Group before and after an act of Congress directed the agency to implement that modified proposal on a pilot basis.[17] Several attempts to include land grant people in the management of national forests in northern New Mexico failed before the innovations of Crockett Dumas and others in the 1990s, and even those successful innovations may become victims of envy, bureaucracy, and downsizing. The diffusion and adaptation of grassbanks has been set back by the failure of Forest Service officials to follow through on their own formal commitments to restore grazing allotments. The Oregon Plan, based on local watershed councils, has been opposed by those who have no better alternative than to press harder to implement the failed recovery policies of the past. One leader in community-based forestry, exasperated by repeated obstructions from local Forest Service officials, suggested half seriously that it was time to shoot the Forest Service and put it out of its misery. This is another expression of cumulating frustrations, not realistic problem solving.

The bottom line is that adaptive governance is a possible but far from inevitable alternative to business as usual and that field officials in federal agencies with jurisdiction over public lands probably are in position to make the most difference. Field officials cannot prevent innovations proposed by community-based initiatives to advance the common interest, but they can decline to participate and block implementation and field testing where their agencies have some authority or control. People in nongovernment organizations such as

The Nature Conservancy, in the news media, and in higher-level government positions (appointed and elected) have had and can have important roles in the diffusion and adaptation of successful innovations, along with community-based initiatives, of course. With some exceptions, the potential of universities and foundations to support innovations over the status quo has yet to be exploited. But in any case, field officials in federal agencies and their decisions account for most of the difference in outcomes between the Klamath Basin and the Upper Colorado River Basin (including the 15-Mile Reach) in implementation of the ESA. They also account for most of the difference in outcomes in the CRRD in the 1990s compared with earlier and later periods in the implementation of approximately the same laws and regulations governing national forests.

If adaptive governance is more constructive than alternative means of dealing with present and future frustrations, then it makes sense to expedite the possible transition to adaptive governance. The initial and continuing strategy, partially implemented in this book, addresses field officials and others in a position to make a difference.[18] First, for those who are satisfied, we have contended that a problem exists. Business as usual has failed to serve any particular interest or the common interest well in recent decades and probably is not sustainable. This might prompt some to undertake a frank accounting of their own experience in light of their own larger and longer-term interests, perhaps concluding that reform, not complacency, is warranted. Second, for those who are dissatisfied but unaware of alternatives to business as usual, we have directed attention to adaptive governance. This might prompt some to compare the newer practices of adaptive governance with established practices of governance, perhaps concluding that established practices do not stand up in a fair comparison. Third, for those who still are skeptical of the newer practices, we provide details on how adaptive governance has worked on the ground and gained support at higher levels in the structure of American governance. This may prompt some to reconsider the basis of their skepticism, but of course there are no guarantees. Real people are involved. They can construe details selectively to defend an established faith or consider the details more comprehensively to open their eyes.[19]

Are there enough people predisposed to overcome their complacency, their lack of awareness, or their skepticism to participate in a transition to adaptive governance? No one can know for sure without implementing the initial strategy long enough and well enough for a fair trial by experience. But if there are enough people, then it is not difficult to imagine how the number of innovations on the ground in natural resource policy can increase, how those that are successful can be diffused as models for other communities to consider, and how adaptations by other communities and additional innovations can be assisted by nongovernment organizations and state and federal governments. All of this already has happened here and there, as documented in previous chapters. If it can happen in more places more often, adaptive governance can become established as the norm rather than the exception, just as bureaucracies and other facets of scientific management were established as the norm shortly after the turn of the twentieth century.[20] To help guide this quasi-evolutionary process, the following section clarifies a basic strategy, one that builds on the initial strategy of catalyzing the latent support of people willing and able to work toward adaptive governance.

## Basic Strategy

A basic strategy indicates in general where we would like to go from the present position and how to get there. Thus it provides stable orientation for the coordination of individual and collective actions amid the many distractions, challenges, and setbacks that surely will arise over time. It also provides guidance for planning and appraising many specific policies adapted to differences and changes in specific contexts. Any basic strategy needs specification because it is necessarily incomplete, reflecting the diversity of contexts and limited knowledge of them. There is no standard map that provides complete guidance in all contexts; there are only better maps for each context. A natural resource policy problem such as recovery of endangered species is not the same problem nationwide, despite the ESA and other national laws and regulations. Each local community has somewhat different soils, waters, plants, animals, and people, and the people have somewhat different interests affected by recovery actions. These differences must be taken into account for recovery actions to succeed. In principle, the following basic strategy provides guidance on any problem in natural resource policy, including endangered species recovery, grazing, and forestry.

### Goal Clarification

The goals for a transition to adaptive governance are both substantive and procedural. The substantive goal is advancing the common interest, beginning with local communities and moving up to larger communities. This goal merits further clarification here as part of the basic strategy. Advancing the common interest does not entail achievement of some ideal, such as unanimity or the inclusion of all interests affected by a decision in making it. As noted in chapter 1, unanimity gives a veto to special interests. The principle of affected interests is impractical and unachievable if real people are involved. Many of those affected typically do not have sufficient time, attention, and interest to participate, even if they are given access and invited to use it.[21] Advancing the common interest means integrating if possible, or balancing if necessary, the valid and appropriate interests of community members who consider their stake in the issue sufficient to warrant their participation in resolving it. The interests are specific to the particular community and cannot be assessed apart from that community. Advancing the common interest is assessed according to a histori-cal baseline in the same community or, with more difficulties, across similar communities. Assessment according to ideal aspirations—ones that cannot be realized—is self-defeating.

Consider some examples of advancing the common interest. The Program-matic Biological Opinion (PBO) in the 15-Mile Reach integrated community interests in endangered species recovery and water development, among others, after the recovery program for the Upper Colorado River Basin was about to fail in 1996. The CRRD Policy included the interests of Hispano land grant communities that historically had been excluded in the management of nearby national forests. Interests in procedural reforms, wood for fuel and building materials, and ecological education, among others, were included without com-promising the valid and appropriate interests of environmentalists or the larger timber companies headquartered outside the local community. After timber har-vests dropped precipitously in the late 1980s, the Community Stability Proposal negotiated in 1993 by the Quincy Library Group would have advanced the common interest of the local community in ecological and economic health, including reduced risk of catastrophic wildfires. Initially, local Forest Service of-ficials served their own interests at the expense of the common interest, locally and nationally, when they delayed implementation of the pilot program based on a modified proposal and enacted by Congress in 1998. Later, after the USFS moved ahead with implementation, environmental groups such as Californians for Alternatives to Toxics, the Plumas Forest Project, and the John Muir Project repeatedly appealed the pilot projects. These recent appeals were denied. The delays continue at the expense of the common interest.[22] The Klamath Project 2001 Annual Operations Plan did not advance the common interest. Accord-ing to the best available science, it is unclear whether the primary interest in protecting endangered fishes was served. It is clear that the plan wreaked havoc on the local economy and everything that depended on it, including migratory wildfowl and bald eagles in national wildlife refuges that depended on runoff from irrigated fields. Such failures to advance the common interest typically are more conspicuous than the successes.[23]

By *community* we mean a community of place such as the area in and around the CRRD. We do not mean a community of interest—better described as an interest group—such as the Santa Fe chapter of the Sierra Club, Hispano land grant organizations, or the Forest Service, each of which represented only part of the community's interest in the CRRD Policy. A community and a common interest exist whenever people and groups are interdependent enough to find it expedient if not necessary to take each other into account. The interest groups involved in the 15-Mile Reach PBO, for example, negotiated because they recognized they were interdependent: What each wanted depended on the others. But they were not friends, at least at the outset. Neither a community nor the common interest depends on whether people and groups feel good about each other or identify with the whole community.

Moreover, the size of a community varies with the scope of the issue over time. When the Quincy Library Group took its proposal to Washington for the second time in 1996, after it was blocked again by the local Forest Service, the community organized around the issue became national in scope: The proposal attracted the participation of people in Congress and approximately 140 environmental interest groups including the Sierra Club. Similarly, the community involved in the Klamath Basin water crisis temporarily became national in scope when local groups disadvantaged by the 2001 Annual Operations Plan appealed to officials high in the Bush administration and their representatives in Congress and involved the national news media and public through such staged events as civil disobedience in Klamath Falls on Independence Day 2001.[24]

These are examples of issue and community expansion, serving as informal means of democratic accountability from the bottom up. Groups unable to protect or advance their interests in conflict with others but unwilling to give up are motivated to expand the issue and the community involved in it. They also are able to do so in an open society. Schattschneider, in a famous formulation, emphasizes "the contagiousness of conflict" under these circumstances.[25] These informal political means of holding field officials accountable to the people are complementary to (and often more effective than) formal bureaucratic means of accountability exercised from the top down. Conflicting laws and regulations are among the factors that tend to devolve effective control to field officials. So are the complexities of particular issues on the ground and the ability of field officials to withhold information from their superiors, even if their superiors have the time and interest necessary to attend to them. But interest in issues on the ground and the time to attend to them become increasingly scarce resources as one moves up the bureaucratic hierarchy.

As these examples suggest, the common interests of local and larger communities are not necessarily aligned, but they can be. If a local community can advance its common interest within the institutional framework, there is little need in practice or in principle to expand the issue or the community nationwide. In practice, diverse community interest groups with a significant stake in the issue are satisfied, as they were with the 15-Mile Reach PBO and the CRRD Policy. In principle, democratic theory favors devolution to the local community: "If a matter is best dealt with by a democratic association, seek always to have that matter dealt with by the smallest association that can deal with it satisfactorily," recommends Robert A. Dahl, a democratic theorist.[26] On the other hand, if a local community cannot satisfactorily advance or defend its common interest, then self-perceived losers among the groups involved have the opportunity and perhaps sufficient incentive to expand the issue. The Forest Guardians and other groups did not have sufficient incentive to expand the issue when Crockett Dumas violated the federal injunction against cutting timber in the Carson National Forest. The Quincy Library Group and others involved in community-based forestry did have sufficient incentive to go to Washington in search of authorizations and appropriations to carry on their work. After hearings, the House passed its version of the Quincy Library Group Forest Recovery Act by a vote of 429 to 1, and a Senate committee reported unanimously in favor of its bill. At that point environmentalists engineered a hold on the bill to block a floor vote in the Senate. However, the hearings and votes taken were sufficient to indicate that the act was expected to serve the common interest at the national level, in addition to the local common interest.[27]

The common interest is a substantive goal compatible with the national framework of laws and regulations. In national forest policy, the multiple uses prescribed in the Multiple Use Sustained Yield Act of 1960 taken together are an explicit statement of a common interest goal. The act itself is an attempt to accommodate the principal valid and appropriate interests actually pursued by participants in forest policy nationwide. The Forest Service mission and motto is a less explicit statement of the common interest. "To Protect the Land and Serve the People" was nevertheless sufficient to guide Crockett Dumas through a series of policy innovations and political controversies in the CRRD. Even the many complementary opposite interests established in the national framework of laws and regulations can be interpreted as recognition of the common interest. However, from a "going by the book" perspective, the framework also can be interpreted as thousands of mandates that defend all established interests against challengers, at least in principle. This interpretation can make it difficult to advance any of them in practice.

The common interest differs from the goals characteristic of scientific management. The latter depends on reducing the multiple goals represented by multiple interest groups in a community to a target, a single priority goal. Perhaps targets are attempts to reduce the policy problem to a technical problem for which scientists and engineers have the requisite expertise to maximize efficiency. Perhaps targets are considered necessary to maximize efficiency through a standard technology. Perhaps targets are attempts to avoid the politics involved in attending to multiple interest groups. In any case, ecological sustainability, the guiding star of the Committee of Scientists, is not equivalent to the common interest of communities nationwide, nor is timber harvest, the Forest Service's historical priority that the committee sought to replace. However, each is one component of the common interest worth taking into account in communities dependent on natural resources. The limitations of ecological sustainability, timber harvest, or any other target become obvious when it is pursued without regard to costs imposed on other interests, prompting their active opposition to further actions.

The procedural goal in this basic strategy is the diffusion and adaptation of innovations that have advanced the common interest in local and larger communities. The point is to multiply the practical significance of successful innovations in natural resource policy and governance by harvesting experience for others in similar circumstances. Without that experience, people willing and able to participate in a transition to adaptive governance have no alternative to reinventing the wheel, an alternative that unnecessarily wastes time and other resources. With that experience, such people can proceed on a more informed basis. This is important because the rate of progress in a quasi-evolutionary process depends on the quality of trials. If people are informed, the quality of trials tends to be maintained in adaptive governance because no one knowingly copies a failed alternative without modification. The rate of progress also depends on the number of trials and their diversity. The number is potentially large because many communities in the American West have pressing problems in natural resource policy and governance, providing opportunities to field test and improve on many trials in parallel. At the same time these problems stimulate the demand to be informed about successful innovations. The diversity of trials can be maintained because the communities differ in important respects and because these differences tend to be taken into account in both the innovation and the adaptation of working solutions. The diffusion and adaptation of successful innovations tend to arise spontaneously, without central planning or control.

Consider some examples of diffusion and adaptation. The PBO in the 15-Mile Reach was diffused by participants to other subbasins in the Upper Colorado River Basin, where it has begun to be adapted. The CRRD's Innovations in American Government award is part of a diffusion and adaptation process institutionalized and funded by the Ford Foundation. The grassbank innovation at the Gray Ranch in the Malpai Borderlands has been diffused through various means and adapted in the Valle Grande Grass Bank in northern New Mexico and elsewhere around the American West. The grassbank innovation also has been incorporated into the programs and policies of the Quivira Coalition, The Nature Conservancy, and to a lesser extent the Forest Service. This is vertical diffusion and adaptation in the sense that an innovation on the ground modifies programs and policies at a higher level, which in turn facilitates further innovation, diffusion, and adaptation on the ground. The Oregon Plan for Salmon and Watersheds facilitated horizontal diffusion and adaptation of particular practices (such as the removal of culverts and riparian blackberry bushes) from one watershed to the next, as well as vertical diffusion and adaptation at the state level to support watershed councils. Moreover, because of the Oregon Plan, the National Marine Fisheries Service found that Oregon coho salmon did not warrant listing, but this unprecedented decision later was overturned in court. Community-based forestry went to Washington and realized some modest changes in national legislation to support practitioners of community-based forestry on the ground.[28]

Innovations that advanced the common interest somewhere are not necessarily adapted elsewhere. For example, the innovations in the CRRD probably were known in the other five districts in the Carson National Forest and in the neighboring Santa Fe National Forest because of geographic proximity, if nothing else. However, the innovations appear to have been restricted rather than adapted there. In the absence of additional information, the outcomes cannot be evaluated on substantive (common interest) or procedural grounds. However, restriction in itself is not evidence of malfunction in diffusion or adaptation processes. The preferred outcome and criterion for appraisal of these processes is expansion of the range of informed choice for potential adapters. It is appropriate for potential adapters to decide that an innovation is not suitable for their own circumstances, which are inevitably somewhat different from those of the innovator. A malfunction would be indicated if the information available on the innovations were insufficiently dependable, comprehensive, selective (or relevant), and creative to inform the choices of potential adapters. A malfunction also would be indicated if the structure of the diffusion network restricted the range of informed choice by failing to reach audiences that were potentially interested or enabled one or a few sources to control or block the flow of information to interested audiences. Thus the priority under the procedural goal in the basic strategy is to identify and correct malfunctions in diffusion and adaptation processes. These processes worked reasonably well by these criteria in the case of grassbanks.

However, it should be emphasized that not all adaptations advance the common interest. Sometimes an adaptation deletes some part of an innovation that is necessary to make the adaptation work. Practitioners of community-based forestry believe this to be the case in stewardship contracting, for example. The pilot programs originally included multiparty monitoring at the local level and for the whole program. When new legislation expanded stewardship contracting programs nationwide, multiparty monitoring at the local level was deleted. However, this multiparty monitoring is an essential part of holding participants in stewardship contracting projects accountable to each other and building trust between them—a way to nurture integrative politics and to avoid appeals and litigation. In its place, Congress inserted an external accountability mechanism, monitoring at the national level, in an effort to ensure that the nation's resources would be used efficiently. Oversight of the stewardship contracting program nationwide has little to do with building trust and accountability in the particular project on the ground.

Whereas innovations that advance the common interest are located in the particular community, the diffusion and adaptation of successful innovations are processes connecting different communities. In particular, appraisals of innovations in one or more decision processes provide inputs to the planning (or more generally, the intelligence) function in other decision processes. Each local community is independent of the others, but as information flows between them, the people involved tend to clarify their common interests at higher levels and to advocate higher-level working solutions accordingly. For example, the Quincy Library Group became part of the Lead Partnership Group of community-based forestry initiatives in northern California and southern Oregon, the Lead Partnership Group became part of the community-based forestry movement in the Pacific Northwest and northern Rockies, and the movement advocated changes in Washington to support practitioners of community-based forestry on the ground. Similarly, working solutions to the endangered species recovery problem in the 15-Mile Reach and other subbasins can be linked together to provide the basis for a solution to the recovery problem for the Upper Colorado River Basin as a whole. These are examples of the architecture of complexity, the hierarchical structure for solving more complex problems more quickly through evolutionary or quasi-evolutionary processes.[29] A transition to adaptive governance can exploit this architecture by relying on many working solutions in parallel from the bottom up as the basis for mobilizing support from the top down.

The procedural goal in this transition differs from the approach characteristic of scientific management. Everett Rogers called that approach "the classical diffusion model," which emerged from the technological successes of agricultural extension services and dominated thinking and action for decades. "In this model, an innovation originates from some expert source (often an R&D organization). This source then diffuses the innovation as a uniform package to potential adopters who accept or reject the innovation." However, Rogers and others recognized that the classic model "fails to capture the complexity of relatively decentralized diffusion systems in which innovations originate from numerous sources and then evolve as they diffuse via horizontal networks."[30] Centralized diffusion and adaptation from the top down can assist in a transition to adaptive governance if the innovations are based on experience on the ground and are not uniform packages to be accepted or rejected as wholes. The procedural goal in a transition to adaptive governance also differs from the emphasis on planning in scientific management, at the expense of appraisal in practice. Adaptive governance necessitates a more balanced emphasis on appraisal, with planning deemphasized to the extent that the relevant consequences of action on a policy cannot be projected with confidence.

## Action Alternatives

No single formula applies broadly to ensure success according to the substantive and procedural goals clarified in this chapter. Aspirations to develop a standard formula from a sample of cases are among the remnants of scientific management, but those aspirations are defeated by the need to attend to differences and changes on the ground, if nothing else. Context matters, in other words. Action alternatives for the transition can be informed by cases that have advanced the common interest well enough somewhere to be considered models for diffusion and adaptation elsewhere. Such models are described in this book and in other sources.[31] A model is sometimes included among the goals of practitioners. According to Bill deBuys, for example, "another goal of our [Valle Grande] grassbank has been to create a working and replicable model of environmentalists, land users, and agency people cooperating for the good of the land, a model that might be exported to other areas of the West and to other sets of issues."[32] Action alternatives also can be informed by selected details of cases if adapters are willing and able to integrate them into a strategy appropriate for their own unique context. Here we inventory some of the details that can be gleaned from cases and knowledge already available. The details draw attention to different means of effecting certain changes for a transition from scientific management to adaptive governance. These are changes in strategies to augment resources, changes in participants and their perspectives, and changes in institutional structures.[33] They are considered in turn in this section.

Even without changes in institutional structures, people ready to try adaptive governance can make substantial progress by changing strategies to augment their resources. Typically they have few important resources at the outset other than some skills in interpersonal relations. Effective control, specific authorities, and funds, for example, often are limited or encumbered. Nevertheless, resources have been and can be augmented by including representatives of a broad range of community interests, by listening carefully to understand their perspectives, and by following through quickly within practical constraints to meet some of their legitimate needs. (This takes more investment of time up front than imposing bureaucratic fiat but can save time in the longer run.) Following through builds trust, step by step; raising expectations and then disappointing them does not. Trust is a resource often squandered or ignored in the practice of scientific management. But it is almost essential for finding common ground on policy innovations, moving into unknown territory to implement those innovations, and surviving external challenges intact. The strategies that have been used in documented cases tend to be similar in these general respects, but the specifics often differ from one context to the next.

For example, after he realized that customary management practices were not working in the CRRD, Crockett Dumas initiated a strategy of horseback diplomacy. He and his employees visited local residents in their homes to understand their needs first hand and followed through with a series of reforms beginning with resident-friendly permitting procedures, a quick and inexpensive innovation. Through additional innovations that worked, participants built up enough trust among themselves to survive the crisis provoked by the region-wide injunction against cutting trees in national forests. Similarly, Ralph Morgenweck and Henry Maddux of the FWS opened up negotiations over the 15-Mile Reach PBO to all interested parties, proceeded at a pace that reassured participants that they were being heard, and resolved each issue before moving on to the next under an informal consensus rule. On behalf of water users, Jim Rooks acknowledged that "a lot of us learned that there are some people in the federal agencies that you can trust and that have clout to convince their superiors that what [local people] are saying is correct and that it can happen that way."[34] Similarly, Bill Coates, Tom Nelson, and Michael Jackson moved their negotiations to the Quincy Library to open them up to all interested parties. The group tolerated intemperate statements about issues but not each other, tabled contentious matters when the shouting got out of hand, and demanded consensus on other matters before moving ahead.[35] As Nelson of Sierra Pacific Industries later explained, "We were perfectly honest with each other from the start. We showed respect for each other too."[36] Several years later, when the Forest Service opened the Barkeley timber sale, no timber company submitted bids because the sale was located outside the area for timber harvest agreed on in the Community Stability Proposal. Bids would have violated the trust built up in the Quincy Library Group, and that trust was important to preserve. Trust is the foundation of solidarity and cooperation within such groups and of their potential for advancing the common interest.[37]

Advancing the common interest is an important but often overlooked base for gaining power, but only where the people are accepted as a potent symbol of authority. From the standpoint of elected officials and their staff, supporting a proposal for advancing the common interest is an obvious choice. It allows them to please many constituent groups and displease none or a few. For example, Senate staffer Kira Finkler observed that community-based forestry "is such a breath of fresh air—a bigger idea than traditional either/or politics. We can have healthy communities and healthy forests. . . . If the people say that's what they want, a bigger piece of the pie will go to natural resources."[38] Some years earlier, Quincy Library Group members organized themselves into groups of three—a timber, environmental, and community representative—to lobby more effectively for the Community Stability Proposal in Washington. Bob Muth, director of the recovery program in the Upper Colorado River Basin, also recognized the political advantages of broad-based support. "When we go back to Congress and ask for funding for the Recovery Program, the water users, the enviros, the Park Service, Fish and Wildlife Service, and others stand toe to toe and fight together for funding the program. . . . We have Environmental Defense Fund people standing next to a water group and saying that we are going to join arms here and fight for this common goal."[39]

At the state level, the Oregon Plan supported watershed councils because they were the most effective means of advancing salmon recovery and accommodating other interests affected by recovery actions.[40] At the local level, Bill deBuys confirmed from experience with the Valle Grass Bank that "partnerships are genuinely powerful. By forming a partnership that bridges traditional divisions, we've been able to attract more money, have more influence, and a get a lot more done."[41] According to Crockett Dumas, "get the job done and you can skirt some rules"—but not rules governing the use of federal funds or property, he advised. The job was to protect the land and serve the people, a common interest goal.[42] Dumas and the community got the job done well enough to take fuelwood from the national forest during the injunction and to avoid prosecution for that act of civil disobedience. Conversely, a failure to advance the common interest can dissipate power. For example, in 1991 Congress authorized a ten-person Wolf Management Committee with a mandate and budget to resolve protracted conflict over wolf recovery in the northern Rockies. But the committee dissipated that power when a majority approved a plan over the objections of the two environmentalists on the committee. They easily blocked further consideration of the majority's plan by advising sympathetic senators.[43]

Gains in power in local and larger arenas have been used to acquire additional resources of various kinds to invest in advancing the common interest. For example, thanks to its effective national representation of the people, the community-based forestry movement has helped protect access to funds through the Economic Action Program and new opportunities to engage in stewardship contracting. The movement also gained some legitimacy through bipartisan support for the Community Based Forest and Public Lands Restoration Act, even though the bill has not been enacted. Thanks to support from Governor Kitzhaber and many others, watershed councils under the Oregon Plan have helped Oregonians develop skills in salmon recovery and a deeper understanding of it. As the governor put it, "This whole thing is about how people in Oregon acquire a deeper level of understanding that how they live their lives affects the environment in which they live. It's about changing the culture."[44] Part of the changing culture is diffusion and intensification of the moral sense that salmon recovery is the right thing to do. Thus individual conscience becomes a bigger asset in salmon recovery. Similarly, the people of the Camino Real developed new understanding and skills in stewardship, thanks to their empowerment through the innovative policies of the CRRD. Using power and these other resources to advance the common interest entails improvisations in the face of uncertainty and adversity. As Crockett Dumas put it, "If you keep running into a brick wall, take two steps over to the side and find the door."[45] Much of that adversity comes from the remnants of scientific management.

Getting more people ready to try adaptive governance is another change needed to support a transition beyond scientific management. People are not interchangeable for policy purposes, as is presumed in the bureaucratic ideal that prizes the impersonal, objective application of laws and regulations. As a veteran of the Forest Service put it, "If you have the right people, they will find or make the tools themselves. If you have the wrong people, the best list of tools will go to waste."[46] Participants and their perspectives do matter. The progress of community-based forestry depended on people such as Kira Finkler and Mark Rey in congressional staff positions, and leaders of the movement such as Lynn Jungwirth, Carol Daly, Maia Enzer, and Gerry Gray. Progress under the Oregon Plan depended on the leadership of Governor Kitzhaber, Roy Hemmingway, and other officials, as well as more than ninety watershed council coordinators including Holly Coccoli, Dana Erickson, and Jennifer Hampel. The diffusion and adaptation of grassbanks depended on people such as Bill deBuys, Courtney White, and Bruce Runnels, as well as Drum Hadley, Bill McDonald, and other innovators in the Malpai Borderlands Group. Crockett Dumas was the catalyst for the success of innovative policies in the CRRD, but he depended on a host of others in various ways, including Mary Mascarenas, Max Cordova, Henry Lopez, and Carveth Kramer. The success of the 15-Mile Reach PBO depended on leaders such as Dick Proctor and Jim Rooks among water users, Robert Wigington and Dan Luecke among environmentalists, and officials such as Henry Maddux, Bob Muth, and Ralph Morgenweck of the FWS and Jim Lochhead of the Colorado Department of Natural Resources. The important decisions are made by real people such as these, not the cardboard caricatures in technical approaches. Multiple, often conflicting laws and regulations do not implement themselves.

Practical realities will continue to prompt changes in the perspectives of participants in natural resource policy and governance. In an epiphany triggered by a remark at Picuris Pueblo, Crockett Dumas abandoned his self-described "authoritarian" or "ranger god" outlook and overnight crystallized many hard lessons into a new point of view. That led to policy innovations in his district. Shocked when he found a rancher on the board of the Santa Fe Sierra Club, Courtney White saw first hand during a tour of that board member's ranch how environmental and ranching interests could be integrated on the ground. That led to the concept of the New Ranch, including grassbanks, and to organization of the Quivira Coalition to promote it. After the recovery program for the Upper Colorado River Basin nearly blew up, leaders of the program focused their efforts and resources on the 15-Mile Reach. That structural decision provided opportunities to solve recovery problems in one basin and eventually others. After being advised that salmon recovery in the Columbia River Basin was too complex for his limited term in office, Governor Kitzhaber visited watershed councils to observe their work first hand. That led to the Oregon Plan, based on watershed councils and a new way of doing business. Facing a host of barriers to exploiting more of the potential of community-based forestry, practitioners put together a loosely organized movement to go to Washington. That led to modest increases in support on the ground and the basis for more to come, including the trust of Republicans and Democrats in Congress.[47]

Changes in educational policies can supplement and reinforce such practical realities to change perspectives. Educational policies broadly construed include harvesting more experience for all who might be interested in adaptive governance, continuing education programs for officials and others already on the job, and graduate and professional education programs that prepare young people for future careers in and around the agencies involved in natural resource policy. This book and others like it are part of the continuing process of harvesting experience that supports further innovation, diffusion, and adaptation. So is the Bureau of Reclamation's 1998 publication, *How to Get Things Done: Decision Process Guidebook,* and other guidebooks like it. However, the influence of continuing, graduate, and professional educational programs on participants has yet to be clarified in any detail in the cases available. For shaping the future in forestry, for example, it would be constructive to examine the experience of new education programs going back at least to the 1980s, arguably the beginning of the end of big timber harvests. How and to what extent have such programs gone beyond the remnants of scientific management? How and to what extent have they succeeded by criteria of adaptive governance? What are the best practices available for diffusion and adaptation within and across agencies? Starting points for answering such questions can be found in the Collaborative Stewardship Program in the Forest Service, the Sustainable Forestry Partnership among forestry schools, and similar programs.

Changes in personnel policies can supplement educational policies in getting more people willing and able to try adaptive governance. It is unlikely that any significant reforms, including those supportive of adaptive governance, can be implemented effectively without personnel willing and able to implement them in and around natural resource agencies. For example, in 1990–1991 about two-thirds of all professional staff in the Forest Service were silviculturists or road engineers.[48] Personnel so trained may have been satisfactory for the big timber harvests of the past, but they are insufficient for a future of adaptive governance, nor are people with skills for "bullet-proofing" Environmental Impact Statements to foreclose appeals and lawsuits by interests adversely affected by proposed actions. In the aggregate, a transition to adaptive governance requires people with a broader range of professional skills, including the interpersonal skills for listening to a variety of interest group representatives and accommodating them insofar as practical. The management of natural resources is largely the management of people in a position to use or abuse those resources.

Personnel policies broadly construed include recruitment, promotion, and transfers. These policies may have been a factor in the diffusion of the 15-Mile Reach PBO to other subbasins in the Upper Colorado. At least there are indications that participants planted seeds of that success elsewhere in the basin, on the model of Johnny Appleseed in American folklore. This suggests the possibility of policy changes to transfer people who have contributed to such success to encourage diffusion and adaptation, to promote them at a higher rate than others, and to recruit more of them into the agencies and related organizations. Increases in the demand for such people can stimulate increases in the supply through changes in programs of continuing, graduate, and professional education. On the other hand, personnel policies were a factor in the lapse of some of the innovative policies in the CRRD. Of more than three dozen employees of the district involved in horseback diplomacy in 1991, only Henry Lopez, a native of the area, remained in the district by 2001. During approximately the same time period, employment in that ranger district dropped from forty-two to seventeen.[49] Replacements who lack understanding or interest in innovative policies are not likely to continue implementing and building on them. This suggests the need for flexibility in personnel policies sufficient to allow practitioners of adaptive governance to stay in place until their innovations are established, without jeopardizing promotions for which they are qualified.

Much more might be accomplished by changing institutional structures to support participants prepared to practice adaptive governance. Practitioners already have demonstrated some capacity for decentralizing decisions within existing institutional structures. For example, under authority of the ESA, leaders of the recovery program decentralized decisions geographically from the Upper Colorado River Basin as a whole to the 15-Mile Reach and within that subbasin decentralized functionally into work groups that allowed several dozen participants to specialize on distinguishable parts of the subbasin problem. Governor Kitzhaber avoided taking on the many jurisdictions involved in the salmon issue in the Columbia River Basin, and he decentralized decisions geographically to watershed councils through the Oregon Plan.[50] Decentralizing decisions in these and other ways provides more opportunities for more people with diverse interests to participate in the decision process. Decentralizing also opens up more opportunities for first-hand observation of the problem on the ground and for face-to-face exchanges of diverse views, both of which facilitate finding common ground.[51] Recall that part of Dumas's strategy was to avoid meetings until contending groups agreed on the factual basis of the problem, preferably after a field trip to observe the problem together first hand. These are among the reasons why decentralization expedites problem solving from the bottom up by quasi-evolutionary means.

In addition, practitioners already have demonstrated the feasibility of networking for horizontal diffusion of knowledge and information about successful innovations on the ground and organizing for vertical diffusion through higher-level reforms in support of adaptive governance practices. Among the available cases, these structural changes have gone farthest in connection with grassbanks, the Oregon Plan at the state level, and community-based forestry at the national level. To supplement what has been accomplished already through networking and organizing, it might be worthwhile to establish resource centers, a suggestion volunteered by Crockett Dumas when asked about reforms for the Collaborative Stewardship Program in the Forest Service. The suggestion is reminiscent of centers established in other policy areas.[52] We are not aware of any specific design in natural resource policy, but there are some obvious design considerations. For example, a resource center might archive in one place books, articles, reports, documents, interview transcripts, and contact information on cases or other aspects of adaptive governance in an agency such as the Forest Service or an area such as grassbanks or community-based forestry. This would provide convenient, one-stop access to relevant information for anyone who is interested—including public officials and citizens in community-based initiatives, students and faculty, reporters and editors, and private foundation personnel—who in turn might be expected to contribute any relevant new material of their own to the archive. Such a resource center could serve a variety of purposes, from university-based education to practical problem solving to research, including independent third-party appraisals. These purposes could be served by passively making resources available or by actively mounting training programs, problem-solving workshops, and research projects. To maintain independence, it would be prudent to rely on multiple sources of funds, regardless of formal sponsorship. Established organizations already engaged in something like this, such as the Quivira Coalition, might be supported as resource centers and networked.

In addition to changes in national legislation already demonstrated by practitioners of community-based forestry, it would be worthwhile to consider a strategy of reform by exemptions to alleviate structural constraints on adaptive governance in the common interest. This possibility is demonstrated to some extent in the 1999 legislation supporting stewardship contracting. For stewardship contracts, the Forest Service was exempted from laws and regulations prohibiting the bundling of timber and service contracts, marking every tree to be cut or left in a treatment areas, awarding timber sales to the higher bidder, and limiting multiyear contracts to five years. The net effect is to gain support for community-based forestry by authorizing flexibility to meet its particular needs on the ground. Similarly, National Fire Plan legislation exempts hazardous fuel reduction work by the Forest Service and the Department of the Interior from laws that for most part allow contracting with businesses only. These agencies now can contract with a variety of nonprofit community organizations, who are expected to hire or train significantly more local people for hazardous fuel reduction.

A strategy of reform by exemptions is suggested by disclosure in July 2002 that then–Senate Majority Leader Tom Daschle (D–S.D.) had included in a defense supplemental appropriations bill provisions to reduce the risk of catastrophic wildfires on about 8,000 acres of 1.2 million acres in the Black Hills National Forest. More controversially, the provisions exempted the work from the National Forest Management Act and the National Environmental Policy Act (NEPA); from notice, comment, or appeal requirements under the Appeals Reform Act; and from judicial review by the courts.[53] Among other Republicans, Representative Denny Rehberg (R–Mont.) complained, "He did it for the Black Hills and yet, what about all the other forests that are stymied under the same red tape?" More than twenty lawsuits, appeals, or reviews, some as old as 1985, reportedly were blocking projects to remove fuel from the Black Hills. In their defense, Senator Daschle and his colleague, Senator Tim Johnson (D–S.D.), noted that the "Black Hills legislation was drafted after lengthy settlement negotiations between the Forest Service, state officials, conservationists and the timber industry. 'If you're going to do what I did legislatively, you're going to have to back up and do what I did through the negotiation process,'" Daschle said.[54] Representative Scott McInnis (R–Colo.) cited the Daschle amendment in support of his HFRA, which constrains the alternatives that can be studied under the NEPA and limits temporary injunctions and the administrative appeals process.[55] The HFRA, passed in November 2003, mandates collaboration in crafting plans to reduce hazardous fuels on 20 million acres of national forest at high risk for wildfire. It remains to be seen how these exceptions are implemented in specific contexts. Abuses as well as successes are expected.

Thus there is a possibility of bipartisan support for a strategy of structural reform by exemption. The difficulty is finding common ground on the purpose of any exemption, crafting an exemption to serve that purpose, and providing safeguards to minimize possible abuses of the exemption in implementation. From our standpoint, the appropriate purpose would be to advance the common interest by authorizing relief from red tape and perhaps appropriating additional funds for management of national forests and other natural resources, under circumstances specified in the exemption. Those circumstances might rely primarily on multiparty planning in a community-based initiative culminating in a consensus on a specific management plan restricted to a small area, as in the Black Hills National Forest, with full public disclosure of the plan and the application for an exemption. The right to appeal a consensus plan might be restricted to those who participated in the negotiations in good faith, providing an incentive for all parties to participate. One safeguard on behalf of the common interest is restriction of the plan to a small area to minimize possible damage to natural resources and communities that depend on them. (This would leave open the option to scale up the area later, to the extent warranted by practical experience.) Another safeguard might require and fund multiparty monitoring and appraisal of each plan. If such specifications create more red tape than they eliminate, it might work to rely on the informal safeguards inherent in the issue and community expansion outlined earlier. Practitioners of community-based forestry and their colleagues in Washington may be in the best position to identify the red tape that stands in the way of community-based initiatives and to evaluate proposed exemptions and safeguards. They also have earned the trust of members of Congress on both sides of the aisle.

In any case, a strategy of reform by exemption appears to be more politically feasible than such large-scale reforms as outright termination of the Forest

Service, as proposed by Robert Nelson; or transfer of sovereignty over federal lands in the American West to people of the West, as proposed by Daniel Kemmis.[56] A strategy of reform by exemption also allows adaptation to differences and changes in context. Thus it is not necessary to presume that we can plan in advance and in sufficient detail everything needed for a transition to adaptive governance. The latter depends on trial and error—learning as we go in many places concurrently—guided by stable substantive and procedural goals that represent the common interest. In his remarks of June 2004, Representative David Obey outlined key elements of this reform strategy (box 7.2), in addition to voicing his frustrations with business-as-usual politics. To the extent that the strategy works, the accumulation of small reforms and trust might provide the basis for more fundamental reform of institutionalized practices that stand in the way of advancing the common interest in the twenty-first century.

Among the practices that might eventually be targeted for fundamental reform are the piecemeal accumulation of mandates for federal agencies that manage natural resources without a commensurate increase in appropriations and other resources necessary to carry out those mandates. Local natural resource officials cannot avoid reconciling responsibilities and resources; elected and appointed officials in Washington might help. The practices also include performance measures that draw down limited resources available, emphasize commodity production in the Forest Service at least, and ignore social and political capital in the form of respect, trust, and loyalty. The institutionalized incentives are to deplete that capital to meet annual performance measures that displace the larger and longer-term mission to protect the land and serve the

---

*Box 7.2. Elements of Reform Strategy*

I have seen intractable differences on forestry matters in my own area resolve themselves in 6 weeks when people are legitimately willing to sit down, deal with each other in an honorable fashion, and recognize that each side has legitimate interests. And I think we have a right as legislators to go to groups on both sides of this issue and say, we have had it, fellows. Get together. Work it out.

Nine times out of ten, the only public policy that can be sustained over a significant period of time is policy which is first worked out in the private sector so that the public representatives can ratify those agreements. Now, once in a while that cannot happen. But these days, we have polarization, polarization, and polarization on every blessed issue that comes before this House.

*Source: Remarks of Congressman David Obey (D–Wis.), ranking member of the House Appropriations Committee, Congressional Record (June 16, 2004), p. H4259.*

people.[57] Finally, the practices include standardized personnel policies and classifications rooted in the Progressive era. At a minimum, advancing the common interest in the twenty-first century requires more flexibility.

### Integrative Politics

Politics are unavoidable in natural resource policy and governance, even if the unrealized aspiration of scientific management was to rise above them. A transition to adaptive governance depends primarily on integrative politics to advance the common interest wherever practical. Integrative politics rely on persuasive strategies that leave the other party with reasonable choices and on indulgent strategies that provide gains (or block losses) for the other party. In contrast, more familiar divisive politics rely on coercive strategies that attempt to leave no choice and on deprivational strategies that impose losses on (or block gains for) the other party. Conventional distinctions between collaborative and adversarial strategies convey some connotations of these functional distinctions. Integrative politics are practical means of advancing the common interest wherever the parties involved recognize that they are interdependent, in the sense that advancing one's own interests depends on accommodating other interests. In the 15-Mile Reach PBO, for example, water users recognized that they had to cooperate with FWS officials and others to secure their historic water rights, continue using the recovery program as a reasonable and prudent alternative, and develop new water supplies. Service officials in turn recognized that to recover the endangered fishes, they had to cooperate with water users, who had authority and control over the water needed by the fishes as well as knowledge and infrastructure necessary for delivering that water to the fishes.

Distinctions between persuasive and indulgent strategies and coercive and deprivational strategies, are not merely academic.[58] Crockett Dumas understood them in practice: "You don't get power from a green Forest Service truck, badge or uniform. You get it from relationships. Bureaucrats want to assert their power to apply the rules by saying 'no' to the public, but they lose public support in doing so. To get power, you must find an appropriate way to say 'yes.'"[59] Governor Kitzhaber understood the efficacy of helping people through the Oregon Plan: "The whole plan is based on getting people to the table, giving them ownership, and then helping them go further than they have to go. . . . [The plan] takes about 50 to 60 percent of the woods out of production in the Coast Range, the feds could never get that kind of a cutback." His advisor, Roy Hemmingway, understood the limitations of imposing on the people: "You don't recover salmon with orders from Salem [Oregon's capitol]. You don't recover them with orders from D.C. either. People on the ground have to want to do it. You can't make them do it. You get it done through long, hard work, stream reach by stream reach, and gravel bar by gravel bar."[60] Similarly, practitioners of community-based forestry sought to distinguish themselves from conventional politics to achieve more. Groups at their Portland meeting agreed that they must draw on the affinity of policymakers to their practice-based approach and their ability to "see it as distinct from interest-based groups who make policy demands based upon their policy 'positions.'"[61] Gerry Gray of American Forests believes their strategy works "in part because it is not an advocacy program but a service that helps our community partners develop and articulate their own views on national policy."[62]

Coercive and deprivational strategies are not sufficient for a transition to adaptive governance but are sometimes necessary to counter entrenched opposition by defenders of the status quo. For example, the principal drafter of the Oregon Plan, Jay Nicholas, recalled that Governor Kitzhaber made a huge commitment to winning state agency support for it in 1996 and applied pressure through the budget process: "He was vetoing so much in his first term that he became known as Dr. No," a reference to Kitzhaber's medical degree and practice of emergency medicine.[63] Similarly, the Quincy Library Group tried from the outset to include representatives of national environmental groups in its intense negotiations and the eventual consensus on the Community Stability Proposal. Environmentalist Michael Jackson was especially concerned that these groups did not join in. Similarly, after its first few meetings, the Quincy Library Group tried to include local Forest Service personnel in the consensus but could not, even after group members went to Washington the first time and succeeded in securing more funds for the local Forest Service. Similarly, in the Camino Real, the Forest Guardians chose to impose their position in courts of law, not to negotiate with other interest groups in the community or even to participate in field trips to agree on current conditions. Where there is no tolerance for other valid and appropriate interests and current conditions are irrelevant, collaborative strategies are impractical, and exclusive reliance on them is self-defeating.[64]

## Another Look Ahead

Not everything will work out as planned in a community-based initiative, in the diffusion and adaptation of the successful innovations, or in an overall transition to adaptive governance. With intelligence and good luck, a plan might realize its goals or make satisfactory progress in that direction. But action on a plan will almost certainly have unintended consequences. And its implementation can be disrupted by unanticipated events in these quasi-evolutionary processes. "Surprise is inevitable," as C. S. Holling insisted.[65] Thus it is prudent not only to consider the potential of adaptive governance to harmonize competing interests in advancing the common interest but also to consider pitfalls that stand in the way of progress. Awareness of potential pitfalls will help practitioners of adaptive governance identify when events are heading off course, signaling the need for corrective action.

## Pitfalls

Goal displacement is a foreseeable pitfall. This is the tendency to turn means into ends, losing sight of the original ends in the process. Ralph Morgenweck recognized this pitfall in the 15-Mile Reach case and cautioned against it. "In essence," he said, "the fish will tell us as time goes on how they are doing. If we are able to improve the fishes' status without meeting those [spring] flow targets, then that is fine because our interest is in the fish. Our interests are not in some number of cfs."[66] Increasing the number of cubic feet per second and meeting the spring flow targets are means of fish recovery, but they are neither necessary nor sufficient given scientific uncertainties acknowledged by the best-informed biologists. Factors other than spring flows, including other fish recovery actions, could turn out to be sufficient for fish recovery with existing spring flows. Factors other than spring flows could prevent fish recovery even with increases in stream flows. Thus means and ends are not equivalent or interchangeable, logically or empirically, and should be carefully distinguished, as Morgenweck has done. There is refreshing humility in recognizing the scientific uncertainties. There is practical wisdom in letting the fish tell us about progress recovery, or the lack of it, by systematically observing changes in their populations.

Consider some of the forms that goal displacement might take. One form is displacement of the substantive goal, the common interest, by practices of adaptive governance. Based on the experience harvested here and elsewhere, we believe adaptive governance practices are superior to scientific management practices for all but the most technical problems. However, practices of adaptive governance do not constitute a complete, determinant, or permanent formula for advancing the common interest. If better practices for advancing the common interest arise, they should be diffused and adapted. A second form is displacement of the common interest by "collaborative conservation" or similar simplifications. As noted earlier, collaborative means do not advance the common interest in all circumstances, and multiple means must be considered in most circumstances. Conservation is an interest worth considering as part of the common interest in any context but is not equivalent to the common interest.

The latter depends on how other interests also are affected by conservation actions. Similarly, delivering water may be taken as the mandate of the Bureau of Reclamation or an irrigation district, for example, but it is not equivalent to the common interest in delivering water. A third form is displacement of the common interest by the pursuit of power. Participation in a power-balancing process easily can focus attention on protecting if not enhancing control over important decisions and divert attention from what the conflict with others once was about. Goal displacements are remnants of scientific management insofar as the remnants attempt to reduce management to the most efficient technology to realize a target, traditional bureaucracies pursue a narrow mandate, and scientists and bureaucrats are caught up in power-balancing politics.

A second pitfall is overinstitutionalization, the standardization or stabilization of practices to the extent that adaptations of policy decisions to difference and change on the ground become unnecessarily difficult or impossible. Some institutionalization is desirable to consolidate policy innovations that advance the common interest. The Camino Real case demonstrates that without some institutionalization, successful policy innovations may fade away as the principal innovators move on to other places. In different ways, people involved in grassbank diffusion and adaptation, the Oregon Plan, and the community-based forestry movement achieved a satisfactory balance between the flexibility needed to adapt and the institutionalization needed to consolidate gains. It is reasonable to anticipate more pressure toward overinstitutionalization of adaptive governance practices to the extent that they succeed by common interest criteria or more parochial ones. Standardization and stabilization are consistent with a long tradition of bureaucratization, providing short-run buffers and relief from the insecurities and frustrations inherent in the growing complexities of our time. But standardization and stabilization exacerbate those insecurities and frustrations in the longer run by inhibiting policy and structural reforms. The appropriate models for the future are not bureaucracies but the more flexible institutional forms that have emerged in other areas.[67] Approximate equivalents are the community-based initiatives in natural resource policy that have demonstrated some capacity to harmonize the competing claims of multiple bureaucracies and other interest groups in a transition to adaptive governance.

A third pitfall is defense through partial incorporation, in which part of an innovation is accepted to defend established practices.[68] The defenders tend to accept what is least costly or disruptive of established practices, often symbols. For example, there is suspicion at least that the symbol "ecosystem management" has been incorporated into the justifying rhetoric of some officials in some natural resource agencies as a substitute for changing practices on the ground. (This backfires to the extent that others predisposed to practice ecosystem management can capitalize on the justifying rhetoric.) Similarly, almost everyone accepts public participation in principle, even if they deny it in practice, since it was mandated by the NEPA in 1969. But public participation in the scoping and comment periods of an Environmental Impact Statement process can be little more than a fig leaf of democratic respectability covering autocratic agency decisions.[69] Finally, to the extent that adaptive governance attracts favorable attention, it is reasonable to expect that adaptive governance will be symbolized as scientific management done right to defend the remnants of scientific management. An important defense against partial incorporation and co-optation by defenders of business as usual is to recognize that words are not equivalent to deeds and to monitor the deeds as well.

## Potential

Adaptive governance has the potential to harmonize once-competing interests with the common interest on a much broader scale. That potential was demonstrated in the Camino Real, where the personal and professional interests of rangers in the district were aligned with the interests of the Forest Service and the local and larger communities. Bill deBuys, who was mostly an observer of the innovations in the Camino Real, offered a vivid account of what happens:

> When you have people that are really interested in their jobs, interested in the people, and their needs, and have the kind of openness displayed by Ranger Dumas where he and his staff went door-to-door. . . . There was a "love fest" for the USFS in Truchas as a result of this. The village of Truchas held a party for the USFS. . . . Career forest people at that meeting were so choked up they could not speak because they were crying because all their careers they hoped something like this would happen and finally it did. These were people who had been working hard for a long time in an organization where it is hard to get the right thing done.[70]

The people of Truchas also had been working for a long time to get the attention of local Forest Service officials by violent and nonviolent means.

To get the right thing done, in this case and in others, it is sometimes necessary to look beyond the proverbial book of legal rules and regulations and interpret them in light of larger ethical considerations. One of those considerations is the Forest Service mission to protect the land and serve the people, or the equivalent in other government agencies. Perhaps another is the idea that the people are the ultimate source of authority in American governance. The people can be served directly by public officials on the ground and indirectly through the implementation of rules and regulations established by elected representatives of the people in Washington. Perhaps another ethical consideration is to serve the land as Aldo Leopold conceived it, a community of interdependent parts including the soil, water, plants, animals, and people. "When any part lives by depleting another, the state of health is gone." On a more personal level, Leopold understood that government alone cannot "bring to bear on small local matters that combination of solicitude, foresight, and skill we call husbandry. Husbandry watches no clock, knows no season of cessation, and for the most part is paid for in love, not dollars."[71] These conceptions of the right thing to do—serving the agency mission, the people, and the land through husbandry—are matters of conscience. Conscience can be served by a transition to adaptive governance.

Adaptive governance also has the potential to help people liberate themselves from the constraints of the past, as demonstrated in the celebration in Truchas. In deBuys's account, career people in the Forest Service and local people in and around Truchas had been working hard for a long time for something like this. They also accumulated many frustrations along the way, but they chose not to replicate the routines of the past: bureaucratic fiat and popular protest, with each reinforcing each other. Instead they chose to participate in constructive reforms that produced more than temporary relief from their frustrations. It took some courage to depart from the routines of the past, just as it took some courage for Native Americans and later Europeans and Africans looking for something better to venture into the unknown territory now known as the American West. But each exploration can yield additional knowledge and information that makes it somewhat easier for those who follow, and explorations in adaptive governance are no exception. One of the pioneers, Ralph Morgenweck, recalled that at the beginning of the negotiations over the 15-Mile Reach, "We all trusted that we were trying to get an end goal of harmonizing our interests. None of us knew how in the world we would get there, but we knew that if we kept at it, we'd get it figured out."[72] That is the spirit that will sustain a transition to adaptive governance by those who are looking for something better.

NOTES

1. See William Ascher, *Forecasting: An Appraisal for Policy-Makers and Planners* (Baltimore: Johns Hopkins University Press, 1978), especially the Conclusion; and William Ascher, "Beyond Accuracy," *International Journal of Forecasting* 5 (1989), pp. 469–484. Declining confidence in forecasts is reflected in rising resort to contingent forecasts (e. g., $X$ will happen only if conditions $A$, $B$, $C$, etc. are fulfilled). Such forecasts cannot be appraised according to post

hoc accuracy unless the contingencies are fulfilled, making appraisal of forecast accuracy increasingly difficult.

2. Richard N. L. Andrews, *Managing the Environment, Managing Ourselves* (New Haven, Conn.: Yale University Press, 1999), p. 196.

3. Robert H. Nelson, *A Burning Issue: A Case for Abolishing the U.S. Forest Service* (Lanham, Md.: Rowman & Littlefield, 2000), p. 8.

4. Andrews, *Managing the Environment,* p. 358. In his chronology (p. 387), Andrews dates the recent environmental era from President Nixon's signing of the National Environmental Policy Act on the first day of 1970.

5. Michael E. Kraft, "Environmental Policy in Congress: From Consensus to Gridlock," in Norman J. Vig and Michael E. Kraft, eds., *Environmental Policy: New Directions for the Twenty-First Century,* 4th ed. (Washington, D.C.: CQ Press, 2000), pp. 121–144, especially pp. 132–133. Appropriations riders are legislative stipulations attached to appropriations bills that must be passed to fund the federal government.

6. Andrews, *Managing the Environment,* p. 361.

7. On the latter see Jeffrey Brainard, "How Sound Is Bush's 'Sound Science'?" *Chronicle of Higher Education* (March 5, 2004), pp. 18–19.

8. Andy Stahl, "The New Question," *Journal of Forestry* 97 (May 1999), p. 23.

9. Robert Gehrke, "McInnis Bill Seeks to Limit Environmental Review in High Risk Forests," *Associated Press State and Local Wire* (September 3, 2002); Anonymous, "Wilderness Society Analysis: Bush's Legislative Proposal on Wildfire," *U.S. Newswire* (September 5, 2002).

10. It is probably still true today, as it was in the late 1990s, that "opinion polls clearly showed continued public support for environmental protection, and opposition to weakening government capacity to assure it; but the polls also showed widespread public dissatisfaction with government regulation and spending in general, and environmental regulation was one of the most visible examples of such regulation." Andrews, *Managing the Environment,* p. 361.

11. Glen Martin, "Klamath Ruling Pleases Salmon's Allies, Growers Say River's Flow Will Stay the Same," *San Francisco Chronicle* (July 18, 2003), p. A3. See also Robert F. Service, "'Combat Biology' on the Klamath," *Science* 300 (April 4, 2003), pp. 36–39.

12. Ibid.

13. Mary A. Munson, "Good News for Wildlife and Ecological Sustainability," *Journal of Forestry* 97 (May 1999), pp. 26–28, at p. 26.

14. Harold D. Lasswell and Myres S. McDougal, *Jurisprudence for a Free Society: Studies in Law, Science, and Policy* (New Haven, Conn., and Dordrecht, The Netherlands: New Haven Press and Martinus Nijoff, 1992), p. 26.

15. Compare Andrews, *Managing the Environment,* pp. 357–358: "In the late 1990s, environmental policy debate in the United States appears to be at a stalemate, between a Congress whose leadership is dominated by opponents of regulation and environmental advocacy groups who can still mobilize strong enough public opinion to block deregulation initiatives but not to achieve positive policy reforms. Neither of these sides appears ready to work together on a positive agenda for further environmental policy development." For some exceptions to these generalizations, see chapter 6.

16. Holly Doremus and Joel E. Pagel, "Why Listing May Be Forever: Perspectives on Delisting Under the U.S. Endangered Species Act," *Conservation Biology* 15 (2001), p. 1260.

17. On these two cases see Christina M. Cromley, "Bison Management in Greater Yellowstone," ch. 4, pp. 126–158, and Christine H. Colburn, "Forest Policy and the Quincy Library Group," ch. 5, pp. 159–200, both in Ronald D. Brunner, Christine H. Colburn, Christina M. Cromley, Roberta A. Klein, and Elizabeth A. Olson, *Finding Common Ground: Governance and Natural Resources in the American West* (New Haven, Conn.: Yale University Press, 2002).

18. Compare the three propositions on factors affecting the probability of ideological change in Harold D. Lasswell, Daniel Lerner, and Ithiel deSola Pool, *The Comparative Study of Symbols: An Introduction* (Stanford, Calif.: Stanford University Press, 1952), p. 4.

19. Compare Machiavelli, who knew something about practical politics, writing in *Discourses I:* "Men are apt to deceive themselves upon general matters, but not so much so when they come to particulars. . . . The quickest way of opening the eyes of the people is to find the means of making them descend to particulars, seeing that to look at things only in a general way deceives them." Quoted in Harold D. Lasswell and Abraham Kaplan, *Power and Society* (New Haven, Conn.: Yale University Press, 1950), p. 106n. See also Daniel Goleman, *Vital Lies, Simple Truths: The Psychology of Self-Deception* (New York: Simon & Schuster, 1986).

20. See Robert Wiebe, *The Search for Order, 1877–1920* (New York: Hill & Wang, 1967). See also Stephen Skowronek, *Building a New American State: The Expansion of National Administrative Capabilities, 1877–1920* (Cambridge: Cambridge University Press, 1982).

21. Robert A. Dahl critiques the principle of affected interests in *After the Revolution?* (New Haven, Conn.: Yale University Press, 1970), ch. 2, pp. 59–103. This critique is included in a discussion of the common interest and applied to an issue in the Quincy Library Group case in Brunner et al., *Finding Common Ground,* pp. 8–18 and 191–93, respectively.

22. Colburn, "Forest Policy." As an example of recent appeals and denials, see USFS, Letter to Patricia Clary regarding appeal number 03-04-00-0046-A217 (February 11, 2004). Accessed July 28, 2004, at http://www.fs.fed.us.r5/ecoplan/appeals/2003/fy03-0046.htm.

23. Similarly, the Joint Management Plan for Yellowstone bison finalized in December 2000 served no obvious interest except relief from exhaustion after more that a decade of struggle between state and federal officials, who denied effective access to citizen groups. See Cromley, "Bison Management."

24. Similarly, the bison management community became national and international in scope after bison roamed out of Yellowstone National Park in search of forage during the severe winter of 1996–1097 and were shot by officials from the Montana Department of Livestock. Televised images of dead bison and blood in the snow prompted protests from around the nation and the world. See Cromley, "Bison Management."

25. E. E. Schattschneider, "The Contagiousness of Conflict," in *The Semisovereign People: A Realist's View of Democracy in America* (Hinsdale, IL: Dryden Press, 1975), ch. 1, pp. 1–19. For compatible accounts, see also Lasswell and Kaplan, *Power and Society,* especially pp. 105–107; James S. Coleman, *Community Conflict* (New York: Free Press, 1958); and Walter Lippmann, "The Making of a Common Will," in *Public Opinion* (New York: Free Press, 1965), part 5, pp. 125–158.

26. Dahl, *After the Revolution?* p. 102.

27. Colburn, "Forest Policy."

28. Similarly, the state of Montana authorized a community-based initiative to develop a plan to accommodate multiple interests in water allocation in the Upper Clark Fork Basin

and enacted the plan almost intact, including a provision to close the basin to new water reservations. See Elizabeth A. Olson, "Water Management and the Upper Clark Fork Steering Committee," in Brunner et al., *Finding Common Ground,* pp. 48–87.

29. See Herbert A. Simon, "The Architecture of Complexity," in *The Sciences of the Artificial,* 3rd ed. (Cambridge: MIT Press, 1996), pp. 183–216.

30. Everett M. Rogers, *Diffusion of Innovations,* 4th ed. (New York: Free Press, 1995), p. 364.

31. See most of the cases in Brunner et al., *Finding Common Ground;* Philip Brick, Donald Snow, and Sarah Van de Wetering, eds., *Across the Great Divide: Explorations in Collaborative Conservation and the American West* (Washington, D.C.: Island Press, 2001); and Jonathan Kusel and Elisa Adler, eds., *Forest Communities, Community Forests* (Lanham, Md.: Bowman & Littlefield, 2003).

32. From the audiotape of Bill deBuys's presentation at the "Grassbanks in the West: Challenges and Opportunities" conference (Santa Fe, N.M., November 17–18, 2000).

33. These are categories in the social process model of the policy science framework. The discussion of resources includes examples of the eight value categories. For an introduction to the framework, see Harold D. Lasswell, *A Pre-View of Policy Sciences* (New York: Elsevier, 1971), ch. 2.

34. Lindy Coe-Juell's interview (September 24, 2001) in Palisade with Jim Rooks, manager of the Orchard Mesa Irrigation District in Palisade, Colo.

35. Similarly, as reported in chapter 5, people in the Applegate community "discovered that we know that we don't agree on this 20%, so let's not keep talking about that. Let's talk about the 80% that we can agree to. There are certain practices, things that we can do, investments we can make in the watershed that will help everyone."

36. Christine H. Colburn's interview with Tom Nelson (February 19, 1999) in Quincy, Calif., quoted in Colburn, "Forest Management," p. 190.

37. Trust is a rectitude value, the expectation that people will behave responsibly. Solidarity and cooperation are, respectively, the integration of diverse perspectives and operations. In the next paragraph, power is participation in making important decisions. Politics is the exercise of power, the giving and withholding of support in making important decisions. For more on these concepts, see Lasswell and Kaplan, *Power and Society.*

38. Jane Braxton-Little, "Congressional Staffers Visit Pilot Stewardship Contracting Projects," *Communities and Forests* 3 (Winter 1999–2000), p. 3.

39. Lindy Coe-Juell's interview with Bob Muth in Lakewood, Colo. (September 19, 2001).

40. Similarly, the Montana legislature gave the Upper Clark Fork Steering Committee a mandate to "balance all beneficial use of water in the . . . basin" and "root water management at the local level." The legislature enacted the committee's plan almost intact a few years later, on that common interest basis. Quoted in Olson, "Water Management," p. 50, from MCA 85-2-338.

41. From the audiotape of Bill deBuys's presentation at the "Grassbanks in the West" conference.

42. From the authors' interview with Dumas (December 2–3, 2001) during a visit to Boulder, Colo., for a seminar on governance and natural resources.

43. Roberta A. Klein, "Wolf Recovery in the Northern Rockies," in Brunner et al., *Finding Common Ground,* pp. 88–125, especially pp. 97–99 and 115.

44. Quoted by Carlotta Collette in "The Oregon Way," *High Country News* (October 26, 1998), p. 11.

45. Dumas interview.

46. Carveth Kramer, personal communication, November 26, 2003.

47. Similarly, the Quincy Library Group was a response to the precipitous decline in local timber harvests and the poor health of local forests. The innovations by Ed Bangs of the U.S. Fish and Wildlife Service and Hank Fischer of Defenders of Wildlife were responses in part to intense opposition to wolf recovery in the northern Rockies, as mandated by Congress. The Upper Clark Fork Steering Committee was a response in part to the alternative no one wanted, legal battles over new water reservations.

48. Paul W. Hirt, *A Conspiracy of Optimism: Management of the National Forests Since World War Two* (Lincoln: University of Nebraska Press, 1994), p. xxxvii.

49. Kirsten Lundberg, "Collaborative Stewardship," in John D. Donahue, ed., *Making Washington Work* (Washington, D.C.: Brookings, 1999), p. 141.

50. Similarly, the Upper Clark Fork Steering Committee met in a central location in the basin, usually Deer Lodge, but also broke into smaller subcommittees that met in six established watersheds. The Gray Wolf Interagency EIS Team, the leader in wolf recovery in the northern Rockies, conducted twenty-seven "issue scoping open houses" in Montana, Wyoming, and Idaho and another seven outside those states. See Olson, "Water Management," p. 75, and Klein, "Wolf Recovery," pp. 99–100, respectively.

51. These are among the factors that can change perspectives. Propaganda alone tends to reinforce compatible predispositions or have no effect. See Lasswell and Kaplan, *Power and Society,* pp. 113–114.

52. See the direction centers proposed in Garry D. Brewer and James S. Kakalik, *Handicapped Children: Strategies for Improving Services* (New York: McGraw-Hill, 1979). Dumas's suggestion was made in a personal communication dated November 11, 2002.

53. Audrey Hudson, "Daschle Seeks Environmental Exemption," *Washington Times* (July 25, 2002).

54. Jack Sullivan, "Some in GOP Draw Parallel from Black Hills to New Forest Plans," *Associated Press State & Local Wire* (May 19, 2003). The quotes from Rehberg and Daschle are taken from Sullivan's story.

55. *Public Lands News* 28 (October 31, 2003).

56. See Nelson, *A Burning Issue,* and Daniel Kemmis, *This Sovereign Land: A New Vision for Governing the West* (Washington, D.C.: Island Press, 2001).

57. On the problems of performance measures in the Forest Service, see U.S. General Accounting Office, *Forest Service: Little Progress on Performance Accountability Likely Unless Management Addresses Key Challenges,* GAO-03-503 (Washington, D.C.: GAO, May 2003). More generally, see Congressional Budget Office, *Using Performance Measures in the Federal Budget Process* (Washington, D.C.: CBO, 1993); and Victor F. Ridgeway, "Dysfunctional Consequences of Performance Measures," *Administrative Science Quarterly* 1 (1956), pp. 240–247.

58. For more on these concepts, see Lasswell, *A Pre-View of Policy Sciences,* especially ch. 2.

59. Dumas interview.

60. See Collette, "The Oregon Way," for the Kitzhaber and Hemmingway quotes.

61. Sustainable Northwest, Watershed Research and Training Center, and Wallowa Resources, *Working Together to Facilitate Change: 2001 Pacific Northwest Community Forestry Public Lands Organizing Meeting* (Portland, Ore.: December 12–14, 2001).

62. Gerry Gray, "Member Profile," *Communities and Forests* 6 (Summer 2002), p. 4.

63. Lindy Coe-Juell's interview (November 5, 2001) in Salem with Jay Nicholas, science and policy advisor for the Oregon Watershed Enhancement Board in Salem, Ore.

64. For more on this point, see Brunner and Colburn, "Harvesting Experience," in Brunner et al., *Finding Common Ground,* pp. 195–196.

65. C. S. Holling, "What Barriers? What Bridges?" in Lance H. Gunderson, C. S. Holling, and Stephen S. Light, eds., *Barriers and Bridges to the Renewal of Ecosystems and Institutions* (New York: Columbia University Press, 1995), pp. 3–34, at p. 13.

66. Lindy Coe-Juell interview (September 18, 2001) in Lakewood, Colo., with Ralph Morgenweck.

67. See Gifford Pinchot and Elizabeth Pinchot, *The End of Bureaucracy and the Rise of the Intelligent Organization* (San Francisco: Berrett-Koehler Publishers, 1993); and Thomas Petzinger Jr., *The New Pioneers: The Men and Women Who Are Transforming the Workplace and the Marketplace* (New York: Simon & Schuster, 1999). See also Errol E. Meindinger, "Organizational and Legal Challenges for Ecosystem Management," in Kathryn A. Kohm and Jerry F. Franklin, eds., *Creating a Forestry for the 21st Century: The Science of Ecosystem Management* (Washington, D.C.: Island Press, 1997), pp. 361–379.

68. Lasswell et al., *The Comparative Study of Symbols,* p. 5.

69. For examples, see Cromley, "Bison Management."

70. Quoted in Lou Baker, *U.S. Forest Service Policy in Northern New Mexico* (MIT master's thesis, 1996), p. 38.

71. Aldo Leopold, "Land Use and Democracy," *Audubon* 44 (September–October 1942), pp. 259–265, at pp. 265 and 262, respectively.

72. Morgenweck interview.

# Index